Absolutely!

everything about

Cowes

The Home of World Yachting - Isle of Wight

by Marie-Claire Baroness von Alvensleben

DELUXE LIMITED EDITION

No. 29   OF 250

Andrew Macomie
with best regards

[signature]

Marie-Claire Baroness von Alvensleben

Absolutely!

everything about

Cowes

The Home of World Yachting
Isle of Wight

by
Marie-Claire
Baroness von Alvensleben

Come to the Isle of Wight
Where, far from noise and smoke of town,
I watch the twilight falling brown
All round a careless-ordered garden
Close to the ridge of a noble down.
You'll have no scandal while you dine,
But honest talk and wholesome wine.

Alfred Lord Tennyson
Written at Farringford, Freshwater

Absolutely! everything about Cowes

Researched, largely photographed and produced
by Marie-Claire Baroness von Alvensleben

with the help of English journalists and writers:
Adrian Searle, Mary McBride, Matt Power, Christian Templer, Patrick Chisholm, Sarah Burdett and Charlotte Hofton
Proofreading by Gay Baldwin, Dick Davis, Andrew Kent and John Medland
Sub-editing: Adrian Searle

Photographers
©Photos MCvA, Beken of Cowes, Yacht Shots, KOS/Carlo Borlenghi, Jon Nash, Colin Kelly, West Island Group,
Christian Février/Bluegreen, Michael Dunkason, Patrick Eden, Hamo Thornycroft
Edward Lloyd, Roger Smith, Rick Tomlinson, Chris Wood, Andreas Hanakamp, Polly Durant,
Franco Pace, Guido Cantini, James Taylor, Jacques Vapillon, Thierry Martinez, Michael Green, Knut Loewe

Additional Photographs Courtesy of
Robin McInnes, Harry Spencer, Ratsey & Lapthorn,
Cowes Maritime Museum, Sir Max Aitken Museum, Newport Classic Boat Museum
The Isle of Wight Council, Isle of Wight Tourism, Geoff Banks, Mayor of Cowes
Cowes Yacht Clubs, Cowes Harbourmaster, CTWT, Claridge and Claridge, the RNLI, the RORC,
East Cowes Marina, GKN Aerospace, AMS Systems, The Isle of Wight County Press,
Murray Dixon, Ian Lallow, Captain Henry Wrigley, Kit Hobday, Heatline (KOÇ Group),
Henri Lloyd, Mumm, Ocean Images/First Results, Nautor's Swan, Rolex Watches,
America's Cup Jubilee: Camper & Nicholson, C&N International, Paul Mason Gallery
The Herreshoff Marine Museum, The Edwin Levick Collection © The Mariners Museum,
The Jubilee Partners: Hennessy (P. Knaup), Moët & Chandon (F.Socha), Phillips Auctioneers,
Edmiston, Asprey & Garrard, Omega, ResidenSea, Louis Vuitton Media Centre,
Lymington Town Sailing Club, New York Yacht Club, Yacht Owners

 The *Thalassa* scarf featured on page 47 and specially created for the RLNI, was designed by Pierre Peron.
HERMES and the logotype of the carriage are registered trademarks belonging to HERMES INTERNATIONAL
PARIS and remains the exclusive ownership of HERMES INTERNATIONAL

Paintings & Drawings
Rodney Charman, Tim Gladdis, Edward Holt, Theodore Walker, Bill Mollart-Rogerson

Cover Picture
Cowes Week 1993 - Scene from the Lawn by Robert King
Courtesy of the Royal Yacht Squadron

Graphic Design
Marie-Claire Baroness von Alvensleben
Avon Imaging Ltd, Bristol
Tony Hollaway, Patrick Convery, Bob Palmer, Chris Sutch, Norman Jaques,
Kevin Butler, Mike Ball, Richard DeMontfort and Colin Reed
Liz Vinycomb Designs, Keith Freeman Typography, Dick Davis

The West Island Group Studio
Mike Ward
John Riddelsdell, Colin Kelly, Peter Gandy, Daniel Woods

Administration, Sales and Marketing
Alan Smith, Marilyn Barrell, Jill Jewell and Mariam Cook

ISBN: 1-904149-05-7

Printed and Published by the West Island Group Ltd
Afton Road, Freshwater, Isle of Wight, PO40 9TT, UK
Tel: 01983 753161 Fax: 01983 754683 ISDN: 01983 753193
e-mail: absolutely@westisland.co.uk www.westisland.co.uk www.absolutelycowes.com

To
My Mother
and
my late friend
Ian Cullerne-Bown

Many thanks
to
Lady Chopard Sain
Hasan F. Abu Jaber
Lord Davis

Peter Harrison
Harry Spencer
Mark Medland and The West Island Group Ltd
Beken of Cowes

Mr Mohammed Al Fayed
for the booksigning at Harrods

Rolex Watches
Avakian Joailliers
Pains Fireworks Ltd
SP Systems

also

My ex-husband and good friend Bodo G. von Alvensleben
Patrick and Lindsay Chisholm · Marie Mollart-Rogerson
Mike Gwyther & Linette Lee of Avon Imaging
Frederick & Pauline Heymann · Chris Young

This book is the first in a series that will endeavour to give readers information about what is known as 'The English Season', as seen by a foreigner. It is meant to be an insider's guide through the colourful calendar of the social season, prestigious events and exclusive venues. A channel to the discovery of traditional events which take place in this country every year, mainly between May and August.

Full of historical details, useful information and anecdotes, and richly illustrated, it will give the international traveller and newcomers, as well as habitués of this country, the flavour of what is called 'the English way of life', enjoyed by a nation of jolly *bon vivants* for whom *Carpe Diem* is a watchword.

This first book deals with *Cowes* on the Isle of Wight and particularly the 150th Anniversary of the America's Cup, which started in Cowes in 1851.

It also introduces von Essen hotels, a private collection of hotels owned by Lord Davis, which are good examples of the lovely country house hotels one can find in this beautiful part of the world. Their fleet of helicopters and luxury cars will provide easy access to Cowes and other parts of the Island.

Marie-Claire Baroness von Alvensleben

Photo © MCvA

Absolutely!

Absolutely!

everything about

Cowes

The Home of World Yachting
Isle of Wight

Contents

Courtesy The Isle of Wight County Press

The annual Brambles Bank Cricket Match
during the Solent's lowest tide of the year

The Isle of Wight

A cameo by
Christopher Bland
HM Lord Lieutenant of the Isle of Wight

It is England's smallest county but this is an island of infinite variety and incomparable beauty. Geologically unique and historically fascinating, the Isle of Wight now fulfils its modern-day rôle as one of Britain's foremost tourist locations while retaining its proud legacy of past centuries. The early Saxons knew the Island as Whitland, but when the Romans took possession, around 43 AD, it became Vectis (the name used by many local companies today). But the Island's geological history far precedes any human occupation, and discoveries dating back millions of years, particularly those of dinosaur fossils, have earned the Isle of Wight geological collection an international reputation.

The Island has always taken advantage of its good climate and fertile soil to sustain a thriving agricultural industry, while the surrounding seas are a plentiful source of shellfish as well as local sole, plaice and cod. In the mid 19th century the Island entered a new era when Queen Victoria and her consort, Prince Albert, commissioned the building of Osborne House as a country retreat. This magnificent estate was left to the nation by Edward VII, and the house and gardens, which provide a superb insight into the life enjoyed on the Island by Victoria and her family, are now the Island's most popular tourist attraction. Royal patronage ensured the status of the Island as a fashionable resort.

Yachting in particular flourished, and the Royal Yacht Squadron in Cowes, whose origins go back to 1815, became ever more prestigious. It is now regarded as the world's most eminent yacht club and is the focus for the annual Cowes Week Regatta, an event renowned today as much for its social whirl and media attention as for its Solent racing.

The Island's population of 130,000 doubles during the summer tourist season and the variety of the Island ensures that it can be enjoyed by all sorts of visitors with all sorts of preferences. There are large seaside towns, picturesque villages, commercial entertainments, magnificent downlands, unspoilt beaches, 60 miles of coastline, nature reserves, historic houses and gardens.

Beyond tourism and its traditional use of sea and farmland, the Island is home to a number of companies that have made their mark on its economy, including a thriving aerospace industry.

The local community has always been proud of its Island identity, an identity which provides a unique ecological and social status within Britain. But while the Island offers an escape from mainland pressures, it also resists isolation. Ferry services are quick and frequent and include the world's only scheduled hovercraft passenger service - the Ryde-Southsea route, which represents a ten-minute journey across the Solent.

St Agnes Church, Freshwater Bay

The Causeway, Freshwater

Whitecliff Bay

Priory Bay

Osborne House

Some of the many attractions and beautiful places to see on the Isle of Wight

The Island provides a wonderful mixture of terrain - downland, forest and wooded vale to the north, open arable land to the south. Discover its unspoilt backwaters, its loveliest and most unusual views.

Dates to remember

Walking & Cycling Festivals
May and September

Skandia Life Cowes Week 3-10 August

Offshore Powerboat Race 24-25 August

Wight Air Extreme Sports Festival October 18-30

Isle of Wight Music Festival 3-16 June

Visit the Isle of Wight Tourism Information Centre Fountain Quay, Cowes or call Isle of Wight Tourism Tel: 01983 813818 www.islandbreaks.co.uk

The Needles

Bembridge Windmill

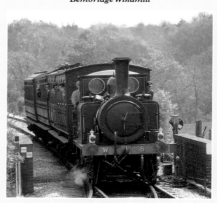

The Isle of Wight Steam Railway

Carisbrooke Castle

Foreword
by
Councillor Vic Morey
Chairman of
Isle of Wight County Council

Minister for Tourism, Dr Kim Howells, MP, with Tim Addison

I must say I am delighted to see this book published, as every year more and more events are added to Cowes' calendar. As there is so much to do in the town, some kind of guide has become essential.

We seem to be having milder winters, and Cowes, in its sheltered position in the Solent, has been well-positioned to make the best of that, offering perhaps the longest yachting season in the UK. And what a season we had in this past year! I think most people will agree that the 2001 Skandia Life Cowes Week was one of the biggest and best ever, and that was closely followed by the America's Cup Jubilee celebrations. These top-ranking international events cemented the reputation of Cowes as a centre of excellence for yachting and drew the gaze of the whole world.

It would, however, be unwise to see Cowes as purely in terms of yachting. It has a rich history and culture, along with dining and specialist shopping opportunities unparalleled anywhere else on the Island.

I hope you will enjoy this book and that it will enable you to get the most out of your visit to Cowes and the rest of our beautiful Isle of Wight.

V-J. Morey

Vic Morey
Chairman, Isle of Wight Council

Tourism
The Heart of the Island's Economy

The Island currently receives approximately 2.7 million visitors per year spending an estimated £260 million per annum. With the business generated by tourism amounting to one-third of the Island's Gross Domestic Product, it is easy to see why tourism is so fundamental to an island that is only 13 miles wide by 23 miles long. The Isle of Wight has a unique location in the South-East; part of the Solent corridor with Portsmouth and Southampton to the immediate north and strategic accessibility to continental Europe. The Island has a population of only 130,000 and during peak season there are an estimated 27 tourists for every Island resident. With a total land area of 146.8 square miles, the Island has more footpaths than roads and over half of the Island is designated an 'Area of Outstanding Beauty'. 53% of the Island's 57 miles of coastline is designated 'Heritage Coast', a title awarded only to beaches of the highest quality in England and Wales. Island landmarks from Osborne House (the Island's own Royal Palace) to the Needles (as featured daily with the BBC hot air balloon) prove a huge draw to visitors. In addition, there are over 70 places of interest including a Norman Castle, Roman Villas and Dinosaur Isle, the first purpose-built dinosaur museum in the country. Events held throughout the year help promote the Island's diversity and because of its microclimate, outdoor activities such as cycling, walking, horse riding and of course sailing are in high demand.

The Isle of Wight remains the only destination in England where all tourism businesses are quality graded and inspected. Whether staying in a busy seaside resort or a peaceful and picturesque village, visitors can rest assured in the knowledge that their accommodation has the 'all clear' from the English Tourism Council, the AA or the RAC. It may only be five miles from the mainland, but the Isle of Wight is a different world. Yes, the pace of life is slower but the outdoor action is intense and with one of the best sunshine records in Britain, the Island really is the first choice for the complete holiday experience. Isle of Wight Tourism is a partnership between the Isle of Wight Council and the Island Tourist Industry Association, with close to 850 members representing a broad range of businesses from hotels and pubs to car hire firms and golf clubs. The Wight Hotline holiday booking service offers a one stop shop to the Island, allowing potential visitors to book their accommodation, ferry and find out all about the Island's events and attractions in one go.

Director, Isle of Wight Tourism

3
Absolutely!

bracelets**V**two

AVAKIAN
GENÈVE

GENÈVE: Hotel Noga Hilton (41) 22 716 15 20
LONDON: Carlton Tower Hotel (44) 20 7235 13 23

EMAIL: info@avakian.com

Opening Spring 2002: London 165 Sloane Street

Cowes
The Yachtsman's Bastion

Some of the biggest names in English literature - Dickens, Tennyson, Keats and many other great Victorian poets and novelists for whom the Island was an unending inspiration - have eulogised about the dramatic beauty of both the inland and coastal scenery of the Isle of Wight. Despite the modernising 'benefits' of the century and more since Dickens penned chapters of David Copperfield at Bonchurch and Tennyson looked towards the after-life in *Crossing the Bar* (a poem conceived on the sea crossing between Lymington and Yarmouth), the Island has, in many respects, changed very little. The pace of life is noticeably less frenetic than in mainland England and the scenery - though subtly altered through the effects of constant coastal erosion - remains as striking as it was in the days when Victoria herself made the Island her home.

The Isle of Wight is a place people tend to return to. Beauty continues to attract beauty - and today, the most beautiful yachts keep coming back to the small but distinguished and elegant Victorian 'home port' of sailing at the mouth of the River Medina. The chic and prestigious reputation of yachting in Cowes was due to several factors - among them the walk along the sea and the Parade leading to the very exclusive Royal Yacht Squadron, and the fact that Queen Victoria decided to spend so much of her long life at Osborne House, which brought many Royals and other well-known personalities to Cowes in the 19th century. There were also the continuing links with Royalty fostered by Edward VII, his famous yacht **Britannia** and the prestigious Cowes Week Regatta, which continues to this day and is part of 'The Season' (after Ascot, Wimbledon, Goodwood, Henley), when Cowes is brim-full of yachts and one can experience some memorable racing.

Last summer's America's Cup Jubilee, which has been generally regarded as the greatest regatta ever seen, and one never likely to be repeated (not for another 25 years, at least), recalled the grandiose Edwardian period and brought back some of the famous yachts of yesteryear .

That is now over, but memories remain. Some are carefully kept in museums, such as the Sir Max Aitken Museum in Cowes High Street, while old firms also recall the golden age of yachting. For centuries they have been known for their superb craftsmanship. Photographers, Beken of Cowes is one of them, while Spencer Rigging and Spencer Thetis Wharf - with founder Harry Spencer still at the helm - have developed an excellent reputation for wooden masts, riggings and booms, bronze fittings, blocks and cleats and all manner of systems which Harry (who some call "a devil of a sailor") has invented or brought up-to-date.

Ratsey & Lapthorn have been making sails since the time of Henry VIII. The firm has equipped (and still does) some of the most famous yachts. Kilometres of hand-woven sails which tell centuries of yachting history. There are many other company names which have long been, or are becoming, synonymous with Cowes, as the reader will discover within the next pages of this book.

Very important for the future of Cowes is **GBR Challenge**, led and organised by Peter Harrison, whose team is building a high-tech boat in its Cowes yard, focusing on a triumph in 2003 which will hopefully bring the America's Cup back to Cowes, where it all started.

Marie-Claire Baroness von Alvensleben

Message from Geoff Banks Mayor of Cowes

Cowes, often called, 'The Mecca of Yachting', still retains that authoritative position as the world's number one destination when it comes to yachting.

Recent years have been no exception and Cowes has taken on the task of promoting the biggest and the best during the past season.

Noted for its annual Hoya 'Round the Island Race' with the largest single racing fleet assembled anywhere in the world, and Skandia Life Cowes Week, an annual pilgrimage for anyone with a yacht, this year Cowes also organised The America's Cup Jubilee. Some several years of planning delivered what must have been the greatest yachting spectacle ever seen. As home of the first America's Cup race in 1851 it was only natural that Cowes should wish to honour one hundred and fifty years of yachting challenges. The town provided a well organised venue for the event which drew past challengers from around the world. It was truly a 'gathering of the clans' and superlatives as to the nostalgic presence of the famous J-Class yachts and over 200 competitors dating from modern times back to 1868 still abound.

Besides over two hundred years of competitive yacht racing off Cowes, the town is also noted for its shipbuilding, dating back to Henry VIII's era. It is also the birthplace of the first commercial hovercraft, the beautiful Sunderland Flying Boats and of many of the world's greatest powerboats in past decades.

As the historic gateway to the Island, and still boasting the greatest number of yacht clubs within any one town, Cowes still very much sets the pace with its yachting prowess, friendly atmosphere and unrivalled yachting history. Always worth a visit no matter what time of year, Cowes remains the 'jewel in the crown' of the Isle of Wight having so much to offer us 'overseas' visitors.

Cllr Geoff Banks
Mayor of Cowes

Photo MCvA

Left: Representatives of Cowes Royal British Legion, the Isle of Wight Polish Society and Cowes Town Council outside St Mary's Church, Cowes, at the Remembrance Day Service on 11th November 2001.

Below: Members of the 'Friends of the ORP Blyskawica Society' during their visit in September 2001 to the destroyer which is now preserved as a Museum Ship in the Polish dockyard of Gdynia.

Photo courtesy of Geoff Banks

Blyskawica
The Polish Heroine

German bombs rained down on the Isle of Wight during the Second World War. Nowhere suffered more than the port and twin towns of Cowes as the Luftwaffe sought to halt the vital ship and aircraft manufacturing outlets of J. Samuel White's and Saunders-Roe, what the enemy propagandists told newspaper readers was "the industrial centre of Great Britain". The enemy launched a particularly savage, two-pronged overnight raid on 4/5th May 1942. Fortunately for the twin towns, the Polish Navy's Cowes-built destroyer **Blyskawica** was in port for a refit when the Luftwaffe struck. Her gunners fired off a non-stop anti-aircraft barrage that night. Without it, Cowes might well have been totally obliterated.

The **Blyskawica** - happily preserved in Poland - is a legend in Cowes. Close links have been fostered in the port with the destroyer and surviving members of her wartime crew through Geoff Banks, Mayor of Cowes. A major commemoration of their heroic action is planned for 2002, the 60th anniversary of the Luftwaffe attack. The Polish Navy has promised to send its marine band and possibly a Naval vessel to the event. It is hoped that Polish yachts will take part in racing on the Solent during the commemoration.

It promises to be quite a tribute.

Painting by Tim Gladdis Courtesy Harry Spencer

The Story of Cowes

by Adrian Searle

Cowes did not really come into its own until the early part of the nineteenth century.
Its original name, Shamblord, is still remembered by Shamblers Road but the present name derives from the stone castles,
or cows as they were then called, built by Henry VIII at the mouth of the Medina and named East Cow and West Cow.
The real growth of Cowes, however, came in the early 1800s when sailing became a popular pastime for the rich and
famous and Cowes was used for supplying the needs of both the Merchant and Royal Navy during the Napoleonic Wars.

Thanks to its long-established eminence as a world centre for yacht racing, Cowes is without doubt the most internationally-known location on the Isle of Wight. Any attempt to recount the history of the place, however, must begin with the fundamental observation that there are, of course, two Cowes - East and West - either side of the River Medina at its point of contact with The Solent, the stretch of sea that separates Wight from mainland England. It is actually on the east bank of the river that any search for the origins of the Island's most northerly settlements must begin.

The broad brush of Wight history does not paint Cowes, East or West, into the picture until the 13th century. By then, the Island, which was probably first inhabited by the Bronze Age Beaker People, had been subjugated by the Celts from Northern France, peacefully ruled for 400 years by the Romans, subjected to centuries of strife and savagery under the Jutes, Angles and Saxons, converted late to Christianity, repeatedly attacked and dominated by the Vikings and then controlled virtually as a mini offshore state by a succession of Norman Lords following the Conquest in 1066. When, after several generations, the Normans became firmly Anglicised, the France of their forefathers lined up as the enemy and the seeds were sown for the necessary development of the two Cowes.

In order to enhance security against the regular 14th century incursions of the Continental foe, it was decreed that there would

The Beaker people are said to have named the Island "Wiht" which means raised out of the sea. The Romans invaded in A.D. 43 and translated "Wiht" into the Latin equivalent "Veho", which means lifting, and called the Island "Vectis".

henceforth be just three recognised trading ports on the Isle of Wight. They were at Eremue (Yarmouth), La Riche (Ryde) and, in between, the newly-developed port of Shamblord - present-day Cowes. Land settlement at Shamblord - the old name is principally recalled today at Shamblers Copse, west of the Medina - seems to have begun in earnest during the 13th century and was probably confined to the east bank of the river. It was spared when, in 1377, a combined French and Castillian force attacked the Island's north coast with devastating effect, destroying the towns of Yarmouth, Francheville (Newtown) and, eventually, Newport in the process. Less than a century later, with the menace of French invasion still a constant threat, the status of Shamblord would be elevated to that of defensive bastion by Henry VIII.

The Tudor King had a string of fortifications constructed to defend the Solent and the land either side of it. To protect the river mouth at the Island's northern tip, two forts, one on each side, went up in 1539, built of the stone from the recently-suppressed abbeys of Quarr, on the island itself, and Beaulieu, on the mainland. There is no trace today of Henry's eastern fort, but its western partner survives as part of the Royal Yacht Squadron's illustrious headquarters. What have also survived are the names given to the Tudor forts - the East and West Cows - which were themselves probably taken from the cow-shaped sandbanks lying off the mouth of the river at the time.

Shipbuilding at Cowes was a logical development in Tudor times, given the geographical location, the adequate depth of available water and the abundance of oak trees from which to cut the frames and timbers for King Henry's ships. In the reign of Elizabeth I, it seems more than likely that the Rat of Wight, one of the fleet sent out to meet the threat of the Spanish Armada in 1588, was built on the banks of the Medina. Demand for Cowes-built ships grew steadily over the next 200 years. From the late-18th century, substantial men-o'-war were being turned out for the Royal Navy in the former Nye yard, already well-respected, on the Medina during its occupancy in turn by renowned Hampshire shipbuilders Philemon Ewer and Robert Fabian. Both were eager to exploit the natural advantages offered by the Isle of Wight's most northerly port. Boats, as well as ships, were constructed - notably, the Cowes ketch, mass-produced throughout the 19th century and widely employed as a versatile workboat, both on the Solent crossing and elsewhere.

Meanwhile, East Cowes had assumed further importance through the development of international seaborne trade and the establishment there of a Customs House for the port - headquarters for the men who waged a constant battle with the smugglers who have plagued the Isle of Wight (and enriched its folklore) for centuries. Most noted of all the Cowes-based Collectors of Customs was William Arnold, who spent 23 years in the post from 1777. He succeeded in substantially reducing the illicit trade, dealing with widespread corruption among his own officers and producing an illustrious son in Dr Thomas Arnold, the famous headmaster of Rugby School, whose own son was the poet Matthew Arnold. Big names indeed, but set to be eclipsed at Cowes with the arrival of the port's most illustrious shipbuilding dynasty via the purchase of the old Nye yard by Thomas White, who moved the long-established family business there from Broadstairs, Kent, in 1803.

The relocation of White's paved the way for the firm's expansion into a multi-faceted business which was to become synonymous with Cowes during 160 years of investment, innovation and industry, providing both a major boost for the economy of the Isle of Wight and a tremendous advertisement for the quality of its products. *"White's-built, well-built"* became a slogan recognised around the globe as the company - particularly after control passed to Thomas's grandson, John Samuel, in 1860 - grew in international stature. Some of the finest fighting ships ever built for the Royal Navy began life in the hands of J. Samuel White's highly-motivated workforce, with destroyers to the fore. Foreign navies also benefited from their expertise, as did the operators of the cross-Channel steamers, offshore lifeboats and a host of other craft which left the Cowes slips.

White's adoption of Cowes as its new base was followed in 1825 by another, equally momentous, arrival. Two centuries earlier, Charles I's sad association with the Isle of Wight had been as a prisoner of the Commonwealth forces at Carisbrooke Castle, prior to his 1649 execution in London. Charles II made an impact on the Island in an altogether different, if indirect, manner, returning from his Dutch exile with the gift of a 52-foot yacht - the yacht had arrived in England! In 1661, the restored monarch and his brother, the Duke of York, contested the first yacht race between Greenwich and Gravesend. Thus were the seeds sewn for the twin social and sporting importance which Cowes proudly retains to this day - though the former arrived well in advance of the latter.

The port had assumed the air of a smart, if small, summer resort early in the 19th century, when sea bathing was newly in vogue and a host of 'fashionables' – the Dukes of Bedford, Portland and Orleans among them - were descending frequently on the place, becoming the first buyers of holiday homes on the Island. Some crossed the Solent in their own private yachts, others hired sloops for the purpose, bringing the family and household staff with them, plus the very necessary horses and carriage (and all for 29 shillings!), while others more modestly used the newly-inaugurated packet steamer service between Portsmouth and Ryde. They were not short of entertainment in Cowes, what with the theatre, concerts in the Fountain Inn (which still stands), balls and firework displays - and when, thanks to Wellington's success at Waterloo; the last of the 'fireworks' with Napoleon's France had brought peace to Europe: fashionable Cowes had really taken off!

It had staged its own regatta in 1813. Two years later a group of aristocrats and gentlemen met in London to form The Yacht Club as a counter to the take-over of London society - and its clubs - by Beau Brummel and the Dandies. The very exclusive yacht club was soon to acquire a Royal prefix. Five years after that, in 1825, it set up home in the Isle of Wight. Its ultimate restyling as the Royal Yacht Squadron followed in 1833, some 23 years prior to the relocation of its headquarters at (West) Cowes Castle, Henry VIII's old fortress, and still at that time the official residence of the Governor of the Isle of Wight (successor to the Norman Lords). With the Squadron's arrival, and the immense implications on social standing which flowed from it, West Cowes stepped up the growth that would eventually, and permanently, outstrip its eastern neighbour across the river. It long ago abandoned the need to add the 'West' prefix. Today, it is pre-eminent as plain 'Cowes'.

The advent of yacht racing at Cowes had been preceded by cruising, a less than serious leisure pursuit undertaken in what were essentially small sailing ships - and ashore at extravagant social gatherings held at Lord Yarborough's sumptuous Appuldurcombe House and other splendid venues. Owners lived aboard their yachts in style and employed crews sometimes in excess of 50! Taking to the sea en masse was virtually unheard of - it was a tediously long process, for one thing - until, in 1821, the Solent witnessed the extraordinary sight of 27 yachts following their leader out from Cowes in a spectacular procession to Hurst Castle, in the western Solent, and back. The first recorded race at Cowes followed in August 1826. A gold cup was up for grabs over a course which ran from Cowes Castle to a mark in the west Solent, thence eastward to No-man's Land and the Nab lights and back to base. It set the precedent for the early-August racing which has famously continued as Cowes Week ever since - a sequence broken only by war.

It has never been an easy thing to gain admission to membership of the Squadron. This was certainly true in the 1820s. Other clubs were quickly needed to cater for those inspired by the maritime exploits of the trail-blazing RYS members. They sprang up initially at Southampton (Royal Southern), in London (Royal Thames whose members frequently raced in the Solent) and at Ryde (Royal Victoria - the Isle of Wight's second club). It was all helped by the proximity of Royalty itself.

By the mid-19th century, the twin towns had attracted some prestigious new residents - with suitably grand accommodation. It is uncertain whether Northwood, the largest house in West Cowes, was designed by the great Regency architect, John Nash. The second East Cowes Castle, successor to the lost Tudor fort, certainly was. Nash designed it as a grand home for his own family. Nearby, the medieval fortress appearance of Norris Castle had actually been created at the end of the 18th century as a summer house for Lord Henry Seymour.

The Victorian Era

Oil on canvas by Edward Holt. Courtesy Geoff Banks, Mayor of Cowes.

America crossing the finishing line off the Squadron, surrounded by a fleet of spectator craft.

Osborne House
Courtesy Robert McInnes

Norris Castle
Drawing Bill Mollart-Rogerson

Princess Victoria who was then 12 years old, spent her first Isle of Wight holiday at Norris Castle, which her mother, the Duchess of Kent, rented in 1831 and 1833. This represented a milestone in the burgeoning reputation of the Island as a fashionable watering place, to rival Brighton - and just about anywhere else in England. This reputation was crowned, almost literally, when Queen Victoria and Prince Albert, having fallen in love with the Island, acquired the Osborne Estate on the fringe of East Cowes in 1845, after a failed attempt to buy Norris Castle. Osborne House, redesigned by the Prince Consort, became a much-favoured country retreat. Few leading figures of the extraordinary Victorian era - British and foreign - failed to put in an appearance at Osborne. With this Royal stamp of approval. resorts developed, railways were built and each seaside town had its own pier. The Island became fashionable venue for the great and the good - Alfred Lord Tennyson, Julia Margaret Cameron, Charles Darwin, John Keats, Charles Dickens, Garibaldi, Karl Marx, Edward Elgar and Marconi who made one of the earliest transmissions from Alum Bay in 1897 - just to name a few. When Prince Albert died in 1862, Queen Victoria went into retirement and was seldom seen in public. It was the twilight of the Victorian era.

The Yacht Clubs benefited from the nearness of the Royal Family. Most had at least one Queen's Cup, presented by the monarch, to offer an added incentive for winning a single race. And then yachting at Cowes was revolutionised by the famous visit from the schooner **America**, which outclassed the top British opposition in the Round-the-Island race which launched the America's Cup. In response, the home yachts were remodelled in the **America**'s image. New ones followed in the same style, giving magnificent employment to boatbuilders and sailmakers of Cowes and adding further to the prosperity of a port bathing gloriously in the radiance of Royalty on its doorstep.

On that famous August morning - 22 August 1851 - 15 yachts, 14 of them British, set off to race eastwards around the Isle of Wight for the Royal Yacht Squadron Cup, also called the 100 Guineas Cup. **America** was the only US yacht to take up the challenge. She won the race and the Royal Yacht Squadron Cup - made by Garrards, the Royal jewellers which became known as the America's Cup, after the yacht which had won it. Queen Victoria witnessed the race and is reputed to have asked who had won. The yacht **America**, she was told "And who is second?" she asked. "There is no second, ma'am," was the reply.

Queen Victoria congratulates John Cox Stevens, Commodore of the New York Yacht Club aboard the yacht America, winner of the 100 Guineas Cup - the event later to be known as the America's Cup

Louis Vuitton Media Centre

The day after the yacht **America** won that first cup race in 1851, Queen Victoria and Prince Albert visited the winner and asked to go below deck. Captain Dick Brown asked the Prince to wipe his feet, saying: "I know who you are - but you have to wipe your feet."

Osborne, Isle of Wight from the Sea
The Royal Yacht 'Victoria & Albert'
by Sir Oswald Brierly (1817–1894)
Print courtesy Robert McInnes

Edward VII

Edward, as has been well-chronicled, was a fun-loving man. Cowes, of course, was a first-hand witness to the lavish lifestyle of 'Bertie' who was naturally drawn to the place by his enthusiasm for the sport of sailing. Along with his Danish wife, Alexandra, he had been no stranger to the town before his accession to the throne. "The Prince and Princess of Wales and many foreign royalties could walk about and amuse themselves without being photographed or mobbed," wrote Jennie Jerome, Lady Randolph Churchill, in 1870's. Queen Victoria herself preferred to keep a telescopic eye on events - a watching brief on precisely who was being entertained by Bertie aboard his yacht *Britannia* - from the terrace at Osborne. Not for her the 'hands on' approach of the son who was to succeed her. Edward's larger-than-life persona was typified by the huge cigars he loved to smoke, the ever-present ebony walking stick and the kindly twinkle in his eyes, a divine shade of blue. He spoke with a slightly guttural German accent and was followed by a glittering entourage which often included the women in his colourful life - Mrs. Alice Kepple, the actress Lily Langtry and, occasionally, Princess Alexandra herself. To some members of the Squadron, the Prince of Wales' jolly bunch of associates were seen as his 'captains of foot' but, whether they approved or not, 'Bertie' undoubtedly brought a new social significance both to the Royal Yacht Squadron and Cowes generally. Thanks largely to his patronage, Regatta Week was established as one of the greatest social occasions of the season. It was said that, when Edward stepped ashore at the Squadron, Cowes would break out into "splendour and gaiety." His private life was the subject of continual gossip. The 'headline' affairs with Kepple and Langtry (and there were, of course, others) together with his frequent borrowing of money, were a source of grave concern for Queen Victoria (who would enquire, no doubt despairingly, about her eldest son's 'goings on') but of general amusement elsewhere, for Edward was regarded as "the most popular fellow in England." Few could resist his charms, though, as recounted elsewhere, the Royal Yacht Squadron proved a rare and notable exception when he attempted to change its rules. He was listened to, of course, but that was as far as it went. The Squadron proved an impenetrable barrier. The dawning of the Edwardian era was, thus, something of a culture shock in England. Following the example of their 'leader' the Edwardians were renowned for their lavishness. Whether they sinned, gambled (for the highest stakes), drank to excess, went bankrupt (often for hundreds of thousands of pounds), or quarrelled (often violently), the top echelon of Edwardian society did it with style! They lived in luxury and kept their wives (and mistresses) in spacious houses, where prodigious meals were served to heavily-laden tables. Their women were dressed in yards of tulle, lace, silk and satin, and covered with sable, chinchilla and ermine. Mink was used in those days for carriage rugs and overcoats. Style was evident, too, in sport - and especially the sport of yachting. In 1893, when still Prince of Wales, Edward had ordered from the Scottish designer, G.L.Watson the large racing yacht which was to become synonymous with his sailing career - and with Cowes. *Britannia* was to play a key role in rescuing the design and subsequent racing of yachts from the 'doldrums' into which it had descended via a succession of narrow 'plank on edge' yachts with immense lead keels and voluminous, largely inefficient, sails. They were big but, unless assisted by particularly hard winds, they were also painfully slow. Edward's graceful new cutter was nothing of the sort. She was fast - very fast - but for one man, she was there to be beaten. Kaiser Wilhelm - whose first racing yacht, *Thistle*, had been crewed entirely by Englishmen, there being no German yacht hands in existence - responded to the launch of his uncle's *Britannia* by having the great cutter *Meteor* built in 1896. She was larger, and had more sail, than her rival and, although skippered by an Englishman, some of her crew were now Germans. *Meteor* was the first of a series of yachts of the same name - each larger and more powerful than its predecessor - constructed as vehicles for the German Emperor's passion for competitive yachting. By the time the series reached *Meteor IV*, construction had shifted to Germany itself, the design was German and the yacht - the Kaiser's first schooner - was entirely skippered and crewed by men of the Emperor's nation. By then, Wilhelm's yachts had more than proved a match for *Britannia*. After a sound defeat by *Meteor* in 1897, a disillusioned Edward sold *Britannia* and ceased yacht racing altogether - until buying her back in 1899, then selling her again in 1900. He was back sailing her at Cowes Week in 1901, the year of his succession, before buying the yacht for a third and final time. *Britannia* remained in Edward's possession throughout his short reign. When he died in 1910, the beloved yacht passed to his son, the new George V. Being a very 'clubbable' man - bored when he was alone - Edward enjoyed the yacht racing more for its associated social gaiety than for the actual sport. He took *Britannia* to the Riviera, where he could race in the sunshine, and felt at ease among his cronies - men and women - who dashed between the casinos in Monte Carlo, Aix-les-Bains, Baden-Baden and other fashionable places. They called him 'Tum-Tum' and he loved his sprees on the 'Continong' where he could smoke his cigars and play baccarat to his heart's content. At home, his ebullience helped Cowes develop tremendously in an exclusive and brilliant way, with many Royals being entertained at portentous balls and dinners. The death of 'Edward the Peacemaker' truly marked the end of an era.

The Royal Yacht

Photo © Beken of Cowes

Standardt

With Edward on the throne, Cowes slotted naturally into the finest grandstand for observers of the Edwardian scene. The King himself, who had become Commodore of the Squadron in 1882, had for some years been entertaining the crowds splendidly in **Britannia**, the most famous of his racing yachts, especially when up against fellow Royals. If Cowes had been waiting for a final, definitive, confirmation of its exclusivity, it came from Edward's love of sailing and - despite his hatred of Osborne - his continued patronage of Cowes. The Regatta Week parties and balls were legendary during the Edwardian era. The whole place sparkled with the sheer brilliance of the occasion. On the water, the Royal Yacht **Victoria & Albert**, with her attendant battleship, dominated Cowes Roads and the yachting fleet around and about her was vast. The Tzar was there in **Standardt**, the Kaiser was aboard his **Hohenzollern** and the King of Spain flew the flag in his racing yacht, **Hispania**. When Edward VII died in 1910, the brilliance of Cowes Week lost a degree of lustre that it would never fully recover.

Hohenzollern

*The Kaiser tried to develop a 'German Cowes Week' at Kiel, encouraging the richest of his countrymen to buy fast schooners such as **Westward**, but he could never reproduce the atmosphere found in the waters of the Solent.*
He was critical of the "over-democratic" conduct of his uncle, famously berating him for "going boating with his grocer" - Sir Thomas Lipton.
Tragically for the world, four years after Edward's death, Kaiser Bill turned his attack on British democracy to more sinister purpose.

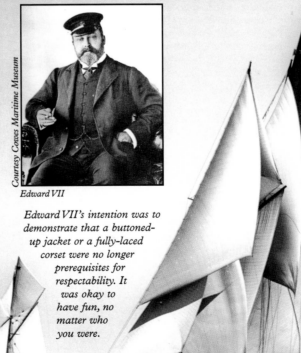

Edward VII

Edward VII's intention was to demonstrate that a buttoned-up jacket or a fully-laced corset were no longer prerequisites for respectability. It was okay to have fun, no matter who you were.

West Country—wherever there was a good berth and good sailing to be had. He reminds us of the great yachts and their owners—crowned, eccentric or just wealthy—who made up the cream of yachting in its golden heyday.

Jacket design by Lyon Benzimra.

BLOND

Cover of Sacred Cowes by Anthony Heckstall published by Anthony Blond, London 1965

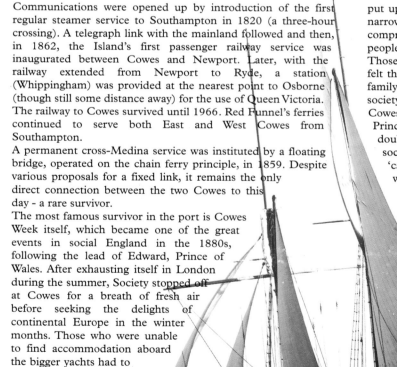

Communications were opened up by introduction of the first regular steamer service to Southampton in 1820 (a three-hour crossing). A telegraph link with the mainland followed and then, in 1862, the Island's first passenger railway service was inaugurated between Cowes and Newport. Later, with the railway extended from Newport to Ryde, a station (Whippingham) was provided at the nearest point to Osborne (though still some distance away) for the use of Queen Victoria. The railway to Cowes survived until 1966. Red Funnel's ferries continued to serve both East and West Cowes from Southampton.

A permanent cross-Medina service was instituted by a floating bridge, operated on the chain ferry principle, in 1859. Despite various proposals for a fixed link, it remains the only direct connection between the two Cowes to this day - a rare survivor.

The most famous survivor in the port is Cowes Week itself, which became one of the great events in social England in the 1880s, following the lead of Edward, Prince of Wales. After exhausting itself in London during the summer, Society stopped off at Cowes for a breath of fresh air before seeking the delights of continental Europe in the winter months. Those who were unable to find accommodation aboard the bigger yachts had to put up with paying exorbitant rents for a single bedroom in the narrow streets of Cowes itself, but all were part of a huge family comprised of what one writer has called "the nicest and prettiest people in England".

Those family members changed little from year to year; outsiders felt themselves to be "intruders upon a private party". Then the family grew to accommodate the American invasion of British society, the cream of which gathered together on the lawn at Cowes Castle - like "a marine Madame Tussauds" - with the Prince of Wales himself the centre of attention (although no doubt relieved to escape the stares of the masses whose own social standing kept them well apart). The lawn became a 'catwalk' for the latest fashions - and the society beauties who modelled them.

Over in East Cowes, brilliance of quite a different sort was emerging in the hands of another major player in the industrial heritage - Saunders-Roe (SARO). The original collaboration of Sam Saunders and Alliott Verden-Roe would eventually present the port, the Isle of Wight, the British nation and the world as a whole with the hovercraft - and much else besides. The story of this enterprising concern is told separately, but it is worth noting here that Cowes' unrivalled association with the hovercraft extended to its own hover passenger link with the mainland. It no longer operates, but the world's first-ever hover service, between Ryde and Southsea, continues to thrive under Hovertravel's management.

Cambria 1870
Courtesy Cowes Maritime Museum

Painting by George Gregory.
Courtesy The Priory Gallery and Robin McInnes

Prince's Green

Photo © Christian Ferrier Private Collection

The Regatta

*The Jerome family ancestors were Huguenots who fled from France.
One of their descendants, Timothy, left the Island for America in 1710.
In 1873 the American Jennie Jerome, her sister and mother met
Randolph Churchill during Cowes Week and two days later Jenny and
Randolph became engaged.
Jenny gave birth to one of England's most famous
Prime Ministers, Winston Churchill.*

Drawing Bill Mollart-Rogerson

The Gloster Hotel

Meanwhile, the port's social and sporting standing flourished up until the outbreak of war in 1914. Indeed, Cowes Week built even further on its international reputation, with yachts now regularly competing from America (notably A. S. Cochran's magnificent schooner *Westward*) as well as many of the European maritime nations. There was a spectacular International Regatta - the last of its kind - in 1911, with parties, balls and fireworks on a grand scale, and trophies given by a plethora of kings and emperors. War, three years later, saw several of them competing against each other for a grossly different type of prize. It truly was the end of an era. For the new British monarch, George V, a great lover of the sea himself, sailing for pleasure slumped quickly down the priority list.

The Bystander, July 26, 1905
A Trial Spin: Yachts Getting in Trim for the R.Y.S. Regatta at Cowes Next Week.

Courtesy Cowes Maritime Museum

ILLUMINATIONS AND FIREWORK DISPLAY BEFORE THE PRINCE OF WALES AT COWES.
Drawn by our Special Artist, Mr. C. J. de Lacy.
THE ILLUSTRATED LONDON NEWS, AUGUST 11, 1897

Pains Fireworks Limited
Tel: 01794 884040
Email: sales@painsfireworks.co.uk
www.painsfireworks.co.uk

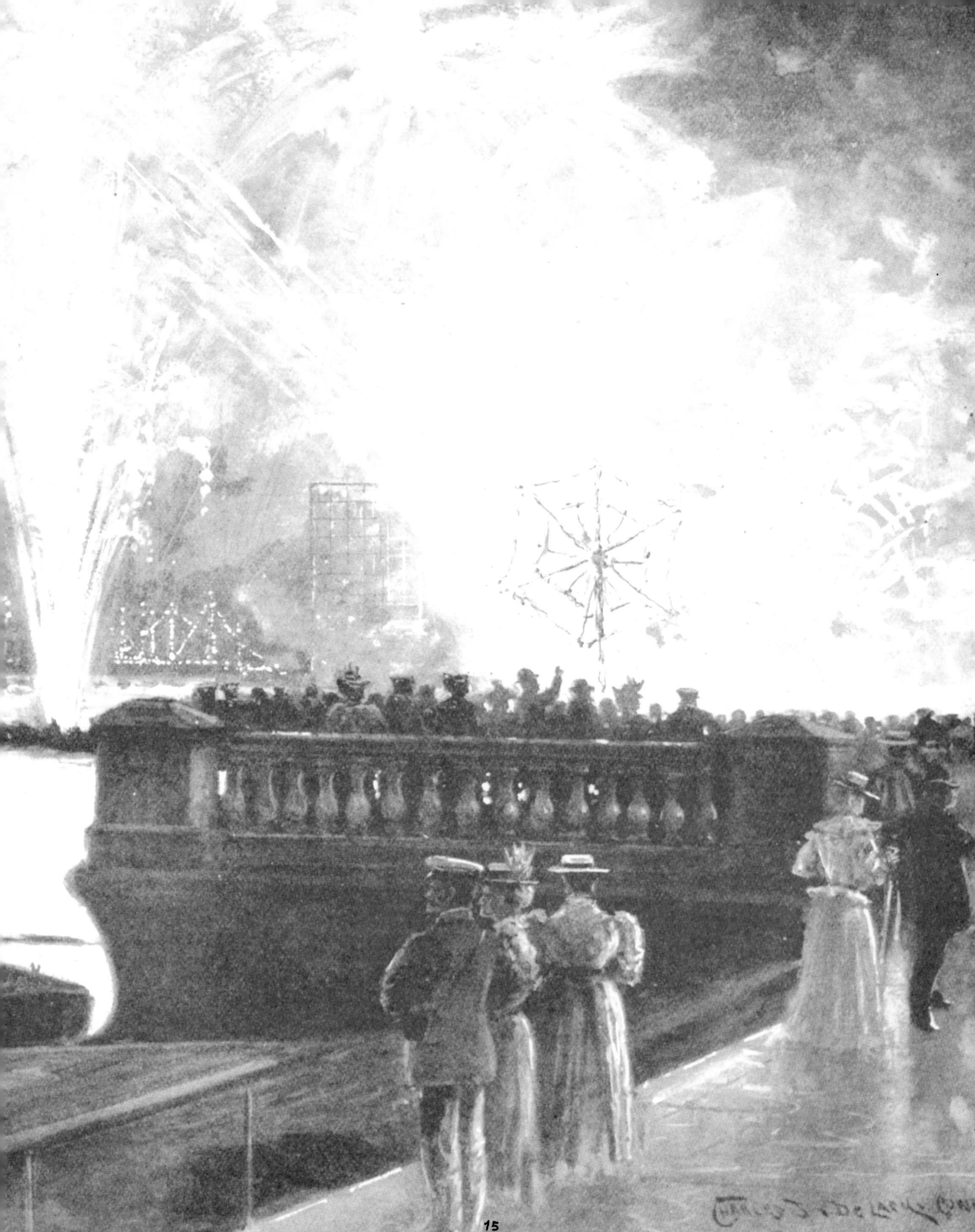

Courtesy Cowes Maritime Museum.

Shamrock III

Endeavour II

Royalty did not return to Cowes Week when the First World War ended. Neither did many others. Young people - those who had survived the conflict - had other interests now. There were no holiday crowds on the esplanade or the nearby green. George V lifted the gloom by ordering a refit for his old cutter, *Britannia*, Tommy Lipton - among the all-time yachting greats - immediately ordered a refit for his famous 23-Metre *Shamrock*, others followed suit (or fitted out brand-new yachts) and Cowes - particularly its shipwrights, sailmakers and ships' carpenters - eagerly anticipated the 'knock-on' effect of the King's decision. Another bright era was dawning for the port at the mouth of the Medina.

However, things were not the same. A new strata of society, newly-rich merchants, shipping magnates, newspaper proprietors and the like, many of whom had either bought or received peerages and baronies for services rendered during the war, now owned the big racing yachts. The old aristocracy could no longer compete financially. Not that it made any difference to the Royal Yacht Squadron - it remained as exclusive as ever. Members may not have been able to afford a first-rate racing cutter, but it remained as true in the 'twenties as it had been before the war - it was still easier to get into the House of Lords than to become a member of the Royal Yacht Squadron!

Getting into the port of Cowes was, for most, a process entrusted to the paddle-steamer fleet of Red Funnel, which continued to link the north coast of the Isle of Wight with the south coast of England. For those with time on their hands, the inter-war 'steam paddlers' - the newest of which, *Gracie Fields*, was doomed to die young off the beaches of Dunkirk in 1940 - would take them in style on more leisurely coastal cruises to places further afield. Bournemouth was a favourite destination. While dwarfed in the Solent by the great Transatlantic liners of the era, the paddle-steamers seem quite magnificent in retrospect. The very last in the Red Funnel fleet, the venerable *Princess Elizabeth*, though withdrawn in 1959, refused to lie down. New owners put her back to work until, in 1967, she had the guts ripped out of her. Thus deprived of the ability to move unaided, the gallant paddler still made it to the River Thames in 1970 to begin life as a floating restaurant, moored just upstream of London Bridge. The fate of most of her sisters was the breaker's torch.

Mourned more widely in 1936 had been the famous old Royal cutter, *Britannia*, beloved of George V, spurned by his sons Edward VIII and George VI, whose dislike of yachting sealed her fate. Their father had decreed that, if found to be unwanted by his heirs, *Britannia* was to be broken up. Launched for the last time from her mud berth at Marvin's Yard on 29th June, she awaited her destiny. It came via a melancholy tow to a final mooring out in the English Channel, south of St Catherine's Point. Charges were laid in her bilge. *Britannia* was blown asunder. She sank, aged 43.

On 8th July 1936, Britannia was scuttled according to the wishes of George V
Photo© Franklin Ratsey - Woodroffe.

George V
The Sailor King and Britannia

*It has been said that no man loved the sea more than George V and that he was probably never happier than when racing aboard **Britannia** with a party of friends. That he seldom found the time to pursue this favourite form of relaxation was a consequence of his ultra-keen sense of duty to the role of Monarch, which became progressively more arduous as the world plunged towards global conflict in 1914. The fun-time era of the Edwardians, personified by George's pleasure-loving father, was replaced by an altogether more contemplative pre-war period which was well suited to the character of the new king - as serious and dull as his father was charming and flamboyant. For the blunt, forthright Naval officer-turned-King, the simple life at Sandringham and Balmoral was preferable to the casinos, cigars and colourful company so beloved of Edward VII.*

George took over the crown in much the same way as he would have taken over the command of a new ship. And, while he loved to race **Britannia**, he would be quickly back on board the Royal Yacht **Victoria and Albert**, post-race, in order to attend to affairs of state. George became Admiral of the Royal Yacht Squadron after his father's death but, unlike Edward, was rarely seen there and was little interested in the social aspects of Squadron membership and office-holding. He did have **Britannia** refitted in 1913, but the outbreak of war a year later confined her to berth for a full six years. George V's greatest contribution to the sport of yacht racing was to provide the springboard for its post-war revival, when he ordered another refit for his old cutter. Tommy Lipton responded by ordering one for **Shamrock**, his famous 23-Metre racer, and the revival was under way. Other yachts were refitted or introduced brand new. Yachting - and Cowes - smiled again. It was the start of another bright new era in the port at the heart of yachting. George continued to foster interest and participation in the sport with still more refits for **Britannia** between 1920 and 1935, though - as with the old aristocracy in general - he was now up against the 'new rich'. The most notable of **Britannia's** inter-war refits came in 1931, when she was re-rigged to conform to the new American Universal Rule and join competition with the other yachts in the newly-created J-Class fleet. Proving that he did have a sense of humour, the King famously commented, with a smile: *"It should have been 'A' for adultery (rather than 'J') because, with the exception of old Davis, I am the only owner in the Class who still has his original wife!"* George's other 'marriage' - the one he enjoyed with **Britannia** - lasted up until his death in 1936, by which time the grand old cutter had been sailed for more than four decades by its two Royal owners. The story of Britannia's scuttling - according to the King's wishes - off St. Catherine's Point is told elsewhere. This sad, still-recalled, event brought Royalty's 'front line' involvement with yacht racing to a symbolic (but, as it would turn out, temporary) conclusion. Britannia would have been spared had George's son and heir, Edward VIII, expressed any interest in sailing her. But Edward had other, more pressing, things on his mind during his controversial short reign. His brothers were similarly disinterested - and so **Britannia** went down. Her gear was sold by auction, the mast was given to the Royal Naval College at Dartmouth, the spinnaker boom went to Carisbrooke Castle, on the Isle of Wight, as a flagstaff and the yacht's racing flags were distributed among various sailing clubs.

*A full scale replica of **Britannia** is being built (see Boat Building page 126)*

Britannia

The Victorian Pier in the middle of Cowes Parade was removed around the 1960s.

Very much afloat - spectacularly so - were the stallions of the sea that raced and graced the Solent waters at this time. Even people with no particular interest in yachting recall the sheer magnificence of the J-class. Criticised by some as fair weather vessels, because of their tendency to remain at anchor while other, smaller, classes competed in perfect racing conditions, the 'Js' were an awesome sight when they did leave their moorings - not least the towering 200 feet of mast. For many they were, and remain, the very epitome of yachting elegance. Remain? Happily, yes. In 2001 came the news that the few surviving 'Js' - plus some very expensive replicas - were to be re-formed, after decades away from the regatta scene, as a strictly limited racing class.

Could there also be a re-formation for the graceful structure that served both as a jutting grandstand for watching the J-class in action during the 'thirties and for catching the pre-war paddle steamer excursion vessels? The rebirth of Victoria Pier at Cowes, or at least a pier of some description, has certainly been mentioned of late. The original lasted just under 60 years, having been opened

in 1902, when the *PS Monarch* called from Bournemouth, and demolished without trace in 1961.

That the pier survived the Second World War, when it was held by the Royal Navy, was something of a miracle. The war demanded a lot from the production and maintenance facilities at Cowes. White's built a string of warships for the Navy (and much else besides), just as it had done during the earlier global conflict of 1914-18. Saunders-Roe supplied many seaplanes, while the smaller boat-building firms based around the port also did their bit for the war effort. Uffa Fox, about whose exploits as boat designer, builder, yachtsman, raconteur and personal friend to Royal princes whole books could be - and have been - written, saved the lives of many an Allied airman ditched in the sea with his parachuted airborne lifeboats. Conversely, the vital importance of the major Cowes industrial sites in 1939-45 inevitably attracted the attention of the Luftwaffe which sought to hold the vital ship and aircraft manufacturing outlets of J. Samuel White's and Saunders-Roe, what the enemy propagandists thought was "the industrial centre of Great Britain". The enemy launched a particularly savage, two-pronged overnight raid on 4/5 May 1942. Fortunately for the twin towns, the Polish Navy's Cowes-built destroyer **Blyskawica** was in port for a refit when the Luftwaffe struck. Her gunners fired off a non-stop anti-aircraft barrage that night. Without it Cowes might have been totally obliterated.

Blyskawica
The Polish Heroine.

Courtesy Cowes Maritime Museum.

Courtesy Ratsey & Lapthorn

Courtesy Max Aitken Museum.

Photo © Patrick Eden

Photo © MCvA

1. John Samuel White
2. Tom Ratsey
3. Ernest A. Ratsey &
   his father George E. Ratsey
4. Clare Lallow & Franklin
   Ratsey-Woodroffe in pleasant
   company at a launch in 1959
   at Clare Lallow's yard
5. Uffa Fox   6. Harry Spencer
7. Sir Max Aitken

Post-war, Cowes saw many changes to its industrial base. Plessey (formerly Decca) Radar emerged as a major employer on the site of SARO's former Somerton airfield base and, despite the closure of the big shipyards, which once employed thousands, the specialists in smaller boat and yacht building and the allied trades of sail and rope manufacture continued (and, in some cases, still continue) to flourish. Many of them - such as the W. A. Souter (now Souter Marine) shipyard and the boatbuilding businesses of Marvins, Clare Lallow and Groves & Guttridge - were known throughout the world for the quality of their craftsmanship, while there are few better-known sailmakers than Ratsey & Lapthorn.

The firm's famous sail-loft in Cowes is now occupied by apartments and the museum dedicated to one of the port's most illustrious yachtsmen, Sir Max Aitken, but Ratsey's continues to operate in Medina Road, as do Lallows, who remain the port's principal yacht maintenance specialists. They still build boats there, too, adding to an illustrious tradition which has included purpose-built racing yachts for Sir Max (*Drumbeat*) and former Prime Minister, Sir Edward Heath (*Morning Cloud*). Uffa Fox's own East Cowes yard, where the variety of craft turned out ranged from the International 14-class yachts - for which the yard became famous - to sailing canoes, survived his death and continued to build yachts for some years under the Groves &

Guttridge banner. Across the river, Marvins' yard in Clarence Road closed to become East Cowes Marina and is also the home of the RNLI's Inshore Lifeboat Centre.

J. Samuel White's itself - the most famous of them all - ceased its ship production line in 1965. The firm's final vessel for the Royal Navy, the Leander class frigate *HMS Arethusa*, had rolled down the slipway in November 1963. When the successor company, Elliot Turbo machinery, itself closed down in 1981, the final link was broken - a sad blow indeed for Cowes. "We have let down our forefathers in allowing shipbuilding to die at Cowes, where it had existed since the 15th century," said Harry Spencer, whose own yacht equipment business happily continues to manufacture masts and spars at Thetis Wharf, once an integral part of the huge and dominating White's empire.

Yet a stroll through Cowes today is all the confirmation required that the port is still very much alive and kicking as a centre for yacht-related excellence and expertise, on and off the water. The famous narrow streets are filled with a host of nationalities during the big week, in August. Indeed, filled is quite the wrong word. The place heaves with its mix of international humanity! And there is still a 'killing' to be made by canny locals, including those who take their own holidays away from the port during August - financed by the rents the 'yotties' pay for hiring their homes.

The Royal Yacht Squadron

by Adrian Searle

With its headquarters at Cowes Castle it is often cited as the world's most exclusive Club - an observation considered worthy of embellishment by one writer, who eloquently described the Club at Henry VIII's Tudor bastion as "the most impregnable fortress ever held by the aristocracy of England against the storms and sieges of the combined forces of the new rich and low bred."

As recounted elsewhere in this book, the Squadron sprang from the desire of a group of 42 gentlemen and aristocrats, tired of the attitudes of the "Dandies" led by Mr Brummel who kept blackballing candidates to gain admittance to White's and Brooke's Clubs, to preserve their exclusivity in society, by forming their very own club. They also had a penchant for saltwater sailing. Assembling at the Thatched House Tavern in St James's Street, London, they set up *The Yacht Club* on 1 June 1815. Qualification for membership was possession of a yacht of not less than ten tons and the payment of an annual subscription of three guineas. Prospective recruits, they decided, would have to submit themselves to a ballot at a meeting of no fewer than ten members. If a candidate incurred the disfavour of two members he was out before he was in. "Two black balls to exclude" was part of the fourth resolution adopted.

The Prince Regent made it past the ballot in 1817. When, as George IV, he became King in 1820, the Club was able to attach a Royal prefix to its title - the first yacht club to enjoy that distinction. George IV empowered members of the Club to wear the White Ensign of the Royal Navy aboard their yachts. Since then, the reigning British Monarch has always been the Admiral of the Squadron, though the title has been twice amended to Patron for Queen Victoria and the present Queen Elizabeth.

Yet the Club initially had no permanent headquarters. Instead, it used a number of different venues for its meetings and social functions. These may have included the Medina Hotel in East Cowes. Did the members, attired in their uniform blue jackets and white trousers, cross the River Medina on that occasion to see what might be available as a fixed Club base in newly fashionable Cowes? Certainly, by 1825 they had decided that Cowes was indeed *the* place to be. The Club secured the lease on a house in The Parade (which later became the Gloster Hotel and has since been converted into apartments) and this remained their headquarters for the next 30 years.

The change of name to the prestigious Royal Yacht Squadron followed in 1833 during the reign of William IV. It recognised an understanding that the Club's larger yachts could be called into service by the Royal Navy in times of war. It was not inappropriate, therefore, that the Squadron should move in 1856 to a former stronghold of defence against enemy attack - Cowes Castle, the West Cow of Tudor times. And there it has remained, making the most of the safe, sheltered harbour with its deep-water anchorage and the attendant facilities essential to the pursuit of sailing pleasure.

That pleasure was linked closely in the early days with the pursuit of something rather more base. Members were challenged to sailing matches, for high stakes - as much as several thousand guineas in some cases. No wonder the majority of yachts carried cutlasses (amid a veritable armoury of weapons!). The matches were keenly contested - to say the least - and a cutlass was useful to hack away rigging when two fiercely competing yachts ran foul of each other. There is a story of rival crews "fighting like wildcats and slashing at each other's rigging with their cutlasses, that flashed and glinted in the light of the fireworks" - being let off in honour of a Royal birthday.

It is difficult not to make the assumption that this swashbuckling behaviour was greeted with a greater degree of approval at headquarters than was a request made several years later by the Prince of Wales (later Edward VII) for hospitality to be extended at the Squadron during Cowes Regatta Week to ladies. Several older members were apparently greatly offended at such an outrage!

Society did, of course, expand under the influence of Victoria's fun-loving heir, but the Squadron did everything it could to remain resolutely exclusive. The Marquis of Hastings was blackballed when he applied for membership. His crime? Presuming acceptance, he had already had the RYS initials engraved on his yacht, *Ladybird*. "A presumptuous impertinence," thundered the members. The flamboyant Earl of Lonsdale fell foul of the RYS

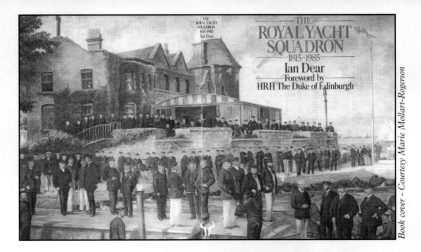

blackballing towards the end of the 19th century. He had opted to purchase the huge steam yacht **Finlandia** in order to entertain the Kaiser during a visit by the German Emperor to Cowes. That was considered over-ostentatious by the Squadron, who accordingly turned down Lonsdale's membership application. The Earl accepted their right to blackball whoever they wished, but complained bitterly that, in so doing, they had denied him the right to enter a Club of which his Royal guest was a member. "Embarrassing . . . without precedent", he stormed. The merits of this argument were accepted by the members. Honour was satisfied and the Kaiser was told the Earl was elected. The Squadron resisted all attempts to relax the rules on the admittance of new members. Even the Prince of Wales tried to convince them that they were too harsh. He called the ballot system "savagely inconsiderate, disgraceful, brutal and uncivilised." The "Pillars of Society", as they were called, listened politely but they wouldn't budge. The old regime clung on to the ideals of exclusivity into, and beyond, Edward's reign. Despite their inability to compete financially with the new rich, in the ownership of first class racing cutters, the old aristocracy were still well represented in the Squadron's ranks after the First World War. The men who could afford to own and race the large yachts found that this was not necessarily the passport to RYS membership. That still depended on the whims of the die-hards. They went too far, however, when they tried to blackball Lord Birkenhead, Lord Chancellor of England and, after the Archbishop of Canterbury, next in precedence to the Royal Family itself. George V found that totally unacceptable and

the Chancellor finally won his place - but it was a rocky ride for him. Women, denied en-bloc the luxury of Squadron membership, were usually allowed only as far as the famous lawn at Cowes Castle - though woe betide any young lady whose attire fell foul of what the members, devoid of any appreciation of modern fashion, considered was appropriate for the hallowed ground. When they spotted on the lawn a member of the fairer sex dressed in sailor's trousers and a sweater, they hastily convened a meeting and promptly banned any trouser-wearing woman from the RYS gardens. This firmly-enforced rule lasted from 1924 to 1938, when it was relaxed so that women in trousers were barred only during Cowes Week, although jeans are still banned today!

An offshoot of the 'no trousers' rule was the Squadron's realisation that, if women were to be barred from the lawn because of the offending garment, somewhere would have to be found at the Castle in which they could change into something more suitable. It seems never to have occurred to the members before then that it might have been a chivalrous gesture to provide convenient accommodation for their women guests within the Castle precincts. Their attempts to buy Castle Rock, a house across the road, in order to resolve this problem were thwarted by a mysterious rival bidder for the property, who offered more money. It was a blessed relief for womankind when the identity of the buyer was revealed as the famous Rosa Lewis, friend of Edward VII and owner of the Cavendish Hotel, in London (said to have been bought for her by the King). She agreed, possibly against her better judgement, to let the Castle Rock ballroom to the Squadron as a ladies' annexe. "While they won't have me on their old lawn, I have

Lord Yarborough was one of the founders of the Yacht Club, the future Royal Yacht Squadron, which moved from East Cowes to Cowes Castle in 1858. The castle had been used as a prison for privateers and other state prisoners and as a house for the Governor of the Isle of Wight.

to let their lady friends into my garden to piddle," was the caustic comment of the irrepressible Rosa.

Women were permitted entry to the Castle itself only on the rarest of occasions - and never without the escort of a Squadron member. They were allowed to view the trophies displayed in the Club and, on the final day of Regatta Week, watch the fireworks from the platform immediately outside.

Other than that, the Club's courtesy to womenfolk extended to tea or iced coffee with cakes, or perhaps strawberries and cream, on the lawn, where they could also listen to the band. Access, however, would only be granted if the women wore the special round cardboard badges issued for the purpose by the Squadron. If you had one of those coveted badges, you were a social success.

It was all completely beyond the grasp of the Americans, who came in large numbers to Cowes during the inter-war years. The men looked in vain for a cocktail bar at the Squadron. They were totally bemused by the lack of even a locker-room or showers at the old-fashioned and monastic headquarters. "Quaint" and "cute" were the best words they could find to describe it. The women were equally baffled by the rigid rules. There was very nearly an international incident when the wife of the renowned American yachtsman Clifford Mallory was found catching up with her mail in the RYS writing room. It was the clearest breach of rule - but Mrs. Mallory was a foreigner. She was also very pretty! The members present were far too gallant to throw her out. They asked the Steward to do it . . . A more enlightened attitude finally forced its way to the surface in the 1930s when Lord Albermarle stuck his neck out by suggesting that ladies should be permitted, at certain times of the year, to take luncheon and dinner in a small room at the Castle. Stern disapproval met his suggestion from certain quarters, but it did have some support. This may well have been helped by the action of whoever it was who decided, in the dead of night, to hoist from the trunk of the RYS flagstaff a pair of pink *crêpe de chine* panties. They were discreetly removed early in the morning... The point was made! Albermarle's proposal was finally adopted, the majority of members accepting the point that a little chivalrous entertaining might help to cheer the often largely empty male-dominated Castle during the cold winter months. Among the many restrictions imposed by the RYS are the famous steps and the pontoon in front of the Club. They are like "holy ground" and can only be used by members and their guests.

While, socially, the Squadron continued to live in the past after the Second World War (until the Duke of Edinburgh's six-year tenure as Commodore from 1961 significantly shook things up), it should not be forgotten that its members were very much up-to-date on the water. John Millar, for example, brought the first hydrofoil to Britain in 1958, four years after joining the Squadron. This type of craft was later to play a key role in speeding up cross-Solent ferry communications in the hands of Red Funnel. Commander Peter du Cane helped to pioneer the development of high-speed craft and the powerboats which were later to forge their own close sporting association with Cowes. Peter Thornycroft, a keen powerboat man himself, was later involved in ground-breaking warship design, while Sir Max Aitken, an outstanding yachtsman and patron of the sport, did more than anyone to bring international powerboat racing to the port.

Sir Max's favourite (and oft-told) story about the Royal Yacht Squadron, however, concerns his application for membership. Ian Dear's acclaimed book on the Squadron's history recalls the remark of one elderly member to another:
"Who's this fellow Aitken, then?"
"Don't you know? He was a Battle of Britain fighter ace. He's a pilot." "Good God." Pause. "A pilot?"
Pause. *"We'll be letting in dirt-track riders next."*

Photo © MCvA

Osborne House
Painting by John Wilson Carmichael, 1862
Courtesy Robin McInnes

East Cowes

by Sarah Burdett

East Cowes lies on the east bank of the River Medina, opposite West Cowes. It is the terminal for the car ferry from Southampton and is also a busy industrial area. Shipbuilding, aeroplane construction and hovercraft development have made the town proud of its industrial heritage and GKN Aerospace still occupies a large site. East Cowes is also where Queen Victoria chose to live, at Osborne House. Other major 19th century developments to shape the town included the construction of Norris Castle, East Cowes Castle and superior housing surrounding the botanic gardens.

In 1539, forts were constructed in East and West Cowes (before they were so named), on the order of Henry VIII. The East Cowes fort cost him £2,000, but the foundations were on clay and the building was abandoned seven years later.

From the 14th century East Cowes had been an important customs post, and by the 18th century the busy port was one of three along the south coast of England where merchant ships from abroad would report to await orders and have their cargo assessed for tax. **William Arnold,** father of Dr Matthew Arnold of Rugby School fame, was the customs collector here for 24 years from 1777. Local shipbuilder Gely was renowned for his fast craft, used by the local smugglers. Arnold had the same firm build a succession of faster craft for the coastguard! The coastguard cottages along the seafront were built in 1881.

In the same year Thomas White bought the Gely shipyard in East Cowes and continued the tradition of building ships for the Navy. His sons continued the firm, which became known as **J.S.White's**. Revolutionary motor torpedo boats led on to destroyers and submarines. In 1944, White's developed the first all-welded destroyers. Eventually the shipyard closed in 1966 and British Hovercraft Corporation bought the site.

At the end of the 19th century, the Liquid Fuel Engineering Company was building steam launches and cars. Sam Saunders bought the yard in 1906 and **Saunders Roe** built the Columbine Shed here in 1935, the main doors of which have the largest Union Jack in the country. Behind these doors important engineering innovations were developed, including many seaplanes, the largest-ever metal seaplane "The Princess", the only British rockets and the first-ever hovercraft. Further along the river the company's yards were building the fastest speedboats in the world, such as *Bluebird* and *Miss England II*.

The **Black Knight** rocket was followed by the **Black Arrow**, which in 1971 launched Britain's Prospero satellite into space. The Government discontinued the project, a fate that also overcame the SRA1 and SRA3 jet planes developed in East Cowes.

The **Hovercraft**, developed by Sir Christopher Cockerell in 1959, was rather more successful. Many hovercraft were built in East Cowes, including the largest in the world - the cross-Channel Princess used to transport 60 vehicles and more than 400 passengers. These craft remained in service for twenty one years.

*The Medina Hotel.
William Daniell, circa 1824. Courtesy Robin McInnes*

In 1861, the Southampton, Isle of Wight & South of England Royal Mail Steam Packet Public Company bought a quay in East Cowes. More usually known as **Red Funnel**, in the 1980's, the company gradually bought much of the old town centre for its car marshalling area as larger ferries were introduced on the route.

The **Trinity House** Engineering Department is next to Red Funnel. Trinity House has had a depot here since before 1845 when it built a fine entrance and pier for Queen Victoria to use. Today, the Depot is at the forefront of hi-tech solar power development - all buoys and light vessels now being lit by the sun.

The cross-river **Floating Bridge** is one of only six chain ferries in England. Operated by steam from 1859, and diesel electric since 1936, the bridge is the only direct link between East and West Cowes. The Council has run the floating bridge since 1901.

The **Royal National Lifeboat Institution** has its inshore boatbuilding and repair depot at East Cowes, together with engineering works and training facilities. It continues the long tradition that the town has had with building lifeboats.

Notable Houses

In 1798 the Regency architect John Nash began building his own home, **East Cowes Castle**, where he entertained lavishly, the Prince Regent and the painter Turner being among his guests. The castle had a profusion of Gothic turrets, towers and ornate castellations, with gardens laid out by Repton. Nash died here in 1835, and is buried by the tower of East Cowes Church - which he also designed. The lodge to the castle, in cottage ornee style, remains in Old Road. The castle fell into disrepair after the Gort family sold it and was demolished in the late 1960s.

Norris Castle, however, still exists. James Wyatt designed it in the Norman style in the late 18th century for Lord Henry Seymour. It is an excellently constructed building in a prominent position overlooking the Solent, and remains a private home.

The Botanic Park Development of 1842 envisaged large houses, perhaps of Gothic style, surrounding ornamental gardens. The road system laid out remains today, the tree-lined avenue leading uphill from the ferry being one of them. Queen Victoria eventually bought many of the houses for members of her family. Kent House was named after her mother, and was occupied until 1921 by Lord Mountbatten and his family. Princess Beatrice occupied Osborne Cottage, and Arthur Cottage was built for the Munshi, the Queen's Indian servant.

Osborne House was developed in Italianate style in 1845 after the Royal couple bought a Georgian mansion as a home of their own. It was here that Queen Victoria died in 1901.

Trinity House

Trinity House has existed in East Cowes since 1842, originally with a view to using the premises as a warehouse for storing oil.

In 1845, Sir John Pelley, Deputy Governor of the Trinity Board gave a directive for the immediate erection of a wharf at East Cowes opposite the old Custom House for the Royal Family to land and embark in private. Even in those days, it seems that they must have had trouble with the paparazzi! Queen Victoria used this facility until her death when she finally left the Isle of Wight via the Depot and her coffin was placed on the Royal Barge and taken out to the Royal Yacht *Victoria and Albert* for her eventual burial in London.

In 1867, the Admiralty granted a free site for the North Buoy store and erected the building for the use of Trinity House. In 1922, the Admiralty conveyed to Trinity House the North Buoy Store as a free gift along with the pier, landing stage and the wharf originally constructed in 1845. This lasted until 1950 when the State canopy over the landing stage was finally demolished. The East Cowes Depot remained unaltered until 1964 when the Depot was completely reconstructed and modernised to cater for more up-to-date requirements.

Trinity House
East Cowes, Isle of Wight, PO32 6RE.
Tel: 01983 203400.
Fax: 01983 294317.

East Cowes Heritage Centre

Run by volunteers from the Isle of Wight Society, this small exhibition looks back over the last two centuries of development in East Cowes through a permanent display. The aim of the centre is to raise public awareness of the wealth of industrial and social heritage to be found here.

The historic houses of the town and the recent housing and industrial development are shown clearly in three-dimensional models. Shipbuilding, aircraft manufacture, hovercraft development, rockets and jet planes all feature in the pictorial display, along with models of some of the aircraft and the sales demonstration hovercraft. The social history of East Cowes is considered, including the influence that Queen Victoria had on the town.

In addition, several temporary exhibitions are held annually, depicting some aspect of the town. Files on more than 50 East Cowes subjects as diverse as schools, regattas, shops, shipbuilding and hovercraft are available for study. Several publications about the town have been produced, which can be purchased. Even if the centre is closed, there can be interesting information to look at in the window displays.

8 Clarence Road (near the umbrella tree).
Opening hours: 10-1 daily, except Sundays.
Other times by arrangement. Entry: Free.
Tel: 01983 280310.

The 'Bat Boat'

East Cowes shipbuilding. An artist of the English school, circa 1860.

Lifeboats
Royal National Lifeboat Institution

The Royal National Lifeboat Institution

The Royal National Lifeboat Institution (RNLI), the rescue service which turns out in all weathers to save lives at sea, has 225 lifeboat stations around the coasts of the United Kingdom and the Republic of Ireland. (Also see other article on page 46) The inshore rigid inflatable craft are made and serviced at the East Cowes RNLI Works, whose large engineering department customizes engines to very high standards specifically for RNLI use. An ongoing training programme is carried out there to enable crews to expertly use and maintain their inshore craft. The Depot is part of the Cowes hi-tech marine industry.
For more information about the RNLI
West Quay Road, Poole,
Dorset, BH15 1HZ
Tel: 01202 663000. Fax: 01202 663167.
www.lifeboats.org.uk.

Cowes Inshore Lifeboat Organisation

Cowes Inshore Lifeboat is an independent group of volunteers. They have been serving Cowes and the central Solent from Newtown Creek to Fishbourne since 1990, attending an average of 50 emergencies a year. They work closely with Solent Coastguard. In 2001 they helped at twelve emergencies during Cowes Week alone. There was an official naming ceremony for the new Cowes Inshore boat during the America's Cup Jubilee week by Mrs Joy Harrison, wife of British GBR Challenge America's Cup bid backer Peter Harrison. He had given £25,000 towards the £80,000 cost of the new boat which was named **Spirit of Cowes**.
The Chairman is Chris Greenham.
For more information, call 01983 298357. A local supporters' group has been set up, and for information on this call Lydia Whittaker on 01983 526760.

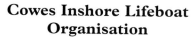

The Folly Inn

On the Admiralty chart of 1783 the Folly public house is shown looking rather like a child's impression of a Noah's Ark. This is because the name is derived from a boat called *La Folie*, which at one time was moored nearby and served refreshment to the barge-masters sailing up river with their cargoes to Newport. One day in a severe storm the boat was washed ashore, and there she stayed. Gradually, the boat became a house, and was extended as the demand for refreshment increased, much within the last three decades of the 20th century.

The word INN painted on the Folly roof has brought joy to the heart of many a sailor, knowing they will find good food and hot showers. Today visitor berths are available at the pontoons west of the inn, but weekend rallies and clubs should book well in advance. Individual moorings can sometimes be obtained.

The Folly Ferry, (Tel.0788 7725922), runs an 'on-demand' service to the Inn pontoon, which is accessible at all states of the tide.

There is a scrubbing berth capable of taking vessels up to 10.67m LOA and a 1.83m draft on spring tides. This can be booked on application to the Medina Mariners Association, (Tel. 01983 866667).

From the Folly Inn there is an attractive walk across the fields up to Whippingham Church, re-designed by Prince Albert when Queen Victoria worshipped there. There is also an exhibition about Whippingham in the Church Hall, open Monday-Friday. Take the road uphill until the first bend and then turn left up the path before the mobile home site, which has a small general shop. Tel: 01983 297171.

EAST COWES
MARINA

Acquired by John Dean & Richard Reddyhoff in 1998, East Cowes Marina has been enlarged and improved by them. The northern end of the marina has been dredged to 2.5 m below chart datum and new pontoons have increased the capacity to 150 visitor moorings.

Weekend rallies are welcome but must be booked in advance, and a DIY barbeque facility is available. In 2001 a new Whitbread pub - The Lifeboat - opened, providing food and drink throughout the day. The usual marina facilities are available - toilets and showers, electricity, trolleys, chandlery, first aid, weather reports and car parking. The site is covered by video camera security. The marina will accept berth-holders' mail and, for a small donation to the RNLI, incoming faxes.

Water taxis provide a service from three taxi stops around the marina for those wishing to avail themselves of the facility. The Marina is a five-minute walk from the floating bridge, Osborne House is a ten-minute uphill walk away.

A crane quay adjacent to the southern basin offers emergency lift-out, and planned storage ashore is available from Small Craft Rigging, (tel: 01983 298269). The area is a sensitive one for dredging and, although Dean & Reddyhoff would like to extend the marina, *English Nature* is against the plans pending a further survey of the river. Financed by the marina, this survey is being carried out in conjunction with the Cowes Harbour Master's office. The firm first developed the 600-berth Haslar Marina, at Gosport, where 25 acres of mud was dredged. Their second marina was developed at Weymouth, and East Cowes is their third project.

The marina at East Cowes was originally the site of a brickworks producing the strong yellow Victorian bricks seen around the town. The site was taken over by Marvin's shipyard. One of the yachts to regularly over-winter here was King George V's yacht, **Britannia**, hence the name Britannia for the road leading to the Marina.

East Cowes Marina, Britannia Way, East Cowes, Isle of Wight, PO32 6HA
Tel: 01983 293983   Fax: 01983 299276
Email: miket@deanreddyhoff.co.uk

FROM TO
RIVER > SEA
the Marine Heritage of Sam Saunders

by RAYMOND L. WHEELER

FROM TO
SEA > AIR
the Heritage of Sam Saunders

by A. F. TAGG
& R. L. WHEELER

Sam Saunders

THE ISLAND HERITAGE
OF GKN AEROSPACE

by Adrian Searle

*The East Cowes premises of GKN Aerospace Services
are obvious to anyone nearing the end of the cross-
Solent passage from Southampton. The giant Union
Flag decorating the hangar doors of the site's principal
waterfront building originally celebrated Elizabeth II's
Silver Jubilee in 1977. It remains there by popular
demand - a startlingly patriotic symbol of a company
which, through a succession of earlier identities, has
done so much to foster national pride in the 100 years
of its extraordinary existence.*

Above: East Cowes waterfront in 1931. The white house in the centre was the Saunders' home for many years.

Left: Alexandra Hall, Sam Saunders' first premises at Cowes.

Right: Syndicate-built boats behind Alexandra Hall.

The record-breaking sea plane, the Bat Boat, was built in East Cowes in 1913.

Sam Saunders

Miss England II achieved 110.222 mph in 1931, gaining the World Record.

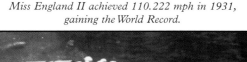

Company origins can be traced to one man. Sam Saunders started the ball rolling in 1901 when the Saunders Patent Launch Building Syndicate was transferred from the Thames to the Island, basing itself in a converted chapel at West Cowes. By 1908, having quit the syndicate, Sam Saunders was operating a new business, S. E. Saunders Ltd., across the river in the Columbine Yard (which remains the successor company's headquarters to this day). Saunders specialised in the development of strong, yet lightweight, high-speed boats, their hulls uniquely constructed through a laminated process in which levels of diagonal plywood planking were sewn together, with copper. This innovative approach led to pioneering work with hydroplanes and proved an irresistible magnet to the men who were developing the concept of the flying boat. A low weight-to-frame ratio was essential for their purposes. Saunders obliged, then seized the initiative by setting up a new department in 1909 to concentrate specifically on design and build for aero navigation. The shift in emphasis from the marine sector to the aeronautical - the transition that would have such profound effects locally, nationally and even internationally - had begun. This move was accentuated by the British Government's decision to channel the expertise of Saunders into aircraft manufacture during the First World War. The company responded by contributing a thousand planes - both land and water-based - to the war effort. By 1917, it was designing its own aircraft. However, marine activity during the war years was confined solely to the construction of lifeboats. Saunders expanded post-war by converting its Folly Works, further down the Medina's east bank, to the manufacture of laminated plywood, but endured a worrying slump in fortunes in the 1920s when it was plagued with the economic harshness of the time. Sam Saunders sold controlling shares to the Vickers company, then did a 'U' turn to regain full control of the firm, but it was evident that the business was in desperate need of a lifeline. It came via Alliott Verdon-Roe, founder of the Avro Company, and John Lord, who were sufficiently far-sighted to spot the potential in a collaboration with Sam Saunders' ailing concern. They were also in possession of that most vital of commodities - money. Their takeover in 1928 led to the formation of arguably the most famous hyphenated name the Island has ever known - Saunders-Roe. Sam Saunders resigned his directorship, remaining as president of the new business, which operated under the chairmanship of Verdon-Roe. The Isle of Wight lost one of its most vibrant 20th century personalities with the death of Sam Saunders in 1933. Not only a key figure in the Island's industrial and employment sectors, he was also active in its property market and was a generous benefactor. It was Sam Saunders who presented the Isle of Wight Football Association with its Gold Cup – reputedly the most valuable football trophy in the world! In the mid-1930s, Saunders-Roe was commissioned by Sir Malcolm Campbell to build the hydroplane *Bluebird* that would successfully capture the world's

The world's largest metal flying boat, the Princess,
was launched in 1952.
She was never to fly commercially.

The first prototype SR.45 Princess being towed on
her final voyage to Southampton to be scrapped.

Left: Saunders-Roe SR.53.

Below: The world's largest hovercraft
SR.N4 Mark 3, used on the
cross-Channel service for 21 years.

Black Arrow 1971,
the only British
rocket to put a
satellite into space.

water speed record in 1937, then break it a year later. But it was the company's considerable reputation for its amphibious aircraft that was called upon when Britain was plunged once again into war in 1939. Seaplanes were urgently needed for the war effort. Saunders-Roe obliged. Initially, the company built the single-engined Walrus amphibian designed by Vickers Supermarine and used by the Fleet Air Arm for reconnaissance and air-sea rescue work. In all, 461 were turned out by Saunders-Roe during the war years, production peaking with 209 in 1942. Next came the much heavier and faster Sea Otter, another Vickers design. The company built 290 from 1943 to 1946. A subsidiary company operated repair works at Solent Works, West Cowes and, after the yard there was wrecked by the Luftwaffe's devastating attack in May 1942, at Forest Side, Parkhurst. The firm's factory at Whippingham produced no less than 40% of the total wartime plywood requirements of the entire British aircraft industry. Employing a wartime workforce of around 6,000 – 40 per cent of them, women - Saunders-Roe also managed some development work on the first-ever jet-propelled amphibian fighter plane before the war's end. It eventually flew in 1947. Post-war, the core Saunders-Roe activity of seaplane manufacture was to culminate with the mighty, and doomed, Princess Flying Boat. It was conceived at a time when the development of water-based planes was still regarded as the way forward for the embryonic long-distance air travel market. Certainly, that was the thinking of BOAC (later, one

of the constituents of British Airways) when Saunders-Roe was commissioned to work on the Princess project amid great expectations. Many advanced features were incorporated in the design of the magnificent two-decked planes. Three were built, the first taking to the air on a test flight around the Isle of Wight in August 1952. However, the aircraft were plagued by engine unreliability - and the thinking had now swung in favour of land-based planes for the Transatlantic route the Princesses were built to fly. It was a bitter blow for Saunders-Roe when the project was cancelled - none of the trio having entered revenue-earning service. The planes that were to have crossed the Atlantic non-stop with their hundred or so passengers survived at East Cowes and Calshot, on the mainland, cocooned until the mid-1960s - moribund, surreal tourist attractions, permanently grounded, symbols of a lost era. But the innovative genius and sheer versatility of Saunders-Roe lived to fight another day. It was, literally, rocket science. The company had paved the way by designing a turbo-jet and rocket-powered fighter plane in the late 1940s. It caught the eye. Saunders-Roe was engaged to develop the Black Knight rocket - the means for testing the re-entry of Britain's new Blue Streak strategic ballistic missile. The company manufactured and assembled the rockets at Cowes and tested them at a dramatic, specially-constructed site above the Needles Battery, in the far west of the Island, prior to fuller trials in Australia.

The famous Hovercraft hanger, with the largest Union Jack in the world.

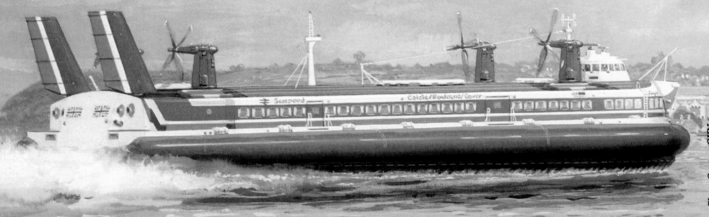

Black Knight was followed by a development called Black Arrow which successfully launched a satellite called Prospero into space in 1971, but Saunders-Roe's next enterprise - and easily its most famous – had far-reaching consequences. It followed the invention by Sir Christopher Cockerell of the annular (ring-shaped) jet. Saunders-Roe was commissioned by the National Research & Development Commission to take Cockerell's brainchild a highly significant stage further by building the world's first manned hovercraft, the SR.N1, in 1959. But, just as the hovercraft arrived on the scene, the proud Saunders-Roe name was swallowed up in a takeover of its major sites by Westland Aircraft (De Havilland Holdings acquiring SARO Laminated Wood Products at the same time). Successor, but still experimental, hovercraft continued to bear the SR.N (Saunders-Roe Nautical) branding in the succeeding years before, in 1964, the company established the world's first commercial hovercraft production line at East Cowes. The SR.N5 was used to launch and, in its 'stretched' SR.N6 version, subsequently maintain, Hovertravel's trail-blazing (and still operating) passenger service between Ryde and the mainland from 1965, before being replaced in 1982 by the larger (and

quieter) AP1-88, another product of East Cowes. In the meantime, Westland and rivals Vickers had merged their hovercraft interests in 1966 to form the British Hovercraft Corporation, based at East Cowes, with Westland holding the majority interest. It was under BHC branding that the biggest hovercraft of them all, the Mountbatten class SR.N4, was launched in 1968. Later 'stretched' to increase capacity, it successfully operated the cross-Channel passenger services from Dover under the Seaspeed (later Hoverspeed) banner. When further reorganisation took place in the early 1980s, BHC found itself transformed into Westland Aerospace Ltd. With hovercraft production now a thing of the past, the successor to Sam Saunders' enterprise has operated since 1994 as the aerospace arm of the massive GKN plc. As such, its output is now the supply of structures, components, assemblies and engineering services to aircraft and aero-engine manufacturers. Recent cutbacks in the East Cowes workforce have threatened the company's status as the Island's largest private employer, but GKN Westland's importance to the local economy is as vital as at any time during the past century.

GKN Aerospace

Castle Street, East Cowes, Isle of Wight, PO32 6RH
Tel: 01983 294101 Fax: 01983 291006
www.aero.gknplc.com

Photos Courtesy Isle of Wight Council

Courtesy Marie Mollart Rogerson

Famous People & Houses

Many famous people have lived in the Cowes area. Some built very fine houses and even beautiful Gothic castles. Lord Henry Seymour lived in Norris Castle, East Cowes, which was built for him by James Wyatt between 1795 and 1805. The future Queen Victoria spent her summer holidays there in 1831 and 1833. Nearby, the famous Regency architect John Nash built and lived at East Cowes Castle, entertaining there on a lavish scale until his death in 1835. It was the Royal stamp of approval for the town, the port and the Island in general when Queen Victoria and Prince Albert bought and completely redeveloped Osborne House. This really brought the Island into its own. It was now a fashionable venue for the 'great and the good.'

Alexandra House

Alexandra House in Birmingham Road was built as a Wesleyan Chapel in 1831. It closed in 1905 when the new Methodist Chapel was built nearby. It was in the rented basement of the converted chapel that Sam Saunders, newly arrived on the Island from Teddington, first set up in business as the Saunders Patent Launch Building Syndicate, forerunner of Saunders-Roe and the present-day GKN. **Miss England,** *which for a time held the world water speed record was built there. Thomas Wilks, who lived at Alexandra House in the late 1960s, was a son of the Wilks family responsible for the development of Land Rover - though on another of Britain's offshore islands. Thomas' father, Spen and his brother Morris lived for a time on the latter's estate in Anglesey and were directors of the Rover Motor Company. Despite the shortage of steel at the end of the Second World War, it was there that they set to work on two ex-Army jeeps and came up with the Land Rover. This is perhaps one of the lesser-known Cowes links with international product development. The story comes courtesy of Michael Henderson, who still lives in Cowes, knew Thomas Wilks personally and who is himself the inventor of the Henderson bilge pump.*

Northwood House

Northwood House, a large, beautiful old building surrounded by parkland and overlooking Cowes and The Solent. combines elements of French, Italian and Grecian design， a grand property indeed. Built by the Ward family in 1838 (as an enlargement of its Bellevue predecessor), Northwood later became a temporary monastery and Red Cross hospital before being gifted to the Town and transformed during the 1930s into local government offices. Trees from many parts of the world survive in the park, thanks to the Wards' grand planting programme. The grounds still feature species of Lebanese cedar, Spanish cork, Turkey oaks, and a massive Scots pine, among many others. Harry Spencer, very impressed, suggested that it would be an interesting and informative exercise to 'name tag' them. Even the gates and gateposts are of interest, with some of them made of teak from wrecked ships. There was once a tunnel running to the east estate entrance and, some say, to the Royal Yacht Squadron. During the Second World War, Northwood House was used as quarters for nurses, scout messengers, ambulance staff and the air raid precautions (ARP) teams. Post-war, little maintenance was carried out by the local council for almost 50 years. Nowadays, Northwood is used for social functions and receptions. It remains a grand setting in its lovely park, but is definitely in need of refurbishment to bring it properly alive for the benefit of the people of Cowes. Harry Spencer, for one, suggested a Marine Museum as well as a Health Centre be built at the back. The upper floor could become a large function room with a stage, and acoustically designed for concerts and banquets. - which the town really needs.

We personally think that it should become a deluxe hotel with a gourmet restaurant - Cowes really needs both and this could also attract investment to restore and improve the building. To keep busy, the hotel could offer a Health Spa - very popular these days - with treatments available to 'outside' clients. And why not a 'Thalassotherapy Centre'? They are very popular in Brittany and there really seems no reason why one could not be similarly popular in Cowes and on the Island. A Marine Museum, with aquatic attractions, could then be housed in a modern building somewhere in the park. Food for thought?

Grantham Court

Lord Grantham - who played a key role in the founding of The Yacht Club in June 1815 - had Grantham Court built on land he owned, known as Prince's Green. G. R. Stephenson, the railway man, son of the inventor of the steam engine, a major benefactor of Cowes, was among its later residents. To commemorate a visit to Cowes by the future Edward VII and his new bride, Princess Alexandra, Stephenson donated Prince's Green to the townsfolk - on condition that it should never be used for commercial purposes. Grantham Court was later run as an hotel and has now been converted into apartments, with beautiful views of the Solent.

Other Famous Houses

Westbourne House *was the childhood home of Thomas Arnold, the headmaster of Rugby School, whose father was the Customs Officer at East Cowes.* **The Commodore's House** *in the High Street was the final home of Uffa Fox, the world-famous yacht designer, after he had lived at Medina House. Uffa used the case of Handel's organ from the Foundling Hospital to trim the entrance to the balcony he built on the harbour side.*

Photo © Beken of Cowes

HRH *The Duke of Edinburgh with Uffa Fox on* **Bluebottle** *1957*

Photo © Beken of Cowes

Bloodhound

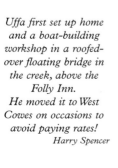

Photos Courtesy Max Aitken Museum and Harry Spencer

Uffa Fox on **Bloodhound**

Prince Philip (second right), Keith Beken (fourth right), Uffa Fox

Uffa Fox at his drawing board

Uffa Fox
The brilliant eccentric
by Adrian Searle

It is hard to conceive of any other Isle of Wight resident in recent (and even not so recent) times with such a rich anecdotal legacy as the remarkable Uffa Fox. The stories of this extraordinary 'son of Cowes' abound - and the catalogue continues to increase.

Uffa Fox, Harry Spencer, Rodney Barton with friends aboard **Fresh Breeze**

Uffa first set up home and a boat-building workshop in a roofed-over floating bridge in the creek, above the Folly Inn.
He moved it to West Cowes on occasions to avoid paying rates!
Harry Spencer

Early Uffa Fox dinghy; left to right; Uffa Fox, his wife and their dog Jack, Alf Todman and Bill Keeping

Courtesy Murray Dixon, Uffa Fox's nephew

As recently as the summer of 2001, an audience at Osborne House were treated to a couple more anecdotes when Prince Charles recalled how his great friend introduced him not only to champagne, but also to the joys of motoring, Uffa-style - the Royal 'learner' receiving his instructions on which way to turn not via the more usual 'right' or 'left' commands, but by being told to 'go starboard' or 'port' at a road junction! That fondly-remembered Royal encounter with the Fox eccentricity took place in the streets of East Cowes, one of the countless 'Uffa' tales that link the man, Cowes born and bred, to his beloved Island and cover so many aspects of his colourful life. To take a random example, one of his more bizarre wartime contributions during the global conflict of 1939-45 was to volunteer, without hesitation, his services to the Local Defence Volunteers (later to become the Home Guard) as one of its first Isle of Wight recruits - simultaneously committing the entire workforce at his Medina boat-building yard to the same cause (almost certainly without asking them first!), calling them the 'Uffashots' and briefing them to protect not only the yard from the enemy, but also the local grocer's shop, the Police station and (very much to character) the Duke of York pub! Yet, for all his eccentric manner, his often outrageous behaviour, his unrestrained *joie de vivre*, Uffa Fox was also an outstanding achiever. Memories of the 'Uffashots' may raise more than a few smiles today, but many Allied airmen, forced to ditch their planes over the sea in the latter years of the Second World War, undoubtedly owed their lives to the master-designer who conceived, developed, introduced - to his immense personal satisfaction - and then refined the brilliant concept of the parachuted airborne lifeboat. "Possibly the greatest contribution I shall ever make to the happiness of others," was his own verdict. Fittingly, it was the airborne lifeboat that was depicted on his gravestone in Whippingham churchyard following the great man's death in 1972. Had it not been for that outstanding contribution to the war effort, the churchyard memorial would surely have featured a yacht. For the name Uffa Fox was, of course, synonymous with the sport of sailing and the design and construction of some of the most competitive yachts to emerge from Cowes. Happily, a reminder of this central part of the Uffa legend is preserved today as the centrepiece of the maritime museum, which shares the library premises in the town. It is arguably his most famous boat, the Flying Fifteen class *Coweslip*, which Uffa designed and then sailed with distinction alongside Prince Charles's father, the Duke of Edinburgh. A crowning glory, indeed. Uffa - hardly anybody in Cowes ever felt the need to add the surname, such was his fame and notoriety! - enjoyed a life-long love affair with the River Medina, stretching back to the days when, as a boy, he swam across its waters from Folly to Werrar to poach swallows' eggs from the brick-drying sheds. As an adult, Uffa was equally at home east or west of the river – literally so, in fact! He lived at Medina House, West Cowes (originally part of the 18th century Birmingham House) before setting up a new home at Padmore, east of the river. It was a sign of the distinctively different status of the 'two Cowes' that Uffa was simultaneously listed in a 1937 directory as a boat-builder in East Cowes and a yacht designer west of the river. In both categories he was a true master. It would require considerably more than a single volume to describe Uffa's various triumphs in the design of marine craft. Apart from those already mentioned, career highlights also included the highly-successful Avenger class dinghy design and - proving his innovative worth in the wider design field of waterborne activity - his contribution to the high-speed hydroplane Maple Leaf project. But it is just too tempting to resist a further excursion or two into the rich anecdotal treasury of Uffa legend. Here's an excerpt from his nephew Murray Dixon's recollections of a (mainly) wartime apprenticeship at Medina Yard, in which he describes the early development of the airborne lifeboat project: "The highlight of the day at Uffa's was afternoon tea, which he turned into a ritual. All the staff of the Drawing and General Offices gathered round a big dining table, where all the snags of the day were sorted out. It was here that the first model folding boat was made - with typing paper and strawberry jam!" From such typically offbeat beginnings grew the Uffa Fox masterpieces. Once he came up with a good idea, Uffa very often went to extraordinary lengths to 'sell' it to others. Murray Dixon reveals how, having conceived and developed a plan for a 'stretched' International Fourteen yacht - naming the resultant craft **My Dainty Duck** - Uffa took her down to Torbay, Devon, where the 1948 Olympics were being held, and "annoyed all the officials by planing round the committee boat when the wind got up!" But, adds the Dixon narrative, at least Uffa and his stretched '14' got noticed. Thus, the Flying Fifteens were born. There were 13 in the first championships. Eccentric he may have been, but Uffa got results.

Cowes is a poorer place without him.

Photo © Beken of Cowes

HRH Duke of Edinburgh and Uffa Fox

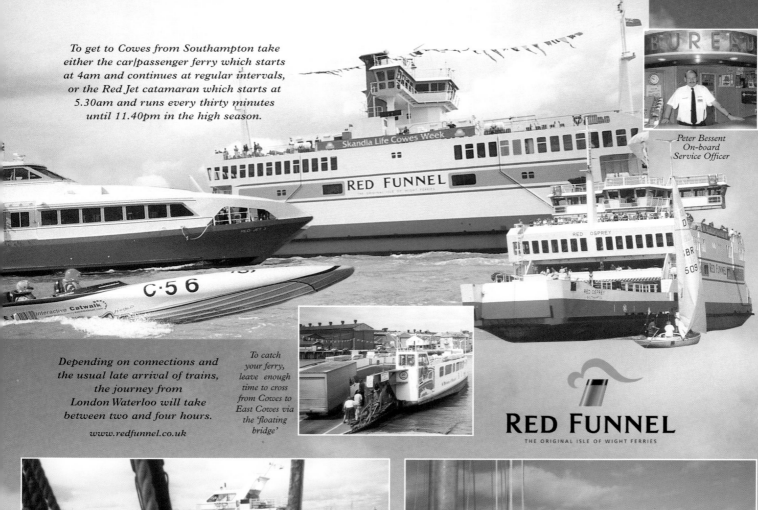

To get to Cowes from Southampton take either the car/passenger ferry which starts at 4am and continues at regular intervals, or the Red Jet catamaran which starts at 5.30am and runs every thirty minutes until 11.40pm in the high season.

Peter Bessent
On-board
Service Officer

Depending on connections and the usual late arrival of trains, the journey from London Waterloo will take between two and four hours.

www.redfunnel.co.uk

To catch your ferry, leave enough time to cross from Cowes to East Cowes via the 'floating bridge'

RED FUNNEL
THE ORIGINAL ISLE OF WIGHT FERRIES

Photos © MG>A

Cowes
The Home of Yacht Racing

Since its first-ever regatta in 1813, Cowes has become firmly established as the spiritual home of yacht racing.
Today, it still hosts many 'top drawer' events in the international yachting calendar.

Cowes Week itself, sponsored by Skandia Life, attracts more than 10,000 participants, while the famous Round-the-Island Race, with sponsorship from Hoya, is contested by a fleet of 2,000. A similar number of boats race for the Little Britain Challenge Cup. The Industry Sailing Challenge, with 150 entries and 36 Sunsail Sunfast boats, grows bigger each year. Then there are the *real* international headline-grabbers. Cowes regularly witnesses the mighty tussles for the Admiral's Cup* and the Rolex-sponsored Fastnet Race, which take place every other year. In 2001, the Volvo Ocean Race fleet set off on the first leg of its round-the-world epic from the Royal Yacht Squadron at Cowes. Topping it all in 2001, of course, was the fantastic America's Cup Jubilee celebration regatta. (All of these major events are featured in later sections of the book.)

Many companies organize their own regattas at Cowes. They include cross-Solent ferry operators Red Funnel and some of the most prestigious business concerns in the UK - including,

There are even small regattas organized from waterfront private houses.

the Bank of England, Price Waterhouse, Ernst & Young, Lloyds TSB and HSBC. The list goes on and on.

Most yachting Classes, too, hold their annual championships on The Solent. Among them are the Swans (the Class's European Regatta is staged here), Etchells, Farr 40s (an event sponsored by Rolex), Sonars, Sigma 33s, Mumm 30s, Sydney 40s, Darings, Contessas, Dragons and Arrows. The racing itself is organised by the local clubs, who join forces with out-of-town clubs for Cowes Week to form the Cowes Combined Clubs.

With its challenging Solent conditions, Cowes plays host to an extensive, and unrivalled, racing programme and provides unique opportunities to test all levels of sailing ability. And it is not only sailing. Offshore powerboat racing has added another important event, styled today as the Honda Cowes Classic, while the colourful competition provided by the Solent Barge Match has also become part of the racing scene. Even in winter, a series of races takes place between local clubs to raise funds for the Royal National Lifeboat Institution.

Cowes Marina can hold more than 500 yachts and offers 300 sheltered harbour moorings for visitors. Extensive boat support repair facilities and sailmaking by some of the world's top specialized companies - such as Ratsey & Lapthorn or Spencer - together with some very good boatbuilders.

All encourage sailors to come to Cowes. There are excellent water taxi services and many corporate facilities. Good hotels and restaurants are, perhaps, few and far between, but there is still a

lot of accommodation and a host of pubs providing entertainment for sailors and visitors alike.

A major survey in 2000 showed that yachtsmen, and visitors in general, attracted by the waterborne activity at Cowes, significantly boost the Isle of Wight's economy. It confirmed that Cowes is a major, and growing, attraction for participants in the sport of racing and cruising and is regarded highly by holiday-makers and day-trippers as a place to visit. According to the report, more than 710,000 visitors (attracted by the yachting) spent in the region of £58.3 million on the Island - spending which supports an estimated 1,850 jobs. In the year 2000 alone, 515,485 people, lured by the array of boats and yachting activity, visited Cowes itself, while some 33,000 yachts and 200,000 yachtsmen, spending millions, came to the town. They spent most heavily on eating, drinking, marine goods and services, mooring fees and accommodation. This had both a direct and indirect economic impact on Cowes and the Island in general. In short, the attraction of yachting at Cowes now accounts for no less than 20% of the Isle of Wight's overall tourism income.

Last but not least, Cowes also attracts Olympic gold medallists. Shirley Robertson, who has bought a house in Cowes, Ben Ainslie and Iain Percy all sailed here in the summer of 2001, during Skandia Life Cowes Week and the America's Cup Jubilee. (They presented prizes at the evening cocktail parties). Indeed, Henri Lloyd, technical sailing manufacturers, who have supported Roberston and Ainslie for many years, have become important sponsors of Cowes events. They have also opened a shop here, which founder and Chairman, Henri Strzelecki calls the "Mecca of sailing."

GBR Challenge

Cowes' premier position as the home of world yachting has been further boosted by Peter Harrison's decision to base the new British America's Cup Challenge here. The multi-million-pound *GBR Challenge* project for the 2003 event is being developed at the former FBM shipbuilding yard on the River Medina.

Cowes Harbour Commission, meanwhile, is working with Harrison to secure the ex- FBM yard as an important next step in the strategic development of Cowes Harbour.

The site is set to become a world class centre of marine excellence, capable of building and maintaining yachts up to 40 metres, together with support services and a visitors' centre. It is also envisaged that a maritime museum will be added.

* in 2002 the RORC decided to stage the event in Dublin,
severing 45 years of history with Cowes

35
Absolutely!

The Royal Yacht Squadron

Ian Cullerne-Bown and Captain Christopher Chamberlen in 1999

Photos © MCxA

The Royal London Yacht Club

The Island Sailing Club

Photos © courtesy of the clubs

The Royal Corinthian Yacht Club

Photo © MCxA

Gurnard Sailing Club

Photo Courtesy RYS

The Lord Amhurst of Hackney

Photo © MCzA

Sir Malcolm Edge KCVO, Chairman of the RLYC and Commodore Peter Cove

During the Regatta Balls, men are requested to wear dinner jackets or 'mess dress'.

Admiral Pat Dyas

Photos Courtesy of the clubs

Edwin Buckley

Cowes Yacht Clubs

Cowes is home to some of the finest traditional yacht clubs in the world. They have played an important role in helping Cowes become the 'Home of World Yachting'.

The Royal Yacht Squadron

The Royal Yacht Squadron, generally accepted as the most exclusive Club in the world, was founded in 1815 by a group of gentlemen at a meeting in the Thatched House Tavern in St James's Square, London. The common bond among its members was that of saltwater yachting and the Club has been based at the Castle in Cowes since 1856.

The Castle, on the northwest point of Cowes, was established on the foundations and battlements of fortifications built by Henry VIII to defend the Medina River. The Prince of Wales (later King Edward VII) became its patron in 1863.

In 1826, the Squadron was the first yacht club to organise yacht races in this country and soon became the world authority to set rules and handicaps. Since that time Cowes and the RYS have become synonymous with sailing, particularly during Regatta Week in August, where it used to be fashionable to be seen.

In 1851, the RYS was the instigator of the America's Cup, which has since become the most prestigious yachting competition in the world, and a Jubilee Regatta was held in Cowes last summer to celebrate its 150th anniversary.

The RYS has a maximum elected membership of 450, together with 80 naval officers and about 40 overseas members. Candidates for election to RYS membership must be invited to join by five established members, together with additional supporters, and are bound by a ballot of the entire British membership. A notable yachting and "impeccable" social pedigree are essential requirements for membership. Like a London Gentlemen's Club, no cash is seen or used and ladies who are the wives and daughters of seafaring men are welcome as associate members, although full membership is restricted to men.

A new pavilion overlooking the Squadron lawn was opened by HRH Prince Philip in 2000. The building has won much architectural acclaim and been used for numerous events at the Squadron, including the traditional black-tie ball held during Cowes Week, generally considered as a highlight of the social season. Restricted to members and a limited number of their guests, it is the most exclusive social event of Cowes Week. A limited number of tickets can be bought for the after-dinner party which starts after 10pm and includes English breakfast after midnight.

The Commodore of the Royal Yacht Squadron (who succeeded Peter Nicholson) is The Lord Amhurst of Hackney, who took up the position in October, 2001, and will hold it for four years.
Tel: 01983 292191.

The Royal London Yacht Club

A Cowes Club with its origins in the capital, the majority of its members still live or work in London. It was founded in London in 1836 by members of the Arundel Yacht Club who raced from "Arundel Stairs", a Thameside waterfront below the Strand.

Its first meeting place was at the Coal Hole Tavern, also in the Strand, but it relocated to Cowes in 1882. Its premises, in a pair of 19th-century terraced houses built by Dr Hofmeister, one of Queen Victoria's physicians, look over the Parade in Cowes, and the traditions of its origins have been balanced by an active and progressive membership. The Club has its full share of social events, with its black-tie ball a glittering regular on the Cowes Week party scene. The RLYC is part of a triumvirate of yacht clubs, along with the London-based Royal Thames Yacht Club and the Royal Southampton Yacht Club.

The Club's Commodore is Mr Peter Cove and the Chairman is Sir Malcolm Edge KCVO.
Tel: 01983 299727.

The Royal Corinthian Yacht Club

Established in 1842, the Royal Corinthian Yacht Club received its Admiralty Warrant in 1872. Neighbour to the Royal Yacht Squadron, its premises in the Castle Rock building above Cowes Harbour command spectacular views of the Solent, where so many great events of the sailing calendar take place.

In 1992, Crispin Lowe who owned the Club, went into receivership. The building was bought back by a consortium led by Admiral Pat Dyas. Now a Members' Club, it has a reputation for good food and service, and its excellent facilities have promoted it as a popular venue for social events and corporate hospitality. A major contributor to Island sailing activities, the RCYC organises both the *Etchells National Championship*, which attracts boats from fleets throughout the UK, and the *Beneteau Cup*. New members, whether temporary or permanent, are especially welcome at the Club, where good parties and congenial company are characteristic of its warmth and hospitality. The RCYC is, like other Cowes clubs, particularly active during Regatta Week, when their programme includes a cocktail party, a ball and a special party for Fireworks Night. Subscription rates are dependent on status (ie, age or place of residence). Island members currently pay £110 per annum. A development levy is also charged to help fund building works to improve the clubhouse facilities. HRH The Princess Royal is the Patron of the Club.

The Commodore is Edwin Buckley and Pat Dyas OBE has been the Admiral since 1978.
Tel: 01983 293581.

The Island Sailing Club

The Island Sailing Club has achieved a popularity which is reflected in its membership figures of around 2,400 with approximately 800 Island members and 200 overseas. Its distinguished history goes back to the late-19th century, when General Charles Baring, a member of the RYS, decided that Cowes needed an essentially democratic club that would cater for all sorts of sailing enthusiasts. Regattas had hitherto been the exclusive province of the wealthy owners of large yachts, and the formation of the Island Sailing Club in 1889 was instrumental in redressing the balance. The founding members reflected this democratic move - in contrast to the exclusive patronage of the RYS, they included both eminent professionals and tradespeople. It was the first club to admit ladies as members.

Among some of the famous members were Lord Dunraven, Lord Lonsdale and Charles Nicholson. Members have also been known for their generosity. During the First World War, twenty members paid for the yearly rental of £40 when they heard the news of possibly closing the Club. In 1835, Bird Cheverton bought 'Seaview House', the next-door premises, and later sold it to the Club at very advantageous terms.

Peter Hedley

Even during the Second World War during which the Club luckily survived the severe bombing, all members paid their subscriptions in spite of the fact that sailing was prohibited and that it was forbidden to cross between mainland England and the Island between 1940 and 1944.

The entrance to the Club's premises is in the central High Street in Cowes, and the building extends through to its water frontage and balcony where there are extensive views across Cowes Harbour and down the eastern Solent. The Club is noted for doing things in friendly style - in 1948 it gave to Prince Philip and his bride, the future Queen Elizabeth II, a Dragon Class boat. To the satisfaction of members who had subscribed the cost of this wedding present, **Bluebottle**, proved its worth by winning numerous trophies for its royal owners, both on the Island and abroad. The Club is almost ceaseless in its round of social and sailing activities. Open every day (except Christmas Day and Boxing Day) it has established a high standard of in-house catering and can accommodate private parties of up to 300 guests. Summer activities, from April to October, are centred mainly around sailing, with a weekly Tuesday evening series for cruisers, day boats and dinghies normally followed by a joyful supper at the clubhouse. The balcony, which has extensive views on the Solent, is a popular place to watch the racing and to entertain. There is also a roof terrace with magnificent views. The Club has a high standard of catering and private parties are held regularly in the 'Centenary Room' or in the marquee in the summer.

The Island Sailing Club has always promoted good living among its sailing activities and the last event in its yachting calendar is the 'Game Supper' in October when members sail to Lymington and dine on their boats. A winter programme of talks and events has been particularly successful, as have Sunday lunches at the Club and a Friday evening 'Happy Hour'. The Club's experience at organising sailing events is tested every year at the Round the Island Race. This event, which takes place in June, attracts about 1,500 entries, and many of the 10,000 crew come back every year to enjoy the challenge and the spectacle of this unique event.

The Club owns a fleet of Sonars, available for hire to members or for corporate events. Its unique location and waterside facilities provide its members with 90ft of mooring space just yards away from central Cowes, while a launch service to swinging moorings operates during the summer. There is also a club dinghy. The slipway and a cradle are also available for hauling out yachts. Visiting yachtsmen from other clubs can use the Club and visitors' passes may be purchased.

While, with a membership as large as that of the Island Sailing Club, there is always pressure on space (its premises reach bursting point on Fireworks Night during Cowes Week), there is residential accommodation available at the Club. Early booking is recommended. There are plans in 2002 to develop a new bar, a beer cellar, a new kitchen and a lift for the disabled.

Among the very respectable members who have been Commodore or Admiral, let's mention Commodore O.A. Aisher (1960-1964). His son Robin Aisher is now the Admiral of the Club. R.T. Lowein was Commodore between 1964-1968 and Sir Maurice Laing was Admiral from 1997 until 2001.

The Club's Commodore is Mr Peter Hedley and Rosemary Joy is Rear Commodore.

Tel: 01983 296621.

Rosemary Joy

*Rosemary Joy, who lives in Cowes, is Rear Commodore of the Island Sailing Club and is the editor of the Club's magazine. But her name is better known outside of Cowes thanks to "The Rosemary Joy Collection", a unique treasure trove of old film footage - now on video tape - of sailing in the 1920s and '30s, with fascinating glimpses into the world of the J-Class yachts, their construction and life aboard. These amateur films were taken from the decks of **Endeavour** and **Velsheda** while racing. They also feature **Britannia**, King George V's yacht. The films were bought by her brother, the racing skipper and yachting enthusiast Dick Thirlby, in 1979 and he passed them on to Rosemary, who studied them for several years, searching for information from old magazines. She then developed a very informative commentary on them. The National Maritime Museum in Greenwich now has the originals and Rosemary has the video copies. She is also a keen collector of anything to do with the J-Class yachts.*

*Rosemary is very proud of a scrapbook in which T. O. M. Sopwith described his almost successful attempt to win the America's Cup in 1934, on **Endeavour**, which was beaten by the American yacht **Rainbow**. The story around the challenge is very colourful. **Endeavour** had to sail across the Atlantic with a last-minute amateur crew, who replaced the professionals who had gone on strike for higher wages. She was accompanied by **Velsheda**, as a trial horse, and the **Aquitania**, Sopwith's yacht. After the defeat of **Endeavour** following a disputed manœuvre around a windward mark, the New York Journal wrote: "Britannia rules the waves but the New York Yacht Club waives the rules." Rosemary, who spent years researching some of the yachts shown on the films, has given many talks in England and France.*

She is also a director of the Classic Boat Museum on The Quay at Newport, which is building an enviable collection of historic yachts and motor boats. Following the Jubilee week she took four restored boats from the museum to Monaco.

She says: "People in Cowes are very blasé. They have seen it all and it is sometimes difficult to have them do something. In fact, what is important here is how well you sail."

Cowes Corinthian Yacht Club

Back in 1948, the great Uffa Fox had a boat-building yard where *Tides Reach* currently stands and 'Tiny' Mitchell, a businessman from the Midlands, who had been instrumental in establishing a clubhouse for the Royal Corinthian Yacht Club in Cowes, was persuaded to have a yacht built. Tiny had a strong desire to make sailing and boating more accessible for everyday people. In other words, a sailing club for the workers.

Adjacent to the yard was a plot of land that Tiny purchased and with his enthusiasm and drive, a clubhouse was built and a 3-ton crane was produced. Tiny certainly never did things by halves! In September 1952, the inaugural meeting took place with some well-known Cowes faces present, including Uffa Fox, Captain Barton (then Cowes harbourmaster) and Keith Beken, with Tiny taking the chair.

Tiny opened the meeting saying that one of the ideas of this Club was to provide cheaper facilities for yachtsmen and the facilities of the club would be available to all yachtsmen and not merely to members of the Club. Membership would be open to any person willing to take an active part in racing, sailing, motor boating, etc. The aim of the Club was to encourage sailing, and therefore, people interested in the club for purely social reasons would not be welcome. Tough stuff when you compare the Club's entry requirements with others in the town. Tiny must have been some character, but there again, Cowes is full of characters. Tiny was immediately elected Commodore and continued to hold that office until his death in 1962, when his widow Blackie succeeded him.

In the 1960s when Gilly Potter was Commodore, a 300ft long steel pier was built and it is the stump of this pier that now forms the access point to Cowes Yacht Haven. By the 1970s, the Club had grown and the original site known as the apron was extended. A new slipway was constructed alongside the pier and a new electric crane was installed on the northern corner. One of the traditions of the Club is that members have taken the tasks of improving the Club, site and facilities themselves. This tradition continues today. Currently, it is the only club in Cowes that can provide marina berths and shoreside boat storage facilities for its members.

The Commodore is Mike Brinton.
Tel: 01983 296333.

Cowes Corinthian Yacht Club

Mike Brinton presenting Admiral Mike Jackson with his Broad Pennant

East Cowes Sailing Club

The Club's aims, laid out when it was founded in 1912, are 'to encourage sailing, good sportsmanship, youth training, racing, fishing and other boating activities'. Its facilities include three inside boatsheds, and hard standing for small yachts, motorboats, sailing dinghies and tenders. It also has drying-out mud berths, for use as appropriate. Social activities centre on its Thursday evening racing programme and its members have established a proud reputation for their sailing skills.

The Commodore is Dave Casson and the Vice Commodore, Barry Watkin.
Tel: 01983 295890

Gurnard Sailing Club

Gurnard is an immediate neighbour to Cowes, and its sailing club is situated two miles west of Cowes. It was founded some 70 years ago, but entered a more modern era when its new clubhouse was recently completed and opened by HRH The Princess Royal.

Its ethos relies on self-help and its membership is a notably enthusiastic and friendly one that looks to the future with a thriving Cadet section. It is particularly renowned for its dinghy sailing activities and for its expertise at running Committee Boat Start and Olympic-style events.

The Commodore is Paul Airey.
Tel: 01983 295169.

Courtesy Gurnard Sailing Club

Captain Stuart McIntosh

Cowes Harbour Commission

Cowes Harbour Commission is the statutory harbour authority. Its jurisdiction extends eastwards from Egypt Point to Castle Point and southwards from the Prince Consort Buoy to The Folly, the public house on the east bank of the River Medina.

Cowes is a Trust Port, constituted by an Act of Parliament in 1897. A Board of Commissioners delegates the day-to-day management of the harbour to the Harbour Master, Captain Stuart McIntosh, who is also the Commission's Chief Executive.

In line with Government policy (*Modernising Trust Ports - A Guide to Good Governance, January 2000*), the Commission has undergone significant changes, with the introduction of new standards aimed at ensuring ports continue to perform a valuable rôle in support of the local, regional and national economy. A new Board of Commissioners is now entrusted with the task of managing the harbour in a safe, effective and efficient manner. While smaller than its predecessor, the new-look Board has a system of advisory committees and continues to operate in an open, accountable manner for the overall benefit of a town whose economy - as outlined in the introduction to this section of the book - is heavily dependent on the waterborne activity in the harbour.

The Commission is confident of its continuing ability to develop the infrastructure required to maintain Cowes' status as the home of world yachting - a rôle helped by the major improvements within the harbour at Cowes Yacht Haven (see later section) and in the redesigned Town Quay basin, where ferry operators Red Funnel's Red Jets have new landing facilities and the number of short-stay visitor pontoons has been increased. As well as Red Funnel, this first-phase development of Town Quay also involved the Isle of Wight Council and the Government's Environment Agency.

Across the Medina, East Cowes Marina (as described before) has also undergone major refurbishment to provide additional moorings and better shoreside facilities, while other key developments have included harbour dredging, extra pontoons and the opening of a new riverside restaurant/pub. Meanwhile, many of the Cowes-based yacht clubs have improved their hospitality facilities.

In addition to its collaboration with GBR Challenge at the former FBM yard (described later), Cowes Harbour Commission completed the purchase in April 2001 of the Shepards Wharf Boatyard, bringing it into quasi-public ownership. Development of this important waterfront site has been boosted by a £150,000 donation from Skandia Life. Shepards Wharf will continue to offer all of its current range of boating support services, but now there is the opportunity to provide more much needed 'walk ashore' moorings, together with good shoreside facilities, for visiting boats.

Thanks to developments such as this, says the Commission, Cowes really does have all the skills, ambience and facilities necessary to successfully host the major events with which it is closely associated - Skandia Life Cowes Week, the Rolex Fastnet Race, the Little Britain Cup in 2001 - together with numerous other regattas and meetings, not forgetting the America's Cup Jubilee Regatta.

In contrast to the bustle of the harbour itself, tranquility is on hand down river at the Folly Reach, where berthing facilities have been considerably improved. "Great efforts are being made," says the Harbour Commission, "to ensure that Cowes remains a major force in the worldwide yachting calendar and a focus for British and international yachting."

*Felix Hetherington
in his beautiful Morgan*

But Cowes is not *exclusively* about yachting. It is also the major Isle of Wight port of entry for commercial shipping. More than 300,000 tonnes of cargo are handled each year from ships of up to 100 metres in length, and with a draft of 5.4 metres. Commercial ship movements can be at any time of the day or night, depending on the tide, and may, as a result, coincide with yacht racing activity - although every effort is made to avoid this at peak racing periods and procedures are in force to ensure safety during race starts (see below). Running to a more rigid timetable are the cross-Solent ferries of Red Funnel, which operate to and from Southampton, serving East Cowes with modern ro-ro car and passenger ferries and West Cowes with a fleet of high-speed catamarans.

Finally . . . Cowes has its own *Customs House*, which endeavours to make procedures easy for visiting yachtsmen. A *Harbour Patrol Launch*, which is 'on station' during the race start procedure (with the Harbour Master and a member of the Race Committee on board) to monitor the movements of all yachts and other vessels, and, in case of difficulty at sea, its own *Inshore Lifeboat* station.

Further information on the facilities available in the port of Cowes is published in the regularly updated *Cowes Port Handbook* and can also be obtained by accessing the Cowes website.

Harbour Master Captain Stuart McIntosh and his deputy, Captain Rory Jackson, can be contacted at:

Cowes Harbour Commission
Harbour Office, Town Quay, Cowes
Isle of Wight, PO31 AS.
Tel: +44 (0) 1983 293952
Fax: +44 (0) 1983 290018
E-mail: chc@cowes.co.uk
www.cowes.co.uk.

Captain Henry Wrigley

From 1966 until his retirement in 1998 Captain Henry Wrigley performed with not inconsiderable aplomb the delicate balancing act required of those who assume the rôle of Harbour Master of Cowes. The old adage of not being able to please all of the people all of the time must surely have crossed his mind at times during his long tenure at the helm of the Isle of Wight's principal sea port.

"Cowes is not only known for pleasure sailing," he is quick to remind you. "It is also very busy with commercial shipping." The Harbour Master controls the movements of all vessels in the harbour, be they small sailing boats, big yachts or the commercial ships that regularly use the port. For the sake of completeness, it should also be pointed out that 'all vessels' also includes Red Funnel's cross-Solent ferry fleet and the humble floating bridge which still connects West and East Cowes. The ferries, of course, have fixed terminal points. For the vessels that don't enjoy this luxury, where they moor in Cowes is another area of Harbour Master control - and vessels have to answer to him for the manner in which they move within harbour limits. Inevitably, there is the potential at Cowes for conflicts of interest (and sometimes worse) between the leisure sailors and the merchant fleet. "Pleasing everybody is not always an easy task!" says Henry Wrigley.

Cowes, of course, has an international reputation as the 'home of world yachting' to maintain. The yachtsmen who visit, and the organisers of the many events, expect to find decent facilities in the harbour. It is down to the Harbour Master to see that these are constantly available. "Their safety is another requirement - it goes without saying that this is of the utmost importance," adds Henry.

Over the years, he has witnessed – and played a key part in - the "incredible growth" of Cowes. He acknowledges the rôle of Cowes Yachting in meeting the challenge posed by competing yachting centres in the South of England. "The aim was to have a big marketing tool in Cowes in order to attract major events and business, and generally breathe new

life into the town. To do so, it was vital to improve facilities and bring in people with the necessary expertise." It worked. Cowes attracted new events, there is now more yachting activity - and more corporate entertaining.

The development of Cowes Yacht Haven has been a major factor. Another, says Henry Wrigley, is "the ability and excellence of the yacht clubs here to organise the racing - a point that was proved again with the staging of the America's Cup Jubilee at Cowes in 2001. It was a really great occasion, very well organised, and has shown the way for the future running of major events."

On the down side was the cancellation of the Admiral's Cup in 2001 owing to a lack of entries. "Rules change and events must reflect this - or be replaced by other events," says Henry, although he is quick to pay tribute to the continuity of the classes that have remained, as he puts it, the "backbone of yachting at Cowes": the Dragons, Etchells, Sunbeams, Mermaids and others of their ilk "which have been attending for years and years." Change, though, must be embraced if Cowes is to continue to thrive - and that applies as much to the allied trades in the town.

"Boats do not have to be built in Cowes. They can be built just about anywhere," he adds. "It was inevitable that some boatyards would disappear and, while we must keep the traditional industry going here - it remains a very important source of jobs - it is good to see the development of new associated industries in Cowes. Everybody benefits, not only in the yachting world, but also the shops, restaurants and hotels in the town."

Having said that, he is anxious to reiterate that some of the traditional businesses in the port of Cowes are "simply irreplaceable." The example he gives is the famed yacht equipment activities carried out at Spencer Thetis Wharf, "who do what very few others can."

Henry Wrigley may be retired now, but he is still a fervent supporter of Cowes. "The America's Cup Jubilee has given us a taste of success. Everyone here wants that feeling to continue over the years to come."

John Power

David Cheverton

Donald Parr CBE

Felix Hetherington

Richard Bradbeer

Morris Barton

Cowes Town Waterfront Trust

Formed in 1991, Cowes Town Waterfront Trust (CTWT) is a charity set up with the aim of improving the town's economy through the progressive regeneration of the waterfront and the High Street premises bordering Cowes Yacht Haven. The CTWT-owned marina is run as an operating subsidiary.

Cowes Marina was formerly owned by the Gardner brothers. They sold it to Crispin Low, whose idea was to develop the site and, among other things, build residential homes. This scheme failed to impress the planning authority and Low's venture ended in liquidation. He was unable to make any progress with his other major purchase in Cowes - the Royal Corinthian Yacht Club. It was a serious situation. If the marina was not retained, the marine industry in Cowes might be devastated.

In order to save it, a group led by Mark Board and John Power approached Sir Maurice Laing, whose Laing Foundation agreed to contribute funding providing it was to a charitable trust. As a result, the CTWT was set up with £1 million from the Foundation and another £1 million from local authorities - half from the former Medina Borough Council and half from the Isle of Wight County Council (as it was at the time). In this context, the new Trust owed much to the help given by Councillor Morris Barton MBE, Leader of the County Council, and its Head of Paid Service, Felix Hetherington. The £2 million enabled purchase of the site, but more had to be borrowed from banks. The resultant overdraft was initially guaranteed by the Borough and County Councils.

Those loans have since been repaid, as is the case with subsequent borrowing. However, recent extensions have incurred another large debt, such is the financial burden of maintaining the marina to the highest possible standards. The many improvements that have been made there have paved the way for a growth in the number and type of events in Cowes. In 1993, 40 rallies and regattas were held in the port during the summer. There are now 150 - spread throughout the year. To date, the Laing Foundation has contributed an invaluable total of £1.3 million to the Trust.

CTWT's Board of Trustees and Directors saw some key changes in 2001. Two former High Sheriffs of the Isle of Wight, Trust Chairman David Cheverton, who also served as Chairman of Cowes Yacht Haven until 1999, and Dickie Bradbeer, men who had been involved with the Trust since 1992, retired. Felix Hetherington, now Chairman of Cowes Harbour Commission, replaced Dickie Bradbeer and Donald Parr, a board member with nominee status since 1993, is the new Trust Chairman. Stanley Malone, another nominee of the Laing Foundation, Morris Barton and John Power remain on the Board, while David Jaggar, a qualified solicitor who has retired as head of the Isle of Wight Council's Development Directorate, is now Company Secretary. Cowes Yacht Haven Ltd, CTWT's operating subsidiary, also elected new members in October 2001. Sir Charles Nicholson became the new Chairman, replacing John Power (who also retired as Chairman of Cowes Yachting). Geoff Wilkins and John Dudley (Dudley Barnes Marine) were elected Directors, while Paul Rudling and Danny Fischer remained on the board. So does board member Roger Granger as Managing Director, in charge of running the Haven.

David Cheverton *OBE, who had chaired CTWT since its creation, is well-known for his work with many committees and was the first Honorary Secretary of Cowes Combined Clubs. A member of Cowes Yachting, he was also High Sheriff of the Isle of Wight and Commodore of the Royal London Yacht Club - just a few of his numerous activities.*

Donald Parr *CBE has been coming to Cowes for the last 25 years where he has kept his boat and a house, although he lived principally in Cheshire. He is a member of the Royal Yacht Squadron and both the Royal London Yacht Club and the Island Sailing Clubs, and has been a past Admiral and Commodore of the Royal Ocean Racing Club.*

'Dickie' Bradbeer

Richard Bradbeer - or Dickie, as his friends call him - has been involved in many associations in Cowes and done much to promote the town. He knows a great deal about the place and can talk about it for hours. As a member of the Cowes Harbour Commission for 20 years and Chairman until 2000, he was an important force behind establishing the Cowes Yacht Haven. He was also the Island's High Sheriff in 1997. Dickie came to Cowes for the first time in 1950, after studying naval architecture at Kings College, Newcastle-upon-Tyne, a college of Durham University. He loved sailing and moved to Cowes to take up a six-month job as a draughtsman at J. Samuel White's . . . He still lives here today. He met his wife, Rosemary, on the Island and it was thanks to his father-in-law, Isle of Wight County Press owner Colonel Wilfrid Brannon, that the couple moved back to the Island in 1955, after a short spell as an assistant yard manager in Lowestoft, on the east coast of England. Colonel Brannon persuaded Dickie to join the *Isle of Wight* County Press, the family newspaper and printing business, which is one of the few independent papers left in Britain. So Dickie followed in the Brannon family tradition and, after a year seconded to the Western Gazette in Somerset to learn the business, he took over as works manager on the Island, later becoming a director, general manager and, since 1987, company chairman. His daughter, Amanda Bradbeer, another keen sailor who started in the Merchant Navy and now has her own chartering business, is now also a director of the Isle of Wight County Press. Talking about Cowes Waterfront Trust and Cowes Yacht Haven, there is still a lot to be done, Dickie is ready to admit. Dickie is also Chairman of Cowes Week Sponsorship. Along with Cowes Combined Clubs' Director, Stuart Quarrie, Harbour Master, Stuart McIntosh, Cowes Yachting Chairman, Chris Troup, Isle of Wight Council representative Mike Fisher, and Cowes Yacht Haven General Manager, Roger Granger, he tries to bring in enough sponsorship to keep Cowes Week (or Skandia Life Cowes Week as it is presently titled, thanks to its current chief sponsors) as the top regatta. Dickie Bradbeer is a member of the Island Sailing Club where he has been Rear and Vice-Commodore. He is also a trustee of Cowes Combined Clubs and was, for 20 years, Chairman of the Solent Cruising and Racing Association. He has his own yacht which he loves to sail in the Solent and in Scotland, but Cowes is very special to him. "Where else can you see so much of the sailing as here," he asks, "within a biscuit toss?"

Cowes Yacht Haven
The Haven's top class facilities make it a quality destination for cruising and racing yachtsmen

Strategically situated in the heart of Cowes, the Yacht Haven is a superb location for boat owners, offering dedicated marine facilities and various services on site. The Haven carries the responsibility for all commercial activity, caring for the area and identifying the future needs of the site. To this end, CTWT has pumped about £4.5 million into the maintenance and improvement of the services and facilities available. Recent activity has included: enlargement of the north basin; the building of a new breakwater and additional pontoons; land reclamation; the creation of easier pedestrian access from the ferries and the High Street and better viewing opportunities for the visitor. Immediate plans include re-cladding the famous boatshed located immediately behind the Haven offices.

Marina facilities include 200 fully-serviced berths, a full level of on-shore services, 24-hour gas supplies, lifting, cleaning and painting, keel and spar repairs, dry sailing, sail making, electronic and electrical work, engineering, surveying, brokerage and insurance, chandlery, clothing and provisions, toilets, showers, launderette, hairdresser, photographer etc .

General Manager Roger Granger, together with Dick Emuss and a staff of 14, manages the entire site, where 30,000 boats visit every year and where more than 100 events are organised. They provide facilities for all the crews and, together with other companies, organise beer tents and hospitality marquees, live entertainment, trade stands and a range of exhibits. "Our organisation has taken steps to improve all our facilities and has enabled the public to walk around and enjoy the yachting in perfect safety," says Roger Granger. "Cowes Week 2001 attracted more than 10,000 people daily, which necessitates that our facilities and events are professionally organised. Advertising banners and bunting, general services, rents, hospitality and berthing fees from around 150 separate events annually make up the main sources of our income. While we were not involved with management of the America's Cup Jubilee, we were home to a magnificent display of yachts and the many spectators who came to watch. We did welcome a new event in the shape of the Euro-North Sea Race, which took place for the first time in 2001, involving the UK, France, Holland and Belgium. We hope that it will include more and larger boats next year."

Cowes Yacht Haven, Vectis Yard, High Street, Cowes, Isle of Wight PO31 7BD
Tel: 01983 299975 Fax: 01983 200332 www.cowesyachthaven.com

Trinity House in London is a Georgian, Grade 1 Listed building in a historic part of London, close to the River Thames and overlooks the Tower of London, one of the United Kingdom's 15 World Heritage Sites.

A special service to mark the 150th anniversary of the America's Cup took place at the Holy Trinity Parish Church in Cowes.

Photo © MCoA

The Corporation of Trinity House

Trinity House in London is the headquarters of a unique maritime organisation dedicated to the safety of shipping and to the welfare of seafarers and their dependants. It traces its origins back over 500 years to the reign of Henry VIII, by whose Royal Charter it was incorporated in 1514. The royal connection persists to this day: the current Master of Trinity House is HRH Prince Philip, Duke of Edinburgh. Today the Corporation is the General Lighthouse Authority for England, Wales, the Channel Islands and Gibraltar, maintaining 72 lighthouses, 11 light vessels and over 500 other navigational aids. It is also a deep-sea pilotage authority and has thriving charitable functions, promoting the safety, welfare and training of mariners.

Trinity House reports not to the Lord Mayor of London, as the City Livery Companies do, but to the Sovereign. Having had its first home at Deptford, near an important naval base, Trinity House moved first to Ratcliffe in East London in 1618 and in 1660, 42 years later, to a City-based location in Water Lane. In 1666, this building was destroyed in the Great Fire of London and a second time, in another fire in 1714.

Today the Corporation is a trustee of registered charities dedicated to the relief of aged and needy mariners, their widows and dependants. It maintains 19 almshouses in Walmer, Kent, which were built in 1958. In keeping with its tradition of maritime education, the Corporation operates a comprehensive Scholarship Cadet Training Scheme to prepare young people for a career in the merchant service. It also makes substantial grants to other maritime and related charities in support of a wide range of causes, including sailing

for the disabled, sea safety for leisure users of coastal waters and, of course, port welfare facilities for seamen of all nationalities. Income from hiring out Trinity House's function rooms makes an important contribution to the upkeep of this historic property and also helps to release funds for the charitable work that has been such an integral part of the Corporation's past and identity.

In East Cowes

Trinity House has existed in East Cowes since 1842, originally with a view to using the premises as a warehouse for storing oil. In 1845, Sir John Pelley, Deputy Governor of the Trinity Board, gave a directive for the immediate erection of a wharf at East Cowes opposite the old Custom house for the Royal Family to land and embark in private. Even in those days, it seems that they must have had trouble with the paparazzi! Queen Victoria used this facility until her death when she finally left the Isle of Wight via the Depot and her coffin was placed on the Royal Barge and taken out to the Royal Yacht Victoria and Albert for her eventual burial in London. In 1867, the Admiralty granted a free site for the North Buoy store and erected the building for the use of Trinity House. In 1922, the Admiralty conveyed to Trinity House the North Buoy Store as a free gift along with the pier, landing stage and the wharf originally constructed in 1845. This lasted until 1950 when the State canopy over the landing stage was finally demolished. The East Cowes Depot remained unaltered until 1964 when the Depot was completely reconstructed and modernised to cater for more up to date requirements.

Tower Hill, London, EC3N 4DH Tel: 0207 481 6900 Fax: 0207 480 7662
East Cowes, Isle of Wight, PO32 6RE Tel: (01983) 203400 Fax: (01983) 294317

UKSA
The United Kingdom Sailing Academy

The United Kingdom Sailing Academy has achieved international status as specialising in the training of sailing professionals. Based in Arctic Road, it is described as the flagship centre for RYA Sailability. There are courses available for everyone of every age and ability ranging from the complete novice to the professional yachtsman. The UKSA is committed to supplying the training that helps students realise their ambitions and has been home to many of the great names in Yachting. Ellen McArthur who was recently voted runner-up in the BBC's Sports Personality of the Year used the UKSA as her base for her preparations for the Vendée Globe. Ian Walker the Olympic Silver medallist and Sailing Manager of the UK America's Cup Challenge, and Shirley Robertson the Olympic Gold medallist have all used the UKSA to achieve their nautical aims.

The centre also provides full on-site facilities for the disabled and has sponsored and hosted the RYA Sailability Disabled Awareness training programme. Paralympic Gold medallist and local sailmaker, Andy Cassell did much of his crews training at the UKSA and benefited from the sponsorship of a UKSA Award of Excellence.

The UKSA
Arctic Road, West Cowes
Isle of Wight, PO31 7PQ .
Tel: (01983) 294941.
Website: www.uk-sail.org.uk.

The Solent Cruising and Racing Association

The Solent is one of the busiest stretches of water in the world with everything from a canoe to a tanker in a relatively small area. Added to all this, clubs, associations and classes are trying to compete in the same stretch of water and more than likely are trying to round the same racing mark. The Solent Cruising and Racing Association was founded in 1895 to promote the interests of yacht cruising and racing in the Solent and is now largely responsible for the co-ordination of the fixtures list of various races and events to avoid clashes and collisions at race marks.

The Association is open to all members and all clubs and publishes the famous Solent Year Book which lists racing fixtures and events throughout the season, as well as all the classes and owners.

President: J. Janson
Chairman of Council:
D. V. Atkinson
Vice Chairman:
M. A. C. Drummond OBE, JP, DL
Hon Secretary and Treasurer:
S. Quarrie

18 Bath Road, Cowes,
Isle of Wight, PO31 7QN
Tel: (01983) 295744 & 293303
E-Mail scra@cowesweek.co.uk
Website: www.scra.org.uk

*John Power,
creator of
Cowes Yachting*

*Chris Troup,
Chairman of
Cowes Yachting*

Cowes Yachting

Cowes Yachting was created by a group headed by local businessman John Power in 1991 as a positive response to the collapse of the Yacht Haven (see earlier sections). Cowes Yachting, now headed by Chris Troup, was formed with the three-fold intention of promoting the town's rôle as an international yachting centre, providing information in support of that rôle and encouraging the availability in Cowes of an international standard of facilities for yachts and their crews.

Cowes Yachting played a vital rôle in the rescue of the marina from receivership by the attraction of finance from the Maurice Laing Foundation, the local authorities and other sources and in the subsequent foundation of the **Cowes Town Waterfront Trust**. Cowes Yachting now acts as a marketing body for Cowes and a point of contact for individuals and organisations to access marine-related information. It helps the organisation of new events and co-ordinates meetings and social activity in connection with them. This work has contributed to the increase in yachting events in Cowes from approximately 40 to over 150, resulting in a full programme from Easter to September.

Back in 1991, Cowes Week had a precarious future and sponsors threatened to withdraw and change the venue of the regatta. Cowes Yachting joined with other agencies in the establishment of **Cowes Week Sponsorship Ltd** which attracted new sponsors for Cowes Week, which has since gone from strength to strength.

Cowes Yachting in its early days created the Port Handbook and Directory, which is now a stand-alone publication of the Harbour Commission. Among other activities it emphasises the importance of yachting at Cowes to the Island, and has commissioned regular market surveys from the Southern Tourist Board. The most recent of these showed that in 2000, yachting at Cowes contributed more than £58 million to the Island's economy.

Cowes Yachting retains seats on the boards of the **Waterfront Trust** and **Cowes Week Sponsorship Ltd**, and since 1993, when planning for the America's Cup Jubilee began, has been represented on the Steering Committee and on the board of **Cowes 2001 Ltd**.

Cowes Yachting benefits from a strong fee-paying membership - currently standing at about 100 - which is drawn from a combination of private, corporate and yacht club members, and is supported financially by a number of commercial sponsors as well as by the Isle of Wight Council. Members and others attend regular monthly lunches throughout the winter, at which there is a guest speaker, and Cowes Yachting arranges conferences as necessary to discuss important topical issues connected with yachting.

John Power

John Power is a prominent figure in the yachting scene in Cowes where he has lived for more than 17 years. He was the main driving force of the creation of Cowes Yachting in 1991 (See article). John still remains actively involved and is a trustee of **Cowes Town Waterfront Trust**.

John is 70, an age when others are contemplating putting their feet up, but not John. On acquiring his bus pass, he was working harder than ever to put Cowes on the map and it is partly due to his tireless efforts that Cowes is the place it is today. John has four grown-up children, two of whom live on the Island.

After a career in business with retirement on the horizon, he moved to Cowes with his wife, but for someone so active, a quiet life tending the garden roses was not for him. An experienced ocean-sailing yachtsman, he was anxious to preserve Cowes and promote the town as a major yachting centre.

He has been involved with the organisation of the America's Cup Jubilee by chairing the Education Programme and has been actively involved in the construction of the Royal Yacht Squadron's striking new pavilion opened in 2000.

Living in Alexandra House, in the heart of Cowes near all the action, John is also a Trustee of the **Jubilee Sailing Trust**, which was involved in the 'Education Programme' of the America's Cup Jubilee. Despite having a busy life style, John even finds time to play the cello and in summer, he relaxes by maintaining and sailing his 42 ft 1959 classic yawl **Kataree** which he has owned for over twenty years.

Chris Troup

Chris is 57 and owns two of the best-known pubs in the town, *The Anchor Inn* in the High Street and *The Globe* on the Parade. He is also in partnership in an outside bar and catering business, with which he has been involved in running the beer tent and entertainment on the Yacht Haven for seventeen years, pioneering the existing format. Chris is now chairman of Cowes Yachting and past chairman of the **Cowes Business Association**. He was also a Councillor and Deputy Mayor of Cowes. As a co-founder of **Cowes Week Sponsorship Limited**, he has been responsible for bringing a number of sponsors to Cowes Week and helping revive the fortunes of the event. He is passionate about Cowes and its future and, like John Power, Chris has played a major part in the promotion of Cowes. He is a keen sailor and, having lived on the Island for twenty years, he now lives in Lymington. His wife Lou-Lou Rendall runs her own marine Press and Public Relations business.

Further information:
Cowes Yachting Centre Ltd., 10 Samuel White's Building, Cowes, Isle of Wight PO3 1 7LP.
Tel/Fax: +44 (0)1983 280770

The RNLI

The Royal National Lifeboat Institution (RNLI), the rescue service which turns out in all weathers to save lives at sea, unlike other rescue services, does not receive Government funding. It must rely instead on donations and legacies * to buy boats, maintain them and train the brave crews.

The RNLI is on call 24 hours a day and, since it was founded in 1824, has saved over 135,000 lives up to the year 2000. The service has 225 lifeboat stations around the coasts of the United Kingdom and Republic of Ireland and the vessels operate up to fifty miles offshore, with more than 6,000 launches every year. Dedicated, highly-trained and mainly voluntary crews man the boats. Despite these volunteers, it still costs £274,000 a day to run the service. The RNLI works closely with the Maritime and Coastguard Agency and other organisations to provide a co-ordinated sea rescue service. The inshore rigid inflatable craft are made and serviced at East Cowes RNLI Works, which also has a large engineering department where engines are customized to very high standards specifically for RNLI use. An ongoing training programme is carried out there to enable crews to use expertly and maintain their inshore craft. The Depot is part of the Cowes 'hi-tech' marine industry.

There are three different grades of membership of the RNLI: Shoreline, Offshore and Governor. Offshore is for anyone who uses the sea for leisure.

RNLI, West Quay Road, Poole, Dorset, BH15 1HZ
Tel. 01202 663000 Fax 01202 663167
www.lifeboats.org.uk

Six out of every ten lifeboat launches are funded by legacies. The RNLI has published a booklet and video which both explain how important legacies are to the future of the lifeboat service, and how easy it is for people to leave a legacy.
Legacy Enquiries Officer: John Marshall
Tel: 01202 663032 Fax 01202 663238
E-mail: jmarshall@rnli.org.uk

Photo: Courtesy of RNLI

![Lifeboats - Royal National Lifeboat Institution]

HERMÈS
PARIS

Hermès and the RNLI

Hermès has had a long association with the sea from which they derive their great inspiration for designs of scarves, ties, beach towels and jewellery. In 1996, with this in mind and in an effort to help raise some very necessary funds towards the RNLI's excellent work, Hermès produced a special edition silk scarf, Thalassa, which was sold exclusively in aid of the RNLI which received a percentage of the sales. Thalassa is regularly included in the Hermès scarf collection.

Everyone works for the RNLI

The RNLI was very lucky in 2001 to be chosen as the charity of two big events: Skandia Life Cowes Week and the America's Cup Jubilee Ball. During Cowes Week, the RNLI offered a free bottle of Mumm champagne to people who joined Offshore. They also had the opportunity to enter competitions to win Henri Lloyd TP2000 offshore Rapid Suits and Timberland boat shoes. During the Jubilee Ball, the £310,000 paid by Bill Koch for the special 'Hennessy Cognac Collection' went to the RNLI at the Phillips auction.

In Cowes many small charity events organised by the 'Cowes Guild' take place regularly, be it lunches in a local restaurant, cocktail parties (sometimes with dancing), a Christmas market at the Royal Yacht Squadron or a 'Yuletide Punch Party' at the Villa Rothsay.

Bill Koch at the auction

John Wortham, a good dancer...

Eve Woodyear

Heather Poynter

John Corby

Valerie Weber

Anne Levi

Lindsay Chisholm

Sue Field

Cowes Guild RNLI Parties

At The Royal Yacht Squadron

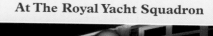

Membership Sec. Mrs Diana Chillcott, Mr Chillcott and Pat Reader

Judge John Wroath and his wife with friends

At Villa Rothsay

Capt. Henry Wrigley receiving an award from Joan Marshall for his help and assistance to the RNLI during 2001

Marie Mollart-Rogerson, Joan Marshall, Joyce Parsons, Rosemary Northlewis

Zoë Langford has lived in Cowes for many years and remembers the lavish social scene and the glamorous parties which were held at the Gloster Hotel among other places.

Zoë Langford with her Morris Minor and John Ward

Photo: Courtesy of The Jubilee Sailing Trust

The Jubilee Sailing Trust

Square Rig Sailing for the Disabled and Able-Bodied

The Jubilee Sailing Trust is a United Kingdom, Southampton based charity, established in 1978 under the patronage of HRH The Duke of York with the principal aim of promoting the integration of physically disabled and able-bodied men and women through the challenge of sailing a tall ship at sea.

To this end the Trust owns and operates two specially designed ships, **Lord Nelson** and **Tenacious**. Both ships are designed, rigged and fitted to enable all crew members on each voyage to share in the ships' daily routines throughout the voyage.

Tenacious, a 65 metre long, 690 tonne, three-masted barque, is the largest wooden tall ship to be built in the United Kingdom in the last one hundred years and has required funding of £14.3 million. It is a masterpiece of teamwork: 36 people worked for over 105,000 hours to complete the hull and decks alone.

Financing of these most worthwhile projects requires substantial support and the Trust relies on charitable donations of all categories. Among the regular benefactors, The Little Britain Challenge, which takes place in Cowes every year, has been donating a great part of its profits to the Trust.

The Trust offers corporate hospitality packages (a day on a tall ship) and each year organises many events, ranging from classical concerts to sailing regattas. It invites sponsorship of events and advertising in the *JST Magazine*, which has a circulation of 30,000, and on a new website (www.jst.org.uk). Membership of the Trust costs as little as £20. Its Chairman is Chris Dunning.

Photo © MCtcA

Mary-Ann, Rodney and Joanna Barton

Fund-raising activities for the Jubilee Sailing Trust are many and varied. At a cookery demonstration organised in her Cowes home by Mrs Mary-Ann Barton, on behalf of the Island Friends of the JST, culinary aspirants could witness the preparation of a whole range of unusual dishes.

The Jubilee Sailing Trust, Hazel Road, Southampton SO19 7GB
Tel: 023 8044 9108. Fax: 023 8044 9145. Email: info@jst.org.uk

Photos © MCoA

Duet

Hartlepool Renaissance

Xylonite

Photos: Courtesy of the Cirdan-Faramir Sailing Trusts

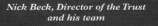

Nick Beck, Director of the Trust and his team

The permanent crew of Queen Galadriel

The Cirdan-Faramir Sailing Trusts

The Cirdan-Faramir Sailing Trusts - sister charities founded by the Rev. Bill Broad in 1983 and 1991 - provide disadvantaged young people with an opportunity for self-development through sailing at sea. More than 17,000 have been helped in this way over the last 18 years. The charities focus on helping to develop life skills by bringing groups of young people to a positive, yet challenging, social and adventurous environment, thus developing self-esteem, independence, responsibility and many other social skills. Sailing and living on large boats fosters these attributes. Four vessels make up one of the largest fleets of historic sailing boats designed to accommodate groups - who are fully involved in working them.

Fullbridge House
3 Candlers Quay, Maldon
Essex CM9 4LF

They are **Hartlepool Renaissance**, a 72-foot Robert Clark ketch, crewing twelve; **Duet**, a 72-foot Edwardian racer/cruiser gaff yawl, crewing seven; **Xylonite**, an 86-foot Thames Sailing Barge, crewing twelve; and **Queen Galadriel**, a 107-foot Baltic Trader gaff ketch, crewing seventeen. Built in Svenborg, Denmark, in 1937, **Queen Galadriel** was purchased by the Cirdan Trust in 1983 and has since carried more than 6,000 disadvantaged young people. She will come out of service in 2003 for a refit taking fourteen months at a cost of £520,000. A fund-raising campaign offering various possibilities for sponsorship has been started. The charities received part of the profits from the 2001 Little Britain Challenge in Cowes. Their President is David Cole and the Managing Director is Nick Beck.

Tel: 01621 851433
Fax: 01621 840045
Email: info@cirdan.co.uk
www.cirdan-faramir.co.uk

The Andrew Cassell Foundation

Award-winning Cowes yachtsman Andy Cassell added another success to his long list in 2001 when he became 'BBC South Yachtperson of the Year' - beating Ellen MacArthur and BT Global Challenge winning skipper Conrad Humphreys. But then Paralympic gold medallist Andy, a director of Ratsey and Lapthorn sailmakers, has been winning things since he was a teenager, when he became national Albacore champion in 1961 - the youngest person ever to win the title and the only sailor without legs ever to do so!

Although Andy was born without legs, it has not stopped him taking on the world at sailing. As well as the Albacore dinghy championship, he has beaten many top sailors in keelboat and big boat classes, winning the Daring Class Championship three times, the Sigma 33 European Championships in 1993 and several top honours in International Dragons.

At the America's Cup Jubilee in Cowes, Andy was a helmsman on the 64 ft *Crusade of Dee*, formerly owned by Sir Max Aitken, which came first overall in its class. He also helmed the classic *Solway Maid*, a 1942 Fife cutter, which won Classic Yacht Week in Palma, Spain, in 1996 he started the America's Cup Jubilee in *Solway Maid* – switching to *Crusade* after *Solway Maid*'s mast fell over the side at the start of the week! Andy was an acknowledged sailing champion before he was invited to take part in events for sailors with disabilities - something never thought of when he started out!

He made his sailing debut at eleven, in a small dinghy with a sail made from his grandmother's tablecloth. From the beginning Andy's success at sailing was boosted by enthusiasm, determination and talent, despite unpromising beginnings. He was born into a

Andrew Cassell, aged 11, out in his canvas dinghy with a table-cloth sail.

non-sailing family just across the River Medina from Cowes on the Isle of Wight. His father, Clarence, farmed at Norris Castle and his mother, Dulcie, was a concert pianist who gave up her career to look after her family. Because of his disability Andy missed a lot of schooling and left when he was 13. Watching the boats at Cowes and reading about the *Kontiki* raft Pacific expedition made him long to take to the water. With a cousin he built a raft – which sank. A family friend bought him a dinghy but his mother was worried he would be swept out to sea and tied it to a 60 ft rope. This could not stop Andy and he cut the rope - to his mother's terror. With £65 savings he bought a 12 ft dinghy to race, progressing to the Albacore. An Olympic campaign followed. Andy was racing against top athletes and his campaign was backed by Tiny Mitchell, of the Royal Corinthian Yacht Club and Cowes Corinthian Yacht Club fame. But Tiny Mitchell died and Andy was left without funding.

Sir Owen Aisher lent him a Daring keelboat and he also crewed for Bill Citron in Dragons. "Because of my disability it took six months to persuade him I was up to the physical crewing needed." Andy's confidence in his abilities paid off and he stayed with Bill for four years, before progressing to offshore successes which included a first in the Royal Ocean Racing Club (RORC) points championships and third in the three-quarter ton world championships. Andy's helming was a lifesaver in the notorious 1979 Fastnet Race, from Cowes, in which 17 sailors lost their lives. Andy was skippering the 30 ft J30 racer *Juggernaut* - not the most stable of offshore yachts - and the yacht was knocked down by a giant wave. Andy steered it through the night, with the boat under water much of the time. "We probably owed our survival to the Herculean efforts of Andy, who drove solidly through to dawn by sheer instinct," said crew Jonathan Sanders.

Andy is probably best known for his 1996 gold medal in the first ever Paralympics - international Olympic events for athletes with disabilities - in Atlanta, USA, and winning the 'Yachtsman of the Year' award. Andy sailed a Sonar keelboat with crew Tony Downes and Kevin Curtis, also disabled, and may well be said to have started the wave of Olympic success which British sailing is currently riding - with enormous help from the lottery fund Sports England. Andy just missed the Sonar sailing medals at the Sydney 2000 Paralympics, sailing with Brian Harding and Andrew Millband, now a rising star in the single-handed 2.4m class. Andy is currently National and European Sonar champion and now has his sights set on Athens in 2004, with crew Brian and Ed Suckling.

Andy and his team nearly didn't make it to Sydney when lottery funding for a new boat fell through. He threw himself into fund raising, with a sponsored swim across the Solent, no mean feat for someone with artificial legs. He received strong support, because of his personal popularity, from the Island Sailing Club, the Royal Corinthian Yacht Club which raised £6,000 with an auction evening, and the Cowes Corinthian Yacht Club, where the Andrew Cassell Foundation is based. The boat was eventually purchased by an anonymous Island Sailing Club member - on condition it be given back to the club after Sydney to be added to the club's fleet of eight Sonars.

It was not until the mid 1980s that Andy had become involved with disabled sailing. Testing a boat for Westerly Yachts, he got together a crew - mainly disabled servicemen - for the 1985 Round-the-Island race. "We won our class and our division, everyone was so excited that I decided I would try to put back into sailing some of what I had got out of it." A few years later he set up the Andrew Cassell Foundation, based at the Cowes Corinthian Yacht Club, to encourage more people with disabilities to go sailing and racing. On the day he won his gold medal in Atlanta, Andy heard that the Foundation had won charitable status.

Since then thousands of pounds have been raised, with help from the Sports England lottery fund. The Foundation has two Sonars used for racing - a third sank in deep water during Cowes Week 2001 and Andy is hoping to replace it with insurance money.

Andy is sure that there is still scope to get people with disabilities out sailing and racing. "But it's not just lottery money to buy the boats, it needs facilities such as suitable toilets and changing rooms in the clubs too. We are currently working with RYA Sailability to find more disabled youngsters."

The Andrew Cassell Foundation, 100 St. Mary's Road, Cowes, Isle of Wight, PO31 7SS
Tel: 01983 292298   e-mail: sue@burgess150.freeserve.co.uk0

The International Etchells Class

Originally designed by Skip Etchells in the USA for the 1966 IYRU three-man keelboat trials for the next Olympics, the new boat won practically every race, but the selection was given to the longer established **Soling**. The Class was granted international status in 1974, having established regular racing fleets in USA, Australia, Canada, UK and Bermuda. Since then further fleets have grown up in Hong Kong, Italy, Switzerland, Israel and, newest and most dramatically, in New Zealand.

There are strict one-design rules but there is flexibility in detailed layout, which has permitted updating in a controlled and acceptable way. There are rules restricting sails acquisition to keep costs within reasonable levels. This fibreglass yacht is just over 30 feet in length and weighs one and a half tons, of which one ton of lead is the fin keel. The boat can easily be trailed by road so transport is easy for inter-fleet competition and assembling for continental championships. There is an annual world championship on alternating continents, easily accessible, as boat and mast fit entirely within a shipping container.

In the late 1950s at Cowes the regular week-end racing was 12-Metre, International One-Designs, International Dragons, X Boats and Flying Fifteens. By the mid-60s the 12-Metre yachts were gone and IODs were dwindling to be replaced by the **Darings**, a fibreglass development of Arthur Robb's 5.5 metre, which built up into a smart and competitive racing fleet.

It was in 1976 that a number of **Etchells**, based on the Clyde, entered for Cowes Week. This caused considerable interest and a Cowes fleet was formed the next year. In the following years the fleet build-up was slow, with resistance from the well-established **Daring** and **Dragon** Classes claiming that an additional class was not needed at Cowes.

Despite the slow start, the originators of the Cowes Fleet were convinced that the **Etchells** had such merit that it would succeed eventually. This proved correct and, by the mid 1980s, it was shown that the **Etchells** was the quickest keelboat, entered for Cowes Week, and became the leading boat for the White Group starts, a position still held today. The Fleet continued to grow so that, for example in 1992, the Cowes Week entries were 46 **Etchells**,

28 **Darings**, 42 **Dragons**, 21 **Flying Fifteens** and 71 **X Boats**. The Cowes Fleet bid for the World Championship for 1996 and obtained the nomination to host the event with the Royal Yacht Squadron. This led to a further build-up of the UK Fleets, now operating at Clyde, Lymington and Burnham-on-Crouch, in addition to Cowes, where the Fleet further increased to be the world's biggest. Cowes Week numbered 64 boats in 1994, which put a huge strain on the White Group start line. The World Championship 1996 at Cowes was well attended and won after very close competition by Adam Gosling (GBR, Cowes), with USA as runner-up, securing only the second British win since Chris Law (Lymington) in Australia 1990. The British Association of the International **Etchells** Class organises area and UK annual championships together with European Championships, which have been held in Italy (Lake Garda) and France (Douarnenez). This year the UK again hosted the 2001 World Championships at Lymington with the Royal Lymington Yacht Club. The racing was held in Christchurch Bay, an international gathering of 65 yachts, won by Stuart Childertey (GBR, Cowes), closely pursued by an Australian. As the Championship followed hard on the back of the America's Cup Jubilee, it was very convenient for a number of America's Cup helmsmen to participate. Many of them find that the **Etchells** gives them the competitive and relaxing situation they need when not out on the big boats.

Sailed by three, but with recent permission for four, the overall crew weight must not exceed 285 kilos. Before this there were a few extreme cases of heavyweight crews sailing fast and upright to the windward mark then sinking on the run; this led to poor racing according to varied conditions. While it is now 35 years since the **Etchells** was designed, it remains up-to-date and yet traditional in many senses of the word. It is fast, enjoyable and testing enough to attract yachtsmen and sailors from club racing level to world class.

The Class is strong with a reasonable turnover of enthusiasts keeping it a relatively young class. Currently there are 1100 registered racing **Etchells** in 55 locations worldwide. The **Etchells**, for some indefinable reason, has remained almost entirely an 'English speaking' boat. It is known as the Class of Keelboat Racing.

The Cowes Fleet Commodore owned K1, K38 and K68.

It's the largest and most popular yacht race of its type in the world and easily the most spectacular sporting event associated with the Isle of Wight. Nothing quite matches the Round the Island Race. Sponsored for the last six years by Hoya Lens UK, this extraordinary race over a course of 50 nautical miles will be held for the 66th time in June 2002. Each year it tests the organisational skills of the Island Sailing Club. Each year, the club rises to the challenge - aided by a large band of volunteers, Cowes Harbour Master, Red Funnel and the Royal National Lifeboat Institution. The number of entries is staggering. In 2001, no less than 1,735 boats took part, well up on the year 2000 - though the record stands at 1,813. That was set in 1989, appropriately the ISC centenary year.

The large entry in 2001 was good news for the Jubilee Sailing Trust, which was chosen to benefit - for the second year running - from the proportion of entry fees allocated annually to a nominated charity, the public interest generated by the scale of the race and events held to co-incide with it. The money donated to the Trust is helping to finance the maintenance of its two square-rigged sailing ships, **The Lord Nelson** and **Tenacious**. Although the Cowes nerve centre of the event is very much at the Island Sailing Club, the thousands of participants (there were around 1,200 of all standards in 2001) start always from the Royal Yacht Squadron line. However, the course naturally provides 'grandstand' views for thousands of spectators all around the Isle of Wight coast.

The Round the Island Race

The annual Round the Island Race, with up to 1,600 boats, brings a flotilla of yachts and sailors together for the 50.2 nautical miles from Cowes to Cowes. It is essential to know the geography, and the tides and winds in the Solent, the most tactically complex stretch of water in the world of sailing. They race for a small trophy mounted on a base of oak taken from Nelson's Victory, and it is much prized by sailors. So many take part that the Solent is a rainbow of colours as the different types of boat compete together.

*It is not generally known that **Shamrock V** sailed round the Island in 3 hours 50 minutes just before the war.*
Harry Spencer

In 2001, they saw Mike Slade's 90-foot high-tech *Skandia Leopard* smash a long-standing record by winning the monohull section of the race in 4 hours, 5 minutes and 40 seconds, a fantastic improvement of more than an hour on the previous best - which was also bettered by a further ten yachts. A new record time for multihulls was also set when D. R. A. Webb's French trimaran *Dexio Eure et Loire* (with Rodney Patterson on board) finished in 3 hours, 8 minutes and 29 seconds - 46 minutes better than the previous record.

Although the present Round the Island Race originated in the 1930s, it did have a forerunner in the Hundred Guinea Cup of 1851. The 19th century event started to the East, leaving the Isle of Wight to starboard. Today's race does the opposite - starting to the West and leaving the Island to port.

Information
The Island Sailing Club
Tel: 01983 296621

Photo © Yacht Shots

Making a first appearance at the race in 2001 was a fleet of five International America's Cup Class (IACC) yachts, including Peter Harrison's *GBR 44*. Three of the others in the class were Sunsail charters while the fourth, Johnny Caulcutt's *Hoya High Voltage*, was skippered by top international yachtsman Eddie Warden-Owen. In keeping with the America's Cup theme was the entry of the beautifully-restored J-Class yacht *Velsheda*, which regularly graced the Solent in the 1930s. A further indicator of the race's high prestige was the appearance of Rod Carr, Secretary-General of the Royal Yachting Association, who competed aboard the multihull *Impulse*.

The boats skippered by today's winners of the coveted Gold Roman Bowl, the principal race trophy - offer something of a contrast to the 7-ton auxilliary cutter *Kalliste* which won the contest for Major Cyril Windeler, the race's founder, in 1939. Some things do not change, however. The event he instigated remains totally dependant on the tide, which means that in some years it is held in May or July, rather than June. That won't be the case in 2002. If you're thinking of entering the race in June, bear in mind that the latest you can do so is one week before the event and, if you do leave it that late, it will cost you more to take part. Normally, the entrance fee is set at £40.

Above: Jacobite gives water to Alvine XII during the Swan European Regatta 2001. Below: Desperado of Cowes at the same event.

The Swan European Regatta

The Swan Class could be described as the sailing equivalent of a Mercedes motor car. Beautifully built sailing yachts with elegant lines and precision engineering, they range in size from 36 ft in length to over 80 ft. Built in Finland since 1966, they are famous for beautifully crafted interiors, excellent sailing performance and sleek good looks, and it comes as no surprise that their owners often sail them year after year with affection. Designed by such famous names as Sparkman and Stephens, Ron Holland and German Frers, they are powerful ocean-going boats and most owners enjoy competitive racing as well as cruising. The Swans also have a legendary reputation for toughness and seaworthiness.

Sixty-one elegant beautiful Swans took part in the Swan European Regatta in Cowes in June 2001. Hosted by the Royal Yacht Squadron, this prestigious event attracted owners from all over the world, and the competitors enjoyed a week of excellent racing in the Solent. Amongst the hot competition were Islanders Graham and Libby Deegan in *Menenes*, a Swan 44, who managed 2nd overall in G Division, and Shirley Robertson who could not resist the temptation to sail in a Swan for the Regatta, such is the lure of the Class.

www.swanregattas.com

The Volvo Ocean Race

The Volvo Ocean Race, formerly known as the Whitbread Round the World Race, and described as the "pinnacle of international offshore racing", is a multi-million pound venture. The total distance of 32,250 miles is a fearsome prospect: in the notorious Southern Ocean the fleet must pass through stretches of gale-strewn water where no land-based aircraft has the range to reach a boat in distress, and where commercial shipping never ventures. The 2001 race started from the Royal Yacht Squadron when a flotilla of eight Volvo 60s bore down, fully powered and hitting speeds of up to 18 knots. The fleet will call at Volvo's home port of Gothenburg, Sweden, before the final sprint leg of the race to the German port of Kiel for the finish.

www.volvooceanrace.org

The Champagne of Yachting
A Toast to Cowes

Champagne Mumm has long had an association with sailing and Cowes. Sponsorship began with power boating before sponsoring the Hermès Mumm Regatta in 1992. In 1993, they started sponsoring yacht classes beginning with the Mumm 36 in 1993 and the Mumm 30 in 1995. The Mumm 36 was a revolutionary new design for a grand prix racing yacht providing close one-design racing at the highest level. This prototype has proved so successful that a new design has evolved. The Mumm 30 has taken the world by storm and is probably one of the most successful international one-design class yachts available. Over 175 of this class have been built to date in the USA and Europe, and recently another boat builder has been appointed in Malaysia, already building six boats to order. It is anticipated that over 200 Mumm 30s will have been built by 2002.

Mumm is a familiar sight in Cowes, particularly during the yachting season. Champagne Mumm provides refreshment for competitors of the annual *Hoya Round-the-Island Race*. A great way to finish a long race! Champagne Mumm are the supporting sponsors of *Skandia Life Cowes Week* and are associated with the *Cowes Classic Powerboat* weekend, providing a link between Champagne Mumm's yachting activities and Formula One motor racing.

www.mumm.com

The Admiral's Cup

The Grand Prix of Ocean Racing, the Admiral's Cup, has acquired a prestige and popularity that very few international yachting events can equal since its conception in the 1950s. It was the brainchild of Sir Myles Wyatt and Peter Green of the RORC, with the aim of encouraging overseas yachts to race at Cowes and in the offshore fleet. Sir Myles was one of five men who jointly donated the cup to the Club, and it was through his position as Club Admiral that the cup took its name.

The Admiral's Cup is a series of offshore and inshore races in the Solent and English Channel for yachts of a certain rating, culminating in the gruelling 605 mile Fastnet race. Back in 1957, Britain's entries for the first series featured the legendary John Illingworth in *Myth of Malham* that was the terror of Ocean Racing, winning everything for 15 years. John's competitive spirit changed the event to the fiercely fought contest it is today. Since then racing yachtsmen have tried all sorts of techniques within the rules to achieve that extra quarter of a knot of boatspeed.

The series is run bi-annually with Britain winning the trophy no less than nine times, and has long featured famous sailing names such as Sir Max Aitken, Eric Tabarly, Dick Nye and Ted Turner. The victorious 1971 team included the then Prime Minister Edward Heath on *Morning Cloud*.

The series continues to attract many of sailing's elite including the likes of Ian Walker, Lawrie Smith, Chris Law, etc. The last series was in 1999, then won by Holland, but sadly the 2001 series failed to materialise due to lack of entries. The RORC is promoting the series heavily to attract entries for the 2003 event, but in January 2002 Cowes received a sad blow when it was decided to switch the venue to Dublin, severing 45 years of history.

The RORC. Tel: 0207 493 2248.

Skandia Life

Cowes Week

On the Isle of Wight

Cowes Week
The Greatest Show
on water

Internationally renowned Cowes Week, in early August,
is considered by many to be the final social and sporting
event of the English midsummer calendar
after Ascot, Wimbledon, Henley and Goodwood
and before the start of the shooting season.

Cowes is a small but historic town on the Isle of Wight, at the mouth of the Medina River, where the Solent provides a twenty-five mile stretch of protected waters within easy reach of London. Here, the yachts assemble for eight consecutive days of racing, converging on Cowes from their home ports on the south coast or from abroad. The town itself is split in two, East and West, situated either side of the entrance to the Medina. West Cowes is the centre of activity and home to the yacht clubs. The two parts are linked by a floating bridge, which is a car carrying ferry.

Patricia

COWES WEEK REGATTA

For hundreds of years, boats have raced at Cowes, which has long been regarded as the premier yachting centre in Britain. Cowes is also home to the Royal Yacht Squadron, the most senior yacht club in the country. Yacht racing has changed a great deal since those early days when customs men were chasing smugglers whose boats were loaded with contraband. Competition began in the late 1700s between gentlemen and peers of the realm with their fast and sometimes armed cutters. The Royal Yacht Club was founded in 1815, and in 1827 won the royal seal of approval from George IV. In 1833 it became the Royal Yacht Squadron, and was housed in West Cowes Castle in 1858. It is now Britain's most established sailing club and its members are entitled to wear the White Ensign on their boats as do the British Royal Navy, while everyone else, including naval ships, must make do with the Red. The first official Regatta was held in 1812, and in 1826 the Royal Yacht Squadron organized the first racing event, later known as the Cowes Regatta, which lasted three days. The following year the Royal family began a long association with the occasion when George IV presented one of the cups. On seeing the success of this event, other yacht clubs based at Cowes began to organize various race days before and after the main event. The regatta continued to evolve in this way and by 1953 the Week had become nine days of hectic confused races. From this time on the Royal Yacht Squadron became the base for all starts and finishes, and the various clubs agreed to race under a common set of rules. The Cowes Combined Clubs was officially formed in 1964 and now runs and organizes the sailing regatta. It has grown to incorporate ten yacht clubs and the Cowes Town Regatta, which, together with the Royal Yacht Squadron, play the dominant role. It is from there that the Skandia Life Cowes Week races are organized. Racing is started from the Royal Yacht Squadron platform, with its distinctive red and white roof, and run under a common set of rules. The gun line on the sea front is made up of 22 cannons from the reign of

King William IV, known as the sailor king. A race committee of more than 60 experienced club members run the proceedings with rule book, computer, radio, flags and cannons in the required synchronization each day. Sailing as a preserve of the rich and well heeled has now become a sport for the enthusiast. British sailing is racing ahead with full sails, especially after the Olympic success and the fortitude of lone yachtswoman Ellen MacArthur along with the announcement of the British America's Cup challenge, the first since 1987. Every year up to five thousand participants in almost a thousand boats enter Cowes Week, 30 or more classes for over 200 races. Boats vary from the latest eighty-foot Maxis, each with 24 crew, through the cruise racer classes to the three and two crew keelboats and Flying Fifteen dinghies. The yachtsmen range from international sailing stars to small club sailors. The yachts on view include the middle of the range to the extremely expensive, and the vast number of the sailing enthusiasts who attend the racing festival are mostly amateur. At its most basic Cowes Week is divided into two main categories: the first, design classes, where the boats are all the same type and size and the first one back wins, and the second, handicap classes, where boats of different sizes and types race together with the final results adjusted by handicap. The Maxis are immensely powerful and graceful racing machines reminiscent of the 1930s when the fabulous J-Class yachts towered above everything else afloat. During Cowes Week silver trophies and prizes are given for every race and series, so there is always competition and the social pace keeps everybody on the go. The town is a sea of flags and banners from the sponsors and suppliers of the event: Skandia Life, Champagne Mumm, Ocean World, Timberland, Carphone Warehouse, Omega, Pimms, Lucozade, B&G, Wightlink, Icom and WNI Oceanroutes. In 2001, Helly Hansen was replaced by Henri Lloyd and Danebury Vineyards came as new sponsors.

Photo © Beken of Cowes

*HRH The Duke of Edinburgh and Uffa Fox sailing **Coweslip** during Cowes Regatta in 1960*

Each year the big yachts create a special atmosphere, lending Cowes that extra aura of glamour. The Royal Yacht Britannia was once always the centre of attention. Now no longer in active use, and moored up in Scotland, Britannia is proving to be irreplaceable and as a consequence the event has lost a little of that special atmosphere, although yachts such as Sir Paul Getty's Talitha G and Sir Donald Gosling's Leander, are hugely impressive.

Cowes Week is one of the greatest regattas of its kind which attracts more than 1,000 yachts and some 6,000 crews, plus family and friends. It is run by Cowes Combined Clubs and is managed from the Regatta Office, and by Director Stuart Quarrie on Cowes Parade. Each day the racing starts at 10.20am from the Royal Yacht Squadron. It is signalled by gunfire and a cannon is fired every five minutes to start each of the 34 classes. Spectators can view the races throughout the day, with the last race starting at about lunchtime, before immersing themselves in the social side of Cowes in the afternoon. Running Cowes Week requires enormous organization: Cowes harbour becomes a bedlam, with not only hundreds of racing yachts, but also leisure and spectator boats, not forgetting the ferries and the commercial vessels for which business goes on as usual. Cowes Week is sponsored by *Skandia Life* (one of the UK's leading providers of unit linked life assurance, investment, pensions and savings plans) which has supported Cowes Week since 1995 pouring £6 million into the event and plans to continue to do so. Its sponsorship has been an increasing success in working with the Cowes Combined Clubs and organizing what is now the country's greatest participation sporting event after the London Marathon, and what Group Marketing Director Bill West calls *the greatest show on water*. "We will be continuing our support for the regatta until 2002. We have funded a new pontoon, off the Cowes parade, to enable competitors to bring their dinghies ashore. We are happy to be providing an additional £150,000 for the development of important shore side facilities," he said. Last year Olympic gold medallists, Iain Percy and Shirley Robertson were actively racing during the regatta. Last but not least, the official charity for Skandia Life Cowes Week 2001 was the RNLI (Royal National Lifeboat Institution), a charity close to the hearts of all those who enjoy their time spent on the water. Cowes Week is the only place in the world where you will find top international 'yotties' racing together on the same stretch of water as weekend family sailors.

'A Great Atmosphere'

Cowes is not just about competitive racing as there is also a lively social side to the week. Since the Edwardian days of Lily Langtry and Rosa Lewis of London's Cavendish Hotel, who owned the house and the lawn that is now the Royal Corinthian Yacht Club, there has been glamour, flirtation and the occasional mild scandal to add spice and grace to the busy scene. The small town is packed with thousands of 'yotties' either dressed to the nines for the cocktail parties and balls or returning, still in their yachting gear, for the famous Yacht Haven 'beer tent' and disco. Cowes social life veers to the extremes. On the one hand tea on the Squadron lawn requires tidy clothes, whilst on the other, wild discos are enjoyed by young crew members and their friends. (The Yacht Haven has an entry fee after 6pm and provides a plentiful supply of drinks and live music until midnight each day). The event is also a mecca for celebrities from the world of film and television and numerous international sporting stars. Parties take place every night and many of the sailing clubs have made an effort to become younger and more casual over recent years. An exception to this is the Royal Yacht Squadron Ball, which is still very grand and formal. The Royal London and Royal Corinthian Yacht Club balls and cocktail parties, held by the competing classes of yachts, turn the week into a continual period of festivity. It begins on Friday with the Royal Yacht Squadron Ball, the most exclusive bash of all, which used to be attended by a party of the Royal family, but, with the Royal Yacht *Britannia* gone, there has been no Royal presence at the ball for the last few years for lack of suitable and secure accommodation. The ball may be attended only by members and their guests. A few hundred 'Happy Few', are

able to attend the dinner before the dance for £200. Others arrive after 10pm having paid £90 for the dancing and the breakfast, which is served after midnight.

A 'ticket holders only' (with the name registered on the Secretary's list) final prizegiving ceremony takes place on Sunday at the RYS.

The Royals at Cowes Week

Although not at the ball, Prince Philip, as Admiral of the RYS, usually attends the Annual Meeting, followed by church and a reception at the Squadron. In 2000, he also opened the RYS's new pavilion. Both Prince Philip and King Constantine of Greece have been regular participants in the actual sailing events for many years, and so have The Princess Royal and Prince Edward. But with no members of the Royal family competing over the past two years, the days of sailing as an élitist sport are over, and the organizers had to turn to new champions to provide the added aura of glamour. However, even when not competing Prince Philip is still a regular at the regatta and is quite at home strolling through the streets of the town in addition to helping oversee the organization of the racing. Since the withdrawal from service of *Britannia*, the Prince has been a guest on a number of luxury motor yachts and in 2000, stayed on *Patricia*. He did not attend Cowes Week 2001 because of his attendance to the America's Cup Jubilee.

And Much More...

Cowes Week is addictive to those who know it and return year after year for the sport and fun. The town and the facilities have been improving over the years and everyone was looking forward to a huge festival of yachts to celebrate the 150th anniversary of the *America's Cup* last August. The Jubilee was followed by the International Etchells 2001 World Championship in Christchurch Bay, sponsored by *Hackett*, which was last held in Britain in 1996 and won at Cowes by Adam Gosling and his team. The Cowes finale is always the spectacular Friday night fireworks at the end of the week (the first fireworks took place in 1827). The next day the *Fastnet Race* yachts set off westwards down the Solent for their three or four day race around the famous Rock of Southern Ireland, ending in Plymouth. Twenty years ago, a terrible storm devastated the fleet and 17 lives were lost. This historic race is held on alternate years, as is the *Admiral's Cup*, which is run on odd numbered years (it was cancelled in 2001). The Regatta is now reckoned to be the largest in the world. Local weather and strong Solent tides introduce challenges to sailing at Cowes, not forgetting the hidden rocks just off the beach along the seafront. That tragic storm of 20 years ago is not the only example of the weather playing havoc with the sailing. In 2000 the second half of Cowes Week saw winds of 25 knots with big gusts of 40 knots leaving a trail of destruction. At least four of the smaller yachts sank and many other craft were dismasted or suffered other damage. These complex tides and high winds offer a great challenge, even to the most experienced of sailors, and the added element of danger can make some of the races that little bit more exciting for crew and spectators alike. The bad weather was blamed on a combination of light and heavy airs, combined with spring tides, which led to the gale-force gusts. In contrast the week ended with the breeze struggling to reach 3 knots, forcing officials to abandon the racing at 1pm on the last day.

After Cowes

As the visiting yachts depart to their home ports after Cowes Week, life returns to normal and the villages of Seaview and Bembridge in turn hold their holiday regattas.

COWES YACHT HAVEN

PIMM'S

ISLAND SAILING CLUB

Photos © MCrvA

cowes radio 106.2 fm
www.yachtradio.com

Peter Ralls, QC - Chairman CCC Committee

Stuart Quarrie - Director

COWES COMBINED CLUBS

This organisation was set up in 1964 as a committee to represent the Royal Yacht Squadron, the Royal Thames Yacht Club, the Royal London Yacht Club, the Royal Southern Yacht Club, the Royal Southampton Yacht Club, the Island Sailing Club and the Cowes Town Regatta Committee, which has been involved since 1869 in racing and has been a member of CCC since its creation. The Royal Ocean Racing Club, which is involved with the start of the Fastnet Race, was later invited to join the CCC and in 1996, the Royal Corinthian and the Cowes Corinthian became members. Every club that makes up the CCC has its own Regatta Day and participates in the running of the races.

The Chairman of the CCC is Peter Ralls. In a break with tradition, this was the first time that the CCC Chairman was not a member of the Royal Yacht Squadron. He has since been elected a member.

Stuart Quarrie is the Director, and Patsy Carter is the very efficient Secretary.

The Royal Yacht Squadron, the most famous club of its kind in the world, was founded on 1 June 1815 by a group of gentlemen in the Thatched House Tavern in London's St James' Street. The club evolved into the Yacht Squadron which met twice a year in London and Cowes allowing these men to discuss and participate in their common interest of salt water yachting. The clubhouse is situated in the Castle on the north-west point of Cowes, built on the foundations and battlements of fortifications constructed by Henry VIII to defend the Medina River, where the club took residence in 1858. Already in 1826 the club was the first to establish organized yacht racing in Britain at its annual regattas. Cowes thus became the headquarters of sailing in the UK and the RYS the principal authority for devising racing rules and handicapping. In 1851, it was the instigator of what would become the most prestigious racing event in the world: the America's Cup. The new pavilion, opened in 2000 by Prince Philip, has become the setting of the many parties held during the regatta on the Royal Yacht Squadron Lawn.

The RYS runs the racing on Tuesday and Wednesday of the week and on Thursday with Cowes Town Regatta Committee.

The Commodore is The Lord Amhurst of Hackney
Tel: 01983 292191

The Royal London Yacht Club was founded in 1838 by Members of the former Arundel Yacht Club who raced from Arundel Stairs on the Strand. Since 1882 the clubhouse has been on the Parade in Cowes in a pair of fine Victorian terrace houses built by Dr Hofmeister, a physician to Queen Victoria. The RLYC is part of a triumvirate with the Royal Thames Yacht Club and the Royal Southampton Yacht Club.

The Commodore is Peter Cove
Tel: 01983 299727

The Royal Corinthian Yacht Club was established in 1872 and was formed to counteract the increasing professionalism in yacht racing. The club also has a fine clubhouse in Burnham-on-Crouch, Essex, and the Cowes branch of the club is based in a superb situation overlooking the Solent. Food and accommodation are considered excellent.

The Commodore is Rosemary Beason
Tel: 01983 293581

The Island Sailing Club was formed on 2 March 1889 after a group of enthusiasts from the Royal Yacht Squadron, led by General Baring, saw the need for a new, democratic club to organize the racing of small craft. The Squadron and the Royal London Yacht Club, the only two clubs in Cowes at the time, did not have the facilities to do this. The club is based on the High Street in Cowes.

The Commodore is Peter Hedley
Tel: 01983 296621

The Cowes Corinthian Yacht Club was formed in 1952 and is unique in so much as it is a club for the working men of Cowes with a common yearning for the sea. The club is based in the heart of Cowes with a unique waterfront position.

The Commodore is Mike Brinton
Tel: 01983 296333

Cowes Town Regatta Committee was in existence even before 1869 and has been involved in Cowes Week ever since. In 1891, by command of Queen Victoria, the Regatta was called the Royal West Cowes Town Regatta and it used to include rowing. The prefix of 'Royal' was used until 1936, when it was dropped on instructions from the then Home Secretary. During the Regatta Shore Sports were also organised on the Green as well as the beach, greasy pole climbing and 'duck hunts' among them. Up to 1939, a water polo match was staged

Ian Lallow

between the Victoria Pier and the Customs House slipway. In 1903, motor boat races were held for the first time. From 1949 until the formation of the Combined Clubs Committee in 1964, the Regatta was organised from the boathouse of the Grantham Hotel. The Committee has been part of Cowes Combined Clubs since its origin. It is chaired by Ian Lallow and has 16 members (local people interested in the town and sailing activities) who meet four times a year. During Cowes Week, they run the racing for the 'White Group' on Thursday together with the Royal Yacht Squadron.

Each of the Clubs that attend Cowes Week enjoys the benefit of security. There are both day- and night-time patrols with police sniffer dogs. The Clubs also have access to emergency radios which are linked directly to the police headquarters in the town. There is a random searching of bags, and fire alarms ring in the event of a bomb warning.
For information about Cowes Combined Clubs - Tel: 01983 295744 Fax: 01983 295329 www.scra.org.uk

Photo Courtesy RORC

The Fastnet Room

The Royal Thames Yacht Club, historically eminent among yacht Clubs, originated out of the Cumberland Fleet that had been formed by the Duke of Cumberland, brother of King George III, in 1775. The Club had been further established as the Thames Yacht Club by 1823 and in 1827, it gained patronage from the Duke of Clarence, which enabled it to become the Royal Thames Yacht Club when he acceded to the throne as King William IV in 1830. Yachting originally took place on the Thames and later the Solent when in the 1850s it became more accessible with the steam train. The Royal Thames held its first regatta during Cowes Week in 1953. In 1973 it organised two days of racing with the Royal London.

Since 1977, with the Royal Southampton Yacht Club it controls the first three days of the week. The Club is involved in a great number of yachting events - both cruising and racing - in the UK and overseas and its Sailing Academy helps younger members develop their sailing skills.

The Patron of the Club is HRH The Duke of Edinburgh. HRH The Prince of Wales is Admiral of the Cumberland Fleet and the Commodore is HRH The Duke of York. Robert Dean is the Vice Commodore. Since January 2002, the Rear Commodores are Patrick Kelly, Clive Chalk and Douglas Harckman. The Secretary is Captain David Goldson.

The Knightsbridge Clubhouse - headquarters of the Club since 1923 - which offers excellent facilities and comfortable 'cabins', organizes a lot of social events. The Club, which is open to men and women of all nationalities, has reciprocal arrangements with leading Clubs around the world, among them the Royal London Yacht Club in Cowes. The Anglo-Belgium Club shares the same premises.

Tel: 0207 2352121

The Royal Southern Yacht Club, which was originally the Royal Southampton Yacht Club, assumed its present identity in 1844. Situated opposite the Hamble River, the Club is in one of the most picturesque sailing locations in the country and it maintains highly-rated positions for its mooring pontoons. It organises the racing on Friday and Saturday with the Island Sailing Club.

The Commodore is R. A. Lovell.

Tel: 02380 450300

The Royal Southampton Yacht Club, based in one of Southampton's most vibrant sailing centres, Ocean Village, was founded in 1866. The Club's history records as one of its most important events the presentation by Queen Victoria to the RSYC of a cup for the 1897 Regatta to commemorate her Silver Jubilee.

The Commodore is Anton Bates.

Tel: 02380 223352

The Royal Ocean Racing Club has as its primary responsibility the organisation of offshore racing - mostly in UK waters - both for members and non-members. It was founded in Plymouth in 1925 after the first Fastnet race and the Fastnet Room in the London Clubhouse is still regarded as the 'holy of holies'.

Given the high-ranking status of Cowes in international yachting, it is entirely appropriate that the Royal Ocean Racing Club should have a presence in the town. In fact, it is considerably more than a mere presence.

Its clubhouse is at St James's Place, in central London, but if members need a room in Cowes, the first port of call will probably be at 82 High Street, within walking distance of the marina, in the house the RORC calls *The Disrespect!*

The RORC is involved with several key events on the Cowes yachting calendar. With the support of the Cowes clubs, it annually organises the *Red Funnel Easter Challenge,* the *De Guingand Bowl Race,* the *Morgan Cup Race* and the *Myth of Malham* event - all from the Royal Yacht Squadron line over to France - along with the *Cowes-Dinard-St Malo Race* later in the summer. Other events run by the RORC from the RYS line include the *Channel Race.* It also has a rôle in the organisation of the *Schroder Channel Race* down to St. Peter Port, Guernsey. And, of course, there is the Rolex-sponsored spectacular *Fastnet Race* to the famous rock off Ireland's South Coast (see separate section).

The RORC also organises a full programme of social activity - lectures, social evenings, dinners and prize givings, all of which feature on the clubhouse calendar. The RORC hosts a cocktail party on the Royal Yacht Squadron's lawn during Cowes Week and other regattas.

So what does it take to become a member?

A good background of racing experience is the chief requirement, and that means completion of at least 500 miles of racing offshore with two or more overnight events and, if possible, at least one RORC race within the five years prior to your application. The Club may offer you provisional membership while you set about the task. You'll need to be proposed and seconded by an existing member before you are granted membership, and sponsored by a RORC committee member or the Commodore of a recognised yacht club. Unlike most other clubs, there is no social membership as such. There again, you do not have to be a member of the RORC to take part in the races it organises.

The RORC, through its 'Rating Office', has become the national authority for measurement and rating of offshore yachts. It is a member of the Solent Cruising & Racing Association run by Stuart Quarrie - the organisation which ensures that racing fixtures in the Solent do not clash - and it relies on a small number of staff who are mostly volunteers for its race organisation. The Club is led by Commodore Peter Rutter and General Manager Peter Wykeham-Martin. Janet Grosvenor is Racing Manager.

Tel: 0207 493 2248 or 01983 295144 (Cowes)

Fax: 0207 493 5252 E-mail: info@rorc.org

CLASSES AT COWES WEEK

The Sigma 38 Class has been running for 12 years and is enjoying a resurgence of interest. A one-design racing yacht designed by David Thomas, the largest fleet is based on the south coast.

The Sunfast 36 Class consists of identical yachts that are used all the year round for corporate charter, hospitality and inter-company regattas, as well as being used for RYA courses and for teaching the fundamentals of flotilla sailing before clients head off to warmer climates.

The Prima 38 Class was launched in 1998 and there are now 15. The Prima is a high performance yacht featuring a wide sterned hull form, carbon fibre mast and high ballast ratio.

The Sigma 33 Offshore One Design Class is a more modern class of boat with the first being built in 1979. It is very popular and there are more than 30 fleets in Cowes.

The Hood 35 Class has its own owners association that was formed in 1999 and the boats raced at Cowes Week for the first time last year.

The Contessa 32 Class consists of boats that were designed as cruise racers in the 1960s and at Cowes this is one of the toughest classes in which to race with some excellent helmsmen pitting their wits against each other. This class also has the reputation for enjoying a party out of the water.

The Mumm 30 Class is for these all-rounders, light, fast and exciting boats. There are some 130 worldwide, with 86 in Europe, 15 of which are based in Hamble.

The Hunter 707 Class consists of low cost, high performance 'sportsboats', measuring just over 23 feet. The 707 fleet continues to grow with well over 100 boats. It is a strictly amateur class and the boat is easy to tow and is also popular with women. All the boats have identical blue and fluorescent pink spinnakers.

The International Melges 24 Class is fast and furious and the boats are sailed by many of the semi-pros of the sailing world. They are also considered to be the sportiest of the sportsboats and one of the swiftest to be sailed at Cowes.

The Sonar Class is a relative newcomer to the UK and Europe. The boat is remarkably agile with an all up weight of 995 kg, (450 kg in the lead keel). They race with three or four people and cater for people of all ages and varied ability.

The National Sonata Class is another of those which features a boat designed by David Thomas. The Sonata is also one of the boats that disproves the theory that sailing is expensive, with secondhand boats being available for very little. They are also easy to tow.

The Daring Class is a class based on the one-design version of Arthur Robb's silver medal winning 5.5 metre boat at the 1956 Olympics. The first Daring was launched in 1960 and there are now 200 class members. For this class owners are required to purchase new sails every 2 years.

The International Etchells Class consists of boats with a waterline of 22 feet and an overall length of 30 feet. As a type they are considered one of the most exciting and responsive keel boats in the world. The boats can carry either 3 or 4 crew, but the weight must be kept within the 285kg limit.

The International Dragon Class race throughout the world (over 13,000 boats in 27 countries) and have 12 major fleets throughout the UK, the Solent Fleet being just one of many. The entries at Cowes usually consist of about 30 boats from the UK, with visitors bringing boats from Holland and Germany.

The Redwing Class has been on the scene for over 100 years. The boats epitomize sailing efficiency and are named after the colour of their sails. Tall and thin they provide the greatest drive with minimum drag.

The Solent Sunbeam Class consists of classic boats built by traditional craftsmanship. 1998 marked the class's 75th year and most of the Sunbeams come from their home club at Itchenor on Chichester Harbour, although there is a growing fleet at Falmouth.

The Seaview Mermaid Class has been racing since the early 1900s. Each boat is a different colour with a matching spinnaker and carries a crew of two or four. The boats have a choice of sails depending on the wind each day.

The National Swallow Class was designed in 1947 for the 1948 Olympics. The boats have a crew of three and are mainly made from glassfibre rather than the original wood.

The Flying Fifteen Class was designed by one of Cowes' favourite sons, Uffa Fox, in 1947. The sleek build of these boats means that in the steep Solent seas there are occasional accidents as the boat sails through rather than over a wave.

The National Squib Class is another type of yacht that smashes the myth that this is a game only for the very rich. The jaunty and economical Squib is easily towed and the strict one-design status means that success is directly related to sailing skill and not the size of your cheque book.

The "X" One Design (XOD) Class consists of 170 different fleets from throughout the south east.

The Victory Class was established in 1954 and has raced regularly at Cowes Week ever since. Rules are tailored to keep the boats relatively simple and affordable and another characteristic is a wet ride on a rough day.

The Thames Barge Class sees the humble Thames Sailing Barge, capable of carrying 250 tons, prove her worth. These boats can sail where other vessels would need to be towed and are considered an important part of Britain's maritime heritage.

The X-99 Class is based on a design by Niels Jeppesen as an offshore one-design in 1985. It offers a unique combination of sportsboat high performance with offshore racing and cruising.

Competition in the Skandia Life Cowes Week is open to any member of any recognised yacht club anywhere in the world. For those who intend to compete and need a mooring in Cowes there are two marinas, Cowes Yacht Haven in West Cowes and Cowes Marina in East Cowes. There are also several boat yards upriver that offer moorings.
Telephone the Harbour Master on 01983 293952 or Cowes Combined Clubs on 01983 295744. Or the official Cowes website www.cowes.co.uk. For the weather www.sailsail.com
Cowes Week 2002 will take place over a nine day period from 3 to 10 August.

Photos©MCvA

2000

Selena Rudge, Paul Volley and Theresa Andrews

Nick Jup and Andy Gomarsall

1. Bill West, Skandia Life
2. Tim Sewell, Skandia Life
3. Rugby players , Andy Gomarsall, Simon Sman, Alex King, Theresa Andrews, Nicki Jupp, Selena Rudge.
4. Edmond Peel
5 & 6. DC Peter Ogden and his team "Spirit of Jethou".
7   John Merrick's father
8.   Ian Walker and Bill West
9.   Christian Roman (Eurosail) and his team: Sebastian Col, William Thomas, Guilhem Joseph, Marc Bouvet, with Bill West.
10. A group of well-dressed young people.
11. Sue Hardwick (PR for Cowes Week)
12. A Chronicle Journalist and Edward Lloyd Hello photographer with Sabine Mollart Rogerson
13. Linda Herbert

André and Julie Oszmann (Skandia Life)

Dubai born Nick Greenstock, whose father Sir Jeremy is the British Ambassador to the United Nations, sailed as a guest of sponsors Skandia Life at the 2000 Cowes Week. Nick and his father spend a couple of weeks on the Isle of Wight each year, sailing dinghies. The Harlequins centre, was pushing then to regain his place in the squad.

The late
Sir Peter Blake

Ω OMEGA

THE SPONSORS

Skandia Life is the principal sponsor of Cowes Week. It took over the title sponsorship in 1995, since which time the event has gone from strength to strength. Skandia has extended its sponsorship and have injected more than £1.5 million into the event. Since 1995 it has provided much more than the all important funding to help run the event and the company's support has been instrumental in developing the regatta into its highly successful format. To quote Bill West, Skandia's Marketing Director: "Our sponsorship has also been instrumental in our record business growth over the last five years." Skandia is one of the UK's fastest growing and leading life assurance companies, with an award winning range of life, pension and investment products. Since launching in the UK in 1979, it has achieved spectacular growth. By the end of 1999, Skandia had become the 14th largest life and pension company in the UK. As leaders in multi-manager investment, Skandia gives more ways for investments to make more money by providing the best investment choice, flexibility and expertise.

Omega are the official timekeeper of Skandia Life Cowes Week following on from its position as official timekeepers of the America's Cup in 2000, when Sir Peter Blake and his crew, Team New Zealand, all sailed to victory wearing Omega Seamasters. Sir Peter was also present during Cowes last year and took to the water on the America's Cup '95 boat in addition to sharing his sailing experiences at the Yacht Haven. Omega also launched a newly designed range of Seamaster watches during the week. It was in 1948 that the first versions of the legendary Seamaster appeared. The blue version of the current Seamaster was worn by James Bond in the blockbuster film *The World is Not Enough*. Omega has also made a long-term commitment to Blakexpeditions and its objective, to create greater awareness of the need to protect the world's great oceans, lakes and rivers. Blakexpeditions were headed by Sir Peter Blake, who had retired from competitive yachting after successfully defending the prestigious America's Cup. Omega has helped to fund the expeditions, a dedicated Internet site and documentary films about each expedition. As Omega President Stephen Urquart said: "Omega is very proud to be associated with such an important cause for the future of humanity". Let us hope they will continue after the sad death of Sir Peter Blake.

Wightlink, the Isle of Wight's largest independently owned ferry operator, offers the most crossings and widest choice of journeys over the Solent. With the most number of routes to the Island its catamaran and car ferry service is the fastest available. Routes include Portsmouth to Fishbourne, Lymington to Yarmouth and Portsmouth Harbour to Ryde. Wightlink carries five million passengers and one million vehicles each year.

Champagne Mumm, which is the official champagne for the Week, has been involved in yachting since 1977 and the Mumm 30 Class races at Cowes Week. Anyone signing for an offshore membership was given a bottle of *Mumm Champagne*.

There are 160 of these one-design yachts and they have regattas all over the world. In the UK they take place at Hamble, Poole, and, of course, the Isle of Wight. As supporting sponsors Champagne Mumm hosts a party and presents an overall class prize. Further information can be found at www.mumm.30.org **Ocean World** of Cowes, the official merchandiser, is supplying the high-quality briefcases for the competitor packs. It offers a huge collection of clothing and accessories, all adorned with the official logo and a comprehensive in-house embroidery and printing service. The firm specialises in new uniforms to match a boat. It created the America's Cup Jubilee logo among others and MD Paul Bertie was running the Jubilee Village.

BT Openworld, BT's new global mass-market Internet business, as well as providing all communications for the event and creating a state-of-the-art media centre, is also streaming Cowes Week radio live onto the web and was the communication sponsor for the America's Cup Jubilee.

Other sponsors include **Timberland**, as official footwear sponsor, **The Carphone Warehouse** supporting the entertainment and the music at the Yacht Haven. **WNI Oceanroutes**, the world's largest commercial weather forecasting organization, supporting all weather-sensitive marine activities and providing an expert marine meteorologist.

Icom (UK) Ltd, importer and distributor for Icom Inc. of Osaka, Japan, supplies radio transceiver, receiver and navigation products for marine and other markets. Another sponsor, **B&G**, the world's leading supplier of marine electronics to racing yachts and boats, supplies wind reading instruments to assist with race management for the week in addition to offering shoreside technical support. Two drinks companies are also among the Cowes Week sponsors and suppliers, **Lucozade Sport**, the UK's number one sports drink, and **Pimm's**. Pimm's home for the week is the Island Sailing Club. It also distributes free chilled cans of Pimm's and lemonade for competitors returning after a hard day's racing.

The 2000 charity was the **John Merricks Sailing Trust**, named after the British Olympic silver medallist who died in a car accident in Italy in 1997. It was founded to advance the education, physical and mental development of young sailors lacking access to necessary resources.

The 2001 charity was the RNLI **(Royal National Lifeboat Institution)**, naturally enough, a charity which is close to the hearts of all who live, work and play on the water.

A 24-hour rescue service which turns out in all weathers to save lives at sea, the RNLI doesn't get Government funding like other rescue services and must rely on donations and legacies to buy boats, maintain them and train brave new crews.

Skandia Life Cowes Week 2001

Julian Bayley and Johnny Woodall

Jerome Pastre and Nigel Croney Champagne Mumm

Mr and Mrs Ernst Piëch and Sebastian

Paul Bertie MD of Ocean World and Chairman of the Jubilee village

Young's Brewery, *one of the oldest brewers in the UK, dating from 1581, have been supplying the beer to the beer tent since 1987. Its Chairman, John Young, in charge since 1962, celebrated his 80th birthday during Cowes Week.*

Chris Troup, Chairman of Cowes Yachting and Director of Cowes Week sponsorship

Skandia Life had daily prizegiving parties in the Hospitality tent next to the Carphone Warehouse stage, where music by top-class performers was played. For the late birds, the party went on at the "Mount Gay Rum Night Club" into the early hours.

Cowes Radio (106.2 FM) team covered the Regatta 24 hours a day with Dick Johnson in his rigid inflatable boat sharing his commentaries with Simon Vigar and Chris Carnegy, while Cheryl Bruggy was doing interviews in the Skandia Life tent.

A Royal Yacht Squadron Security Guard watching over The New York Yacht Club Challenge Trophy

Sue Hardwick Public Relations Team

Cowes Week 2001 registered more than 1,000 entries and attracted famous yachtsmen and women such as Olympic gold medallists Shirley Robertson, Iain Percy, Steve Redgrave and Ellen MacArthur, Ben Ainslie, Adrian Stead and Jo English. Many of them were also guests of **Henri Lloyd**, official clothing suppliers. This year the rules had been changed and upper limits increased in order to accommodate the big yachts which had already arrived for the Jubilee.

The most celebrated yacht competing at Skandia Life Cowes Week was the 12-Metre *Australia II,* with Skip Lissman, and John Bertrand at the helm, which won the 'Auld Mug' in 1983 from the Americans after 132 years. 1995 winner **NZL-32** was also there, as well as 1987 British America's Cup challenge 12-Metre *Crusader* owned and sailed by Richard Matthew and skippered by Harold Cudmore. It had just gone through a ratings make-over by yacht designer John Corby. Don Wood's *Italia*, another 12-Metre, was helmed by Chris Law.

Among the other big boats of Class 0 and Class 1, which drew a lot of attention, the glories of the course were the 90ft. **Skandia Leopard,** led by sympathetic Mike Slade, and the impressive all black **Stealth** belonging to Fiat boss Gianni Agnelli. Among the Farr 52 was **Bear of Britain** of Kit Hobday and Tim Louis, sailed by Mark Campbell-James, **Chernikeeff 2** headed of course by buoyant *GBR Challenge* boss Peter Harrison and David Lowe's **Loco.**

Among some of the most remarkable in the Swan Class let's mention **Desperado,** owned by Richard Loftus (helmed mostly by Johnny Caulcutt after his own IACC yacht **High Voltage** was rendered out of order by the strong winds and choppy seas), Peter Ogden's **Spirit of Jethou, Island Flying** skippered by Simon Dudley, and **Aera** belonging to Greek Nick Lykiardopulo. Among other foreigners were Sebastian and Ernst Piëch with their **Danebury First Challenger** sailed by Richard Bagnall, Dutch Frank Van Beuningen on **Hestia**, and American Edward Sawyer on **Clairvoyant** etc.

Last but not least, beautifully restored Classic J-Class **Velsheda, Endeavour** and **Shamrock** were also in Cowes.

However, among the 1,008 smaller and more 'down-to-earth' dayboats were all the classes such as the Etchells 22 getting ready for their championship in Christchurch, the Hunter 707, the XOD, the Beneteau 40, with some racing in the IRC Class 3 and the Melges 24. Another nice sight was provided by the graceful **Thames Barges** which have been part of the maritime heritage, since the 19th century.

Zaca A Te Moana

Sponsors

Among the new sponsors in 2001, *Henri-Lloyd*, world leader in foul weather, sailing and leisure clothing is official technical clothing suppliers of Cowes Week for the next three years. It owns Melges 24 *Henri Lloyd Rapid Breathing*, campaigned by Chief Executive Paul Strzelecki and his crew.

Danebury Vineyards, owned by Ernst Piëch since 1993, was the only one out of 390 English vineyards to participate actively in Cowes Week. Danebury is a six-acre vineyard, 3 miles North West of Stockbridge, Hampshire. The oldest vines were planted in 1988 and the grapes are used to produce the Pyrrhus.

Sailing artist Tim Shepard designed a special montage of an English vineyard for the *Seafood and Wine Bar*, where Mumm Champagne and Danebury Vineyards were selling their champagnes and wines together with seafood provided by *Phillips Fine Food*. Ernst Piëch, who is of Austrian origin, was there with his wife and his son, Sebastian, who sailed the *Danebury First Challenger*. The Piëch family has a very interesting story which we shall write about in a future edition. In the meantime, try to find their 1996 *Pyrrhus* and *Cossack*, which are delicious English wines.

Tel: 01264 781851 www.danebury.com

Nicorette - The Nicorette team, winner of the Sydney-Hobart 2000 and current Maxi One Design World Champions, sailed under the banner 'Competing for a smoke-free world.' After Cowes Week, Olympic champion Shirley Robertson joined the crew for her first Fastnet Race, and the third for skipper Ludde Ingvall, who also sailed during the America's Cup Jubilee.

Among other participants in the Skandia Life Cowes Week was *International Air Charter plc*, a private air travel and exclusive company which charters private planes. Its owner and Chief Executive, Hugh Courtenay was sailing a Mumm 30 called *Nautilus*.

Tel: 01843 822833 www.aircraftcharter.com

The Ardberg Distillery, which belongs to a private family which also owns Glenmorangie, presented its 10 and 17-year-old whiskies as well as the 1975 limited vintage *www.ardberg.com*

Merrill Lynch HSBC also had a stand encouraging people to open an account with them. *www.mlhsbc.co.uk*

Cups and Trophies

The Skandia Life Young Skipper's Trophy went to Archie Massey's *Skua* in the National Swallow Class, crewed by Douglas Pattison.

The Britannia Cup was won by *Chernikeeff 2,* Peter Harrison's Farr 52.

The New York Yacht Club Challenge Cup sailed for by the combined Class 0 and 1 was won by Richard Loftus' *Desperado*, skippered by John Caulcutt. *Spirit of Jethou* was second and Adam Gosling's *Yes! T&G* was third.

Other cups included the Henri-Lloyd Challenge Cup, The Red Funnel Trophy, the Mumm Cup, the Champagne Nicolas Feuillatte Trophy, the Emirates Trophy, the Chisholm Challenge Cup etc.

The Royal Yacht Squadron 'opened up' for the first time. Cowes Combined Clubs (with the kind permission of the Squadron), invited some sailors and media to witness at first hand the fascinating and normally behind-the-scenes set-up for course setting, timings and Black Group broadcasts from the Platform, where races start at the Squadron.

An extraordinary gesture considering how restrictive and inaccessible the Squadron can be towards outsiders and foreigners.

A 'Seafarers Service' took place at the Holy Trinity Church for the Mission to Seafarers. Lady Pigot, Chairman of the Island Lifeboat Board, Peter Nicholson, Commodore of the Royal Yacht Squadron, Captain Stuart McIntosh, Cowes Harbour Master were among those present.

Rev. Richard Emblin, Commodore & Mrs Peter Nicholson and Mr G.J. Banks, Major of Cowes.

Photos © MevA

Photos Courtesy: Henri-Lloyd

Rapid

Henri with Shirley Robertson and Ben Ainslie

Ben Ainslie

HENRI-LLOYD

*In 1963 Henri Strzelecki in partnership with Angus Lloyd founded Henri-Lloyd Limited.
Today, Henri Strzelecki's two sons, Paul, who is a keen sailor, and Martin, who is a golfer and
sportsman, keep the company abreast of state-of-the-art developments,
reinforcing its product as a world-class brand.*

Henri-Lloyd has been supplying crews racing at Cowes Week for over thirty years. At the 2001 Regatta, Henri-Lloyd was appointed official technical clothing supplier to Skandia Life Cowes Week. The company yacht, a Melges 24, named **Henri-Lloyd Rapid Breathing** was campaigned by Joint Chief Executive Paul Strzelecki and his crew and won the Melges 24 Class.

In May 2001, the company opened a retail outlet, The Henri-Lloyd Sailing Store in Cowes High Street. The company sponsors some of the world's top sailors who help to test and develop new fabrics and designs at Cowes, including Olympic Gold Medallists Ben Ainslie and Shirley Robertson.

Oracle Racing Team has appointed Henri-Lloyd the official outfitter of technical marine clothing, lifestyle sportswear and accessories to the Oracle Racing Team, challenger for the 2003 America's Cup. Having been the world leader in ocean, offshore, coastal and dinghy racing clothing for more than thirty years, Henri-Lloyd distributes the Henri-Lloyd/Oracle Racing range of products at selected retail stores throughout the world. Apart from protective jackets and suits, the range of accessories include T-shirts, shorts, deck-shoes, deck-boots and luggage.

Four out of the eight crews in the Volvo Ocean Race are wearing Henri-Lloyd's 'breathing'™ Ocean Racer One-Piece Suits.

The company displayed the full range of yachting clothing at the 2001 Southampton Boat Show, which is being worn by **Amer One, Amer Too, Assa Abloy** and **SEB** for the heavy weather legs of the Volvo Ocean Race.

Henri-Lloyd have supplied many round-the-world race crews. They have sponsored many famous people in the sporting world, including Sir Francis Chichester, Robin Knox-Johnston, Chay Blyth, Dame Naomi James, Ben Ainslie, Mike Golding, Emma Richards, Miranda Merron and many others. In 1967, Sir Francis Chichester made history by completing the first solo circumnavigation, wearing his Henri-Lloyd Consort Original Jacket.

Henri-Lloyd's association with the America's Cup and with Cowes goes back nearly forty years. In 2001 the company was chosen to be official technical clothing supplier to the America's Cup Jubilee Regatta and has produced a range of clothing to commemorate this unique event. Winning skippers of past America's Cup events were presented with an exclusive America's Cup Jubilee Limited Edition Jacket.

Photos Courtesy: Henri-Lloyd

Sir Robin Knox Johnston

Sir Rannulph Fiennes

Photo © MGvA

Henri Strzelecki MBE

A Personal Profile

Henri Strzelecki was born at Brodnica in Poland on 4 October 1925. Mr Henri, as he became internationally-known, came to England in 1946 as a Polish soldier, after serving with the British Eighth Army in Italy. Henri chose to settle in England and went on to study and work in the textile industry.

As a keen sailor in the Sixties, Henri was quick to spot the potential of a newly-developed fabric called Bri-Nylon as an alternative to the more traditional heavy cotton 'oilies'. He put forward ideas to his employer, but Henri's proposals were rejected. As a result he decided to form his own company.

In 1963, Henri Strzelecki founded Henri-Lloyd Limited, in partnership with Angus Lloyd. From a converted chapel on the outskirts of Manchester, the company developed a number of sportswear firsts. Henri's remorseless eye for detail and desire for perfection in craftsmanship ensured that the highest possible quality was achieved.

Henri-Lloyd were responsible for many design firsts which are now accepted as industry standards, such as the use of Velcro as a closure, the first non-corrosive zip, the first integral safety harness jacket and the reliable taping of seams.

Henri-Lloyd continues to pioneer the development of performance fabric technology and garment design. In 1994, Henri-Lloyd launched its breathing range incorporating the latest in GORE-TEX™ membrane technology. This started a breathable revolution which significantly increased the comfort and performance for sailors. Henri-Lloyd has since exclusively

developed its own TP breathable fabric technology and offers a wide range of foul weather gear protection for all sailing activities. Henri Strzelecki has now retired but still follows Henri-Lloyd's development very closely. His two sons, Paul, who is a keen sailor and Martin, who is an enthusiastic golfer and sportsman, manage the business and have reinforced their father's company as a world-class brand. Ironically, they set up a business and factory in Henri's home town Brodnica in 1993, following the opening up of Eastern Europe.

Henri thanks God for having given him so much. "I have got everything and I even feel guilty for having so much. I do a lot for charities and I try to help people as much as I can; I enjoy doing this. I also like to advise people and to give lectures. Otherwise, when I am alone, I pray, I meditate, I contemplate, I go to church. I have some guiding principles: live and let live, don't do to others what you would not like them to do to you and treat people as you would like them to treat you. I am in fact, a very simple man."

One of Henri's principles is that "two and two do not make four, they make either three or five. Why? Because when you talk about costs it should be five and when you talk about profitability it should be three . . . you never know in advance what the results are going to be."

He remains close to his Polish origins and tries to help fellow countrymen whenever he can, like supporting a Polish ex-Service club in Manchester. He is very proud of the fact that the Polish army was the fourth largest during the Second World War.

Mike Slade

Mike Slade and his wife Heather
with Diana Montegu and David Rendall

Skandia Leopard

Leopard, an innovative carbon fibre water ballasted 90ft racing Supermaxi yacht campaigned by Mike Slade, has been sponsored for the last two years by Skandia Life.

During Cowes Week 2001, the **Skandia Life Leopard** raced with crews including Olympic medallists Ben Ainslie, Iain Percy and Shirley Robertson. On 9th August, the 175th Anniversary of the first ever race sailed at Cowes Week in 1826, the **Skandia Life Leopard**, skippered by its owner Mike Slade and helmed by Iain Percy, was first to cross the finishing line. Also on board was Peter Ralls, Chairman of Cowes Combined Clubs and Director of Cowes Week Sponsorship Ltd.

Built by Green Marine at Spitfire Quay, Southampton, this unique Riechel/Pugh designed yacht is an ultimate high performance racer capable of competing with the fastest racing yachts in the world. The standard of luxury on board rivals that of the best superyachts thanks to the latest construction and engineering techniques developed by *Ocean Marine* and an interior scheme by Ken Freivokh Designs. Mike Slade, Chief Executive of *Helical Bar*, the office development specialist, said: "It has taken many years to establish Ocean marine as a successful charter business and it is only with recent advantages in technology that we were able to consider building a boat of this size that can fulfill our requirements for an outright racing boat and at the same time be fitted out to a very high level for luxury charter work. The days I host on **Leopard** offer the ultimate combination of excitement and luxury entertainment, as our guests can enjoy being on the UK's foremost racing yacht which also offers the safety and comfort of a luxury charter boat. This may well explain why we see growing demand for one-day charters."

The yacht has a towering 135ft carbon fibre rig, which allows her to carry masthead asymmetric spinnakers that dwarf everything else in the Solent. It is the largest UK owned racing yacht built for many years.

The radical monohull was racing again last year in Skandia's colours, not only during Cowes Week, but also at the Cowes St. Malo and Channel Races, the Fastnet and the America's Cup Jubilee. In June, Mike skippered the **Leopard** to victory in the Hoya Round the Island Race and completed the race around the Isle of Wight in a record breaking 4 hours 5 minutes. During Cowes Week 2001, **Leopard** raced with crews including Olympic medallists Ben Ainslie, Iain Percy and Shirley

Robertson. On 9th August, the 175th Anniversary of the first ever race sailed at Cowes Week in 1826, **Leopard**, skippered by its owner Mike Slade and helmed by Iain Percy, was first to cross the finishing line. Also on board was Peter Ralls, Chairman of Cowes Combined Clubs and Director of Cowes Week Sponsorship Ltd.

The design brief of **Leopard** began from the prerequisite that she must be a self-sustaining viable entity in her own right via commercial charters and it was demanded that she should be water ballasted to keep her stable for charter guests, as well as fast on the water.

Green Marine of Southampton built the hull, deck and primary structures with other aspects of the build managed in-house by Slade's own team, *Ocean Marine Ltd*, led by project manager John Bremner, plus naval architect Rob Papworth, who looked after design co-ordination, and captain Chris Sherlock. *Southampton Yacht Services* ran the systems design and implementation and *Fairlie Restorations* fitted the teak decking.

Leopard has been built and equipped by some of the leading maritime firms and names represented on board include *Hall Spar, North Sails, Edson, Lewmar, Spinlock, B&G* and *Deckman*, to name but a few.

Interior appointments include a bright and spacious saloon, comfortable dining area and two sizeable guest cabins. There is a full-beam master cabin forward of the guest accommodation, while the galley, navigation station and crew accommodation for four are housed aft of the main companionway.

An excellent variety of watersports equipment available for guests' use includes fishing, waterboarding, waterskiing, two windsurfers and scuba diving gear.

Despite her innovative design technology and cutting-edge performance, **Leopard** still requires only a small crew of her captain and three others.

Photo © Beken of Cowes

HRH The Duke of York with Kit and Georgie Hobday

Photos © MGtvA

Tom and Sally Louis, Susie and Kit Hobday

Legend has it that the bard Merlin foretold of a great king
who would restore glory and honour to the people of the
island of the mighty. His name - Arthur the Pendragon, lord
of the war host, Bear of Britain.

Celtic Myth AD 450

Bear of Britain

Bear of Britain *is the culmination
of more than ten years endeavour
supported by Tom Louis and his wife
Sally together with Kit and Susie
Hobday and many other people such as
Peter Harrison and Peter de Savary.
She is sailing under the burgee of the
Royal Thames Yacht Club, whose Vice
Commodore, Robert Dean has been
very supportive. Mostly crewed by
young members of the club,* **Bear of
Britain** *provides them with experience
of amateur international yachting at
the highest level. HRH The Duke of
York, who is Commodore of the Royal
Thames Yacht Club, was present at the
London naming ceremony in April
2001.* **Bear of Britain**, *a Farr 52, is
in fact an amateur version of the
America's Cup boats. With her
spectacular Union Flag spinnaker, she
has already participated in most of the
important races in her first season. She
sailed in the Hoya Round the Island
Race, the Champagne Mumm World
Cup, Skandia Life Cowes Week, and
the America's Cup Jubilee, where she
won several prizes and, to the delight of
the whole crew, was declared the overall
winner. A great achievement for a
boat sailed by amateurs and young
crew only.
Everywhere, the talented on-board
piper, Hugh Carter, who even produced
a Bear of Britain March, created quite
some atmosphere.*

Kit Hobday

English born, on 14th July 1931, Kit Hobday spent some
of his younger years in Belgium, where his mother
was married to Colonel Edward Stiers. He
became besotted with sailing at 13 when his
father bought him a boat and, at 17, he
founded the Thorpe Bay Yacht Club
which became one of the top dinghy
racing clubs in the UK.

After a spell as a merchant, he
became a journalist and then
created his own PR company
(KH Publicity), which was lucky
to have Peter de Savary as one
of its clients. Having taught
him how to sail, Kit served
as Deputy Chairman on Peter
de Savary's *Victory* America's
Cup campaign in 1983.

Talking about Peter Harrison
supporting a new British
Challenge, he said: "At the
beginning, I tried to dissuade
him from doing it. But he is
doing very well, I wish him the
best of luck."

Kit Hobday would like to
organize an 'amateur' version of
the America's Cup, a strictly
amateur race in identical boats. It
will probably take place in 2002,
with the backing of the Royal
Thames Yacht Club. After trying
unsuccessfully to organize it with the
New York Yacht Club, Kit is finalizing a
challenge from an Australian syndicate
for a new trophy. The first match should be
sailed at Cowes and the second leg in Sydney
by competing yachts of the Royal Thames Yacht
Club and an Australian club.

Photo © Beken of Cowes

I think it's time for a drink...

With HRH Prince Edward and Patrick Chisholm

With John Caulcutt on 'Right Time' in 2000

NICK BONHAM

Six generations of Bonhams have knocked down all kinds of treasures to the highest bidder at the Knightsbridge-based auction house. Nick Bonham, a boyish 52-year-old, started working for his father when he was only 17 and held his first auction aged 19. In 2000, Bonhams and Brooks - the two British family enterprises - merged to form the fourth largest auction house, combining tradition and the comprehensive national structure of Bonhams (founded in 1793) with the powerful international sales platform developed by Brooks since its creation in 1989 as the world's largest vintage car auction house. In November 2001 Bonhams & Brooks merged with Phillips Son & Neale UK, creating an extensive worldwide network of salerooms and offices: Knightsbridge, Bond Street, Bayswater and Chelsea in London and 40

Bonhams sites across the UK, not forgetting offices and representatives all over the world. The new Bonhams is half-owned by Louwman Brooks (the holding company for Bonham & Brooks) and 49.9% by LVMH Art Investments. Roger Brooks is the Chairman of the new Bonhams while Nick is Deputy Chairman.

Nick Bonham's talents have made him the darling of the charity auctions and he is now regarded as one of London's most sought after auctioneers, attending more than 30 society functions from high profile balls to fashion shows throughout the year. When not involved in auctions, Nick is a passionate sailor and supporter of the Cresta Run in St Moritz. He is still one of the youngest contestants ever to have completed the gruelling Run - at the age of 14. "Two days later my mother went down there dressed as a man," he laughs. "That was when women were banned." Equally, each year he competes in Cowes Week Regatta with his friend and former neighbour Patrick Chisholm in the Etchells Class. One Cowes year, when sailing with Prince Edward, he suffered the indignity of going aground right in front of the Royal Yacht Squadron. "Now that's something I won't do again in a hurry," he says!

John Caulcutt and his crew in 2000

High Voltage in 2001

John Caulcutt with Peter Harrison and Bill West being presented with the NYYC Challenge Trophy

JOHN CAULCUTT

The 'Right Time' for a 'High Voltage' challenge

The thrilling spectacle of two big America's Cup yachts racing off Cowes added an extra thrill to Skandia Life Cowes Week in 2000. John Caulcutt, owner of the **Young America Yacht** (formerly **Il Moro 4**) and Oyster Marine boss Richard Mathews, owner of **Tag Hoya**, two yachting enthusiasts who had bought the world-class boats and shipped them back from New Zealand to Cowes, were hoping that the sight of them would boost Great Britain's chances of mounting an America's Cup challenge for 2003. The two boats were renamed **About Time** and **Right Time**, referring to a potential America's Cup challenge, and John had gathered a very good international team who had sailed with him before in transatlantic and offshore races as well as in Antigua for the last five years. They came from England, Ireland, Scotland, South Africa, Canada, the USA, Mexico, Poland and St. Martin, and they were all professionals.

Two further America's Cup Class boats (bought by Chris Gordon) **France II** and **France III**, built for the 1995 race, were there to be used with the other two to help train prospective America's Cup crew.

John Caulcutt said when interviewed in 2000: "Britain invented the Cup in 1851 and we lost it. It is bad that a maritime nation like Great Britain has not had an America's Cup challenge in the past 14 years, while a small nation like New Zealand has managed to take the Cup from America and successfully defend it. That is why we have launched a campaign called **'It's about time, it's the right time'**. We are here in Cowes to prove what we can do for potential investors and sponsors. To fund the first part of a two-boat campaign we need £10 million. There is plenty of money around and we must give people who have got that money tangible evidence that there is a will and a chance that we could win. We are a maritime nation with 55 million people and more than a thousand new millionaires. We aim to persuade these people that England must regain the oldest high profile yachting trophy in the world. It is important that we are professional and have everything operating in harmony with the Royal Yachting Association. We might not win the first time. But we must attempt to get the trophy back for the prestige and the national pride of our country." According to John, the America's Cup Jubilee in

August 2001 "should have been the platform for a fresh British challenge." With his background in the marketing business John was planning to treat the project like a brand.

His message was certainly understood by Peter Harrison who, in 2001, created *GBR Challenge* for the 2003 America's Cup. In the meantime John has renamed his yacht **High Voltage**.

During Cowes Week strong winds and choppy seas put his yacht out of order and he sailed Richard Loftus's **Desperado**, winning Class 1 overall, as well as the coveted New York Yacht Club Challenge Trophy and the Bathsheba Trophy. **High Voltage** was back for the America's Cup Jubilee where she sailed with other IACC yachts which had come to Cowes.

John Caulcutt has built up his public quoted company called **Watermark**, which operates in the marketing and communication sector. Although his mother is American and met his English father during the war, he claims to be totally English. Caulcutt has always been passionate about sports. In the 1976 Winter Olympics he represented Great Britain in the bobsleigh team, and in 1982 he tried for the Summer Games, coming second with David Howlett in the Star Class Olympic trials. He has built a number of boats over the years, including the first ever RIB - when just 22-years-old at Atlantic College - a design which was then adopted by the RNLI (the *Atlantic 21*) for coastal rescue, something he now wishes he had patented. With his childhood friend, Graeme Dillon, he went on to build a concrete boat, a larger more stable boat for a three-year world sailing project, and later bought the American 12-Metre **Columbia**, a post-war design which had won the America's Cup in the 1950s.

John Caulcutt has always done unusual things, and is presently planning the fastest trip round the world on water in 2004. The record currently stands at 71 days, and he believes it can be done in 35. The parallels between him and his most famous client, Richard Branson, are not hard to see. John is married and has a ten-year-old daughter, who loves sailing. He says he has high hopes that she may one day become a champion like her father. He lives with his family and spends time between homes in Hampshire and on the Isle of Wight. Other interests include skiing and playing guitar in his 1960's Rock 'n' Roll band, which has raised many thousands of pounds for charity events.

The 2001 Royal London Yacht Club Ball

Sir Malcolm Edge KCVO, Chairman of the Royal London Yacht Club and Commodore Peter Cove

Richard and Sonia Carver who own a boat called 'Marie-Claire'

Derek Hodd Treasurer of the Club

Mark Fear and Kate Christie

Vice Commodore Patrick Kelly of the Royal London Thames Yacht Club and Mrs. Heather Kelly.

Bill Andrea-Jones, QC with Debbie Phillips

Kenneth Kendall

For the balls, 'Mess Dress' or dinner jackets are a must!

Jane Terry

John Terry and Bill West

Larry Lugg with Claus and Michael Anderson

Mike Brown, Julia Holmes, Susie Fannon and Lizzie Lockhart

Andrew Holmes & Julian Beauchamp

Honest George

Jane Grace and Brian Knivett

Iain Percy and Sue Hardwick

Having fun... gambling... for fun...

Davinia Bulford-Coope and Alexandra Barbour

Sue Field and Ken Beken

Christian Février and Karren May

Photos©MCzA

74

John and Jane Terry

June Abbey

Firework Parties
at
John and Jane Terry's
beautiful harbour house

John and Jane with their sons, Nick and Simon,
David and Jenny Kelley, and Libby Milling.

Ken Newman

Belinda and Richard Phillips, David Sherriff and John

John with David Gower, Clare Sherriff, Dr. Elisabeth Dancey
and Gwynne Lawrence

Captain Henry Wrigley and his wife Sheila

Patrick Chisholm,
Lucy and John

Cowes Week always comes to an end with traditional spectacular fireworks. In 2000, to mark the occasion of the Queen Mother's 100th birthday the traditional firework figure of the Queen's head was replaced by a display dedicated to the Queen Mother. Thousands of people and a huge flotilla of boats watch the fireworks which each year cost the Isle of Wight Council over £30,000.

Pains Fireworks

The company who is responsible for the pyrotechnics, used to train Royal Marines in the use of fireworks so that they could provide a display each summer for the Queen Mother on the Royal Yacht Britannia.

Pains are the oldest and largest fireworks display company in the UK and have been putting on the prestigious Cowes Regatta fireworks show for almost 140 years. It is one of the top three annual fireworks shows in the country. They received great accolades for their part in the spectacular opening of the 267m high Al Faisaliah Tower in Saudi Arabia and the opening of the Burj Al Arab in Dubai, the tallest and the only seven star hotel in the world.

Tel 01794 884040
www.painsfireworks.co.uk

Photos©MCvA

Ellen MacArthur

When you have a dream...

After they have weathered the harsh elements of the Southern Ocean against fierce competition or competed neck and neck against fellow sailors in the Olympics when inches count, Cowes has made celebrity sailors so welcome that they have decided to make their homes there. Ellen MacArthur was recently made a Freeman of the Port of Cowes after her epic solo adventure around the world and Gold Medallist Shirley Robertson has fallen so in love with the place that she too has decided to settle in Cowes.

Round-the-world yachtswoman Ellen MacArthur (25) was made a Freeman of the Port of Cowes. as it was from here that her great adventure in the 'Vendèe Globe' single-handed non-stop circumnavigation was masterminded -

With Kos on Lady Christine

and it was to Cowes that Ellen returned for her first night back in Britain, after her triumphant sail back up the Solent in **Kingfisher**. At just 24, Ellen had become the fastest woman and youngest person ever to race around the world non-stop single-handed, beating the previous record by ten days and finishing a close second in the formidable race.

The previous year she had won the single-handed Trans-Atlantic race. But it was when she met up with Islander Mark Turner that her ambitions began to attract the heavyweight backing for a serious campaign. An experienced offshore sailor himself, Cowes-based Mark dedicated his efforts to helping Ellen secure £2 million sponsorship from retail giant Kingfisher plc, owners of B&Q and COMET in the UK. There were times of struggle when Ellen sent 2500 letters to find sponsorship and could hardly afford the stamps. A brilliant communications campaign run from Cowes by Ellen and Mark's Offshore Challenges Team, has enabled millions of people world-wide to follow Ellen's progress day-to-day on board **Kingfisher** - via the Internet - and she is now writing a book *Taking on the World* to be published in the Autumn.

Photo © Kos

Photo © Kos

Photo © Terry Martinez

Taking On the World

Ellen's love of sailing started when she was just eight years old. She loved it immediately and decided that dolls and dreams of becoming a ballerina were not for her, but a life on the ocean waves most definitely was. Later she saved all her dinner money in order to buy a small sailing dinghy, a measure of her determination that was to stand her in good stead in years to come. At age 18, she sailed single-handed round Britain and won the BT/JA Young Sailor of the Year award. Two years later in 1997, she bought a 21ft yacht named **Financial Dynamics** and sailed her across the Atlantic. Her achievements and determination have bought her world-wide fame and recently she was voted runner up in the BBC's Sports Personality of the Year award, only a whisker behind footballer David Beckham. At the end of 2001 she was awarded the MBE. Ellen endeared herself to the public by showing signs of frailty, and the determination to overcome them when the going got tough. But she would never give up. She says: "I simply wasn't going to give up. That's not what I do".

In November Ellen participated in the Transat Jacques Vabre on Alain Gautier's 60ft trimaran **Kingfisher-Foncia,** and the monohull **Kingfisher** was co-skippered by Mark Turner and Nick Moloney. After leading for much of the race, Ellen narrowly missed victory in the final hours due to gear failure but still recorded second, and the boys took a good third place in the 20 strong monohull fleet.

Photo © MCxA

At the 2002 London Boat Show Ellen MacArthur announced that she is to attempt the Southern Ocean non-stop round-the-world race for the Jules Verne Trophy. The current record stands at 71 days and 14 hours. Ellen's sponsors, the Kingfisher Retail Group (which also confirmed another five-year sponsorship programme), have chartered a giant 110ft catamaran for Ellen and her 12-strong crew to attempt the challenge in 2003.

Photo © Jacques Vapillon

You can follow Ellen MacArthur's projects at www.kingfisherchallenges.com www.ellenmacarthur.com

www.gbrchallenge.com

Photo Courtesy: GBR Challenge

PETER HARRISON
A big heart and a passion for sailing boats

Yachting enthusiast and Chairman of **GBR Challenge Company,** Peter Harrison has 'kick-started' Britain's entry into the 31st America's Cup, which he calls "The World Cup of Yachting" Britain's first America's Cup Challenge for 15 years, by putting £10.4 million in to get the company started. A lot of money but he says "It has been a dream and I had to try to win that famous 'Auld Mug' and bring it back to where it all started in 1851. I also hope to capture the hearts and minds of the British public and gain their support in our campaign."

Harrison, (64), has the business skills, creativity and finances, after realising £300 million from the sale of his company which he had built up over 24 years. In 1976 he bought Chernikeeff, which then specialized in marine speed and distance log systems for the Royal Navy, and some 23 other navies in the world and in 1978 he founded Chernikeeff Networks - a company that he developed to design, build and support computer inter-networking systems. In 1999 he sold 49.9% for £100 million, and the remaining 50.1% for £200 million in 2000, having bought Chernikeeff outright in 1979 for £133,000. In 1987, he won a £10 million contract from the Home Office to build the Emergency Communications Network (ECN) connecting all the fire, ambulance, police and civil defence emergency services throughout the UK. It gave him enough cash to negotiate an exclusive contract with *Cisco Systems* in San Francisco which was then a new 'start up' company with a total of twelve founders and employees, in October 1987. This was a brilliant move as it was then a quantum leap forward in computer inter-networking technology, which now drives approximately 80% of the UK Internet activity.

Born in Cheshire, Peter grew up in a wartime family. His father was in the army for six years, and like most families at that time there was never much spare money around. For his first work experience, in 1954, Peter was paid £1 a week as an articled clerk, five years later qualifying as a Chartered Accountant. He commenced his industrial career with Ford Motor Company in forward market forecasting and product planning in 1961 and eventually acquired Chernikeeff in 1976.

Peter Harrison Foundation

His philosophy is to "share my success with others" and to do this he has created the Peter Harrison Foundation, into which he has gifted £30 million to help build the skills, confidence and self-esteem of disabled and disadvantaged people through sport, education, research and special facilities for young people. He has also been very generous in sponsoring the British Admiral's Cup team in 1999, the Chernikeeff RYA National Match Racing series and the RYA Sailing Regatta and Olympic Trials in 2000.

The GBR Challenge for the 31st America's Cup

The first British Challenge since 1987 has been made possible by Peter Harrison who set up the GBR Challenge Company Ltd (GBR Challenge) in October 2000. The official British entry has been made through the Royal Ocean Racing Club (RORC) and the series will take place in Auckland, New Zealand from October 2002 to January 2003, with the winners of the Challenger Series being awarded the Louis Vuitton Cup and the right to take on the defenders, in February, 2003.

Strategy and Organisation

Knowing that the America's Cup Class design rules had totally changed in 1992 from the old 12-Metre rule and realizing that the British design and sailing team had a large technology and sailing experience gap to fill, the immediate problem was how to gain some 'catch up' experience. Harrison was aware in September 2000 that the former Nippon Challenge Syndicate was not going to be able to mount another challenge in the 2002 series and solved this problem by purchasing all their assets in December 2000. This move gave the GBR Challenge two 2000 generation plus one 1995 America's Cup Class (ACC) - yachts which competed in the last America's Cup challenge rounds in New Zealand in January 2000. Additionally, the assets included seven 40ft containers comprising the necessary support equipment, engineering work shops and gym equipment. Four masts and four RIB support boats - two 8m one 12m and one 14m - which were shipped from Japan to the GBR Cowes base in March 2001.

Photos © MGxA

Peter Harrison and his crew, winners of the Britannia Cup, Skandia Life Cowes Week August 2001

Peter Harrison and his wife Joy

Peter Harrison with Ian Walker

Peter Harrison with John Caulcutt and Bill West

Presenting the Skandia Life 2001 Young Skipper of the Week award with Olympic gold medallists Shirley Robertson and Iain Percy

These yachts have enabled the GBR Challenge sailing team to undertake a match racing and training programme in Solent waters throughout the summer months. In January 2001, Harrison also purchased the nine acre, former FBM Shipyard in Cowes, to house the design, administration, training base and building sheds which are being used for the construction of the new ACC yacht to be completed in April 2002. In addition, Harrison acquired the lease of the Base Eight compound in the Viaduct Basin at Auckland to serve as the GBR Challenge base in New Zealand, to which the two ACC 2000 generation yachts, **GBR 41** - shipped in July 2001 and **GBR 52**, together with the necessary support containers and RIBs, was shipped after competing in the America's Cup 150th Jubilee Regatta in Cowes. This enabled the GBR-Challenge Sailing Team to continue their two boat match racing training programme in the Haruki Gulf, gaining valuable experience and knowledge of the New Zealand waters and weather conditions prior to the arrival of the new GBR Challenge ACC 2002 yacht in early summer 2002.

Management and Team Organisation
On the management side, Harrison has appointed five times America's Cup expert, David Barnes, a New Zealander as General Manager and Ian Walker, the British Olympic double Silver Medallist at the 1996 Atlanta and Sydney 2000 games, as Sailing Team Manager. Legal and administration is headed by Julia Harrison-Lee, Peter's daughter, who is a solicitor. Julia has also been appointed to the Board of Directors of the Challenger of Record Management company - CORM - which was set up to organise the racing series, the racing rules and the TV and media rights, on behalf of all the challenging teams. Ian Walker was briefed to recruit the best of British sailors with the accent on youth to create a potentially strong team for future campaigns - or the defence? - in 2006. The management team also decided to recruit athletes from outside the sailing world and brought in two rowers: Greg Searle - Olympic Gold Medallist - and Ian Weighell, an Oxford Blue, as grinders. GBR Challenge has also signed up the two former Nippon senior design engineers, Taro Takahashi and Akihiro Kanai who, together with Jo Richards, the British Bronze Medallist in the 1984 Los Angeles Olympics, and Derek Clark, who was

involved in formulating the ACC rule in 1992, form the technical design group. The yacht design team includes the UK designers Stephen Jones, Simon Rogers, Hugh Welbourn and Rob Humphreys, co-designer of Ellen MacArthur's **Kingfisher**. Most importantly Harrison has organised a tank testing programme to be carried out by the Wolfson Marine Unit at the Qinetic (formerly DERA) facility in Gosport during which a series of four scale wood models of hull shapes and appendage designs provide performance data to help the technical and design group to determine the final yacht design. Harrison has also contracted the British Olympic team meteorologist Fiona Campbell to the campaign and signed an agreement with the Meteorological Service of New Zealand Ltd for detailed weather support data during the upcoming six month training programme in New Zealand and for the Challenger Series.

National Campaign and Sponsorship Opportunities
"I have set up a strong team and organisation which I am sure will enable the British Challenge to be on the start line for the Louis Vuitton Cup - the Challenger Series for the America's Cup in October 2002 - which I estimate will involve total campaign costs in the order of £20 million. I have run my own companies for 24 years and I know how to build teams and run businesses. I have been a sportsman all my life, playing rugby into my 50's, and I have always been a competitive person. I see this as the ultimate challenge, the World Cup of yachting. We have already achieved a major boost to our campaign, at the 150th America's Cup Jubilee at Cowes in 2001. When **GBR 52**, **Asura**, was first in the America's Cup Class repeat of the 1851 Round the Island Race, beating *Prada's* **Luna Rossa** and **Team New Zealand** into second and third places. I hope that the GBR Challenge will attract TV and media coverage, plus Government and national support from other UK companies wishing to benefit from this national team campaign. There is a wide range of promotion and sponsorship opportunities for companies wishing to project a global marketing image, in what will be a highly publicised and prestigious event. Sponsors already supporting the team include P&O NEDLloyd, who have shipped the yachts and equipment to New Zealand, Red Funnel, Peters & May, Musto and Dragon".

GBR Challenge Sponsorship & Partnership Opportunities
• *Make history with the GBR Challenge*
• *Build a global brand awareness campaign around this unique opportunity*
• *Heighten brand awareness in Great Britain and overseas*
• *Become a member of the GBR Challenge Business Club*
• *Purchase exclusive GBR Challenge merchandise via the website or from Musto Stockists*

The GBR Challenge Business Club
During the 2002 London Boat Show, Peter Harrison launched the official GBR Challenge Business Club at the Royal Ocean Racing Club. The Club gives companies who are not in a position to become sponsors an opportunity to support the GBR Challenge. In return for a donation of £25,000, Business Club members will benefit from a range of networking, hospitality and promotional activities for their business and brand.
Tel: 01983 531465
www.gbrchallenge.com
e-mail: info@gbrglobalchallenge.co.uk

Photo © Beken of Cowes

Chernikeeff

Sir Donald Gosling presenting a certificate of competence to Hugo Lidbetter with John Evans, Leander's Executive Officer

SIR DONALD GOSLING ON LEANDER

An habitué of Cowes Week, we met Sir Donald Gosling on his super yacht *Leander* which was moored off the Royal Yacht Squadron. The co-founder of National Car Parks, who is worth an estimated £450 million, was elected to the Squadron in 1999. With other members of the club, he helped the Jubilee Sailing Trust finance their new training ship *Tenacious*. Donald Gosling was knighted for his generous donations to various naval charities.

The *Leander*, which was named after a cruiser Sir Donald served on during his time in the Royal Navy, was bought for $47 million and is now worth $55 million after an extensive refit and major improvements at Devonport dockyard in 1998. For those who can afford her, she can seat 100 diners on the aft deck and has a crew of 24 to cosset up to 22 guests. Sir Donald charters the yacht for £280,000 a week, though he says he is very selective about to whom as it is like a home to him. Sir Donald and closest friend and business partner for over 50 years Ronald Hobson, have been involved in a variety of projects over the years but they are better known for their development of National Car Parks, which they sold three years ago. "We are still very much business partners," says Sir Donald, "and we are currently involved in a variety of property through our company *Consolidated Property Investments*. As he says: "We are investors and not speculators. That is what happens when you get older, you also get wiser."

Thanks to modern communications systems, Sir Donald can travel, especially on his yacht, and be in touch with his office at the same time. He likes to spend his summers in the Mediterranean, the French Riviera and Turkey. When on the Riviera he says: "I love *Tetou* in Golfe Juan (there is nothing like it in the world), *Le Ruban Bleu* in Juan Les Pins (very simple but they always know where to find me!) and *Rampoldi* in Monaco, where I have a home in Rocabella. I prefer to go there out of season when it is less crowded, in the autumn and at Christmas. In Cannes I like *La Chunga* because of its atmosphere and the dancing, although I'm not very good at dancing!" Sir Donald also enjoys the open air, shooting and sailing (especially with his son Adam) and swimming, something he does every day. He has three sons: Mark (42), who is in property and has two sons himself with his wife, Donna; Adam (39), who is a very good sailor and has won several championships including Antigua and La Nioulargue in St. Tropez (now Les Voiles de St.Tropez); and David (38), who runs *Countrywide Events* and is married to Lois. Sir Donald finished the interview by saying: "I'm not at all sophisticated and I like to tease people. I enjoy Cowes because it has certain standards and people come properly dressed." During Cowes Week he normally hosts private receptions for Royal Yacht Squadron members, for private guests and for Adam's birthday on 4th August.

©MGvA

LEANDER
AN OUTSTANDING LUXURY YACHT

The 75 metre (245ft) Leander was built in 1993 by West German yachtmaker, Claus Kutsch, in the former East Germany, at the Peene shipyard by the Polish border. It was the first craft ever to emerge from the yard with a mission of peace. The yard was the wartime home of Hitler's guided missile programme and was renowned for building sophisticated Soviet and East German warships and missile boats during the cold war. The yacht's reputation has been enhanced by Sir Donald's demands that the ship be manned by a professional, highly trained, experienced and disciplined crew, and under Captain Giles Cope this is always in evidence, particularly when the ship enters and leaves harbour. A nucleus of the senior crew has been with Leander since she was built. Leander is a showcase of modern engineering technology. It boasts an 18 knot cruising speed with no vibration and a noise suppression engine with an exhaust silencer. The steel hull and aluminium superstructure conceal 5 decks and hide an interior that is as spacious as it is sumptuous. There are three distinct living areas which allow the different groups to be unaware of each other, a complete environment reserved for the owner, a second for his guests, and one containing the technical areas and crew accommodation. The guest quarters are designed in the style of a relaxed, informal world of an English country house and contain a fine collection of nautical art and artefacts. The owner's section covers the main and boat decks and contains the master suite, two further state rooms, and an observation saloon which has a view of a full 270 degrees through its tall windows and opens directly onto a private deck. The owners suite starts with the study which leads into the master stateroom and from there into a dressing room with massage bench and a luxurious bathroom. Backing onto the master stateroom joined by an interconnecting door is the principal guest stateroom. The third stateroom is a smaller, twin bedded room with ensuite bathroom that is well suited to children as there is an adjoining 'nanny's' cabin. This cabin has also been known to be used for servants and bodyguards. The vast size of the owner's quarters does not detract from the scope of the guest quarters which contain a further seven staterooms, four twins and three doubles, all with ensuite. Four of these cabins can be interconnected in various ways to meet the personal needs of the guests, and two of the larger double state rooms can be joined to form a suite by opening a sliding wall between them. This area also contains a dive centre with changing rooms, store rooms and a decompression chamber that a doctor can enter to treat a casualty as well as a vast hull port that forms a diving platform or dock. The yacht's public areas consist of the main saloon, dining saloon and boat deck saloon. Designed to be used for both formal and informal occasions the decor is such that they are not overbearing, although consisting of some very fine art work. The aft boat deck has an informal dining and sunbathing area around the large, raised spa pool and the forward part of the deck has a gymnasium. This area also houses self contained accommodation for the Captain and First Officer, and the radio room and bridge. The radio room is the most impressive technical area within the boat and contains three satcoms, computers running PC Weatherfax, Morse decoding and Wayplanner software, SSB and VHF radios, security monitors fed by low light TV cameras, the ships computer system that can direct information screens to TV's in guest areas and an impressive bank of TV and radio tuners that feed the ship's piped audio and video system. To keep an eye on all this there is an electronics engineer in addition to the radio officer. And, as all decent yachts should, it has a helicopter deck to accompany the 9-metre, 600 horse powered custom tenders, three inflatables and water sports equipment including four wet bikes and a hobie cat.

***If you can afford to charter her, for more information,
e-mail: myleander@compuserve.com***

*The engine room, which the Chief Engineer loves to show off, is regarded as the finest and
best kept engine room in the yachting world.*

82
Absolutely!

©MCvA

©MCvA

One of the private parties given by Adam Gosling for his **Yes** team in his house overlooking the harbour

1. *Adam and Donald Gosling, Michael Parker, George Brown, Stig Granger, Dale Naylor and Boris Marlow.*
2. *Denis Boyd and Boris Marlow, in the back, Daniela Di Nora, Anna Raggioli and Donald Gosling*
3. *Boris Marlow's birthday - Happy Birthday!*
4. *Adam Gosling and Susie Lister*
5. *Marie-Claire Baroness von Alvensleben 'Star of the Day' chosen by Simon Dudley and Steve O'Farrell*

Photos © MCvA

Adam Gosling

Sir Donald's sailing son Adam, a former Etchells 30 foot world champion, has a house in the former High Street Post Office at Cowes. During Cowes Week 2000, he sailed a rented Farr 40 yacht, renamed **Yes!** *like all his boats, and chartered his own Sydney 60 craft, which was also called* **Yes!**, *to United Airlines, sponsor of several Olympic sailors. His own reason for not considering the next Olympics was simply a lack of time, insisting that he was too busy to put the full time training in over a three-year period.*

During Cowes Week 2001, he sailed **Yes! T&G** *and during the America's Cup Jubilee Regatta, he was part of the crew on the 23-metre* **Cambria**.

Adam has won several championships including the 1996 Etchells World Championship and the Round the Island Race.

The Rolex Fastnet Race

As Skandia Life Cowes Week came to an end, another spectacular and famous race, the Rolex Fastnet Race, set off from Cowes in August 2001 for a 608-mile epic offshore haul. The race took more than 200 yachts along the south coast of England out into the Atlantic to the southern tip of Ireland and back again, to finish at Plymouth.

Held in alternate years, as the major offshore event of the RORC, the Rolex Fastnet Race is one of the best known races in the world. Taking part were several Volvo 60s getting ready for the Volvo Ocean Race, many world-famous America's Cup sailors, Olympic gold medallists, billionaires who had brought their superyachts to Cowes ready for the America's Cup Jubilee and thousands of keen sailors who just wanted a chance to be a part of possibly the finest fleet ever gathered together for one race.

Since its beginnings in 1925, the Fastnet has been an icon in the world of yachting – it has been described as the most difficult ocean race to win, the sailors' Everest, and offers a great challenge to those racing small boats or large across some of the most treacherous waters in the world. Some people say you are not really an experienced sailor until you have 'done' the Fastnet.

The 2001 Rolex Fastnet was the first big offshore race for Olympic sailing gold medallist Shirley Robertson, who lives at Cowes and who won her medal at Sydney sailing a single-hander Europe dinghy. Shirley was guest helm aboard Ludde Ingvall's maxi yacht **Nicorette**, which won the Fastnet Challenge Cup in 1995. The race set off from the Royal Yacht Squadron start line at Cowes on a breezy Sunday afternoon, with waves whipped into spray by the wind and yachts. First to go were the brightly coloured Volvo 60s, newly arrived in Britain for the start in September 2001 of round-the-world Volvo Ocean Race. They were closely followed by the Maxis including Hasso Plattner's 80ft Reichel-Pugh design **Morning Glory**, with members of the defending New Zealand America's Cup squad aboard, Italian Gianni Agnelli's all-black 92-ft carbon yacht **Stealth**, Mike Slade's 92ft beauty **Skandia Leopard** and **Nicorette**. But as these fabulous monohulls raced down the Solent they were overtaken by the 60ft trimaran **Eure et Loir**, sailed by French ocean racer Francis Joyon and British Olympic medallist Rodney Pattisson, which loomed up behind them out of the spray and whizzed past into the distance - the last time they would see the tri until the race had finished. **Eure et Loir** was first boat back to Plymouth, on Tuesday morning, in just 1 day 18hrs 19mins, failing to beat Loick Peyron's 1999 multihull record by two hours after light airs at Bishop Rock slowed the boat. Line honours for first multihull to finish went to Gianni Agnelli's **Stealth**, which had overtaken the Volvo 60s and beat them back by two hours. Onboard was skipper Paul Standbridge, a Whitbread veteran and now a member of the GBR Challenge America's Cup squad, along with American Kenny Read. **Stealth's** time was 2 days 10 hrs 58 mins, five hours outside the record. She was followed in by **Morning Glory** and **Nicorette**. But while the focus is always on the big boats racing to be first home, the top prize is awarded to the yacht recording the best time after handicap adjustments have been made. The Fastnet Challenge Cup went to Dutch skipper Piet Vroon, sailing his 20th Fastnet Race, on the blue-hulled Lutra 52 **Tonnerre de Breskens**. Not exactly the tortoise and the hare, but Piet's comment: "We didn't break anything, we had an exceptionally good crew and the boat revels in tough upwind offshore conditions" showed the truth of the old adage that the boat that doesn't make any mistakes or break gear will win - even in a race as tough as the Rolex Fastnet.

Information: www.rolex.com

The Rolex Commodores' Cup is one of the biggest international team racing events in Europe for pro/am crews and is sailed in even years, at Cowes. The next event is due to take place in August 2002. Organised by the Royal Ocean Racing Club, the Rolex Commodores' Cup is a three-boat team competition that acts as a focus for some of the keenest sailors in Britain, Europe and further afield. Over its 10 year history, teams from Argentina, Australia, Belgium, England, France, Germany, Hong Kong, Republic of Ireland, Netherlands, Scotland, Scandinavia, Spain, the USA and Wales have competed. Some crews even build new boats and plan their summer sailing schedule so as to raise a Rolex Commodores' Cup team and qualify for the event, which gives amateur sailors a chance to compete on the grand prix stage alongside top professionals. The Rolex Commodores' Cup in its present form has been going since 1992 and was conceived as a major team regatta for the years when there was no Admiral's Cup. But the trophy for which the teams race, the impressive and elegant Commodores' Cup, has an older history than the current event.

The Rolex Commodores' Cup

The cup was bought by a fleet of Island Sailing Club commodores in 1978 - the then current commodore, John Wroath, who still lives in Cowes, plus four former commodores; Derek Boyer, Sir Owen Aisher, Bobby Lowein and Mike Henderson - as the trophy for an event run by the Island Sailing Club.

That was also an international team event, raced for the first and last time at Cowes in 1978. It was won by an Irish team skippered by Harold Cudmore, then a young rising star of international sailing.

But because of poor interest in the 1978 event - it was contested only by Britain and Ireland - it was not raced again and the grand trophy sat in the Island Sailing Club's vaults.

When RORC developed afresh a new international team event, the name Commodores' Cup seemed appropriate for the trophy and so it has been ever since. In previous Rolex Commodores' Cups the three boats making up each team have been divided into size bands, so that each team fielded a small boat (around 30-36ft, possibly a Mumm 30 or Mumm 36), a medium-size boat (typically a Farr 40 or Sydney 40) and a big boat (40-50ft).

The Rolex Commodores' Cup trophy was won in 2000 by a team from the Channel Islands. The three victorious boats were Tony Buckingham's *A Bit of a Coup* (Farr 40), Rennie Miller's *Dignity* (Farr 40) and Tony Buckingham's *Easy Oars* (Mumm 30). Teams taking part in that event included two representing England and one each for the Commonwealth, France, Scotland and Europe, with 21 boats and seven teams competing. The 2000 event was the first major regatta to be raced under the new IR2000 IRM measurement rule, a system of yacht handicapping developed to encourage designers to build fast yachts purely for racing, rather than cruiser/racers.

The Rolex Commodores' Cup incorporates a strong pro/am element, with a rule which requires a minimum of 50% amateur sailors in the crew of each boat. An amateur is required to helm the boat throughout inshore races and at the start of offshore races. The intention is to encourage crews to come together earlier in the season to train together and to help amateur sailors improve their skills by working closely with professionals. The format for the August 2002 Rolex Commodores' Cup will be much the same as last time, with three-boat pro/am crews making up each team, but the IRM handicapping rule has been replaced by IRC to encourage more foreign teams to compete. The banding of boats into size categories has also been abandoned, allowing more flexibility in choice of yacht design and, RORC hopes, making it easier for semi-professional teams to be put together. The RORC and Rolex are keen to maintain wide interest by meeting trends in sailing dynamically. The changes made for 2002 address this need and, perhaps, will even set some trends for the future.

Information: www.rolex.com

The Rolex Farr World Championships

Cowes was the venue for the Rolex Farr 40 World Championships in September, 2001. Competition was top rate, with many of the world's leading sailors still in Cowes after the excitement of the America's Cup Jubilee a few weeks before and the Etchell's World Championships raced in the Solent the previous week. The Farr 40 is very popular in the USA and fast-growing in Europe and elsewhere. It is a one-design class, which means that all the boats are of identical design and specification, so it is the skill and teamwork of the skipper and crews which wins or loses the race. And the owner/driver rule means that it is the boat owner who steers the boat for most of the time, so it is not just a matter of who can afford the best professional crew.

It was this element which gave the greatest satisfaction to eventual Rolex Farr 40 Worlds winner Ernesto Bertarelli, head of the Swiss Alinghi America's Cup Challenge. He had won the Prada 12-Metre World Championship during the America's Cup Jubilee, with his crack team headed by two-times America's Cup winner Russell Coutts, on *South Australia*. But for the Rolex Farr 40 World Championships Mr Bertarelli himself was at the helm, much to his delight. With a smile a yard wide he compared his Rolex Farr 40 victory with the 12-Metre win. "The 40s win is better than the 12s," he declared, "because I was helming." He beat the defending Australian world champion, John Calvert-Jones on *Southern Star*, by 15 points. Third place went to American Jim Richardson, with *Barking Mad*. It was only the second regatta for Ernesto Bertarelli and the Alinghi crew and in their first outing, the European Championships, also in the Solent, earlier in the year, the team had managed only tenth place. This time, one observer commented, it was as though they were able to change gear, accelerate and pick their way through to the front of the race. Mr Bertarelli admitted that he had found the Farr 40 tricky at first, but had now mastered the technique of helming. I just put the bow straight and Simon Daubney and Warwick Fleur steer the boat for me with their trimming," he said. Tactician on board was Russell Coutts with Whitbread veteran Curtis Blewett on the bow.

Information: www.rolex.com

Photos Courtesy Rolex Watches

The Rolex Transatlantic Challenge
The Round the Island Race

A race across the Atlantic has always been one of the most exciting and enticing challenges facing serious sailors and the NYYC/ Rolex Transatlantic Challenge is probably the most spectacular of the lot, with fabulous ocean-going superyachts crewed by the cream of the yachting establishment. The event challenges yachts of 85 feet or more in length to break the 1905 west-east monohull racing record, set by the 185-ft yacht *Atlantic*, for a crossing of 12 days 4 hours 1 minute and 19 seconds, raced from New York to The Lizard, on the south-western tip of England.

Cowes was the final destination for the 1997 Transatlantic Challenge presented by Rolex. After the ocean race, which finished off The Lizard, the fleet sailed on up the Channel and anchored off The Parade at Cowes, giving a fabulous foretaste of the America's Cup Jubilee which was to follow four years later. The final highlight of the 1997 event was a race eastabouts around the Isle of Wight in a re-enactment of the 1851 race, won by the yacht *America*, which gave birth to the America's Cup.

Transatlantic line honours in 1997 went to the 165ft schooner *Adela*, which beat the early favourite, the 183ft three-masted *Adix*, built with Atlantic's record in mind. But neither boat managed to beat that 1905 time, *Adela* taking 14 days 15 hours 57 minutes and 25 seconds to reach The Lizard. The Royal Yacht Squadron's entry, the 86ft ketch *Sapphire* skippered by round-the-world hero Sir Robin Knox-Johnston, retired with damage as did *Globana* and *Never Say Never*. Winner on corrected time was *Sorcerer*.

A Classic Yacht Race to break the record time of 12 Days 4 Hours 1 Minute 19 seconds, set by the yacht 'Atlantic' in 1905, sailing from New York to the Lizard, England.

Absolutely!

Photos Courtesy Rolex Watches

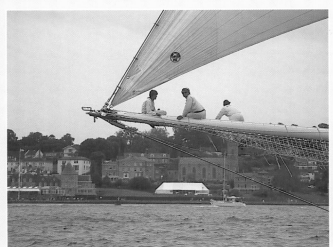

In the classic division, the replica of the original 1851 yacht America and Tom Perkins's beautiful 1915 Herreshoff-design *Mariette* were among several yachts which were forced to retire. Winner was Robert Towbin's *Sumurun*, second *Thendara* and *Belle Aventure* third.

The next NYYC/Rolex Transatlantic Challenge will take place in May 2005. The Transatlantic race will be preceded by festivities in Newport, Rhode Island. The competing yachts will then rendezvous off Sandy Hook, New York before racing across the Atlantic to a timing point at The Lizard and continuing on to the finish at The Needles, off the Isle of Wight. A further period of celebration will take place culminating once again in a race around the Island.

Information: www.rolex.com

Photo © Polly Durrant, Courtesy Heatline

Photos © MGvA

Alex Norford, Kevin Phipson, Erol Usten,
Bulent Yazici, and Ibrahim Yazici on 'Heatline'

Nick Colwyn-Foulkes, Chairman LBCC 2001
and Peter Thompson, Chairman in 2002

The Little Britain Challenge Cup (LBCC) Regatta is open to crews whose businesses are directly involved in the construction industry. In the spirit of the event, the number of professional sailors/charterers is limited to one per boat for yachts under 40 feet and two per boat for those above that length. The professionals are not permitted to helm. The Cowes-based event is organised around the successful formula of a three-race series in the Central Solent area. The Royal Yacht Squadron sets the courses and is in charge of race organisation, which has the added excitement of 'Squadron line' starts. The event was started in 1988 by Peter Thompson, Steve Green and Phil Davis, consultants for the Little Britain Office Development in London. The original wager for the single race was the price of a dinner! Today, the LBCC Regatta is the biggest in England after Cowes Week and easily the largest European industry yachting event. It still, however, meets its founders' objectives and remains a 'fun event' where it is the taking part, rather than the winning, that counts the most. It is the volunteer committee's task to maintain these standards and ensure the LBCC remains a premier event in both the yachting and construction industry calendars. While having their fun, participants are also raising substantial sums of money for the event's chosen sailing charities.

In 2001, the event saw 60 new teams and more than 220 yachts taking part, raising a massive £125,000 for the Jubilee Sailing Trust and Cirdan-Faramir Sailing Trusts. Two local organisations, the Island Youth Water Activities Centre and the Sea Cadets, also benefited by £2,000 apiece. The committee had the support of major sponsors from the construction industry and related business interests (Tarkett Sommer Ltd., Finnforest, Building Design, Plus Wall Ltd., S. J. Berwin & Co, Colwyn Foulkes and Alexander Forbes)

A wide range of social activities (including a Champagne Mumm reception at the Royal Yacht Squadron) took place over the regatta weekend in a marquee around 25% bigger than anything ever before erected in Cowes! There were more than 1,500 guests on the Thursday and Friday nights, while the attendance for the Saturday gala dinner was in excess of 1,800. A charity auction, live music and dancing were all laid on, and 3,000 bottles of wine consumed. Yet, the attendance was even higher for the Sunday trophy presentation!

Over the years the LBCC has generated more than £300,000 towards the building of the Jubilee Sailing Trust's Tenacious. The Trust's *Lord Nelson* put in an appearance during LBCC 2001, as did the Cirdan Sailing Trust's *Queen Galadriel*.

The Little Britain Challenge Cup

Paul Perkins,
Press Attaché

Mary Scott-Jackson and her PR team

Martin Kemp, Nick Colwyn Foulkes and guests

*Party on
Colwyn Foulkes'
yacht*

Bill Edgeley, Nigel Morley and John Durden

Martyn Cox, Bruce Sweeney, Alan Harding (Jayhard) & Kevin Phipson

*Roger Whitney,
Ibrahim Yazici
(CEO of Beko UK),
and Mustafa Findik
(GM of Heatline)
Heatline is the
heating division of
Beko UK Ltd, a
Turkish company
which is part of the
Koç Group.*

Erol Usten (MD Beko UK) and Alex Norford

*The WS Atkins Team – Above: David Thomas, Michael Jeffries (Chairman), Chris Dacey,
Andrew Albutt, Martin Jochmann
Below: Wayne Adams, Nick Seaton, Peter Thorn*

*In 2001, Stuart Quarrie
and Cowes Combined
Clubs were appointed to
act as Race Director for
the event, ensuring liaison
with the Royal Yacht
Squadron and input into
the racing format and on
courses set in the Central
Solent Area from the
Squadron start line.*

*Keith Webster and Richard Hayden
of Asprey Estates*

Honda Cowes Classic Powerboat Race

The Cowes Classic, inarguably the world's most prestigious offshore powerboat racing festival, celebrated several key milestones over the August Bank Holiday weekend in 2001 - powering into the future by retreating into the past! A highlight on the Cowes maritime calendar for the last four decades, this international spectacle took the sport back to its roots with a reversion to the Cowes-Torquay-Cowes and Round-the-Island race format originally devised by the late Sir Max Aitken. Equally significant was the handing over of race organisation to the newly-formed British Powerboat Racing Club, which has Lady Aitken as its first President. Happily, Tim Powell, retiring as event organiser after 22 challenging years at the helm, remains 'in touch' in the role of Club Vice-president. To quote the Earl of Normanton, who chairs the Club, the Powell legacy is one of "innovation and excellence," not the least part of which was his success in attracting Honda (UK) to become title sponsors for a three-year period. How fitting, then, that the reinstated Cowes-Torquay-Cowes race in 2001 should be won by none other than Tim Powell himself - a long-cherished ambition realised for the 63-year-old former race director. Invited to drive the 55-foot RIB of Italian designer and powerboat legend, Fabio Buzzi (who navigated), Powell survived a late scare during a splendid return to the Solent - when the boat's failed satellite navigation system required hasty repair work on Buzzi's part - to finish first at the Royal Yacht Squadron in 2 hours 52 minutes 54 seconds and lift the coveted Beaverbrook Trophy. Powell regularly raced in the 1960's and 1970's, and was a winner of many events, but success in the Cowes-Torquay-Cowes had eluded him until its reinstatement after a ten-year gap in 2001. The event most closely associated with offshore powerboating was first won in 1961 by Tommy Sopwith, who finished ahead of the 26 other craft which had lined up for the start off the Squadron. Back then - not altogether surprisingly, given the Aitken/Beaverbrook connection - the race was sponsored by the Daily Express. Sopwith added to his initial success with two subsequent wins. The boats in which he and the other early pioneers of powerboating competed bear little resemblance to their modern equivalents and the race itself has undergone several changes. When Tommy Sopwith won it, the event was contested over a one-way course from Cowes to Torquay, becoming a two-way marathon in 1968 and later developing into a packed programme of international and national races, though minus the Cowes-Torquay-Cowes element itself until its recent revival. In 2000, the original concept was re-enacted by a fleet of Ribsters, which competed over the full course to Torquay and back. A unique atmosphere prevailed and, with the subsequent formation of the BPRC, the decision was taken to reinstate the 'there and back' marathon in 2001 as the key element of the Cowes Classic festival, when the UIM International Marathon Endurance fleet (contesting their World and European championships) were joined in Cowes by a big entry of RIBs and other fast production monohulls for the 1 September spectacular. While the main event, attracting large crowds of spectators, took place, RYA British National Championship classes, including the Honda Formula 4-Stroke boats, competed within the waters of Wight for their own trophies.

The 2000 **Cowes Classic**, celebrated its 40th anniversary in August. Damon Hill, the British Formula 1 Champion flew in to race with World Champion Steve Curtis in the celebrity Honda Formula 4 Stoke class race. V-24 driver, Steve Cunningham, who used the occasion to highlight his future attempt at the World Blind Water Speed Record: his eyes for the event were Mike Mantle. Winners from the past 40 years came for a celebration dinner at the Royal Yacht Squadron. Famous faces included international rally driver Paddy Hopkirk, World Air Speed record holder Peter Twiss, Vittorio Missoni of the Italian clothing dynasty Missoni, Don Shead, Tommy Sopwith, Bill Shand-Kydd and 4 time race winner Renato Della Valle. On the Sunday, a flotilla of military World War II powerboats paraded off the Royal Yacht Squadron line with Eve Branson (Richard's mother) joined by her husband Ted. As a young Signal Wren stationed on the Island during World War II, in 1944, Eve operated from the last signal station at Yarmouth Pier on the Isle of Wight as the D-Day invasion fleet left for France. The Solent was crammed with the ships of the Allies' Invasion Force and Eve signalled the fleet using semaphore flags, a light flasher and an Aldis lamp.

Among the previous Cowes Classic Powerboat Race winners were Tommy Sopwith, who won the race 3 times, in 1961,1968 and 1970. Stopping Sopwith from taking 3 consecutive wins was American Don Aronow in his boat, Cigarette in 1969. In 1976 Charles Gill won before it was dominated between 1982 and 1985 by Italian, Renato Della Valle. Frenchman Jean Pierre Fruitier won the race in 1987 and Stefano Casiraghi won it two years later for Monaco. In the 1990s David Allenby and Charles Burnett III were both double winners for Great Britain. Allenby in 1993 and 1999 and Burnett in 1995 and 1996.

The Honda Cowes Classic will take place between 22nd and 26th August 2002. www.cowesclassic.com

The 2000 Offshore Festival of Speed

Eve Branson

Damon Hill and Steve Curtis

Anthea Powell

Lunch at The Prospect hosted by Ray Mac Enhill

Lady Aitken

Ted Davidson, Andrew Hedges, the Earl of Normanton, Alex Foster and John Henry Falk.

Marie-Claude Parnaud (ex PR Harry Winston)

A bunch of party goers...

...at Rawlings

Ros Nott, Charles Burnett III (the "King" as he is called), Shannon Tobin, Charles Gill, Marie-Claire von Alvensleben and Michael Mantle

Ray Mac Enhill Tim and Anthea Powell

Dinner at the Royal Yacht Squadron

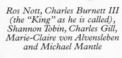

1. *Ted Davidson & Graham Peck*
2. *Andrew Hedges & Mike Mantle*
3. *Tony Miller, Tim Powell & Ray Mac Enhill*
4. *Sue Field & Ken Beken*
5. *Miriam Burnett Jnr, Charles Burnett III & Shannon Tobin*
6. *Robin Culpan, Alex Foster & Lady Aitken*
7. *John Irving*
8. *Lord John Smither (Lanson)*
9. *Eric Hall & Alan Stileman*
10. *Graeme Dillon & John Caulcutt*
11. *The Hon. Laura Levi and Martyn Levi*
12. *Steve Curtis & his parents*

Laura Aitken

Photos© MCvA

Watercolour by W. L. Leitch showing Osborne in 1850

Sir Max Aitken Museum
The Prospect

The Museum houses a collection of fine marine paintings, nautical instruments and yachting memorabilia gathered by Sir Max Aitken. Pieces in the museum include The King's chair, designed by Edward VII to fit on the top step of *Britannia's* main companion way and used by the Czar, and Kings of Spain, Norway, Denmark, Greece and Germany.

The property containing the museum was bought by Sir Max Aitken in 1947. It used to be the premises of Ratsey & Lapthorn. The subsequent restoration is part of the Conservation area of the Cowes river frontage that is admired by thousands each year. The museum is also part of a trust, a registered charity, that is managed by *Laura Aitken*, Sir Max's daughter. Other exhibits include a long table, in the main area of the museum, placed where the sails were made in the past, and above the table *Britannia's* gaff. Throughout there are numerous half models and full models, including many of Sir Max's own yachts. A gimbled cradle made for the infant King of Rome, son of Napoleon Bonaparte and Marie-Louise of Austria is also on show as is the cradle, designed by Uffa Fox for Laura, Sir Max's daughter. Many items in the museum are from Nelson's day, including a letter written by him on April 26th 1804, and a copper bolt from the timbers of *HMS Victory*. There is a figurehead, Belle, of the Island of Guernsey, wrecked in 1787, numerous paintings and even Queen Victoria's croquet set from Osborne House. Intriguingly there is also the tiller of *Meteor*, owned by the Kaiser, who entered the yacht for races to be held from August 4th to 7th 1914 when ironically the date of the outbreak of the Great War was August 4th.

The museum runs guided tours from May to September and visits by parties of up to 12 can be arranged between October and April.
Sir Max Aitken Museum
The Prospect
83 High Street Cowes
Tel: 01983 295144
Fax: 01983 200253

Osborne House
Queen Victoria's favourite home

Osborne House was built in 1845 as a seaside home for Victoria and Prince Albert, who both adored the place. Queen Victoria, great-great grandmother of the present Queen, died at Osborne House on 22 January 1901 and the Centenary of her death was commemorated in 2001. Part of the celebration project included the restoration and conservation of her family holiday home, bequeathed to the nation by her son Edward VII and now, managed by English Heritage. Already re-opened to the public in June 2000 was the "Table Deckers Room" beneath the Dining Room which offers the opportunity to take a peek at life below stairs in the servants quarters at Osborne. The Victorian walled garden, restored by English Heritage, was opened allowing visitors the chance to walk in the fruit and flower garden which has been replanted with plants of the period. It also contains glass houses installed by Albert, a great moderniser, who helped make their home up-to-date. The Prince Consort seems to have been a pioneer in many things, such as built-in wardrobes, with sliding doors. The 'Durbar Room', with its stunning Anglo-Indian interior, contains some of the gifts given to Queen Victoria by Maharajas when she became Empress of India in 1876 (she was given the Koh-I-Noor diamond by Maharaja Duleep Singh). She never went to India but surrounded herself with Indian servants and cooks and, with her Indian secretary Abdul Karim, even learnt Hindi. The lack of daylight lends an evening atmosphere to the house and the exterior was repainted its original colour, resembling warm bath stone. Other highlights include the Queen's dressing room with her Minton porcelain dressing table set, and the looking glass that Albert gave her for Christmas in 1853. The 'Drawing Room contained a piano and it is claimed that Prince Albert would sometimes slip into the seat, whilst the Queen pulled out some music books, and they would sing and play German or Scottish music until Queen Victoria was tired and moved to the round table. At around 11 o'clock the Queen retired and the ladies were then free to go to bed. The bedroom in which the Queen died has also been recreated as it was just after her death: for the first time, presentation models of the heads of Victoria and Albert, and her silver and crystal communion set are on display. The bed was decorated with palms and flowers until the end of 2001.

Much of the house, with the exception of the restoration, has been untouched since Victoria's death and so offers a unique insight into the organization of the Royal Household.

For further information:
Osborne House,
East Cowes
Isle of Wight
PO32 6JY
Tel: 01983 200022
Fax: 01983 281381
www.english-heritage.org.uk

Cowes Maritime Museum

Cowes Maritime Museum is situated in Cowes Library. It houses collections of regional significance which trace the town's maritime history from its early days as a customs port through to its heyday as an important shipbuilding centre, to its rôle today as a yachting Mecca.

Much of the museum's collection consists of the J. Samuel White's archives. White's shipyard was a major employer for two centuries, producing modern, medium-sized ships such as Naval destroyers, freight carriers and ferries. The yard closed in 1982 and a large selection of plans, drawings, photographs and models has been rescued by the museum.

Cowes's yachting heritage is also explored in the museum. Cowes was home to the yacht designer and *bon vivant* Uffa Fox. Three Uffa-designed dinghies, *Cub*, *Avenger* and Prince Philip's flying-fifteen *Coweslip* are on display.

The museum is home to a large photographic collection of William Kirk, a photographer who worked from the town in the early twentieth century. His work rivals that of the renowned Beken of Cowes and a selection of his photographs of the J-Class yachts from the 1930s are on display.

Cowes Maritime Museum
Beckford Road, Cowes, Isle of Wight, PO31 7SG.
Tel: 01983 293394.

Collection Enquiries:
Tony Butler, Curator of Human History
The Guildhall, High Street, Newport, Isle of Wight PO30 1TY
Tel: 01983 823433. Fax: 01983 823841

The Classic Boat Museum

The Classic Boat Museum, which houses a unique collection of historic small craft and marine memorabilia, is nationally-registered as a Charitable Trust, with the aim of providing an Island centre for the restoration and exhibition of all types of unique and historic craft, many with an Isle of Wight link. Inevitably, a number of these will have been designed or built at the Uffa Fox yard and so, early examples of an *International 14*, *National 12*, a *Firefly*, an *Albacore*, a *Jollyboat* and even Uffa's own personal dinghy are on display. Many of the original cotton sails shown were made by Ratsey and Lapthorn of Cowes. The 1935 tender to *Bloodhound* is exhibited and the Museum has on view the restoration of an early Airborne Lifeboat which was also designed and built in East Cowes in 1940, and which was dropped by parachute to rescue aircrews who had 'ditched' in the sea.

The power section of the museum exhibits a classic *Riva* and Lady Docker's Chris Craft, *Silver Arrow*. The museum archives hold early photographs of engines built at J. Samuel White's and numerous small artefacts relating to the boat design and boat building activities on the Island.

There is a restoration shed where visitors can see work in progress on the old lifeboats, while videos show the boats sailing in regattas. You can become a 'Friend of the Museum' and help the restoration work.

The Classic Boat Museum
Newport Harbour, PO30 2EF.
Tel: 01983 533493. Fax: 01983 533505.
E-mail: cbmiow@hotmail.com.

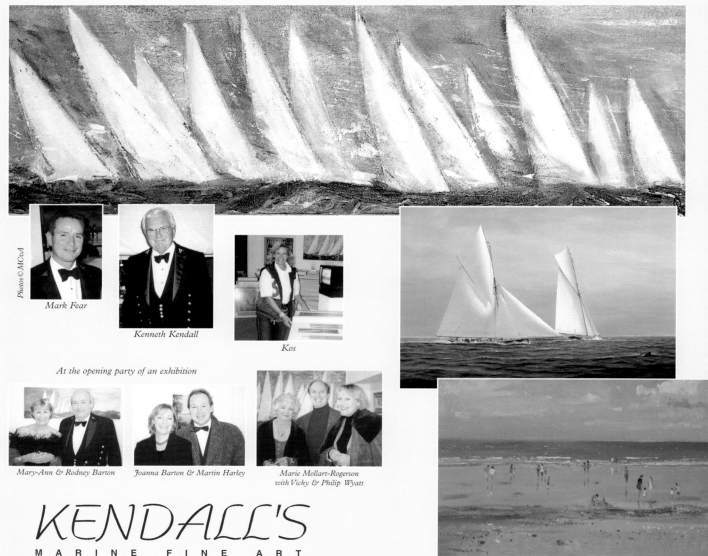

Photos © MCvA

Mark Fear

Kenneth Kendall

Kos

At the opening party of an exhibition

Mary-Ann & Rodney Barton

Joanna Barton & Martin Harley

Marie Mollart-Rogerson
with Vicky & Philip Wyatt

KENDALL'S
MARINE FINE ART

Contemporary marine art dealers Kenneth Kendall and Mark Fear, who opened the gallery at Bath Road, Cowes, six years ago, specialise in contemporary marine art and present over 80 artists with paintings ranging from £200 to £200,000. Many of the artists are members of the "Royal Society of Marine Artists", of which Kenneth Kendall and Mark Fear are lay members. Their "Internet Gallery" is also updated every month. In their second gallery just opposite, they often show paintings of one single artist. In August last year, renowned marine artist Tim Thompson was the one-man show.

Most of the artists the gallery represents also work to commission and paintings are regularly shipped to the USA. During the spring and autumn the gallery holds shows in Central London and exhibits at various art fairs throughout the year. In September 2001, they held their second show at Barney's Gallery in Greenwich, Connecticut.

Their next exhibition will take place in London in the autumn. Mark used to have a modern painting gallery in London and Kenneth, who is originally from Cornwall (but was born in India), was a BBC newscaster. They both enjoy living on the island, "Britain's best kept secret" as they say, where they meet people who come to sail but also to shoot and to hunt.

During the Jubilee Regatta, they featured the book **'20 x 20'** by Kos. This large carbon fibre, which celebrates 20 years of Kos's marine photography, must be one of the most extraordinary books ever published, both in content and sheer enormity (520mm x 630mm). It weighs nearly 10 kilos and costs £750. Many of the 200 beautiful images have been taken from the top of a 180ft mast - one of Kos's favourite vantage points. It was printed as a limited edition of only 1,000 copies with a foreword by HSH The Aga Khan.

Bath Road, Cowes, Isle of Wight PO31 7QN
Tel: 01983 281414   Fax: 01983 282992
Email: gallery@kendallsfineart.co.uk   www.kendallsfineart.co.uk

Kenneth and Keith Beken

Frank Beken

Keith Beken

Beken of Cowes

Marine photographers

Keith Beken, the son of the founder, is now 87. He still drives to the shop every day in his own car, but he stopped taking photographs in 1999.
He recalls: "With the old camera we could only take 30 pictures, so we had to be careful to get the perfect pictures in one shot.
Black and white photos were of better quality then because of the silver used in the emulsion and the chemicals used in the processing.
Today the quality has gone down but of course colour pictures are made more fashionable.
Our job is not easy: you have to be a yachtsman and a photographer!
But I love the sea and looking at the sea.
I must have salt water in my veins!"

Frank Beken was born in Canterbury in 1880. His father Alfred, already a chemist and photographer, moved to Cowes on the Isle of Wight in 1888 where he eagerly pursued his hobby, photography, and was soon afloat in a 14ft. dinghy photographing the fine vessels that plied the Solent waters. He quickly realised that the early bellows cameras of the day were just not suited to photography at sea, so he set about designing his own camera to withstand the seawater and the harsh treatment anticipated afloat. This new camera had three focus settings, 'Dinghies', 'Yachts' and 'Liners'! It was held up with both hands and the shutter fired by biting a rubber ball gripped tightly between the teeth! Frank's son Keith joined the company in the 1930s. He adapted the cameras to take colour film and started the worldwide travelling to selected regattas to broaden the field of the already large archive. Keith's son Kenneth started his photographic career in 1970. With him came a change to more modern cameras. Hasselblads for their classic portraits and 35mm Canons for close-up action images. Slower motor boats made way for high-speed powerboats and helicopters. Attendance at international sailing events is now a regular occurrence and the Beken Archives now house over 250,000 different images from over 100 years of maritime history.

Each generation of Beken has been awarded the prestigious title of 'Fellow of the Royal Photographic Society' and three Royal Warrants hang in their shop awarded by Queen Victoria, King George V and HRH Prince Philip. In their shop one can find all manner of their marine photography from a humble postcard to magnificent framed hand made limited edition prints. Their calendars and posters can be found in good outlets all over the world or sourced on their website. Two London galleries exhibit their work, *Atlas* in the City and *Trowbridge* in the Kings Road and early examples of Beken photography have achieved high prices at London auction houses.

Waterwitch

Absolutely!

BY APPOINTMENT TO
H.R.H. THE DUKE OF EDINBURGH
MARINE PHOTOGRAPHERS

BEKEN *of* COWES

Beken of Cowes

Limited Edition Photographs

Beken of Cowes are proud to launch their selection of a Limited Edition of 250 photographic prints from each of 72 of the finest images held within the Beken archives dating back to 1888. Each negative is hand printed onto archive paper, hand tinted, retouched, dated and titled, embossed and numbered. Each is then approved and signed by Beken. The images may also be viewed at the Atlas Gallery in London.

Beken of Cowes

Calendars

Beken of Cowes Calendars offer a taste of the sea for everyone. Take a dip into the nostalgic past by enjoying turn of the century studies in our Classic Calendar. Enjoy the grace and splendour from square-riggers and schooners in our Tall Ships Calendar. Be captivated by the thrills and spills of the wilder side of sailing in our Marine Action Calendar. The Beauty of Sail Calendar depicts yachts with a more traditional style of elegance and the Yachting Calendar portrays images from both sides of the Atlantic.

Beken of Cowes

Collection of Hand Made Photographs

The images selected for the Beken Collection have been carefully chosen from the Beken Archive of original glass plate negatives. Each has been carefully printed by hand and sepia-toned. Quality archive mounting board is then matched and sized to each print making it ready for framing.

Beken of Cowes

America's Cup Collection

Following the success of the 150th Jubilee celebration, Beken of Cowes, in collaboration with Omnimage Editions, has published a superb limited edition boxed set of fifteen classic America's Cup photographs. The covering of the box is highly appropriate being in the form of cloth from a headsail of Endeavour, the 1934 America's Cup challenger provided by Ratsey & Lapthorn.

Beken Maritime Services Ltd, 16 Birmingham Road, Cowes, Isle of Wight PO31 7BH
Tel: +44 (0) 1983 297311 Fax: +44 (0) 1983 291059
E-Mail: beken@beken.co.uk Website: www.beken.co.uk

Absolutely!

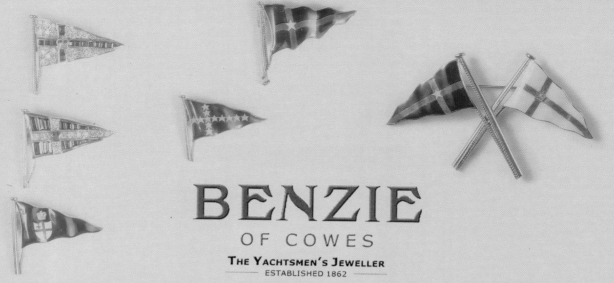

BENZIE
OF COWES
THE YACHTSMEN'S JEWELLER
ESTABLISHED 1862

MANUFACTURERS OF QUALITY
NAUTICAL AND SPORTING JEWELLERY

Simpson Benzie founded and established Benzie of Cowes nearly 140 years ago, in 1862 and the firm has been world renowned for producing unique items of jewellery of the highest possible standard. Its craftsmen have enjoyed patronage by the most demanding of clientele, as can be seen from a list of eight Royal Warrants, including Queen Victoria, George V and the Duke of Edinburgh, thus proving the company's success. In 1934 Benzie was commissioned to make a silver model of the famous yacht *Endeavour*. Anecdotally, Lord Louis Mountbatten, Governor of the Isle of Wight, was unable to gain access to the Royal Yacht Squadron. He therefore used to watch the sailing from the observation tower at the top of the Benzie premises in Cowes.

Since the 19th century Benzie has created jewellery and nautical insignia for many famous yachtsmen and their clubs all over the world including the Royal Yacht Squadron, the Royal London Yacht Club, the Island Sailing Club (Cowes), the New York Yacht Club and the Seawanhaka Corinthian Yacht Club (Long Island). Today, under the leadership of Bernard Taylor who has been with Benzie for more than 50 years, the traditional quality and craftsmanship have become famous the world over. Bernard is supported by Will Souter, a goldsmith, and his son Jamie in the workshop, where the famous Benzie range of nautical jewellery is produced. Hand-made to the clients'

instructions, each Benzie piece is given a unique registration number which is entered in the Benzie book.

Following 139 years of trading in Cowes, and by way of a 'thank you' to the town, Benzie constructed a brand new Mayoral chain in Sterling silver and enamel which was presented to the office of the Town Mayor.

In August 1998, James W. Muggoch with his partner, Subash Lodhia, bought Benzie of Cowes. Since then, turnover has increased fivefold and the staff has doubled. "What was destined to become a museum is now a living, breathing entity," says James Muggoch. Of Scottish origin, James had done many jobs in his life until he decided to buy Benzie. A real coincidence, (or was it fate?) as he had come to Cowes to sail, went for a walk, discovered Benzie, learned it was actually on the market and decided to buy the business. "I want to make our yachting and nautical jewellery the best in the world. We have the name, the right people and the ambition to produce it. The America's Cup Jubilee was a great opportunity to gain new customers and I am going to follow it up by going to New Zealand for the next America's Cup; after all, my wife is from New Zealand."

Benzie of Cowes has another shop in Richmond (West London) which specialises in antique and fine second-hand jewellery, together with individually made diamond and gem set rings. Both Cowes and Richmond shops offer an excellent repair service for clocks and watches, jewellery and silverware, plus valuations for insurance and probate. The shops also offer friendly advice provided by fully trained staff.

61 High Street, Cowes, Isle of Wight, PO31 7RL
Tel/Fax: 01983 293932

1 Dome Building, The Quadrant
Richmond-on-Thames, Surrey, TW9 1BP
Tel/Fax: 0208 9405005

Email sales@benzie.co.uk
Website: www. benzie.co.uk

*Benzie is sole stockist
on the Island
for Rolex Watches.*

Simpson Benzie

A great team of craftsmen

Friendly service

The Benzie Trophy for the fastest boat in the
UBS Jubilee Round-the-Island-Race, won by Stealth,
was given in absentia to a member of the Agnelli
family at the Royal Yacht Squadron in September 2001.
The trophy, a copy of the yacht America,
was manufactured and gifted to the Royal Yacht
Squadron by Benzie.

James Muggoch and Subash Lodhia, owners of Benzie of Cowes, presenting the
Benzie Trophy to Commodore Peter Nicholson of the Royal Yacht Squadron.
With them, Jamie Souter, Rebecca Hanwell, Will Souter and Bernard Taylor

Ratsey & Lapthorn
The driving force of sailing

To anyone seriously involved in yachting, the name of Ratsey & Lapthorn is legendary. From the earliest days of yachting on the Solent, the company has been a major force in the development of the sport.

RATSEY & LAPTHORN
Sailmakers
COWES
SAILMAKING SINCE 1790

While contenders for the America's Cup have come and gone, many with egos dented and ambitions thwarted, one reputation remains intact: that of Ratsey & Lapthorn. Indeed, until the 1960s every British challenger for the America's Cup was equipped with Ratsey & Lapthorn sails, while from 1903 all American defenders wore their canvas. For over two centuries, the firm has been involved with international yachting - an influence which far eclipses even the most long-lived yacht designers. It's surprising then that this contribution to the sport is often overlooked, for Ratsey & Lapthorn has without doubt been the single most important name in sailing. George Rogers Ratsey originally established the firm of Ratsey's in 1790 and for a long time, the enterprise was very small-scale. The earliest archives of the firm, from 1813, show that Ratsey's supplied sails for a wide variety of working boats, including smacks and cutters.

"The history of Ratsey & Lapthorn is synonymous with that of yachting. The firm's first sail loft preceded the establishment of yachting and for over two hundred years, the world's leading yachts have set the firm's canvas. From its origins in Cowes and early involvement with the Royal Yacht Squadron, the firm grew to establish lofts on the British mainland and in New York. For a hundred years Ratsey & Lapthorn were sail-makers of choice for yachts competing for the America's Cup. Members of the Ratsey and Lapthorn families sailed on the greatest yachts and liaised with a client base that included Kings, Emperors and tycoons."

William Collier

Photo © Beken of Cowes

Cambria

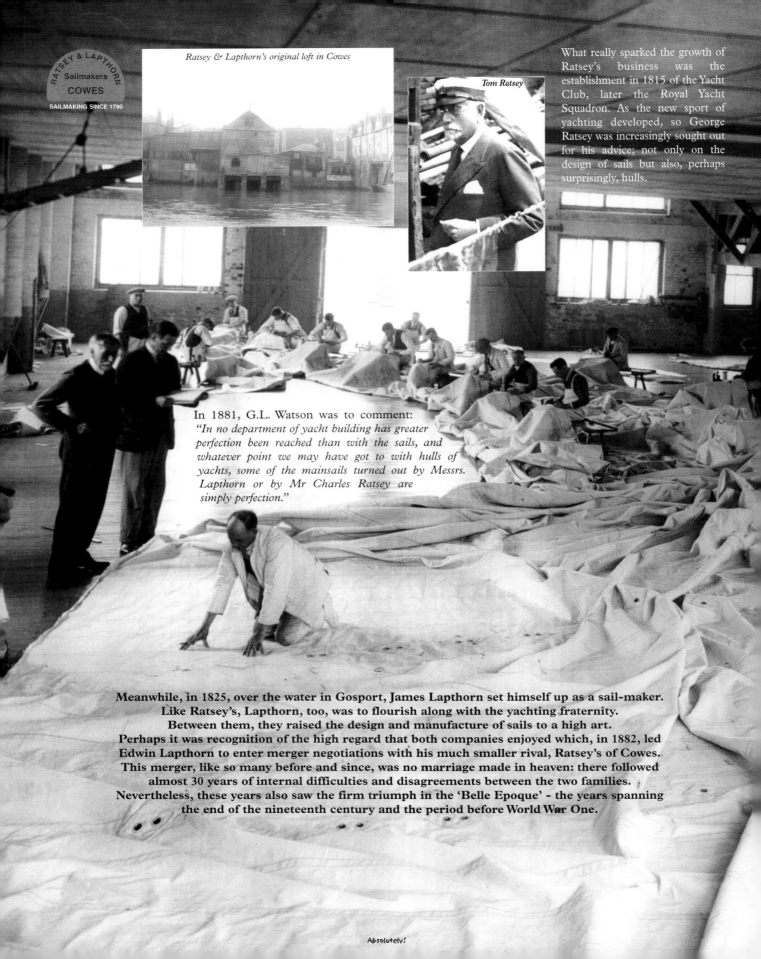

Ratsey & Lapthorn's original loft in Cowes

Tom Ratsey

What really sparked the growth of Ratsey's business was the establishment in 1815 of the Yacht Club, later the Royal Yacht Squadron. As the new sport of yachting developed, so George Ratsey was increasingly sought out for his advice; not only on the design of sails but also, perhaps surprisingly, hulls.

In 1881, G.L. Watson was to comment:
"In no department of yacht building has greater perfection been reached than with the sails, and whatever point we may have got to with hulls of yachts, some of the mainsails turned out by Messrs. Lapthorn or by Mr Charles Ratsey are simply perfection."

Meanwhile, in 1825, over the water in Gosport, James Lapthorn set himself up as a sail-maker. Like Ratsey's, Lapthorn, too, was to flourish along with the yachting fraternity. Between them, they raised the design and manufacture of sails to a high art. Perhaps it was recognition of the high regard that both companies enjoyed which, in 1882, led Edwin Lapthorn to enter merger negotiations with his much smaller rival, Ratsey's of Cowes. This merger, like so many before and since, was no marriage made in heaven: there followed almost 30 years of internal difficulties and disagreements between the two families. Nevertheless, these years also saw the firm triumph in the 'Belle Epoque' - the years spanning the end of the nineteenth century and the period before World War One.

Absolutely!

Ernest A. Ratsey & his father George E. Ratsey

RATSEY & LAPTHORN
Sailmakers
COWES
SAILMAKING SINCE 1790

James Stanley Lapthorn

James F. Lapthorn

In 1902, Tom Ratsey opened the firm's loft in New York,
thanks to the support and encouragement of Robert Jacob,
who owned a substantial yacht maintenance business on City Island.
The business was an almost immediate success and Ratsey & Lapthorn
graduated to the international stage. Indeed, the firm established a monopoly on
America's Cup sails on both sides of the Atlantic which lasted until the 1950s.

In the late 1960s Ratsey & Lapthorn's mobile service van helped maintain the standard of customer care that clients required.

Sail making

Absolutely!

Photos © MCvxA

Andy Cassell and Mark Ratsey-Woodroffe

Ratsey & Lapthorn's involvement in the Beken America's Cup Collection is as fine an example of serendipity as one could wish to find. While trying to find a suitable material to use to cover the box for the collection, Allan Jones of Omnimage Editions called Ratsey & Lapthorn for advice. When they found out what he needed 'sail cloth' for, it was suggested that they had an original sail in their loft from which the covers could be made. In the event, the material used was from one of the sails of **Endeavour II**, *Tommy Sopwith's marvellous America's Cup challenger from 1937. One could hardly wish for a more elegant or fitting protection for the collection.*

The fascinating history of Ratsey & Lapthorn has been researched from the myriad archive entries by Dr. W. Collier who published *Classic Sails*, an extensively illustrated book.

Ratsey & Lapthorn,
Medina Road, Cowes,
Isle of Wight, PO31 7BY.
Tel: +44 (0) 1983 294051
Fax: +44 (0) 1983 294053
Email: ratseysails@ratsey.com

Photo © Franco Pace - Courtesy of Ratsey & Lapthorn

Mariette

Absolutely!

Photo © Hamo Thornycroft

*Mark Spencer towing Mr Gucci's **Avel**, after launching, to Thetis Wharf for masting*

Photo © Patrick Eden

Harry Spencer

Photos and text © Marie-Clare Baroness von Alvensleben and Harry Spencer

Spencer Rigging
The Story of
Harry Spencer
'The man who gets things done'

"When Harry Spencer talks, his eyes blaze vivid blue, his ears waggle, he blows out his cheeks, flaps his lips in the breeze and sticks out his tongue, while rubbing his hands over his shining pate."
Elizabeth Meyer, Publisher.

One of the characters who make Cowes the centre of yachting excellence, traditional style, is Harry Spencer at Spencer Thetis Wharf in Cowes Harbour and Spencer Rigging in the town's St Mary's Road. As Elizabeth Meyer, the well-known publisher and classic yacht owner, wrote: "Spencer's is obviously more than just a company. It is more like a state of mind in which ordinary standards of what is and is not possible do not apply. Spencer's is simply a necessary extension of Harry's personality: a mere blend of artistic sensibility and brute force, his unerring sense of the right way to do a thing, his uncanny skill in managing any impossible job the world brings his way." To many of the classic yacht owners visiting Cowes for the America's Cup Jubilee - even those who had never previously been here - Harry was an old friend.

Maurizio Gucci at *Avel*'s launch

Harry Spencer is completely unfazed by his first-name-term acquaintance-ship with the very rich and famous. "I look on people as equals," he said, "and I give respect where it is due but I just try to be myself."

Maurizio Gucci's '*Avel*'

Harry works 12-hour days overseeing both workshops and, if necessary, will make an urgent delivery to Gatwick, climb a mast or work in the roof of a local church.

He will occasionally wear a jacket!

Cowes born and bred, Harry left school at 14 and has spent a lifetime working on yachts - a circumstance which has put him on first-name terms with many of the richest and most famous people in the yachting world. For Harry - boatbuilder, rigger and problem-fixer - and his Spencer Thetis Wharf and Spencer Rigging have been responsible for restoring, fitting and rigging many of the world's most famous and beautiful sailing yachts. Thirty years ago Harry had a strong feeling that yachts would go the same way as classic cars, with growing interest in restoration - and he has been proved right, with a healthy classic yacht programme here, in the Mediterranean and the States. "I was one of the first to see that people with money would want the beauty and tradition of sail," says Harry, who established his Spencer Thetis Wharf in Cowes 30 years ago. "At that time people said I was mad to concentrate on wood and the lovely old fittings of yesteryear - they thought the future was going to be all modern alloys, fibreglass and carbon."

Photo © MCvA

Harry Spencer with Mohammed Al Fayed

Harry Spencer and Spencer Rigging have been associated with Mohammed Al Fayed for the last 33 years. When Mohammed Al Fayed's grandfather bought a 235-ton American schooner in the early 1950's, she was harboured in Greece and called Kira. After his grandfather passed away, Mr Al Fayed set about rebuilding her to her former glory and called her Dodi. The boat was taken to Genoa in 1968 for a complete overhaul of all the rigging and masts, which was carried out by Harry Spencer at Spencer Thetis Wharf. She was renamed Sakara. Harry has been looking after her ever since, carrying out a yearly survey of the masts and rigging, wherever she is moored. Mohammed Al Fayed's brother Ali has a 90-ton yacht Jasali, for which Harry and Spencer Rigging carry out a similar service.

Sakara

SPENCER RIGGING

'Bounty' replica
fitted out 1978-1979,
all made in Cowes,
masted and rigged
in New Zealand

With the equally prestigious *Spencer Rigging* in Cowes, Harry and his team are the force behind many famous restorations, including the J-Class *Endeavour*, *Velsheda* and *Shamrock*, the 23-Metre *Cambria* and top beauty, Tom Perkins' *Mariette* of 1915.

Harry with Rafe in the mast shop

Mark and Rafe Spencer

Third generation - young Harry Spencer

Harry and Mark on Spencer barges

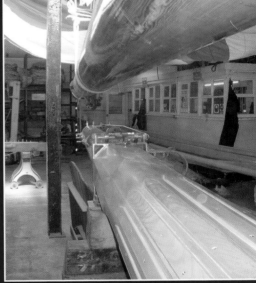

Sculpture/Masts at Limerick University

Harry has been married twice and with his second wife, Ross, has two sons, Mark, (31), and Rafe, (28), who work in the business with him. Mark, previously an engineer, now manages the towing side of the business as well as being company secretary and becoming influential on the rigging side. Rafe, with Martyn, runs the spar and block workshop operation. With both sons married, Harry and Ross already have one grandchild (Mark and Vicky's son, little Harry) and another (Rafe and Kathy's) was due early in 2002. Mark and Rafe are both directors of the company and are keen to see Spencer's continue to grow stronger for the future, with their own knowledge and expertise. "I want to see the company thrive so that my children also get the chance to take over from me one day," says Mark. Harry still takes a big rôle in the business but he and wife Ross are also busy outside work with their own artistic interests. Ross has a sculpture studio and Harry has a workshop for carpentry, metalwork, painting and varnishing. Together, they complement one another perfectly.

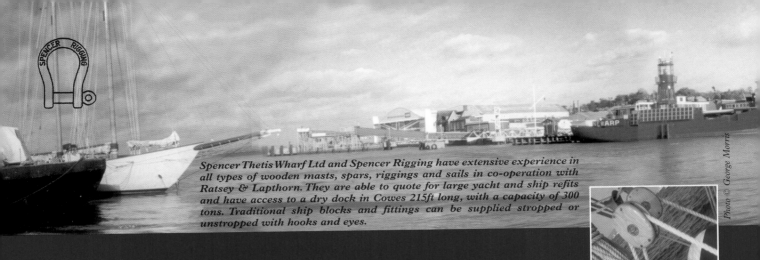

Spencer Thetis Wharf Ltd and Spencer Rigging have extensive experience in all types of wooden masts, spars, riggings and sails in co-operation with Ratsey & Lapthorn. They are able to quote for large yacht and ship refits and have access to a dry dock in Cowes 215ft long, with a capacity of 300 tons. Traditional ship blocks and fittings can be supplied stropped or unstropped with hooks and eyes.

Photo © George Morris

Born on 4 September 1925, the son of a former shipwright working at Saunders and White's in Cowes, Harry was educated at Denmark Road School. But five years before Harry was born, his father had taken up a career as the golf professional at Cowes Golf Club. It was a change of lifestyle for the family and Mr Spencer became an exceptional golfer - which also meant he could earn more in one hour giving lessons in golf than he would take home for a week's work in the shipyard. He taught the young Harry how to play from the age of four but with the outbreak of war in 1939, such frivolities finished. Instead, the Spencer's became engaged in useful work in the shipyards. In 1939, at the age of 14, Harry started work as a pattern maker at J. S. White's Shipyard in Cowes. He started a lot of extra-work activities and became a fitness fanatic running, swimming, rowing and sailing. Later, in 1952, he would row the seven miles between Cowes and Hamble twice a day, to get to work and back to see his girlfriend. After the war Harry became involved in many jobs, such as delivering RNLI lifeboats all round England and Scotland, serving as second mate in coasters, (English coast and Continental), then sailing as a bosun's mate and sailmaker aboard a troopship running to Singapore and Hong Kong.

Back in Cowes, Harry worked for five years for twin brothers Robert and Wallace Clark, handling repairs including new masts and rigging. After another year working for the legendary Tiny Mitchell, Harry decided he wanted to work for himself and established a loft at the rear of the old National and Provincial Bank, nowadays the NatWest - with the impressive address of 1 Bank Chambers. The telephone number was an equally simple Cowes 15. Working sometimes 22 hours a day - Harry says he was fortunate in not needing much sleep - he built a reputation for reliable rigging work and an ability to take on marine projects, including building test-tank models for a fast patrol boat, working all night if needed to get a job done on time. He would then carry on working all day rigging, towing, climbing masts and sailing 12-Metre yachts. Another of Harry's tasks in those days was to run the fast boat for Sir Robert Hobart, then aide-de-camp to Sir Hugh Fraser, owner of the house of Fraser and later Harrods. Offers of posts at sea came and went - including work on the new *Oriana* liner and for Captain Irving Johnson on his schooner *Yankee* - but Harry was not to be

tempted by long-term contracts or even a fifth-share in the schooner. Instead, he became busier and busier in Cowes, as the orders poured in. Soon, Harry was well-established making test tank models for American test tanks and for the British Hovercraft Corporation and Southampton University, among others. The Spencer Rigging premises in St Mary's Road - once a cinema - were set up when Harry was working with the meticulous boatbuilder Tony Hendy. Tony, with Dick Appsley, eventually bought out the model-making side of the business, as Woodforms in Newport.

In the 1960s Harry's rigging expertise was called on for a different sort of mast - the radio masts of the pirate radio stations Radio Caroline North and South, which broadcast pop music to British teenagers from off the Essex coast, and Radio Scotland. Harry has a lot of anecdotes of those times. He bought Spencer Thetis Wharf with Ratsey's, the sailmakers, and when J. Samuel White's yard in Medina Road was sold he bought premises there, creating Thetis Engineering. This later had to be sold. After setting up Spencer Rigging in 1958, Harry started Spencer Thetis Wharf to go back in time, making not only masts and spars but wood-shelled blocks with bronze fittings and deck work in nickel alloy bronze, matching the high standards of 19th century and early 20th century boatbuilders in Britain and the United States. Harry's reputation grew in the world of classics and he has refitted the yachts of some of the richest people in the world: Maurizio Gucci, Harrods owner Mohammed Al Fayed, Baron Bentinck and Elizabeth Meyer, among others. Mr Al Fayed calls Harry 'donkey', but Harry says: "A donkey will give you years of good service if you treat him well." He has built two aerial tramway rides for the Sultan of Brunei's garden; rigged and fitted a 200-ton arab dhow for Dr Zowawi, an Omani gynaecologist; and negotiated the sale of **Shamrock** between the Newport Maritime Museum and a Frenchman. In 1977 film director Dino de Laurentis approached Harry to survey an 18th century replica warship, **Rose**, for films he wanted to make, and the next year de Laurentis asked Harry to build the rig for the film *Mutiny on the Bounty*, with Anthony Hopkins. He designed the masts and spars, rigging and blocks in 1790

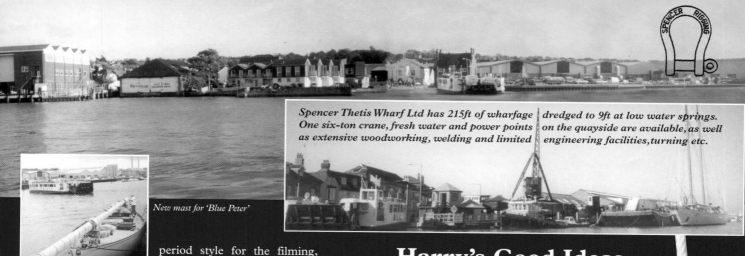

New mast for 'Blue Peter'

Spencer Thetis Wharf Ltd has 215ft of wharfage dredged to 9ft at low water springs. One six-ton crane, fresh water and power points on the quayside are available, as well as extensive woodworking, welding and limited engineering facilities, turning etc.

period style for the filming, most of which was done in New Zealand. For the storms and other dramatic shots, a one-fifth-size replica was used in a tank with Harry overseeing the sailing aspects at Pinewood Studios.

Square-rigged vessels, including training ships, were another speciality of Spencer's, helping to keep around 30 employees in work. Problem solving has always been one of Harry's strengths and it has got Spencer's involved in projects ranging from gas pipelines under the Solent to lifting the roof of the Groves and Guttridge building. The property had been bought by the Gardiner brothers, who wanted the roof raised - literally - without disturbing anything inside. Everyone, says Harry, reckoned it couldn't be done but, of course, he did it and for just £1,500, a sum he reckons he should have trebled in the circumstances. Harry's reputation for dealing with unusual tasks grew even further when he carried out changes to the round steel structure housing the foghorns at St Catherine's Lighthouse, on the southern tip of the Isle of Wight. Have a problem with a large object, not necessarily a boat? Call Harry and he will solve it. To quote Elizabeth Meyer again: "The more Herculean or more unusual the task, the more Harry will revel in it." His physical strength is amazing and he has shown it many times, especially in the 1969 Fastnet Race when he raced in Arthur Slater's *Prospect of Whitby*.

Northwood House is a beautiful big old building surrounded by parkland which was donated to Cowes by the Ward Foundation. Squire Ward had insisted that there should be an example of every tree in the world in the park. Harry Spencer was so impressed that he suggested putting name tags on the trees. Harry has also proposed that a marine museum be built on the ground floor, with a health centre at the back. The upper floor could be a large function room with a stage, and acoustically designed for private and public functions.

Harry's Good Ideas

Over the years Harry Spencer has come up with many ingenious suggestions to improve the way things are done around Cowes. He has suggested replacing the chain ferry across the Medina with river buses, and removing the slipways which cause bottlenecks. He has also presented plans to alter the Town Quay, extend the marinas and build new breakwaters.

Harry says: "Being a local and older inhabitant of Cowes, I am not opposed to new developments and do not think everything should remain as it always has been - as some do. I have travelled and I have seen what can be achieved if the financing is there. Cowes Harbour has terrific potential. There is enough talent and expertise in Cowes without having to pay expensive outside experts. Leisure activities and commercial interests must be kept in balance - yachting brings in revenue but little work and there has been a serious erosion of facilities in the port. Something should be done to have the ferries come into new terminals outside the breakwater, so as not to interrupt racing and to diminish risks to small yachts moored in the harbour. If the Red Funnel ferries went outside the breakwater, the vacated area could be made into a quay where ships and large yachts could berth, giving East Cowes a new attraction - restaurants there would offer some of the best panoramic views of Cowes Harbour. A small ferry could run between the east and west terminals, the 'penny struggle', as it used to be called. I would love to see the existing breakwater made into a 30-ft wide quay wall. I would stabilise the river bank and dredge the useless area of mud flat to allow training vessels and large yachts to berth there. That would put East Cowes on the map. People might say that this would need big money... but so many other projects get funding, why not this one? The money would come back within the next 20 years. We have the reputation but we badly need the facilities to bring profitable work to Cowes. Large yachts are now refitted in Portsmouth, Southampton and Falmouth, or in other countries. We need the facilities to get them back here, to get them out of the water and under cover. We have the position, the reputation, the expertise, so let's make plans for the future and bring back the activities that made Cowes so well known in the past." Will the Council listen to him...?

The *Creole* Story

Photo © David White

1. **Creole** arriving at Cowes in 1980 with a broken mizzen mast. She then belonged to a Danish school as a training ship.

Photos Courtesy Harry Spencer

2. **Creole** arriving stern first to receive her new mizzen mast.

3. The new mast being quickly lifted in by a special crane.

4. **Creole** with her mast temporarily stepped, leaving Spencer Thetis Wharf to prevent her going aground at low tide. She has a 17ft draught.

5. The new mast being built.

6. **Creole's** new mast nearly in position.

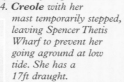

7. **Creole** leaves Cowes re-masted after 16 days.

8. A few months later **Creole** had all her other masts and booms replaced. This is a picture of her new foremast being lifted off the quay.

The Gurnard Church Story

The base of Gurnard church steeple was found to be rotting. A new base was built from hardwood. The steeple was then lifted off the old base and bolted to the new taller base. The new steeple assembly weighed two and a quarter tons and was replaced without scaffolding using a crane with a 28-metre boom.

Spire with old base being lifted off

Harry, Mark and Rafe Spencer all at it.

Rev. Graham Morris with Harry

Spire with new base being lowered into position.

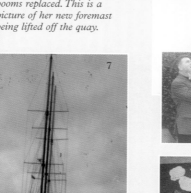

Photos © MCvA

Everyone seems happy, it all went well!, especially Harry's wife Ross

Kathy, Vicky and baby Harry!

Photos Courtesy Harry Spencer

Sculpture/Masts arriving at Limerick University

Mark and Harry preparing to lift Number 2 mast

*Tug **Hofland** and barge **Malaya** with **New Zealand** mast, from London to Falmouth*

***Hispania**, salvaged from a mud berth in Essex and taken to Southampton, used to belong to the former King of Spain, King Juan Carlos' father.*

Some vessels rigged or supplied by Spencer (masts, rigging, blocks)

Adix
Creole
Fleurtje
Velsheda
Shamrock
Altair
Aetos
Mariette
Moonbeam
Sakara
Thendara
Ketty Iona
Kentra
Aile Blanche
Belle Aventure
Vagrant
Tuiga
Seven Seas
Flica
Trivia
Annabel J
Rona
Avel
Fidelis
Merry Dancer
Puritan
Shenandoah
Jezebel
Discovery
Aquarius
TS Captain Miranda
TS Captain Scott
TS Lord Nelson 1
TS Lord Nelson 2
Garden
Audela
Eric Borgmann

Concorde 1
Concorde 2
Concorde 3
Colombaio Sun
Colombaio Star,
Lulworth
Brooke Yachts
Cambria
Allobeta
Centurian
Sylvia
Young Endeavour
Tunas Samudera
Blue Leopard
Valdettaro 1
Valdettaro 2
Valdettaro 3
Valdettaro 4
Jankel
Ploutis 1
Ploutis 2
Sintra
Onyx
Royalist
Varuna
Saharet
De Brabander
Ticonderoga
Bounty
Halloween
Al Masroora
Angel Aline
Barbarossa
Karantia
Winston Churchill
Malcolm Miller
Duet
Dulcibella
Rosa
Raven of Maine
SS Great Britain
HMS Warrior 1860

***Domino** has been a vital tool in many of Harry's enterprises and adventures. He bought the 30ft towboat in 1957, when she was already 23-years-old, from HM Customs and had her completely refitted. Since then she has proved very useful - and is still in action today. He says she is like an old friend. At one time Harry moved a 170-ton Princess flying boat, with a 200ft wingspan, across the river, using the 70-horsepower boat. **Domino** has towed the J-Class yacht **Endeavour** and **Norsaga**, among others, and has travelled to France, Holland and Germany. Harry has also bought another tug - this one with an ocean-going licence - and with **Domino** and the new tug he towed **Endeavour** to Cowes from Calshot Spit, then to Holland.*

***Domino** in the 1960s*

Ben Bradley

SPENCER RIGGING

Created in 1958, Spencer Rigging has gained expertise in supplying rigging to many diverse industries on a world-wide basis. Both the Cowes and Southampton rigging lofts are fitted with an extensive range of rigging machinery, making them some of the best equipped in Europe. The company is involved 65% in yacht rigging and 35% in architectural and industrial rigging.

Yacht Rigging

Spencer rigging is equipped in every way to specify and manufacture rigging for the smallest sailing dinghy or the world's largest sailing vessels. Whether the yacht is a modern racing machine using rod rigging and hi-tech ropes or a vintage gaff cutter fitted with deadeyes and lanyards, Spencer's have the necessary stock, machinery and skilled workforce to undertake whatever specification is required. The rigging personnel and Harry himself, travel to foreign countries to supply yachts with new or replacement items. They retain records of the rigging specification supplied to all the yachts they have worked on. The rigging lofts contain large stocks of wires, ropes and associated chandlery and also serve as retail outlets. Spencers are continually evaluating new materials and, with the 'feedback' from some of the world's top owners, skippers and designers, are able to offer their customers the latest in materials and technology. They act as consultants to naval architects and associated trades for all aspects of yacht rigging, and undertake surveys for surveyors, insurance companies, yacht brokers and private owners. They can supply a complete above-deck package including spars, furling units, sails, winches, deck gear and ground tackle all complete with on-site rigging service.

Hi-Tech Rigging

Parallel to the expansion of yacht rigging there has been the development of a commercial market for rigging assemblies and lifting equipment used by the construction and engineering industries. Nitronic and Navtec Rod Rigging is now used extensively in modern buildings on large structures such as glass walls and roofs as load carrying ties. Stainless steel wire rope assemblies are used extensively on balustrading and as ties and support wires in various ways such as supporting mezzanine floors and open plan suspended staircases. The advent of flexible structures and large tented buildings has created a substantial market for wire ropes and associated hardware. Spencer Rigging is approved by the Factory Inspectorate to manufacture and supply lifting equipment accompanied by the necessary certification. Their many other activities include the onsite testing and certification of factory lifting equipment and the lashing and securing of deck cargoes. Spencer Rigging also supply specialized assemblies to the aerospace, submarine and nuclear industries, equipment to the RNLI, offshore and oil spillage as well as farming and horticultural industries. They also act as consultants regarding the design of specialised lifting equipment and material selection.

Photos © MCxA

Gerald Wildish, who has been with Spencer since he was 17.

Ian McCully

Neil Brinsdon

Plantation Place
Tower Beacon,
London.

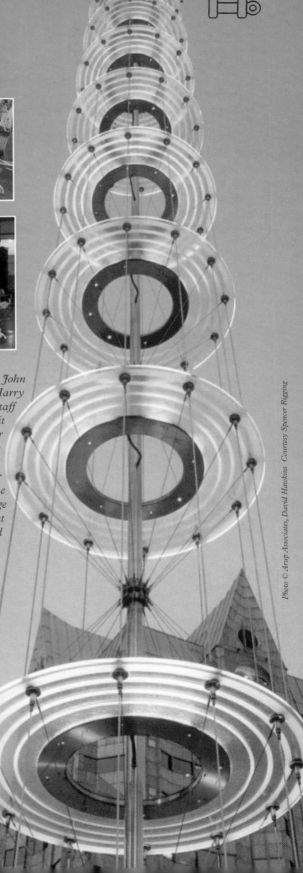

Photo © Arup Associates, David Hawkins Courtesy Spencer Rigging

Ben Bradley

Ben Bradley is the Managing Director of Spencer Rigging. After doing his apprenticeship as a naval architect while he worked at J.S. White, at the end of the 50's he started working for Harry Spencer and became part of the crew formed for the Red Duster Challenge when Harry was the skipper of *Norsaga* (now *Trivia* again). Sailing tests were done for the new boat that was supposed to be built (but P&O, persuaded by Harry, dropped the challenge in the early 60s). Norsaga's first mast was too heavy and was added to 'Radio Yorkshire', the last pirate ship that Spencers rigged. The others were Radio Caroline North/South and Radio Scotland, all masted, rigged and serviced at sea by Spencers. When John Powell started making aluminium masts he needed stainless steel rigging and that's how Spencer Rigging mushroomed with new business. Many yards were building yachts, so there was a big demand. He remembers the tiny workshop they had in those days behind the Bank. Their telephone number was Cowes 15 (Ratsey and Lapthorn's was Cowes 1). In the 60s they moved to St Mary's Road. Nowadays there is a big replacement market and they get a lot of requests for classic boats which need re-rigging, even if they have an aluminium mast which is the case with *Adix* or a carbon fibre one in the case of *Velsheda*.

Tom Archer   Raymond Field

Ben Bradley, with Ken doing the quotes and John the accounts, has run Spencer Rigging since Harry started the wharf 30 years ago. Many of the staff have been with Spencer Rigging since it started. Simon Dunford has run the store for the last ten years; very conscientious men like Gerald Wildish, Ray Field, John Alder (retired), Ian McCully, Neil Bransome, Peter Martin and Chris Friel have travelled the world, rigging craft from small boats to large square- rigged ships. Some started straight from school when they were 12 or 13-years old and have been there 30-40 years. Young men like Tom Archer are growing up in the same tradition. Others will be trained to continue the reputation. It is not only marine work that is carried out. Ben has obtained a great deal of civil engineering work from well-known architects: hotel facades, bank entrances massive tent structures and a tower beacon. All have added to the extensive range and capabilities of Spencer Rigging. Both it and the wharf have full order books and are quoting the whole time. Surveys of masts and rigging are conducted world-wide for insurance companies, brokers, private owners and other surveyors. Obviously, staff will retire but Spencer's two sons, Mark and Rafe, are determined to see the Spencer reputation continue.

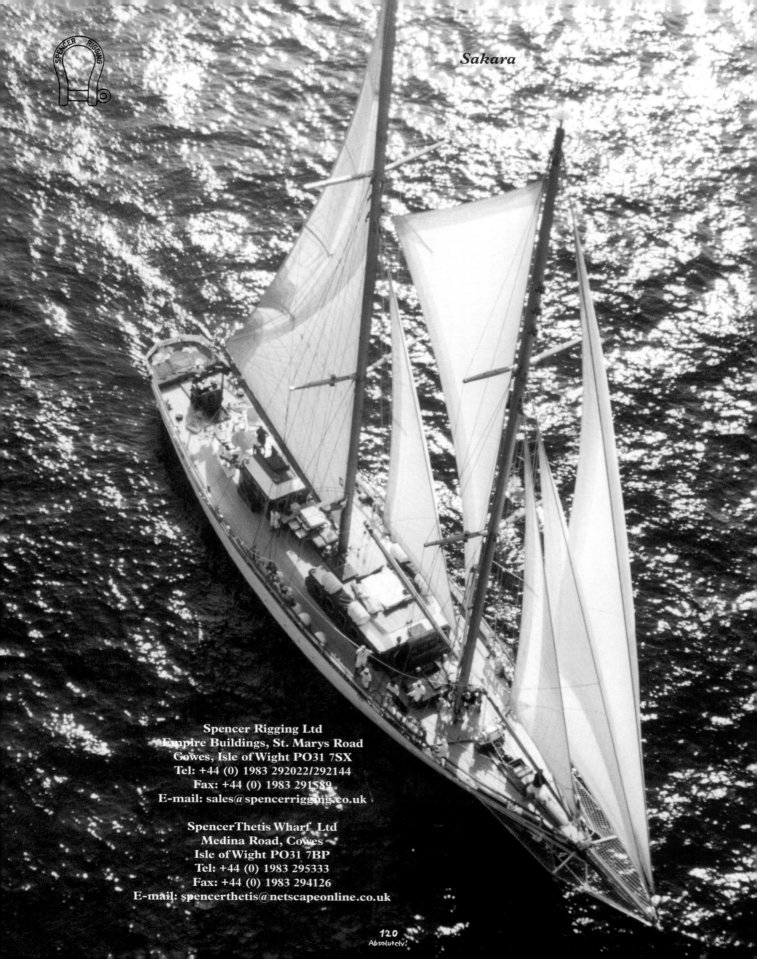

Sakara

Boatbuilding

Until the end of World War II, the major employers in Cowes, J.S.White's, Saunders-Roe (SARO) and Plessey Radar employed some 8,000 people: boatbuilders, rope and sail makers in the maritime industry but also in shops, building firms and other allied trades. Other companies engaged in yacht and boatbuilding were W.A.Souter, Marvins Yard, Lallows, and Groves & Guttridge.

Before the War, many large schooners as well as steam and square-rigged vessels were moored in the harbour: *Sunbeam* (renamed the *Flying Clipper* by the King of Norway) the Guinness barque *Fantôme* (renamed *Belle Amie*) and the most famous of all, *Britannia*, which was regularly maintained and re-planked by Marvins in Cowes, to name but a few.

J.S.White's, the huge shipyard which had a good reputation for well-built Naval ships, used to employ 5,000 men. The engineering sheds alone covered 12 acres on the riverside, south of the floating bridge. It helped the 1914-18 war effort by churning out warships and weapons. In the 1920s J.S.White's had received an injection of new shipbuilders from the north. White's was later taken over by an American company specialising in petrochemicals who modernised the site, but later sold it.*

North of the floating bridge, in West Cowes, was Pickford's Wharf (now Thetis Wharf) where goods were discharged, the SARO-seaplane factory (which also had premises in East Cowes, next to Trinity Wharf), Shepards Wharf and Lallows yard, the main yacht-servicing yard in the port. Both are still operating today.

Next to Lallows was Uffa Fox's yard where, in the 1930s, sailing canoes were built as well as the International 14-foot Class boats for which they became famous. Their construction method was adopted for the airborne lifeboats. Next to Uffa Fox was Groves and Guttridge (with other premises in East Cowes), they too building boats.

There was also a Ratsey's sail loft (now replaced by apartments and Sir Max Aitken's Museum) but this was moved to Medina Road.

Among other companies was David Cheverton, who had set up a yacht and boat-building business. He also designed workboats.

In East Cowes, there was Marvin's Yard, bought by Mr Willmot, which became East Cowes Marina and the RNLI Inshore Lifeboat Headquarters. Saunders-Roe (SARO) had the larger hangar workshop and slipway. They were known for a variety of craft including high-speed boats. They built the biggest seaplane ever, the *Princess* (144 tons with a 220 ft. wingspan) but it was discontinued. After the last War *Princess* was mothballed, covered in plastic and sprayed silver, becoming a landmark for years at the West Cowes SARO site (now GKN Westland Aerospace). The site later became a hovercraft terminal.

After the War major changes took place, not only in the industrial situation, but also in the transport of freight.

Shipbuilding was in decline in England. Out-of date machinery and methods could not compete with those of Germany and Holland. Shipyards which should have been modernised either concentrated on engineering or closed, abandoning a business which had existed for 400 years.

Newport Navy Barges were replaced by car ferries. Red Funnel and Wightlink ferries were now carrying hundreds of vehicles, replacing the old paddle steamers which used to carry, at best, 12 cars and two lorries.

Most of these changes in fast transport were introduced by Sir Robert Hobart with the Red Jets and the hovercraft. The ferry terminals became a focal point. Red Funnel first used a sidewall version of the hovercraft but abandoned it because of problems. Then they bought the Cowes-conceived but Italian-developed hydrofoils which were used until the Red Jets entered regular service.

Today, much has changed. Big yards have disappeared and facilities in the port are declining. We have let our forefathers down and let it all die where ships were built since the 15th century!

However, with the injection of capital in the last ten years by the local councils and, among others, the Laing Foundation, the yachting business seems to have recovered, and Cowes, including those older companies which have survived, offers some very good facilities for visiting yachtsmen.

Harry Spencer

Many inventions were created on the Island: among them, the hydrofoil by Mr Hook, and the hovercraft by Sir Christopher Cockerell (built by SARO)

The Mast of Norsaga (now Trivia) put in a field by Harry Spencer as a test rig for Ratsey & Lapthorn

*At the beginning of the 1970s Elliott TurboMachinery, which had bought J.S.White's, closed it. This was a sad blow for Cowes after 120 years! The 12-acre site with all the workshops was sold for £400,000 to a consortium of Christopher Bland, Mike Souter and the Isle of Wight Council. Christopher Bland moved from Clarence Yard to the vacant J.S.White's site and later sold it.

Photo © Beken of Cowes

Clare Lallows' Cowes yard in 1952

Photo Courtesy Ian Lallow

Clare Lallow with Edward Heath

Photo Courtesy Ratsey & Lapthorn

Clare Lallow (left) at the launch of Franklin Ratsey-Woodroffe's ocean racer 'Misty'

Ian Lallow

Photo © MCvA

Lallows
A Cowes Institution

Situated on Medina Road near the chain ferry, Lallows boatyard is timeless and as you peer inside the dimly lit sheds, you take a nostalgic step back in time. Images of gentlemen's graceful yachts with topsides like bone china, teak decks bleached and scrubbed snowy, and sails a dazzle of white on spars pale as peeled willow immediately come to mind. Built like Chippendale furniture to that yacht broker's favourite phrase 'Lloyds 100A1', Lallows boats became famous all over the world. Beken's photographs often depict them sailing to windward, their bows peeling back the sea like scissors through silk. The owner was, and still is, addressed as 'Sir' and more often than not, 'Sir' never questioned the bill or haggled in any way. Gentlemen didn't do that. It is rumoured that the final bill was not sent to 'Sir' until the yacht had won her first race. So how did it all begin?

Clare Lallow, the great-grandfather of Ian Clare Lallow, founded Lallows shipyard on their existing premises in 1867. Originally they came from Clermont Ferrand in France and the family name 'Clare' has been passed down through the generations to Ian's young son Charlie Clare. In 1907, the yard was almost completely destroyed by fire - but the premises were rebuilt and the yard survived. Ian's father, Clare, took over in 1948 and Ian Clare started working in the yard in 1961. In 1977, Clare retired and Ian took over the management before relinquishing the reins in 1996.

Throughout the 1950s, 60s and the early 70s the yard built fine yachts for many well-known people, including Sir Maurice Laing, Sir Max Aitken and two **Morning Clouds** for Sir Edward Heath. The yard became famous building boats by such legendary designers as Sparkman and Stevens and Charles Nicholson. Lallows also built several of the well-known South Coast One Design Class, or SCOD, the Jolina Class, and other designs by Charles Nicholson. More recently they have built XODs and Dragons with varnish work that resembles the colour and patina of fine French polishing.

In addition to building boats Lallows provided a 24-hour emergency service, especially during Cowes Week, when masts would be replaced and gaping holes temporarily repaired overnight to keep the boats racing. A 'phone call at any time would bring assistance to just about any need.

After 35 years of busy boatyard management, Ian decided that it was time to retire. "Business is not what it used to be after GRP took over as the most popular boat-building material and increasingly stringent rules and regulations could close the firm overnight. Long working hours and no weekends was the final deciding factor." Ian wanted more time for sailing and the pleasures of life, so the business was sold.

Ian is chairman of Cowes Town Regatta Committee and is a competitive Dragon sailor. As well as managing racing , he also organises the annual cricket match which takes place on the Brambles Bank at the lowest spring tide of the year in mid-summer, originally started by Uffa Fox.

On hearing the news that Lallows was to be sold, Cowes folk feared that one of the town's greatest institutions was going to be replaced by yet more waterside development. Lawrence Boarer, the current owner, took over in the spring of 1996, having worked in the business in the early '70s, and now maintains its timeless tradition.

The craftsmanship continues to this day. Several of the loyal workforce have built boats there for 40 years and more. Each winter sees the shed full with Dragons, XODs, Darings and larger craft in for refurbishment, and each spring sees them emerging immaculate, ready for the season ahead. Despite the decline in traditional wooden construction, the yard remains busy with refits and restorations using their renowned skills to restore one of 'Sir's' yachts to its former beauty. The phrase 'Built by Lallows' will always be synonymous with quality, fine craftsmanship and service.

Photo © MCxA

Shepards Wharf

Ships and Boats have been built in Cowes since the 15th century. Fishing craft, opium smuggling craft and HM Customs cutters; sometimes built next to each other, on the same slipway, in the same yard. Since the term 'yacht' was invented, people have built boats in Cowes, and the ones that survive are as varied as women's fashions. Some of them are steeped in history that goes back to the great days of yachting, the J-Class era. Graceful dinosaur-sized yachts owned by rich gentlemen, had mainsails that weighed over a ton and huge lofty rigs that required a crew of over thirty men to handle. It is said that if a candle flame blew out, there was too much wind to go sailing. If the flame stayed alight, there was not enough. Dismastings were frequent - which kept the yards busy. Nowadays, there is something in Cowes for everyone. Whether you want to win big league ocean races, have a Sunday afternoon 'round the buoys' or an up-the-creek coastal potter, there is a boatyard in Cowes that can provide a yacht to suit your needs.

Matt Power

Shepards Wharf

Shepards Wharf boatyard (now owned by the Harbour Commission) is run by the friendly Lucas brothers, Greg and Jonathon. This yard equipped with an 18-ton travel hoist, is specially run to cater for the DIY yachtsman. The yard has no restrictions on any outside labour working on the yachts. A Sunday afternoon stroll round the immaculate boat park reveals all sorts of aspiring dreams and high and low budgets. There is an increasingly wide gulf between hi-tech and low-tech, separating the world of plastics, alloys, microchips and precision engineering from the mud and gumboot scene - the third world of boating. These are the people who are happy just to be afloat, and being afloat is their reward for the hammering and banging, the improvisation and ingenuity that puts a tired old boat back on the water for yet another season. With its clean toilet facilities and smart hard standing, Shepards Wharf is far from being third world and in its friendly way it caters for all.

The yard has no full-time engineers or boat-builders but there are several small businesses operating on the yard's premises which can repair everything from making curtains for the saloon to complete engine rebuilds and hull repairs.

Currently the yard is home to the Etchells Class, competitive day racers that, in order to maintain their porcelain-like underwater surfaces, are slipped every Monday morning and launched every Friday afternoon ready for the weekend's racing. Tel: 01983 297821.

Run by Richard Pierrepont and Keith Brettell, **R.H.P. Marine Ltd** is an engineering company on the Shepards Wharf site specialising in mechanical and electrical repairs and installations. Tel: 01983 290421.

David Wager runs the **Saltern Sail Co.**, a traditional sailmaking company specialising in all aspects of sailmaking and repair but with the accent on covers, sprayhoods and interior upholstery. Tel: 01983 280014.

Shipwright Eddie Richards is part of the **Clarence Boatyard** in East Cowes but he is often to be seen in Shepards, wreathed in pipe tobacco smoke, putting his expert shipwright skills into practice, altering, repairing or improving. Tel: 01983 299740.

Souters

Souters Yard originally started in Arctic Road in 1947, beginning by building small dinghies and yacht tenders and introducing the cold-moulding method of boat-building which made the yard famous. The process involves laminating thin plys of wood over a mould, using modern synthetic glues to bond the layers rigidly and permanently together. The yard graduated to building cold-moulded light but strong ocean racers and powerboats. Among the many ocean racers the yard has built were **Outlaw** for Sir Max Aitken in 1963 and several designs by Illingworth & Primrose and Sparkman & Stevens. Souter-built ocean racers were selected for the Admiral's Cup in 1963, 1971, 1973 and 1975.

Several powerboats were built for the Classic Cowes-Torquay-Cowes, the 1969 Round Britain Power Boat Race, and the 1966 world champion was built by Souters. In 1986 Souter Shipyard was formed, at which time it purchased the assets of W. A. Souter and Son Ltd. It now builds high quality power yachts and commercial vessels in steel, aluminium and FRC polyester epoxy. The yard's largest vessel to date was an auxiliary yacht trimaran which was 25 metres long, with a 10 metre beam. The yard also specialises in refits of RNLI Lifeboats.

Tel: 01983 294711.

Photo © MCxA

Souter MARINE LIMITED

17-29

Chris Ratsey in front of Bear of Britain

UK McWILLIAM SAILMAKERS

Cowes Yacht Haven

Ocean racing is a high-pressure league of nautical lawyers and mathematical wizards who study each rule change more closely than Hebraic scholars working on the Dead Sea Scrolls, and Cowes Yacht Haven is home to them all. Roger Granger, the Marina's manager, capably runs a bustling hive of activity throughout the year with several rallies and events such as the Admiral's Cup and finds space for everybody in Cowes Week.

In the Marina complex, **David Wroath** repairs and installs electronics, and can provide a total rewiring for your yacht. Tel: 01983 281467.
Mel Colwell of **Powerplus Marine**, also in the Marina complex, is frequently to be found in the engine compartment of some yacht, planning, installing or servicing. If you have a mechanical problem, then Mel is your man. In fact, if it cannot be done in Cowes, then it cannot be done at all. Tel: 01983 200036.

UK/McWilliam Sailmakers

Run since 1979 by Chris Ratsey, **UK/McWilliam Sailmakers** are part of the UK Sailmakers group that has lofts all over the world and makes the sails of many modern top class racers. They have been at the forefront of sailmaking technology using their Tape Drive system of manufacturing. Tel: 01983 281100

Harley Racing Yachts

Successful builders of racing yachts, including Cowes Week twice winner *Reflex 38* and *Reflex 28*, the *Mustang 30*, *Corby 33* and *Corby 25*, **Harley Racing Yachts** also build bespoke, one-off craft and specialise in lightweight multihulls. They have recently launched their first venture into motor boat production with the very successful 25ft *Harley Cowes Classic*.
Tel: 01983 280060 Mobile 07808 256254

Yacht Designers

Among the racing wizards are **Christian Stimpson Yacht Designs Ltd** and **John Corby Designs Ltd** (See separate article). In hot demand as a racing tactician, **Jo Richards** is also a boat builder but not related to Eddie at East Cowes. Jo is currently part of a team building the new *GBR Challenge* boat for the next America's Cup, in the former FBM yard which has now become the GBR Challenge base. The build team of 22 people is led by Australians Jason Akers and Brandon Linton who are using the latest technology and materials for a possible triumph in 2003. (See various articles elsewhere in the book.)
Cowes Yacht Haven: Tel: 01983 299975

Adrian Stone

Situated just across the boat park, Adrian Stone can provide all sorts of repairs from hi-tech Kevlar to wood. Adrian has been in business for over twenty years and specialises in refits and restorations on all kinds of vessels, from steam launches to a 120 ft schooner. Adrian can turn his hand to any boat, but his heart lies in traditional vessels. He did a superb job in restoring the original *Kelpie* built in 1903, and if you gave him a similar project now, he will be your friend for life. He is currently busy restoring *Zaca A Te Moana*.

Adrian Stone Yacht Services
Cowes Yacht Haven
Cowes, Isle of Wight, PO31 7BD.
Tel: 01983 297898. Fax: 01983 280499.
E-mail: adrianstone.yachts@virgin.net

Harry Spencer & Mike McMillan

Mustang Sally

John Corby
a prolific race winning designer

Destined to follow in the wake of legendary yacht designers Sparkman & Stephens. John Corby started his own yacht design business in 1988 after having worked briefly for an established designer. Corby-designed yachts were an instant success right from the beginning, winning all the major trophies and, 13 years later, his designs, both old and new, continue to win all the silverware. John's talents also extend to boat-building although he only builds one of his designs, preferring to subcontract any others to reputable yards. He works closely with SP Technologies on structural design.

John's first design was **Waveplane** and her sister yacht **Skytrain** were launched for the 1989 season as two 27ft foam/glass yachts intended to race under CHS, but in retrospect they became the original sportsboat. Twelve years on, they are still winning but John's big break came in 1995 with the launch of the 36ft **Mustang Sally**. She swept the board during her first season with an impressive record of 33 wins out of 53 starts.

From then on, whether large or small, a Corby-designed stern has always been a familiar sight to fellow competitors. The 40ft **Cracklin' Rosie** launched in 1996 once again frightened all the competition by winning all the major events and was recently awarded Irish Yacht of the Year for the second time running. (3rd time for a Corby design). In 1997 the recently launched **Independent Bear** scooped all the trophies during Cowes week and after some updating, is still winning. **Incisor**, a 45ft design launched in 1998, once again collected all the prizes, continuing John's success. By 2000, John's designs had attracted sponsorship and Barlo Plastics Ltd were sufficiently impressed to back a new 41½ footer for Oyster Marine boss, Richard Matthews. Under the management of legendary skipper Harold Cudmore she proved to be another Corby Design winner. The yacht has since been sold to

Carphone Warehouse boss Charles Dunstone and renamed **Nokia Communicator**.

John's recent projects include a new 48ft Ocean Racer for Richard Matthews who had been so impressed with **Barlo Plastics**, and a production 33ft design to be built by fellow Cowes boat-builder Harley Racing Yachts. Corby-designed yachts' racing achievements make impressive reading and in the last two years, they have won over 14 major series all over the country. John is a futuristic innovative designer and is currently working on various keel designs for improved efficiency.

John has two children, but sailing and boats are his passion. He regularly participates in many yachting regattas all over the world.

Corby Boats
88 High Street, Cowes,
Isle of Wight PO31 7AW
Tel: 0044 (0) 7798 753962
www.johncorbyboats.com

Before she won the Fastnet and other honours at the America's Cup Jubilee, **Stealth**, owned by G. Agnelli, had been checked over at the Camper & Nicholsons yard.
Below: **Atlantide**

Leonardo Ferragamo and Luciano Scaramuccia

Camper & Nicholsons

One must differentiate between Camper & Nicholsons International, which is the brokerage company with offices in London, Monaco, Palm Beach etc, and Camper & Nicholsons Yachting Ltd, the historic yard in Gosport, which, since July 2001, has been owned by the Nautor Group, chaired by Leonardo Ferragamo. Chairman of Camper & Nicholsons Yachting Ltd is Luciano Scaramuccia, Managing Director of Nautor. The new owners want to re-establish the company as a major yachting influence and the focus at the yard is on custom yacht-building, major restoration and refits, while Nautor's Swan Service Centre has a separate repairs and commercial hit squad.

Mumby Road, Gosport, Hampshire PO12 1AH
Tel: 0239 2580221 Fax: 0239 2601145
E-mail:design@enyachts.co.uk www.enyachts.co.uk

A SPLENDID NEW BOOK!

**Camper & Nicholsons
Two Centuries of Yacht Building**
is an invaluable reference book on the history of yachting and describes the many remarkable achievements of the Nicholson family.

Boat Building & Restoration

England has always been a centre of excellence in boat building and restoration. Apart from Camper & Nicholsons, many other shipyards have a good reputation.

Britannia reborn

A full-scale replica of **Britannia** is to be built in the UK for the owner of the Fife ketch **Belle Aventure**. The new yacht, to be called **Harlequin**, is being designed by Dutch naval architects, Gerard Dijkstra and Partners, working from original drawings. Project managers Theo Rye and Steve Hammond intend to have the yacht available for charter in 2004.
E-mail:harlequinproject@cs.com.
Another replica of the famous Royal Yacht is being built in Russia by Norwegian Sigurd Coates. Cowes-based Mark Downer is overseeing the project and the yacht is due to be completed in 2003. She might be named **Maud**.
Find out more by telephoning 00 47 69 255575.

£30m yacht for US Tycoon

The Vosper Thornycroft Yard in Southampton is building a £30m yacht for US tycoon Joe Vittoria, a former chairman of the car rental firm Avis. **Mirabella V** will have a 295ft mainmast, a 1680 square metre mainsail and a keel weighing 150 tonnes. She will cost around £210,000 a week to charter.
Tel: 0238 0426000, Fax: 0238 0421539

The Maritime Workshop

This boatyard, situated in Gosport, has been building boats since the reign of George I and continues this long tradition. Run by Bill Puddle, the yard also undertakes construction and refit work using modern techniques. Recent projects have included the extensive rebuild of the late Sir Francis Chichester's **Gypsy Moth IV**, the ketch in which he made his epic voyage around the world. Other restorations include a pulling boat and a new upper deck for **HMS Warrior**, and a replica of Captain Bligh's launch. Extensive work has been carried out by the Company on **HMS Victory** and they have restored a 1911 Steam Pinnace, believed to be the only one in existence, for the Royal Naval Museum. The yard is fully equipped for restoration, refit work and construction of vessels up to 50 tons. A registered charity, it works closely with maritime heritage organisations.

50 Ferrol Road, Gosport Hants PO12 4UG
Tel: 0239 2527805 Fax: 0239 2586822

Hi-Tech Marine Industries

To most people, Cowes appears to be a bustling hive of nautical activity, particularly during the summer.
Beautiful people sailing beautiful yachts give the place an air of opulent fashionable affluence,
an atmosphere that has existed for over one hundred and fifty years.
During Cowes Week and other big regattas, the elite of the sailing world and spectators pack the little town to bursting point.
Hotels, shops and businesses have their best week of the year and barmen and waitresses can earn a fortune in tips.
In mid-winter, life in Cowes adopts a more sleepy tone, not quite hibernation, but a town earning a well-deserved rest after a
busy sailing season. The yachts are laid up and the Parade is almost empty apart from a few local dog walkers.
There is, however, a lesser-known side of Cowes that maintains a steady beat throughout the year, perhaps gaining tempo
during the peak weeks of summer. In all sorts of buildings in and around Cowes there are engineers, scientists, designers and
technicians, all involved in research and manufacturing advanced hi-tech products,
not just for the yachtsman but for all sorts of applications.

'PlayStation', record-breaking super cat fitted with
twenty LCM designed load cells and sensors to monitor
and control the rig.

Spinlock Fittings

Mooring line load monitoring and berthing systems are
part of Strainstall's complete service to port operators.

LCM Systems
Newport Road, Cowes
Isle of Wight PO31 8PB
Tel: 01983 299737
Fax: 01983 298283
Email:
info@lcmsystems.co.uk
www.lcmsystems.co.uk

Spinlock Ltd
Birmingham Road, Cowes
Isle of Wight PO31 7BH
Tel: 01983 295555
Fax: 01983 295542
E-Mail:
ProSupport@spinlock.co.uk
www.spinlock.co.uk

**Strainstall Engineering
Services Ltd**
Denmark Road, Cowes
Isle of Wight PO31 7TB
Tel: 01983 203600
Fax: 01983 291335
E-mail:
sales@strainstall.co.uk
www.strainstall.com

LCM Systems

LCM Systems specialise in the design and manufacture of load measurement and instrumentation systems, from the one-off load cell and simple analogue amplifier to a fully integrated microprocessor system. They have supplied load cells and electronics to a diverse range of customers, including many of the main OEM's in the process, offshore and safety fields. They lead the world in the manufacture of load cells for very demanding environmental conditions, where high integrity waterproofing and high reliability are essential. All the facilities are housed in their factory at Cowes, which includes calibration traceable to National Standards, up to 300 tonnes. Collaboration with external facilities also allows them to calibrate externally to 3000 tonnes.

Spinlock

For over thirty years, Spinlock has been a world leader in rope - holding equipment for every size of sailing yacht and dinghy. The company manufactures a wide range of systems for effective sail control and the company's products are widely seen, particularly on the racing circuit. There is an extensive range of equipment to suit all types of deck layout and applications. In fact, everything to fit out a yacht in terms of rigging hardware, including cleats, clutches and jammers, headsail furling controls, bullseyes, organisers, jammer blocks, tiller extensions, boom vangs, padeyes and rigging screws.

Spinlock rope holding systems are finding their way into an increasing number of applications in industry where new high strength ropes are providing innovative solutions.

Strainstall

Strainstall have been at the leading edge of load measurement and strain and stress determination for over 30 years.

In the marine environment, the company monitors mooring load and berth-management systems for jetties, single point mooring buoys and ship hull stress monitoring to classification rules. For industrial purposes, the company can design, supply and install crane-weighing equipment and overload protection. A team of experienced engineers is available to carry out on-site installation, testing and analysis for all disciplines of engineering - commissioning and calibration of Company systems.

The Company is both national and international, having bases in Bath, Aberdeen and Norway with agents throughout the world.

Vikoma
The Pollution Solvers

Vikoma International Ltd
Place Road, Cowes
Isle of Wight PO31 7AD
Tel: 01983 296021
Fax: 01983 299035

Sales Office:
Vikoma International Ltd
21/22 Britannia Chambers
Town Quay, Southampton
SO14 2AQ
Tel: 02380 828 900
Fax: 02380 211 644
E-Mail: sales@vikoma.com

Since the early 1970s, Vikoma International Ltd has been designing, developing and manufacturing oil containment and recovery systems. From its manufacturing base in Cowes, the company has supplied equipment and product training to over 160 countries worldwide. Vikoma can supply everything from small oil skimmers to complete sea-going craft and also provides small skimmers for use in industrial applications such as refineries. These skimmers can separate oil from water to 98% efficiency.

Vikoma International Ltd continues to develop, manufacture and supply products and services to marine and industrial sectors worldwide, to prevent and combat oil pollution. Today, the Company supplies turnkey projects consisting of complete packages designed to meet requirements laid down by International Maritime Organisations.

SP Systems

Composite
Engineering
Materials

SP Systems

Performance driven technology

In the 1980s there was a revolutionary change in boatbuilding techniques, as some builders moved from aluminium and conventional glass reinforced polyester to advanced composites, based on materials such as carbon fibres and epoxy resins. SP Systems, formed in the late 1970s on the Isle of Wight, was instrumental in driving this change with their development of advanced composite materials that could be used in standard boatyard facilities. The use of these materials for racing yachts, combining high strength with lighter weight, proved successful, and their usage has now spread throughout much of the marine industry. For example, SP's materials have been used for the construction of all the RNLI's rescue boats since 1989.

SP moved into purpose-built premises in May 1999, from where it headquarters its global business, employing over 300 people. The eight-acre site in Newport now houses most of its manufacturing work, research and development and operational activities. The Australian sales office opened in the late 1980s and an additional manufacturing plant, based in Albacete, Spain, opened in early 2001.

SP does not specialize solely in the marine industry, but has broadened its reach to include other areas that also rely on more advanced materials and processing technology. The principle markets in which SP is active include marine, wind energy and automotive.

The potential for composite materials is huge, as manufacturers try to develop structures that are stronger, lighter and higher in performance than ever before. SP believes its 'Integrated Materials Approach' is key to its success, and combines skills from three major areas: material science, structural design and process engineering. It is this approach that SP will carry into the future as it continues to provide its customers with what they have come to expect from the company - a commitment to the development of cost effective, high performance composite materials that will stand the test of time.

SP Systems, St Cross Business Park, Newport, Isle of Wight PO30 5WU
Tel: +44 (0) 1983 828000 Fax: + 44 (0) 1983 828100 Email: info@spsystems.com Web: www.spsystems.com

Recovery of a Boeing 747 - Kai Tak airport - Hong Kong

Inflatable buoy - Power Boat Race, Cowes

Photos Courtesy Seaflex

Photo Don French - Courtesy Seaflex

Water ballast bags load testing a bridge

Seaflex
The story behind the stories

Some of the more unusual projects undertaken by Cowes-based buoyancy specialists Seaflex have been sufficiently spectacular to make national - indeed, international - headlines. You cannot help but be impressed by its company literature. Seaflex projects are the stories behind the stories.

Remember the Boeing Jumbo that crashed in bad weather a few years back while attempting to land at Hong Kong's international airport? The aircraft overshot the runway and ploughed into the nearby harbour. There it sat, in shallow water, obstructing the flight path, until air lift bags were used to refloat, tow and moor the plane in a safe position. Those lift bags had been flown out from Heathrow, but originated from the Seaflex factory in Cowes. The order was taken at 3.35 pm. Less than four hours later, 304 tonnes of fully enclosed lift, bags packed on air freight pallets, was on its way. Seaflex prides itself on its ability to respond rapidly to large orders and customer 'specials'.

Just as newsworthy in 2001, though less hectic in the build-up, was the company's involvement in the raising of Donald Campbell's jet-powered *Bluebird* from Coniston Water, 34 years after the crash which turned an attempt on the world's water-speed record into a tragedy etched deep on the psyche of the British nation. *Bluebird* had to be brought up from its watery grave in a bed of silt 152 feet down. The salvage operation was filmed for a BBC television documentary. There was some controversy over the ethics of this - but no doubts at all about the expertise and equipment involved in the salvage operation. Once again, just beneath the headlines, were the specialists of Seaflex.

The man behind Seaflex Ltd is Mark Board, who first arrived in Cowes to sail, before launching a children's adventure holiday business called Venture Creek at Newtown. His next step was to save Seaflex - set up in the early 1980s by an experienced commercial diver - from closure, by purchasing it from the previous owner. Today, competition within this specialist field is restricted to just one other British company and another two in the USA.

Apart from the underwater buoyancy systems, the product list includes drogues and flexible fuel tanks, inflatable racing marks, flexible water tanks, fenders and the patented SeaSerpent system for floating submarine cables. A recent development has been the introduction of the Seaflex WaterLoad© range of water filled test weights up to 35t.

To quote its own publicity, the company has grown beyond recognition, becoming incorporated in 1987 and moving to its own spacious Cowes premises in 1996. However, the original concept of a safe, simple, economical product, well built and delivered on time, remains the principal objective.

As for the busy, yet always jovial, Mark Board himself, the objectives since he arrived at Cowes have not been confined to the development of his business. The town has good reason to be grateful for that - particularly for his leading rôles in rescuing Cowes Marina from collapse and in the development of Cowes Town Waterfront Trust, described elsewhere in this book. "We have achieved a lot, but we still need more facilities," he says, putting a breakwater and permanent pontoons to attract more and bigger boats at the top of his priority list. But what about the commercial side?

"Cowes should be better known for its hi-tech marine industries", is Mark Board's not entirely surprising response. "Some of the local companies such as BAE Systems, Vikoma, Spinlock, Westlands, Strainstall and ourselves have world reputations in our own fields of specialised products. There is nothing new about this Island excellence - in the past we've built the first hovercraft, the fastest racing yachts and the biggest flying boats - today we build the best radars, best buoyancy systems and grow better potatoes than Jersey Royals.'

The sign that hangs above his office desk declares: 'Hope for the best - prepare for the worst - hang on to what you've got - then get some more.' If that's the philosophy behind Mark Board's approach to life, it seems to have served him well.

Seaflex Ltd, Samuel White's, Medina Road, Cowes, Isle of Wight PO31 7RA
Tel: +44 (0) 1983 290525   Fax: +44 (0) 1983 295853   E-mail: info@aflex.co.uk   www.seaflex.co.uk

Nick Edwards

Alenia Marconi Systems
Radar Development at Cowes

The Isle of Wight has been at the forefront of radar innovation since its highest point, St Boniface Down, was chosen as a key location - the western-most when built - in the coastal chain of Radio Beacon Finding stations developed in great secrecy at the start of the Second World War. RAF Ventnor, as the station was formally known, was the forerunner of several other radar sites on the Island which played a vital rôle in the nation's defence against Nazi Germany. It was also an irresistible 'magnet' for the Luftwaffe, whose Stuka dive-bombers wreaked havoc at St Boniface in 1940.

Post-war radar development was initially in the hands of Decca, operating in the early 1960s from the former Somerton airfield just outside Cowes. In 1964, Plessey acquired the business, achieving considerable growth and establishing itself as a world-class supplier of heavy radar for both civil and military applications. Then, in 1989, the parent Plessey company was taken over jointly by GEC and Siemens, the Somerton operation subsequently trading under the Siemens Plessey Radar banner. Eight years later, the defence activity of Siemens Plessey was put up for sale and, after intense competition, was sold to British Aerospace in 1998.

Following a change of company name, the business then formed part of BAE SYSTEMS Combat and Radar Systems Division, which became part of Alenia Marconi Systems' joint venture between BAE SYSTEMS and Finmeccanica of Italy in December 2001.

Overall, AMS/BAE SYSTEMS is now the second largest defence contractor in the world, with home markets in the UK, USA, Saudi Arabia, France, Italy, Germany, Sweden, Canada and Australia, and many international markets beyond. It has more than 100,000 employees, working at some 100 sites, and generates a turnover in excess of £12 billion, with forward orders of more than three times that figure. Alenia Marconi Systems designs and produces radars for land-based air traffic control, meteorology, air defence, battlefield and naval applications, as well as a number of specialist radar systems. At the most recent count, total radar system deliveries to date had exceeded 1,000, of which well over 50 were three-dimensional, long-range air defence radars.

Cowes is an integral part of the picture. Most of the Royal Navy ships seen regularly in the Solent or in Portsmouth Harbour are equipped with radar made by BAE at the Cowes site. Similarly, the majority of Britain's airports and military airfields control their aircraft using Cowes-built systems.

AMS/BAE SYSTEMS' hi-tech operation at Cowes contributes significantly to the Isle of Wight economy. Nick Edwards is one of several senior managers who actually live on the Island. Like so many before - and since - he first came to Cowes 18 years ago to sail. The town made such a good impression on him that he decided to settle there. "A lovely place to be when you have a family," he says. Certainly more pleasant than when the Island played such a key rôle in the pioneering use of Radio Direction Finding back in the dark, battle-scarred days of the 1940s.

Alenia Marconi Systems
Newport Road, Cowes,
Isle of Wight, PO31 8PF.
Tel: 01983 294141. Fax: 01983 202326
www.amsjv.com

Rod Hillier.
Beken & Son

Where to shop
in
Cowes

An 18 carat gold Rolex watch or a humble Timex?
Designer outfits or a bargain T-shirt?
In the High Street the yachtsman can buy all he needs
from top quality oilskins down to a tiny shackle.
But the shops in Cowes are not just for the sailors.
Here is our selection of recommended retailers.

Photos © MCvA

For addresses
not included
in this book!

Andy Willard

Chandlers

Established in 1799 and believed to be the oldest chandlery in the world, **Pascall Atkey & Son** has everything for the yachtsman including a wide range of quality branded sailing clothes, general chandlery, safety equipment, charts, shoes, and code flags. The chandlery is owned by Brian Roberts and his German born wife Vera (tel. 292381).

Aquatogs, a fully stocked chandlery, also offers waterproofs, leisurewear, footwear and safety equipment. Retailers of the well known Helly Hansen brand of sailing wear (tel. 294949), the shop is part of the **Shipmates Group** which has other branches on the South Coast. (tel. 295071).

Sports Clothing

Most sports shops in Cowes obviously offer sailing and water sports clothing, wet suits, dry suits, oilskins, hats, bags and shoes, angling wear, life jackets, etc. Among the best sources of sporty clothing are **Henri-Lloyd** (see separate article in Skandia Cowes Week), **Ocean World** (see separate article in America's Cup Jubilee section), **Helly Hansen** at Aquatogs (see above) and **Slam-Lay Line** (see next column).

Marine Pool has clothes for all kinds of water sports (tel. 299940), **Musto** at **Shipmates** known for its safety kits, manufactures merchandise for GBR Challenge (tel. 292259), **Quba Sails** offers elegant sailing clothing and bags manufactured from recycled sail cloth (tel. 299004) **T&G Clothing** sells smart casual sailing wear (tel. 280077) and **Crew Clothing** not only sells sailing wear but also leisurewear for skiing and horse riding (tel. 280830). Last but not least, **Timberland** offers an extensive range of sailing shoes and boots (tel. 292161).

Ladies Wear

Artigiano has a wide range of elegant formal and informal day clothing for the fashion-conscious. (tel. 297773). **Bailey's of Cowes** stocks good 'every day' clothing (tel. 292592) while **Mantrap Ladies Boutique** can help you out for stylish clothing, including evening outfits - and this is also the place to bring your dry cleaning* or - if the seamstress is available - clothes for repair. (tel. 295813).

Beauty & Hairdressing

The best place is **Wavelength**, next to the Red Jet terminal, where they offer a wide range of services (tel. 200114). Otherwise, **Mahogany** in Gurnard Pines Holiday Village, is well-equipped (tel. 282520). For hairdressing only, **Jean's** (tel. 293102) has been around for more than 50 years (tel. 293102).

Ocean World Ltd

Official clothing supplier to most of the major events featured in this book, Ocean World also offers a worldwide embroidery and manufacturing service for crew clothing. Visit its website for details and see Skandia Life Cowes Week and America's Cup Jubilee sections in this book.

46 High Street, Cowes,
Isle of Wight, PO31 7RR
Tel: 01983 291744
Fax: 01983 297252
E-mail: info@oceanworld.co.uk
Website: www.oceanworld.co.uk

Slam-Lay Line Ltd

Founded in 1980 in Italy by a group of friends with a shared passion for sailing, Slam-Lay Line has developed an advanced technology fabric from which it produces waterproof, windproof, 'breathable' and thermal-regulating garments. Crew and corporate discounts are available on the company's wide range of fashionable sailing clothing and footwear.

3 Shooters Hill, Cowes
Isle of Wight, PO31 7BE
Tel: 01983 291141
Fax: 01983 291141
E-mail: slam_cowes@hotmail.com
Website: www.Slam.it.

Taxis

During the high season, finding a cab in Cowes can be a nightmare, they are few and far between - however, if you call **The Alfa Group** quoting this book, Roger Coombes will sort something out for you. (tel. 0800298 5421). Other friendly taxi firms include **Martin's Taxis** (tel. 281111), **Anywhere Taxis** (tel. 291711), **Island Limousines** (tel. 873979), **Gill's Taxis** (tel. 292678) or **Jones Taxi Service** in East Cowes. (tel. 282822 or Mike on 07971391525). **Amar Taxis** have a Rolls Royce for hire (tel. 520968).

For **Water Taxis**, call **Cowes Harbour Taxi** on 293952 or 07050344818, **Folly Ferry** on 07887725922 or **Sally Water Taxi** on 07831331717.

The Alpha Group

The Alpha Group, created by Ron Humphries - now a manager - has been progressively developed since 1997 by Roger Coombes. The group's taxis and small coaches are equipped with uniformed drivers. There are plans to introduce wheelchair-accessible cabs in 2002.

Freephone: 0800 298 5421
Tel: 01983 524616 Fax: 524616
E-mail: ail@thealphagroupiow.co.uk
Website: www.thealphagroupiow.co. uk

And Also...

Visit renowned marine jewellers, **Benzie of Cowes** (tel. 293932). **Flagstaff Antiques** which has some nice pieces for sale (tel. 200138) and **Kendall's Fine Art**, the best local gallery for marine art (tel. 281414). **Beken of Cowes** is of course *the* marine photographers'. (tel. 297311). Other good marine photographers are **Patrick Eden** (tel. 290366), **Christian Février** at **Bluegreen** run by Karren May (tel. 282233), **Yacht Shots** in Yarmouth (tel. 760444) and **Michael Dunkason** in Ryde (tel. 612129) You can have your films developed at **Beken & Son** off the Parade (tel. 297181) or by **Cowes Photographic (Kodak)*** in the High Street. (tel. 295680). **J.C.B. Imaging** in Freshwater will develop any film in a few hours. (tel. 756313).

Galerias Segui has a wide choice of kitchenware, pottery, paintings and all manner of gifts (tel. 292148).

For newspapers and magazines, **Morrells Newsagent** (tel. 292240) next to the Red Funnel terminal, opens early and closes late. On the parade, Mike Shea at **Tradewinds** will deliver (tel. 293448). At **Chivertons of Cowes** (tel. 292013) you can also play the National Lottery. If they are closed go to the Co-op which stays open late (tel. 281472).

Last but not least, if you are Catholic, **St Thomas of Canterbury** Catholic Church is right next to the Co-op (tel. 292739).

Good Food

If you want to eat on your own, Debbie at **Prime Food** will provide just about anything you need in the way of good food, with delicacies from all over the world (tel. 291111).

For fresh fish, go to **Phillips Fine Food** where the very helpful owner, James Dove, offers 40 years' experience. He supplies the best fish and seafood products imaginable from local fishermen, Scotland, France and further afield (tel. 282200). Here's a suggestion - how about a *Fruits de Mer* Restaurant in Cowes, serving fish and seafood fresh from the tank?

For fresh fruit and vegetables try **Dave Hill Greengrocers** in the High Street. It's the next best thing to shopping in an open market, which unfortunately does not exist in Cowes (tel. 290215)

*Anyone thinking of opening a business in Cowes, should consider a dry cleaning business, or perhaps another photo processing shop, for it is impossible to have clothes dry-cleaned in the town or an Advantix film developed within a single day. The latter apparently have to be sent to Newport or even as far as the mainland! Food for thought?

Cowes Business Association

Created in 1990 by Paul Bertie to attract more yachtsmen and visitors to Cowes, and to increase the prosperity of the town, the CBA has grown over the years, and has developed a series of projects to further its aims.

The Association draws revenue from the flagpole and banner sites in the High Street which they rent to sponsors. All income to spend on projects and interests of the Town! Cowes Business Association (CBA). Tel. 01983 280972

Andy Willard, CBA Chairman, has various businesses involved in outside catering and mobile canteens. He also runs the very successful Morrells Newsagent next to the Red Funnel passenger terminal.

Renting

Renting a property in Cowes can be expensive during regattas. Book your accommodation well in advance as the available properties go fairly quickly.

Letting agents

Linda Herbert   Tel. 01590 616216
Sarah Marshall   Tel. 01983 291369
Mrs D Gordon   Tel. 01983 293756
Carole Walker   Tel. 01983 280632
Kuki Waterstone   Tel. 01983 280060
Sally A Warwick   Tel. 01983 291919
Steven Caudle   *Marvins of Cowes*
        Tel. 01983 292114

Real Estate

Property on the Island is generally cheaper than on the mainland although any characterful old house in Cowes and the surrounding countryside is much sought-after. Prices are creeping up but a purchase could prove a sound investment especially as letting - particularly during Cowes Week - is very lucrative.

Several estate agents offer tempting properties and give valuable advice but **Waterside Properties** in the High Street has probably the biggest selection and the staff there are most helpful. (tel. 282222).

All Photos © MCvA

Left: Oliver & Mark at Mojac's
Below: Peter & Eileen Tibbetts

The Globe on The Parade

Brian & Fran Bracken of Murrays

John Bodley (right), Wendy Cragg, Manager, and the team at The Red Duster

Where to eat in Cowes

Cowes does not have a huge choice of restaurants, as the yacht clubs traditionally have always catered for all the yachtsmen's needs and this still continues. However, there are a few good establishments offering excellent food for hungry sailors and visitors alike. Away from the bustle of the High Street, gourmet cooking can also be found at several of the hotels including a substantial carvery at Villa Rothsay and delicious Châteaubriand at the New Holmwood. There are plenty of pubs for the gregarious with many of them offering live music on a regular basis and others where you can talk to fellow yachtsmen. All are packed during regattas, giving Cowes a carnival atmosphere.

Continental and Traditional English

Mojac's

Mojac's which opened in January 2000 and was named after Mark Baldwin's two children, Tom and Jack, boasts an elegant décor with stylish glassware and cutlery. Mark's previous experience includes the *Café Royal* and the *Auberge de France* in London. He also worked on the *QE2* where he was responsible for special orders. Mark concentrates on presentation in his cooking as well as interesting flavours. The restaurant offers a good selection of wines and there are 40 covers. It is run by a small team, which includes Penny, who manages, and Kate. Oliver acts as deputy. The menu includes delicious fresh-baked sardines, Tournedos Rossini and Raspberry Pavlova.

10a Shooters Hill   Tel: 01983 281118

Café Mozart

More than just somewhere for a bit of lunch, the Café Mozart is described as 'the café that thinks it's a restaurant'. It was originally opened in 1997 as an Austrian pâtisserie and restaurant. In 1999, Peter and Eileen Tibbetts purchased the property and, with their culinary expertise, gave the Mozart a little *je ne sais quoi* atmosphere. During the day, the Café Mozart offers quality home-made cakes, afternoon tea, and delicious light lunches of hot and cold specialities.

In the evening, it transforms into a restaurant serving fine wines and superb freshly-cooked seasonal foods. Peter has had over 30 years of experience working at the best London hotels under some of the great *chefs de cuisine*.

48 High Street   Tel: 01983 293681

The Globe

Owned by Chris Troup, the Globe has both excellent cuisine and outstanding panoramic views of the Solent. The sunny terrace is always packed during the summer season. Chris, a well-known businessman, also owns the popular **Anchor Inn**, and used to own the lovely **Bugle Inn** in Yarmouth.

The Parade   Tel: 01983 293005

Alexander's

Just a few steps away from the Royal London Yacht Club, this restaurant offers *crêpes* and pancake specialities, English and international cuisine with traditional ales and an extensive wine list. The candle-lit restaurant has an informal atmosphere and some spectacular views of the Solent. Owned by Alan Miller and his wife, the restaurant has considerable potential as a French brasserie which Cowes currently does not have. A menu could include some nice *choucroute, saucisson* and mouth-watering *plateaux de fruits de mer* and could have a lot of success.

The Parade   Tel: 01983 296246

Seafood

The Red Duster

This charming little restaurant gives the impression of being on board ship. English-born John Bodley used to teach catering and by coincidence came to Cowes where he took over the restaurant, with the aim of providing a good standard of cooking. His trademark is good, simple food using all fresh ingredients. Pâtisserie is a speciality, together with 'modern English' cuisine and seafood specialities. The menu includes the most delicious mussels. The restaurant is closed from Christmas to mid-March.

37 High Street   Tel: 01983 290311

Murrays

Originally opened by Murray Dixon in 1975, this well-established restaurant is now run by Brian (who acts as Chef) and Fran Bracken. Brian gained experience in several hotels and restaurants before venturing out on his own. He came to Cowes to sail and fell in love with the place so much that he decided to stay. The restaurant is open all year except for Christmas and the menus change regularly. Seafood is a speciality, including oysters, prawns, crabs and lobsters, supplied from Devon, Scotland and France. The 'Catch of the Day' is a feature of the menu and Brian believes in presenting his fish simply. A favourite sweet is the strawberry and champagne Mumm speciality ice cream.

106 High Street   Tel: 01983 296233

Photos © MCvA

Baan Thai

Manager
Tom Ramley and his
assistants Rachael
and Rowena
make sure that
everyone has a good
time at Rawlings.
Tel: 297507

Manée &
Russell
Spencer

Douglas
'Dougie'
Peterson
of
The Alamo,
and
Patrick
'Le Mex'
with dog
Mocca

Pubs

The Duke of York

The atmosphere in the Duke of York seems timeless but, with a well-stocked bar and a wide range of ales, this is definitely the place to swap stories of the sea. Owned by Barry and Sally Cass, it is famous for its Sunday lunches and extensive fish menu. It also offers good comfortable accommodation with 14 en-suite bedrooms.

Mill Hill Road
Tel: 01983 295171

The Pier View

Ideally placed for thirsty sailors in the High Street, the Pier View has a great atmosphere and is frequented by sailors and non-sailors alike. Run by Sue Wescomb since 1993, the Pier View offers excellent home-made burgers and seafood. It is very popular and often packed during regattas. Definitely the place to be seen in and to catch up with all the racing gossip!

25 High Street
Tel: 01983 294929

And also...

Among other well-frequented places in Cowes let us mention **The Anchor Inn** (tel. 292823), **The Fountain Hotel** which has a very popular terrace overlooking the Yacht Haven (tel. 292397), **The Waterside** with great views on the Solent(tel. 293269), and **Painters Arms** which is a hang-out for sailors. (tel. 297229).

Italian

Tonino's

The place to visit for a taste of Italy, Tonino's is the only Italian restaurant in Cowes. Owners Tonino Roscino and his wife fell in love with Cowes 22 years ago and acquired the restaurant, since when they have become a household name. Despite being located in Shooters Hill, at the top of the High Street, it is hard not to imagine that you are in Italy. The cuisine is a must for lovers of pasta, and the extensive menu will satisfy the most discerning Italian gastronome. Bed and breakfast accommodation is also available.

8 & 9 Shooters Hill
Tel: 01983 298464

Indian

Bahar Tandoori

Mohammed Abdul Bahar first came to Cowes on holiday and is of Bangladeshi origin. He liked the town enough to open a business with a partner in 1988. Bahar Tandoori was opened in March 1997, specialising in Balti food, cooked with spices bought by Mohammed himself. The restaurant is closed for Islamic holidays and it does not have a licence, but patrons are able to take their own wine or beer. The restaurant has some distinguished clientele (such as Sir Richard Branson) who find it friendly and enjoy the food. There are 95 covers on two floors and the restaurant is open until midnight.

44 High Street
Tel: 01983 200378

Thai

Baan Thai

As its name suggests, Thai cooking is a speciality that has made this restaurant famous throughout the yachting world. Owners Russell and Manée Spencer, from London and Bangkok respectively, established this excellent restaurant in 1989. Their reputation for quality cooking has spread like wildfire and many sailors and residents from all over the Island and mainland frequent the restaurant. Baan Thai takes you on an imaginary journey from Cowes to the Far East. The surroundings are relaxed, with a convivial atmosphere, and Manée and her Thai chefs cook all the delicious food to order. Evenings only, but lunch groups can be arranged. Booking advised.

10 Bath Road
Tel: 01983 291917

Mohammed Abdul
Bahar

Tex Mex

The Alamo

Born in Pennsylvania ("I left as soon as I could"), Douglas Peterson - 'Dougie' to his friends - lived in Texas, New York and London before he decided to move to Cowes, where he had been sailing. He opened The Alamo in 1998 with over forty shareholders, most of them friends from all over the world. Rumour has it that John Caulcutt, Robin, the owner of *Ciao Bella* and Patrick, alias 'Le Mex', are some of them. The Alamo is one of the most popular places in town and is almost always full with locals who have been very supportive. As you would expect, the cuisine definitely has an American flavour with steaks and burgers a speciality.

15 Shooters Hill
Tel: 01983 298754

Delicatessen

Prime Foods Ltd

Located in the High Street, opposite the Island Sailing Club, it is difficult to walk past this shop and not be attracted by its mouth-watering delicacies, a lot of which have been imported from all over the world. Debbie Phillips, the lovely and friendly proprietor, started the business four years ago and in that short time she has achieved a renowned reputation for fine cuisine. Her home-made sandwiches are coveted by sailors each breakfast and lunchtime.

62 High Street   Tel: 01983 291111

Debbie Phillips
with some of her
imported cheeses

Sally and Patrick, the Chef at the Salty Seadog

The Woodvale, Gurnard

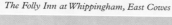

The Folly Inn at Whippingham, East Cowes

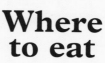

The Gibbs Family. The Crab & Lobster The Horseshoe Bay House & Café

Typical Island thatched house

Where to eat on the Isle of Wight

If you fancy a change from sailing and the sea, then it is well worth venturing inland and sampling some of the menus the Island has to offer. There are some good quality restaurants and quintessential English pubs with excellent ales all within a short taxi ride from Cowes. The pubs that abound are great places to eat, drink and relax after a day's exertions and each has a certain character. Listed here are just a few to whet your appetite.

Gurnard

The Salty Seadog
This restaurant, which has a grandstand view of the yacht racing start line, is directly on the Solent sea front. Originally called Sea Lights it has been renamed by Sally and John, who have enlarged it and created a barbecue terrace. Patrick, the Irish chef, offers a menu which includes lobster and crab from Bembridge, mackerel and sea bass from Cowes, and specialities which change according to the season.
31 Marsh Road   Tel: 01983 200330

The Bowsprit
Located on the seafront with views over the western Solent, this is a nice little place to enjoy lunch or a snack and watch all the action. The Bowsprit provides a good setting for a romantic dinner while watching the sunset. The restaurant specialises in traditional home-cooked food. Owners John and Judith Murray also offer delicious home-made cakes and desserts.
21 Princes Esplanade   Tel: 01983 291933

The Woodvale
With its spectacular waterfront location, the Woodvale is an ideal place to watch the sailing and the sunsets, while enjoying good food. Owners Doug and Sue Parkin are renowned for their hospitality. Live music is a regular feature and the pub offers good food and a wide selection of ales. (See Cowes Hotels section)
Princes Esplanade   Tel: 01983 292037

East Cowes

The Folly Inn, Whippingham
Situated in a rural setting upriver between Cowes and Newport, the Folly has long been a favourite with sailors. Conspicuous by the name INN painted on the roof, sailors and travellers have sought sanctuary in this hospitable establishment since 1783. Famous for its good food, the Folly also has moorings and showers available for visiting yachtsmen and can cater for clubs and rallies. Book well in advance!
Folly Lane, Whippingham   Tel: 01983 297171

Bembridge

The Priory Bay Hotel
This picturesque secluded hotel serves superb food in elegant Victorian surroundings. *The Priory Oyster*, near the beach is open in season only, specialises in a 'Catch of the Day' and is renowned for its seafood and barbecued lobster.
(See Hotels on the Island)
Tel: 01983 613146

Foxes
Classy stylish restaurant frequented by the sailing fraternity.
Tel: 01983 872626

The Crab & Lobster Inn
Specialising in seafood, with the accent on lobster, this excellent pub has such a reputation for food that people fly in just for lunch. The beach is down just a few steps and there are five en-suite rooms.
Tel: 01983 872244

Frank & Rosemary's
Recommended by *Les Routiers*, Frank & Rosemary's offers a warm welcome, excellent food and value for money.
Tel: 01983 872303

Bonchurch

Baywatch on the Beach
Open from mid-March, this is a nice place for fresh fish and seafood.
Tel: 01983 873259

Horseshoe Bay House and Café
With stunning views of the Channel and voted the best seaside location on the Island, the Horseshoe offers delicious lunches featuring freshly caught crab, lobster and grilled sardines. Famous for its cream teas.
(See Hotels on the Island)
Tel: 01983 856800

Seaview

Seaview Hotel & Restaurant
Excellent food, cooked by owner Nicola Hayward, considered by some to be the best on the Island.
(See Hotels on the Island)
Tel: 01983 612711

The Old Fort
Owned by Peter Hall, this nice pub and restaurant, overlooking the sea, specialises in fresh fish. Nice terrace.
Tel: 01983 612363

Ryde

Joe Daflo's
This popular wine bar serves good cuisine and has a huge selection of wines. Owned by Ian Whitehead, there is also a branch in Newport.
Tel: 01983 567047

White Hart, Havenstreet
Serves traditional English food that includes fresh garden vegetables and a good selection of real ales. Recommended by Ian Lallow.
Tel: 01983 883485

Ventnor

The Royal Hotel
A 'must' for the discerning gastronome, this splendid hotel is renowned for its excellent food and service.
(See Hotels on the Island)
Tel: 01983 852186

The Spyglass Inn
The pub, which has two lovely terraces overlooking the sea, offers fresh local crab and lobster among other dishes. It has a wide range of ales, and regular live music. It is part of the Gibbs Family Group which has several other pubs on the Island.
Tel: 01983 855338

The Red Lion

The Fat Cat on the Bay

Jo & Peter Green at Salty's

'Yellow Room' at Foxhills

Pavarotti's

Royal Essex Cottage

The Blacksmiths Arms, and Edgar Nieghorn, its popular Bavarian landlord

Freshwater
The Farringford

This lovely hotel with excellent food and beautiful surroundings is full of atmosphere and is a great place to dine and relive the days of Tennyson. (See Hotels on the Island)

Tel: 01983 752500

The Sandpipers Hotel

Excellent food is served at the **Fat Cat on the Bay** restaurant. Families and pets are made welcome and the hotel even has a qualified nurse for child care.

(See Hotels on the Island.)

Tel: 01983 758500

The Red Lion

This traditional English country pub with origins dating back to the 11th century is run by Michael Mence. It serves excellent food cooked by Lorna, the Head Chef, and is recommended by Egon Ronay. Michael's brother Myles is a famous local artist who regularly exhibits his work at the Royal Exchange Art Gallery. Myles lives very close and visits to his studio from the Red Lion can be arranged. Voted Isle of Wight Dining Pub of the Year in 1995, 1998 and 1999.

Tel: 01983 754925

Totland Bay
The Waterfront

Right on the water's edge, the Waterfront Bar and Bay View Restaurant are open every day during the season.

Evenings and week-ends only in the winter. The manager is Gareth Ashton.

Tel: 01983 756969

Shorwell
The Crown Inn

This attractive and popular country pub has a very pleasant garden with a stream, a spacious interior and excellent food.

Tel: 01983 740293

Shalfleet
The New Inn

Voted Isle of Wight Dining Pub of the Year 2002, this historic inn dating from 1743 is a 'must' for its fish dishes and the wide selection of wines. It also offers four real ales including the local brew *Ventnor Golden*. The owner is Martin Bullock.

Tel: 01983 531314

Yarmouth
The George Hotel

For a memorable meal, The George offers top quality cuisine in the restaurant, the attractive brasserie and the seafront garden. Definitely the place for gourmet cooking. Three rosettes in the AA guide 2000.

(See Hotels on the Island)

Tel: 01983 760331

Salty's

This lively and excellent fish restaurant located above a bar serving fish snacks, is right next to the Wightlink ferry terminal and the harbour. Recommended by Sir Donald Gosling and Bill Andrea-Jones, QC. Ask for 'Salty', the owner.

Tel: 01983 761550

The Wheatsheaf

Close to the ferry, this popular pub has a variety of dining areas including a large conservatory where families can dine.

Tel: 01983 760456

Shanklin
Foxhills

Foxhills is a gastronomic delight offering superb cuisine and wines. The small restaurant serves only 20 and offers exceptional value for money. Private parties of up to 12 people. Non-smoking.

(See Hotels on the Island)

Tel: 01983 862329

The Steamer Inn

This nautical pub on the Esplanade belongs to the Gibbs Group and serves good traditional dishes and fresh fish.

Tel: 01983 862641

Pavarotti's

With 164 dishes on the menu, this traditional Italian restaurant will spoil you for choice.

Tel: 01983 863528

Newchurch
The Pointer Inn

This traditional village pub, with excellent home cooking using fresh vegetables from their well-tended garden, is recommended by Ian Lallow.

Tel: 01983 865202

Godshill
The Royal Essex Cottage

This is a very popular restaurant with an excellent reputation. Open from Easter.

Tel: 01983 840232

Calbourne
The Blacksmith's Arms

Dating back to the 16th century, this pub was originally a blacksmith's workshop. In the 18th century it became a hunting lodge and was a staging post for smugglers who used this area to transport their contraband. Legends and myths abound and, even in the early 1960s, a former landlady was murdered. However, don't be put off by the spooky stories as you get such a warm welcome from Bavarian landlord Edgar Nieghorn and his wife Donna that this excellent pub's sinister past fades into insignificance.

The pub is unique in having this German atmosphere and has a wide selection of German draught and bottled beers. In fact it is believed to be the only British pub which offers all six genuine *Oktoberfest* beers, brewed in Munich specifically for the world-famous German Beer Festival. The pub's *Island Oktoberfest*, at the end of September, is a truly Germanic experience. Edgar and Donna revitalised the pub and offer excellent German cooking, including *sauerbraten*, *rinderrouladen* and *pork schnitzel*, all prepared by Donna. Delicious Mexican and English cooking is also served, and live folk music is featured regularly. Families are welcome.

The pub has won several awards, including the coveted CAMRA (Campaign for Real Ale) Island branch Pub of the Year award for 2001. For an evening of fun and for something just that bit different.

Tel: 01983 529263

Newport
The Bargeman's Rest

This famous nautically-themed pub is part of a group owned by Andrew, Neil and Stephanie Gibbs and Jane Simmonds, which includes **The Spyglass Inn** at Ventnor and **The Steamer Inn**, Shanklin. They all offer good traditional pub food. In May 2002 they will open a countryside pub at **Arreton Country Craft Village**, on the Sandown road from Newport (tel: 528353).

Tel: 01983 525828

Where to stay
in
Cowes

*Cowes and the Island have numerous hotels to suit all tastes and budgets.
Some offer distinguished Victorian comfort with modern facilities while others
provide a more informal, relaxed atmosphere.
In Cowes itself, **Villa Rothsay** and the **New Holmwood Hotel** give you the chance of a
perfect view of the sailing from the comfort of the lounge, without getting wet!*

Rawlings

Situated right in the heart of the old part of Cowes and owned by David Crowther, Rawlings is ideally placed close to shops and yachting facilities. It offers a friendly, convivial atmosphere. Live music, played by anyone who feels in the mood, is a frequent occurrence in the bar. As a result, spontaneous parties are the norm. Tom Ramley the manager recommends membership, as Rawlings is ideal for those party-goers who love a good night out. The hotel and bar stay open until 1 am or later for residents and members.

Tel: 01983 297507 Fax: 01983 297507

The Fountain Hotel

Owned by the Greene King brewery and managed by David Hill, the Fountain Hotel has 20 en-suite well-equipped bedrooms, a 60-seat restaurant serving good traditional food and a well-stocked bar. It is conveniently situated in central Cowes adjacent to the Red Funnel passenger ferry terminal. There is a nice terrace overlooking the Solent, very popular on sunny days!

Tel: 01983 292397. Fax: 01983 299554

The Woodvale
Gurnard

Perched on the Esplanade at Gurnard, near Cowes, this small hotel enjoys truly magnificent views across the Solent, a perfect place for those romantic evenings to watch the sun go down. The bedrooms are en-suite and breakfast can be served on the balcony in fine weather. Good food is served all day with an extensive menu and a wide range of ales. There is live entertainment on Friday and Saturday evenings.
A recently refurbished function room is available for that special occasion. The Woodvale, owned by Doug Parkin and Sue Brockwell, offers a relaxed, friendly atmosphere. Transport to and from the ferry terminal can be arranged.

Tel: 01983 292037 Fax: 01983 292037

Villa Rothsay

Built in 1873, the Villa Rothsay is an elegant Victorian hotel with magnificent views of the Solent. Sir Philip Hunloke, the sailing master for King George V on *Britannia*, spent his childhood at the Rothsay, where he acquired his taste for the sea watching the large yachts racing. The hotel was often frequented by the great personalities of the age. Edward VII so enjoyed his visit that he gave his name to the house through his title, the Duke of Rothsay.

Throughout the hotel, the Victorian period is evident, with original antiques and a distinctive architectural style supplemented with modern comforts. All the bedrooms have en-suite facilities and are individually decorated, with stunning sea views. Several are available with balconies. The Rothsay's drawing rooms are furnished with an interesting collection of maritime memorabilia, consisting of signed photographs, antiques and original paintings, and have a superb view of the Solent.

Owned since 1973 by a family partnership - April and Margaret Ankers and Miranda Courtney - Villa Rothsay is renowned for its superb food, specialising in local produce for its imaginative menus, cooked by Miranda and her team. Intimate dinners can be enjoyed in the Admiral's Room, which can seat eight people, providing an atmosphere similar to a large distinguished country house. Larger parties can be catered for and the hotel also has conference facilities available for up to twenty delegates.

Tel: 01983 295178/291568   Fax: 01983 290352
E-mail: margaret@villa-rothsay.co.uk

New Holmwood Hotel

Situated on the water's edge at Egypt Point and with unequalled panoramic views over the Solent, there is no better place than the New Holmwood to see the action. Originally built in 1832, it became a hotel in the late 1950s and has been enlarged with renovations and improvements ever since. The hotel owns two deep-water moorings for those who wish to anchor nearby, or a pre-booked courtesy car is available for arrival and departure at the Red Jet terminal and West Cowes Marina.

Proprietors David Titley and Sheena Lamont offer you a warm welcome and will make your stay a truly memorable one and, while the sailors are getting cold and wet, you can relax and spectate from the lounges and terraces.
The hotel restaurant enjoys superb Solent views and is open daily, offering both *table d'hôte* and *à la carte* menus. The lounges and terraces offer an extensive bar snack menu or simply a drink, whatever your preference. With a purpose-built function room, the hotel specialises in wedding receptions, conferences, dinner parties and corporate events.

Tel: 01983 292508   Fax: 01983 295020
E-Mail: nholmwdh@aol.com

Where to stay
on
the Isle of Wight

Familiarity does not so much breed contempt as dull acceptance.
It is all too easy to forget what treasures lie 'on the doorstep'.
In an uncertain age, it is perhaps time to rediscover the simple pleasures of British holidays.
Why not on the Isle of Wight, which reeks of nostalgia?
Away from main traffic routes, people still drive on the open road at 30 mph
and find the time - and the carefree opportunity - to walk their dogs. An outline of a duck or a tractor
on road signs warn of approaching rural 'hazards' while Island cafés still serve Prawns 'Marie Rose'.
Maybe it is time to recall memories of long summer holidays, when school did not seem to exist
and return to the Isle of Wight - to those happy days that stick in the mind.
Some hotels on the Island recapture the days of Victorian grandeur and will make it a short break to remember.

The Priory Bay Hotel
Seaview

The magnificent Priory Bay Hotel overlooking the eastern Solent takes its name from the 11th century St Helens Priory, which originally occupied the site. The Cluniac monks at the Priory enjoyed the revenues from the estate until the reign of Henry V, when all foreign religious orders were banished from England. Edward IV then granted the revenues to Eton College, a situation that prevailed until 1799, when the Priory was purchased by Sir Nash Grose, founder of the Grose-Smith family, who constructed a splendid mansion on the site. The family lived at the Priory until the late 1920s. The subsequent owner became a victim of a City financial crash and the Priory passed into the hands of an American lady - known as Mrs St George because of her fascination with the patron saint of England! Mrs St George made some fine improvements to both the house and the grounds, including the building of a swimming pool and other amenities. Although she had the front entrance porch built, it may well be of 14th century origin. Mrs St George acquired the porch in France and had it rebuilt at the Priory stone by stone.

Mrs St George died in 1938. The Priory was occupied by the military during the second World War and up until 1946. In 1981, Mr and Mrs Battle, of Yorkshire, bought it and used the buildings as a family hotel business until 1997, when it was sold to Andrew and James Palmer, owners of *Le Roussillon* Restaurant in London. The hotel then underwent major refurbishment until 1998, when it was reopened as the Priory Bay Hotel.

Nothing remains of the original building, but continuous modifications throughout the ages merge together to form a unique architectural style. Strolling round the hotel, there is evidence of the different periods of architecture. The farmhouse and the fireplace in the reception area are both Tudor, providing a pleasant contrast to the modifications undertaken by the Grose-Smiths and Mrs St George. The hotel offers a range of excellent food, served both in the restaurants and out on the terraces. The Priory Oyster Seafood Bar in the woods, just above the hotel's adjacent beach, specialises in *fruits de mer*, local crab and lobster. The hotel also has a 9-hole par 3 golf course, tennis courts and outdoor swimming pool. Cowes is 30 minutes' away by car (and five by helicopter)!

The Priory Bay Hotel, Seaview, Isle of Wight, PO34 5BU
Tel: 01983 613146   E-Mail: enquiries@priorybay.co.uk   www.priorybay.co.uk

Photo © MCvA

Jacki Everest
General Manager

John Illsley &
Jeremy Willcock

The George Hotel
Yarmouth

Set in the heart of historic Yarmouth, The George offers unparalleled views of the western Solent from its splendid location. Yarmouth has the distinction of being the oldest planned town and seaport in the Isle of Wight, having been constructed in the early years of the 12th century when the Island was ruled by the Normans. The town has had a turbulent history, having been burned down by the French at least twice, and was subject to all the fluctuations in fortune of a major port.

Throughout the centuries, The George, situated as it is, close to the harbour, has been pre-eminent. Although it did not become an inn until 1764, the building has been of significance since the very earliest days. In 1206 and 1214, King John stayed at Yarmouth in a house on Quay Street. It later became known as 'The King's House' and is where The George Hotel currently stands. In 1668, Admiral Sir Robert Holmes was appointed Governor of the Isle of Wight, with ambitions to transfer the seat of power to Yarmouth, as opposed to the traditional Carisbrooke Castle. Holmes, who wanted to live beside the sea, proceeded to build himself the handsome house which today functions as The George. The architectural style which distinguishes The George and makes it Yarmouth's most outstanding building owes much to Sir Christopher Wren and the return to a classical form which was becoming popular towards the end of the 17th century. There are several elegant houses of this type in the West Wight, all believed to have been constructed by a builder named Stephens who lived in Yarmouth. The Holmes family themselves lived in Yarmouth (at The George) until 1764 and a plaque on the front of the Town Hall is a memorial to the last of them, Thomas, Lord Holmes.

The first licensee of The George was John Wilson, who prospered as a publican and established it as one of the most popular inns in the town, a reputation which continues today. In 1894, the houses occupying what is now 'The Square' were demolished, thus opening up a view of Yarmouth Pier and the delightful gardens of the hotel. Three years later, during Queen Victoria's Diamond Jubilee, the name of The George was changed to the Pier Hotel. This was not popular with the locals and in the late 1920s it was changed back to The George, to the satisfaction of just about everybody in town.

Now owned by Jeremy Willcock and John Illsley, with Jacki Everest as General Manager, The George's reputation as one of the most popular hotels on the Island is helped by the expertise of Head Chef Kevin Mangeolles, a mæstro of the culinary art. In either of the two restaurants, you can be sure of a meal to remember. Since Kevin joined the hotel in 1996, it has been awarded three rosettes in the AA guide.

Jeremy and John also run the Master Builder's House Hotel (owned by Lord Montagu), in the New Forest, offering similar high standards of luxury and comfort.

The waterside garden at The George, with views of the yachtsman's playground that is Yarmouth Harbour, provides a stunning backdrop for a 'sundowner' while the traditionally-styled bedrooms - accessed by the unique four-abreast staircase - are all en-suite with modern facilities. The hotel owns a luxurious motor yacht *The Master George* that is available for charter in summer. In winter, roaring open fires and beautiful 18th century panelling in the lounges make a visit to The George definitely one to remember.

The George Hotel, Quay Street, Yarmouth, Isle of Wight, PO41 0PE
Tel: 01983 760331   Fax: 01983 760425   E-Mail: res@thegeorge.co.uk   www.thegeorge.co.uk

Photo © Alfred Dewing

The Chapel

The Royal Hotel
Ventnor

This imposing building was built 150 years ago as an inn to accommodate travellers who had come to Ventnor for the sake of their health, as the region is renowned for its fine climate. In 1833, the Royal Hotel - then called the Ventnor Hotel - was run by John Fisher. During Mr Keatly's ownership in 1844, Queen Victoria took refreshment before visiting nearby Steephill Castle. A succession of owners then followed, during which time the hotel was improved and enlarged. In late 1885 bankruptcy had forced the hotel into decline. In 1917 it was bought by the Home Counties Public Trust (later called Trust House Forte). By 1965, the hotel, still under the ownership of Trust House Forte, was offering sumptuous accommodation for 55 shillings (£2.75) a night. Ah, the good old days!

The decline of the Island railways had a detrimental effect on the hotel and visitors became fewer and fewer. The once splendid building was in a sad state when William Bailey, the current owner, set about restoring it to the magnificent hotel it is today. The Royal has regained its former Victorian grace and splendour and is now credited with having two AA rosettes for outstanding cuisine, plus various awards for quality and service. It is also the first hotel on the Isle of Wight to be awarded four stars from the AA. Alan Staley, the head chef, will serve you a meal to remember as each of his dishes are expertly prepared and beautifully presented. Small parties can be catered for, as well as large functions for up to 150 people. Conferences and banqueting services are also available, with several conference rooms suited for both large and small events.

The splendid views from the Royal provide a romantic spectacle from the rooms which are individually furnished, with modern facilities. Enjoy the superb cuisine, beautiful gardens and elegant décor.

Tel: 01983 852186   Fax: 01983 855395
E-Mail: royalhotel@zetnet.co.uk
www.royalhoteliow.co.uk

Swainston Manor
Calbourne

A short distance from Cowes, the Swainston Manor offers a secluded setting in 32 acres of unspoilt countryside steeped in history which stretches back to AD 735. During the reign of Edward I, the charter granting the Parish of Newtown to the Bishops of Winchester was served at Swainston. Through the ages, there has been a distinguished list of owners, including Richard, Earl of Warwick, George, Duke of Clarence, Sir Fitzwilliam Barrington and Sir John Simeon, who was described by Tennyson as a "Prince of Courtesy". Then living at Farringford, Freshwater, the great poet was a frequent visitor to Swainston and is reputed to have written part of *Maud*, his favourite poem, while sitting under the cedar tree in the garden. On Sir John Simeon's death in 1870, Tennyson composed a poem *In the garden at Swainston* as a tribute to his long-lasting friendship with him. The Simeon family continued to live at Swainston until 1941. The house suffered bombing during the war and subsequently became a school and a country club. In 1982, new owners, Fred and Margaret Woodward, bought the estate and set about the restoration. Through their efforts and determination, the hotel is now reminiscent of the splendid building it was in the days of the Simeons. Sadly, Fred recently died but Margaret continues to run Swainston Manor and maintains its excellent reputation as a high class hotel.

Adjoining the main building is a 12th century Bishop's Chapel that is ideal for marriage blessings, since Swainston Manor is licensed for the conduct of civil marriages.

Today, centrally-heated throughout, Swainston Manor offers high standards of comfort and hospitality while retaining the charm associated with a grand historical building. Beautifully appointed with superb amenities, Swainston provides all manner of recreational facilities, including horse-riding and swimming in a beautiful wall-painted indoor pool.

Tel: 01983 521121   Fax: 01983 521406
E-mail: hotel@swainstonmanor.freeserve.co.uk
www.hotelsiow.co.uk

Seaview
Hotel & Restaurant

The Seaview Hotel offers traditional Victorian seaside elegance and a relaxed atmosphere. Proprietors Nicholas and Nicola Hayward are proud of their hotel's deserved reputation for fine cuisine. Dining out at the Seaview is a memorable experience, where the restaurants offer a fine selection of seafood and other exotic specialities prepared by Nicola. One of the restaurants, has a collection of clocks, silver, paintings and gracious white linen, while the Sunshine Room features ship models. Before or after dinner, relax in either of the two bars: the main bar is in the style of a naval wardroom with pictures of hundreds of old warships and liners, plus memorabilia. The polished wood, brass-adorned public bar is decorated with all manner of nautical artefacts.

Tel: 01983 612711
Fax: 01983 613729
www.seaviewhotel.co.uk

Biskra Beach Hotel
Ryde

It was a great loss when, after the 'Good Hotel Guide 2001' had nominated it as one of the top 50 hotels in the UK, this simple but stylish hotel had to close. It offered views of the Solent, with lovely rooms and self-catering flats, friendly service and good food by chef Lisa Roberts. Managers Barbara Newman and Hamish Kinghorn were always welcoming. Hopefully this lovely hotel will soon be reopened.

17 St Thomas's Street, Ryde
Isle of Wight, PO33 2DL

FARRINGFORD
ISLE OF WIGHT

THE HOME OF TENNYSON

Come to the Isle of Wight:
Where, far from noise and smoke of town,
I watch the twilight falling brown
All round a careless-ordered garden
Close to the ridge of a noble down.
You'll have no scandal while you dine,
But honest talk and wholesome wine

Thus wrote Alfred Lord Tennyson from Farringford, his home in Freshwater Bay. What could better describe this perfect rural setting? As you approach Farringford with its beautiful grounds, you will appreciate why Alfred Lord Tennyson chose this immensely charming house as his home.

Farringford is set within 33 acres of parkland with uninterrupted views over some of the finest countryside in the UK and offers the perfect retreat for holidays or breaks throughout the year. Farringford has retained all its authentic charm enjoyed by the Poet Laureate, Alfred Lord Tennyson, but offers guests a traditional quality service with all the facilities and comforts expected from a renowned countryside hotel.

Soak up the atmosphere of Tennyson's original library where he sat and wrote many of his memorable works, beautifully restored, it now offers the perfect place to enjoy a quiet private moment.

The Drawing room commands superb views across the outstanding gardens and golf course. A perfect place to sip a sundowner on a glorious summer evening. The Bar offers a friendly and welcoming retreat after a long day exploring the West Wight's many secrets.

The en-suite bedrooms are stylishly decorated complete with splendid period furniture, many of which offer stunning countryside and sea views. The Downs Restaurant which benefits from views across to Afton Down and into the Bay is famous for its cuisine and service and has long been a favourite eating place for both residents and visitors of the Island.

The Hotel is licensed for civil marriages and can accommodate intimate parties and banquets for lunches, dinners or conference meetings. Whether you are with a party of friends, guests or on a company conference, Mr Kevin Gauvine, the respected Channel Island Chef will make your meal one to remember. Through his efforts, the Hotel awaits the coveted AA Rosette Dining award.

A Great Place to Relax

Not only is the Farringford renowned for its fine cuisine but it offers superb recreational facilities. It is the only hotel on the Island offering a nine hole Golf Course with no fees for the residents. To compliment it there is also a 9 hole putting course in the grounds and Freshwater Bay Golf Club provides an 18-hole course close to the Hotel. If you feel like a swim, then try the hotel's superb outdoor pool, which becomes a real suntrap for guests.

There is a Tennis court, a croquet lawn and a bowling green for those long summer days and the adjacent land offers stunning coastal and downland walks over National Trust conservation areas surrounding the Hotel. The famous Tennyson trail starts from the green gate at the edge of the grounds leading east across to Freshwater Bay and West to the Needles headland. Horse riding, fishing trips and cycling can also all be arranged. If the swim provides you with an appetite then try one of the excellent lunches at Shallots Bistro surrounding the Pool area.

The beautiful West Wight is an area of outstanding natural beauty protected by the National Trust and it is small wonder why Tennyson chose to spend a large part of his life there. Nearby is one of the Island's oldest ports, Yarmouth. Overlooked by Henry VIII's Castle, this quaint bustling port is steeped in history and local folklore. The ancient Military road runs along the south coast of the Island from Freshwater Bay and offers spectacular scenic views of the Channel and its many secluded beaches. Alum Bay and the Needles at the most Western tip of the island are famous landmarks while further inland offers quintessential English Villages and beautiful walks.

While you are enjoying your stay in this beautiful area it is all too easy to think of Tennyson and what inspired him to write some of his most famous works.

The present owner Lisa Hollyhead a chartered accountant by profession has made enormous improvements in recent years retaining the authentic charm so much enjoyed by the Tennysons. Enlisting the help of Mr Brian Kerr, General Manager, they are striving to sustain the highest possible levels of customer care and satisfaction.

Alfred Tennyson was born on August 6th 1809 at Somersby Lincolnshire. He was the fourth of twelve children of an alcoholic minister. In 1827 he followed his brothers to Trinity College Cambridge to escape from a troubled family background. In 1850 after the success of his "In Memorandum", he was established as the most popular poet of the Victorian era. After marrying Emily Sellwood in 1850, Alfred, his wife and their newly born son moved to Farringford. Alfred and Emily Tennyson had searched long and hard for their perfect home. Arriving at Farringford they were instantly attracted by its sweeping majestic drive flanked by mature trees leading to this most beautiful stately home.

It was just what they were looking for, somewhere peaceful with breathtaking scenery and secluded private grounds, just right for the inspiration needed for creative writing and bringing up his family. In a letter to Queen Victoria, Tennyson wrote, "We go no further, this must be our home". And so it was for almost 40 years.

In 1853 Disraeli and Gladstone offered him the title of Lord but he declined until Queen Victoria in 1883 insisted he accept it. He died after a long illness on October 6th 1892 at the age of 83 but the alluring charm of Farringford still lives on to captivate many visitors today.

Bedbury Lane, Freshwater Bay, Isle of Wight PO40 9PE
Telephone (01983) 752500, Fax (01983) 756515
E-Mail: enquiries@farringford.co.uk
Website www.farringford.co.uk

Foxhills is run by Paula and John Morton, who used to be a racing car designer.

Foxhills
Shanklin

A few minutes from Shanklin seaside, this late-Victorian honey-coloured building provides year-round facilities in a peaceful environment. Decorated in a contemporary style with eight en-suite bedrooms, comfortable lounge and airy garden rooms, the hotel offers health and beauty treatments. The sunny gardens are great on a warm summer afternoon. The small restaurant seats twenty and offers exceptional value for money.

Tel: 01983 862329
Fax: 01983 866666
E-Mail: foxhills@foxhillshotel.co.uk

Windcliffe Manor
Niton Undercliff, Ventnor

Run by David and Jean Heron, this is a lovely Victorian manor hotel offering spacious rooms, elegant décor, a swimming pool and delicious food prepared by the hotel's renowned chef, Graham Clow.

Tel/Fax: 01983 730215
E-mail: enquiries@windcliffe.co.uk

Horseshoe Bay
House & Cafe
Bonchurch, Ventnor

The Horseshoe Bay House and Café has a spectacular seaside location that has been voted best on the Island. Owned by Howard and Christine Smith, its atmosphere is relaxed and informal. The conservatory restaurant and patio are just feet from the water's edge and offer stunning views of the English Channel. Bedrooms all have panoramic views and are fully equipped.

Tel/Fax: 01983 856800
E-Mail: howard@horseshoebayhouse.com

Freshwater Bay

Freshwater Bay - which is within a designated Area of Outstanding Natural Beauty (AONB) - has fine coastal and countryside walks along the Tennyson Trail, secluded bays, rugged coastline and uncrowded sandy beaches. The Julia Margaret Cameron Photographic Museum (Dimbola Lodge) displays her famous Victorian photographs. The bay area offers all kinds of water sports and has an 18-hole golf course.

The Albion Hotel

Set within a stone's throw of the sea, The Albion Hotel enjoys a unique position and is steeped in four centuries of history. In the 1600s 'The Cabin' - one of the earliest parts of the building - was a local ale house for smugglers. By the late-1800s, during the reign of Queen Victoria, the 'Royal Albion' was proudly displaying the coveted 'By Appointment' crest. This is no longer the case. But even so, because of its its prime location the hotel could become one of the best on the Island. All the more so if it offered a thalassotherapy centre. The majority of the 40 bedrooms have their own balcony or terrace facing the bay, affording outstanding sea views. This also applies to the restaurant, where traditional food is served. The hotel offers a large indoor heated pool as well as a jacuzzi.

Tel: 01983 755755 Fax: 01983 755295

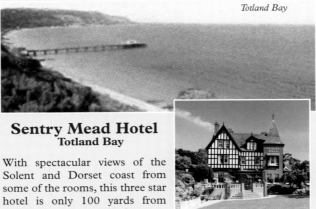

Totland Bay

Sentry Mead Hotel
Totland Bay

With spectacular views of the Solent and Dorset coast from some of the rooms, this three star hotel is only 100 yards from Totland's beach. All fourteen bedrooms are well appointed with modern en-suite bathrooms. The stylish dining room offers imaginative five-course dinner menus that combine the best of English cuisine, some European dishes and the hotel's own culinary flair, cooked by owner Julie Hodgson. The conservatory and terrace are great places to relax after your gourmet meal. Totland Bay is a popular bathing beach and attracts many visiting yachtsmen throughout the summer.

Tel/Fax: 01983 753212   E-Mail: brochure@sentry-mead.co.uk

Sandpipers Hotel

Sandpipers is run as an extension of the proprietors' own home, where you can relax knowing that you are being well looked after. Sandpipers was built in 1861 as a Victorian temperance hotel and named after the wetlands bird. In a sheltered spot just 50 yards from the waters' edge, it has excellent sea views from its Four-Poster en-suite bedrooms. Owned by Jay and Kelly Chapman, who are a local family who understand the needs of children, early teas, drinks and meal times to suit your itinerary. A qualified nursery nurse can be available on request to help you with your children should you want some time to yourself. After a day's exertions, you can relax in the 'Fat Cat Bar' or enjoy an exquisite meal in the restaurant 'Fat Cat On The Bay' set in a garden of fountains and ponds. They specialize in home-cooked Aga baked food, second to none - their Chef being renowned on the Island for his traditional dishes. They offer table d'hôte and à la carte menus, where 'homemade' really means 'homemade', including a traditional breakfast, to your room if you like. Freshwater Bay's 18-hole golf course is a short walk away, with discounts available for residents of the hotel. Water sports, riding, a walk in the Afton Nature Reserve or even hang-gliding can be arranged, nothing is a problem. Wave goodbye to the mainland and relax at Sandpipers.

Tel: 01983 758500
Fax: 01983 754364
Website: www.fatcattrading.co.uk

Norris Castle

East Dormers

The Gloster Hotel

Egypt House

Swainston Manor

Gatcombe House*

Quarr Abbey

William Mollart-Rogerson

William (Bill) Mollart-Rogerson grew up on the Isle of Wight. He left the Island to serve in the forces during the Second World War. He eventually retired to Cowes and began drawing churches and manor houses on the Island. He completed some 65 churches, manor houses and many other drawings, which reflect his love and appreciation for this beautiful English Island. His wife, Marie, who was born in Belgium, still lives in Cowes at Grantham Court and so does his sister Zoë Langford, at the family home, East Dormers.

Bill and Marie
Zoë and her brother

* HM King Juan Carlos of Spain stayed at Gatcombe House during the Jubilee

The Isle of Wight

The Isle of Wight has always attracted tourists, especially those with a passion for sailing. The Victorian façades of Ventnor and Ryde have been preserved, and the thatched cottages of Godshill and Shanklin restored. The landscape which once inspired poets and painters now attracts movie makers. In 2000 the Isle of Wight hit the headlines as the location for the new television series, *Reach for the Moon*, filmed exclusively on the Island. Film maker Anthony Minghella was born on here, which accounts for his Oscar acceptance speech for *The English Patient*, when he said "this is a great day for the Isle of Wight!" His passion for the Island was born from both the landscape and slower pace of life, and the warm welcome that the Island, with easy old-fashioned charm, extends to all. Film and Opera Director Ken Russell also admits to being "quite a fan of the Isle of Wight", after holidaying there as a child. "I loved the old paddle steamers and I used the last of them in my first film," he recollects. The Island is special as it is such a small area (23 miles long and 13 miles wide) and yet encompasses the best of England's landscape features. It has been described as "The Best of Britain in Bonsai". More than half the Island is recognized as an Area of Outstanding Natural Beauty, while much of the coastline with its fantastic beaches is designated Heritage Coast. Some 800 km of bridleways and footpaths can be explored and discovered on foot, bike or horseback. There are *Walking* and *Cycling Festivals* every year. The Island is home to numerous historical buildings and sites, many maintained and restored to their former glory by the National Trust and English Heritage. Around the varied coastline there are sandy bays, secluded coves and rockpools. Deep ravines known as 'chines' slash open the cliff faces. A Mecca for sailors, the Island hosts, in August, the internationally renowned *Skandia Life Cowes Week* as well as the international *Offshore Powerboat Race*. Visitors can enjoy water-skiing,

©*John Hinde (U.K.)*

Photos © Isle of Wight Tourism

bodyboarding, jetskiing, snorkeling, diving, canoeing, fishing, paragliding and hang-gliding. For golfers there are eight courses to choose from. The *Wight Air Extreme Sports Festival* is scheduled for October. The Island will also host one of the country's biggest music festivals - *The Isle of Wight Music Festival* - which will incorporate a varied range of music from Jazz, Blues, Rock and Pop, to Folk and World Music, in venues across the Island. The new attraction, *Dinosaur Isle*, is housed in a specially designed pterodactyl-inspired building in Sandown. Both entertaining and educational, it will interest visitors of all ages. Dinosaurs are just part of the interesting history of the Island; it teems with fossils and dinosaur remains, Roman villas, beautiful parks, gardens and Castles. *Carisbrooke*, where Charles I was imprisoned, is one of the most popular, and *Dimbola Lodge*, the home of photographer Julia Margaret Cameron, a close friend of Lord Tennyson, is also impressive. Other popular spots include the Castle at *Yarmouth* and *Brighstone* with its lovely wild scenery and thatched roofs. On the other side of the Island there is the Victorian town of Ryde and Queen Victoria's island home, *Osborne House* at East Cowes. *Sandown*, *Shanklin* and *Ventnor* are all popular beach holiday resorts. Private planes can land at Sandown Airport which is 40 minutes from Cowes. *Seaview* is a secluded village with many retired residents and a discreetly exclusive Yacht Club. *Bembridge* attracts an upmarket clientele because of its marina and airstrip. Ventnor air was considered the best in Britain for poorly lungs and the quarter-mile long Royal National Hospital for Diseases of the Chest once stood here. Thanks to the microclimate, winters are mild and the vegetation luxuriant. The Isle of Wight has a reputation as Britain's sunniest isle. Combined with its relaxed atmosphere and pace of life, it is not difficult to understand why it is such a popular summer destination.

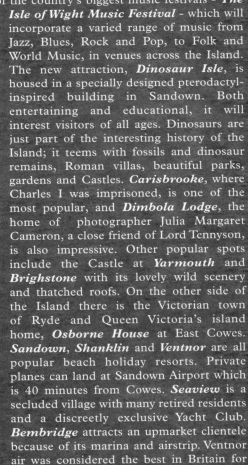

Thalassotherapy
by Hazel Knox-Johnston

There is enough seaweed on the Island...

Photo © MGvA

The Lodge & Spa

Photos Courtesy The Lodge & Spa

*'Thalassa' is the Greek word for sea water.
'Thalassotherapy' is a combination of the Greek words for sea and medical treatment.
First invented in England in the 17th century under the guidance of Doctor Floyer, the
practice of 'taking the waters' grew throughout the 18th century with the work of
Doctor Charles Russell, who wrote the first modern treaty on Thalassotherapy.
He believed that sea water, rich in algae and oligo-elements would assist
in the regeneration of the body. Today, Thalassotherapy is not only used
for medical purposes, but also for general health reasons.*

For those unfamiliar with Thalassotherapy, treatments involve the medical use of heated seawater to restore health and vitality. The theory behind the practice is that fresh sea water, when heated to a certain temperature, will open the pores and cause an exchange of minerals between the blood and the sea water. The benefits are well documented medically and the programmes available are devised and supervised by the spa doctor and his team. Not just anybody can open a Thalassotherapy centre to qualify as a member of the *Institut de Thalassothérapie*. The spa must have seawater pumped directly from the sea and not transported, a centre by the sea and medical supervision.

The centre is normally divided into private rooms with highly sophisticated equipment. These include baths, seawater jet showers, algae application, cryotherapy, pressotherapy, electrotherapy and marine bruminisation, a therapeutic heated seawater pool and all its particular attractions, a counter-current swimming area, waterfall, geyser, airspa, microbubble and underwater massage seats, neck showers, underwater jets, and an aquagymnastic area. Within the health complex there is often a fully equipped gym, hammam (steam room) and sauna. To promote health, well being and a sense of vitality, personal programmes are worked out by the medical team in accordance with the individual's needs.

*Hazel Knox-Johnston and her husband Michael
own the Lodge & Spa at Inchydoney Island, Clonakilty, in West Cork, Ireland.
It is the only official Thalassotherapy Centre in the UK and Ireland
which offers the best of both worlds - seawater health treatments,
as well as mouth-watering menus.
At The Lodge & Spa, guests really feel they have arrived in paradise...*

*Lodge & Spa
at Inchydoney Island*

The Lodge & Spa, Inchydoney Island, Clonakilty, West Cork, Ireland
Tel: +353 (0) 23 33143   Fax: +353 (0) 23 35229   www.inchydoneyisland.com

A superior room at Ston Easton Park; haute cuisine at von Essen hotels; luxury cars: Sue Plaisted, General Manager of New Park Manor; Nicholas Romano, Director of Operations, von Essen hotels; friendly staff and Brian Jarvis, General Manager at Thornbury Castle.

Andrew Onraet, architect in charge of developing the Spas and the Thorne Island Project

Each hotel in the **von Essen hotels** Private Collection has its own distinctive style and character, offering the highest standards of service, decor and charm.

von Essen hotels
A PRIVATE COLLECTION

Created in 1997 by Lord Davis and Countess Erika von Essen, von Essen hotels specialises in the care, restoration and operation of historic buildings as high quality country house hotels, and numbers in its portfolio properties which each offer particular interests. von Essen hotels' objective is to establish a collection of 20 hotels, each individual in character and providing uniformly high standards of service and on-site facilities from high quality fine dining in formal style to a more informal bistro style with a Mediterranean influence linked to the hotel leisure spa, as well as conference and function facilities discreetly located.

von Essen hotels is also upgrading the existing portfolio of properties. In each hotel, *Michaeljohn* of Mayfair, the well respected market leader in the beauty, hair and health spa business will provide high quality leisure facilities. Michaeljohn have recently launched their new Salonspa range, which will be available in all von Essen hotels spas in due course.

Ston Easton Park near Bath is a superb Palladian mansion set in classical parkland, on the edge of the Mendips.

Thornbury Castle near Bristol is a magnificent 16th century Tudor castle.

Congham Hall near Sandringham, Norfolk is an elegant mid-18th century Georgian manor house set in 30 acres.

New Park Manor at Brockenhurst, New Forest was once Charles II's favourite hunting lodge and is now a gracious country house, where fallow deer graze in the park.

Mount Somerset in Taunton nestles high on Stoke Hill, overlooking the beautiful Vale of Taunton, Somerset.

von Essen hotels recently bought **Bishopstrow House & Spa** at Warminster in Wiltshire which already operates the Ragdale Clinic, the only existing *Michaeljohn* Spa located in an English country house hotel.

Among future projects, **Thorne Island** off the Welsh coast will be the first contemporary von Essen hotel, decorated in association with the exclusive French House of Hermès.

©MCvA

Congham Hall was built in the mid-eighteenth century, an elegant Georgian Manor House which remained a private residence until 1982 when it was sympathetically transformed into one of the finest Country House Hotels. Nestling in thirty acres of parkland, finely manicured lawns, orchards and a renowned herb garden, Congham Hall has retained the rare luxury of a fine country house, where guests feel at home, enjoying a fine tradition of hospitality, excellent food and luxurious comfort.

In the Orangery restaurant a team of award-winning chefs creates imaginative dishes using a wide variety of fresh local produce. The famous Herb Garden is a traditional Victorian working kitchen garden with over 700 different varieties of herbs. An abundance of flowers, both fresh and dried, are grown for the House and in the preparation of unique pot-pourris.

The area has many places of interest within easy reach, such as Kings Lynn, Holkham Hall, Sandringham, Ely and Norwich as well as the beautiful unspoilt Norfolk coastline.

Elegant lounges and luxurious bedrooms offer peace and tranquillity in surroundings of fine antiques and paintings, with views out across the lawns and gardens beyond.
Fakenham and Newmarket race-courses are easy to reach, excellent golf is available locally and clay pigeon shoots can be arranged. Croquet, tennis and swimming are all available at Congham Hall.

©MCvA

STON EASTON PARK

Ston Easton Park is a Grade 1 listed Palladian mansion built in 1740 and is set in a classical Humphry Repton parkland, dating from 1793. Once the seat of the Hippisley family, it has been sympathetically restored to its former glory in the past 30 years to create a 20 bedroom hotel of great distinction. It also has a further 3 guest suites sited in separate buildings in the grounds. The estate has extensive woodland, river fishing and a kitchen garden.

In 1982, Ston Easton Park was opened as one of Europe's finest country house hotels evoking memories of a more leisured age, offering the elegant surroundings, friendly service and warm welcome one would associate with a magnificent private country house full of exquisite furnishings and paintings. The decorations are by Jean Monro, an authority on 18th century style. The award winning cuisine uses fresh vegetables from the Victorian kitchen garden. There is also a Georgian kitchen, complete with sparkling copper pans where guests can enjoy candlelit dinners. Some bedrooms have genuine four-poster beds, others coronet beds, all with enticing views of the landscaped gardens and the parkland beyond, where interesting historic features and some beautiful cedar trees can be seen. A *Michaeljohn* Spa is to open in the near future.

As one would expect in such a romantic setting, weddings are a speciality of the hotel. But whether for business or pleasure, Ston Easton is the perfect place to be. Ston Easton village is situated midway between Bath and the cathedral city of Wells.

NEW PARK MANOR

New Park Manor was a former and favourite hunting lodge of Charles II. It later became one of the principal residences of the New Forest. The hotel was extended some 20 years ago and now provides 24 bedrooms but the timeless beauty of its unique setting has been carefully preserved. Located in the centre of the New Forest the hotel stands in 200 acres of pasture, which also houses the New Forest Showground and Polo Fields and herds of fallow deer graze in the parkland. The Hotel also owns and operates an on-site equestrian centre and stables for 30 horses, providing riding into the forest, as well as croquet and tennis. Clay-pigeon shooting can be arranged.

The building, which is listed Grade II, was acquired in 1997 by **von Essen hotels**.

The 24 bedrooms offer everything from period four poster beds to cottage-style rooms with low beamed ceilings to the modern inspired look.

The elegant, panelled restaurant features a traditional log fireplace bearing the Coat of Arms of Charles II, where dishes with a classical influence are offered. Game and wild mushrooms from the surrounding Forest are special features. There are also two private Dining Rooms which cater for parties of almost any size, making them perfect for both family and corporate entertaining with a Conference Room that can cater for 150 people.

A *Michaeljohn* Spa, health and fitness suite is being developed and will include informal dining in the Orangery.

©MCvA

THORNBURY CASTLE

Thornbury Castle resonates with history. It dates from 1511 and is one of only two castles in England occupied as an hotel.

It was built by Edward Stafford, 3rd Duke of Buckingham, Constable of England who was accused of treason in 1521. His lands were confiscated and Thornbury Castle was appropriated by Henry VIII and retained as a royal demesne for 33 years. In 1535 Henry stayed at the Castle with Anne Boleyn. Mary Tudor also lived there and when she became Queen Mary I, she returned the Castle to the descendants of the late Duke in 1554.

It is today a magnificent first class hotel with roaring fires, delicious modern cuisine and sumptuous accommodation, where the wealth of the past is combined with the luxury and comfort of a modern hotel.

The restaurant has three dining rooms, which are baronial in style, with panelled walls, heraldic shields and large open fires.

The main apartments have large Tudor fire places, and spectacular views over the walled gardens. Many bedchambers have four-poster or coronet beds.

The Castle is licensed for civil weddings. For that extra special ceremony, the Summer House, located in the oldest Tudor gardens in England creates a memorable setting.

The Castle was acquired from Baron Taylor of Portlethen by **von Essen hotels** in 2000, since when the hotel has increased in capacity. Conference and business facilities were also added. A *Michaeljohn* Spa will soon include a separate bistro restaurant.

Thornbury Castle is ideally situated for exploring the West Country. Bath, the Cotswolds and South Wales.

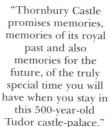

"Thornbury Castle promises memories, memories of its royal past and also memories for the future, of the truly special time you will have when you stay in this 500-year-old Tudor castle-palace."

The Mount Somerset

Mount Somerset Hotel stands high on the Blackdown Hills with unparalleled and unique views overlooking some of the most beautiful countryside in England.

It was built in Tudor times and an Italian architect was later commissioned to design the classical structure of a Regency country residence which has been carefully preserved and cherished, and complemented by fine antiques and soft furnishings.

A home more than a hotel, it is a place to relax and unwind. The landscaped gardens are home to exotic peacocks.

The bedrooms are furnished with style and rich in colour-co-ordinated fabrics and carpeting. Some of them have four-poster beds. Most of the spacious and luxurious en-suite bathrooms have whirlpool spa baths.

In the gracious, intimate Dining Room or the delightful Garden Room guests can enjoy imaginative, inspired dishes, created by a team of young enthusiastic chefs. The hotel provides facilities for business meetings, presentations, private dining and small wedding parties.

Located in the heart of the West Country, The Mount Somerset Hotel provides the ideal base for visiting the numerous places of interest throughout Somerset and Devon such as Taunton Racecourse, the historic town of Bath, Woodbury Park Golf and Country Club, Cheddar Gorge - home of Cheddar cheese, or the many celebrated cider makers.

©MCvA

Thorne Island

A romantic retreat on the Welsh coast, Thorne Island is set within the Pembrokeshire Coast National Park, adjoining a marine nature reserve, a third of a mile off the mainland.

The Castle, at the top of the island, will be converted into a hotel linked to the mainland by a cable car. It will be the first fully contemporary von Essen hotel designed by architect Andrew Onraet, decorated in association with the exclusive French House of Hermès. The resort will encompass a fabulous seawater spa run by *Michaeljohn* of London, a preview cinema with editing suite, a seafood restaurant hosted by a celebrity Chef and numerous facilities to provide relaxation and activities for all guests.

von Essen hotels
A PRIVATE COLLECTION

Congham Hall
*Grimston, King's Lynn,
Norfolk PE32 1AH
Tel: 01485 600250
Fax: 01485 601191
reception@conghamhallhotel.co.uk
www.conghamhallhotel.co.uk
An elegant mid-18th century Georgian
manor house set in 30 acres of
beautifully tended Norfolk parkland
and gardens.
OS 132 TF 712 229
N52° 46.8 E000° 31.9*

New Park Manor
*Lyndhurst Road, Brockenhurst,
New Forest, Hampshire SO42 7QH
Tel: 01590 623467
Fax: 01590 622268
enquiries@newparkmanorhotel.co.uk
www.newparkmanorhotel.co.uk
Once Charles II's favourite hunting lodge
and now a gracious New Forest country
house and equestrian centre, where herds
of fallow deer graze in the park.
OS 196 SU 295 045
N50° 50.3 W001° 34.9*

Thornbury Castle
*Thornbury, Nr Bristol,
South Gloucestershire BS35 1HH
Tel: 01454 281182
Fax: 01454 416188
info@thornburycastle.co.uk
www.thornburycastle.co.uk
A magnificent 16th century Tudor
palace castle in south Gloucestershire,
built by the Duke of Buckingham and
home to Mary Tudor for some years.
OS 172 ST 632 907
N51° 36.8 W002° 32.5*

The Mount Somerset
*Lower Henlade, Taunton,
Somerset TA3 5NB
Tel: 01823 442500
Fax: 01823 442900
info@mountsomersethotel.com
www.mountsomersethotel.com
A fine country house hotel nestling high
on Stoke Hill, overlooking the Vale of
Taunton, taking in some of Somerset's
finest countryside.
OS 193 ST 273 231
N50° 59.9 W003° 02.2*

Ston Easton Park
*Ston Easton, Nr Bath,
Somerset BA3 4DF
Tel: 01761 241631
Fax: 01761 241377
enquiry@stoneaston.co.uk
www.stoneaston.co.uk
A superb, Grade 1 listed Palladian
mansion set in classical parkland, on
the edge of the Mendips, close to the
city of Bath.
OS 183 ST 624 540
N51° 16.9 W002° 32.5*

Bishopstrow House & Spa
*Warminster, Nr Bath
Wiltshire BA12 9HH
Tel: 01985 212312
Fax: 01985 216769
enquiries@bishopstrow.co.uk
www.bishopstrow.co.uk
This quintessential English country
house near Stonehenge offers a private
river frontage and the Ragdale Spa
for complete relaxation.
OS 184 ST 898 443
N51° 11.8 W002° 08.9*

Helicopter services

For speed and convenience, arrive or depart in style using one of the von Essen hotels fleet of single or twin-engined unbadged helicopters. Each hotel has a heli-pad in the grounds. For business, pleasure or convenience, the reception at the hotel will arrange transfers to and from international and regional airports, private homes, company headquarters and other venues. Pleasure flights can also be arranged for a memorable view of sights otherwise never to be seen.

Luxury Cars

The hotel offers a selection of the most desirable classic cars in the world for you to drive - making for a very special experience: Aston Martins, Bentleys, Rolls-Royces, Jaguars, Ferraris and even a TVR and a Lotus to choose from.

Leisure Spas

In each of the von Essen hotels, *Michaeljohn* of Mayfair, the well respected market leader in the beauty, hair and health spa business will provide high quality leisure facilities including their recently launched Salonspa range.

admin@vonessenhotels.com   www.vonessenhotels.com

Thorne Island
*Angle, Pembroke,
Pembrokeshire SA71 5BE
Tel: 01646 641225
Fax: 01646 641448
admin@thornisland.co.uk
www.thornisland.co.uk
A romantic retreat on the Welsh coast,
adjoining a marine nature reserve.
OS 157 SM 846 038
N51° 41.0 W005° 06.9*

The America's Cup Jubilee

150th Anniversary
(1851–2001)
Cowes 2001

"From all over the world, a great armada of the finest yachts were planning their routes to Cowes, bringing back memories of the schooner America's famous victory, against all comers, 150 years ago."

Maldwin Drummond
Chairman
America's Cup Jubilee

The Old versus the New
1909 Owl
and 1996 Stealth

Photo © James Taylor

Photo: Michael Dunkason, Courtesy Paul Mason Gallery

The America's Cup Jubilee
Cowes 2001

Chance conversations often lead to great events. I was walking down Cowes High Street and bumped into Keith Beken of the world famous family of yachting photographers. Keith asked me what the Royal Yacht Squadron was going to do about the 150th anniversary of the America's Cup that would take place in August, 2001. We were then enjoying the summer of 1993 and I was the Commodore of the Royal Yacht Squadron. I felt bound to reply in a positive way, though the thought had never crossed my mind. "We will certainly consider the best way of marking the great event" I said brightly, as though I had been waiting for someone to ask the question.

Walking back to the Squadron's Castle of West Cowes, I remembered that the Club had occupied the Gloster Hotel, almost next door, in the magic year of 1851. Magic it was too, because the Prince Consort, Prince Albert, Queen Victoria's husband, had organised the Great Exhibition in that year, "where science, industry and art, the three hand maidens of progress", as they were then described, had been gathered from all over the world in the newly built Crystal Palace. America was to be represented by modem machinery devoted to agriculture, printing, and the art of the gunsmith, in the form of the Colt revolver, and in the medical field by an articulating artificial leg. Added to this was the schooner America, a development of the famed New York pilot boats, which was given the honour of showing how great was the skill of the United States in naval architecture, ship building, sail making and seamanship. American prowess was illustrated in a chromolithograph entitled "American Superiority at the World's Great Fair" with the yacht America taking pride of place in the centre. The schooner was ordered by a syndicate of six members of the New York Yacht Club, under the Commodore, John Cox Stevens.

I also remembered that the Royal Yacht Squadron was about to join with other yacht clubs in Newport to celebrate the sesquicentennial of the founding of the New York Yacht Club in 1994. Perhaps the Squadron could persuade the New York Yacht Club to cross burgees with us and join in a celebration of the 150th anniversary of the first America's Cup. After all, the Squadron had arranged the original race round the Isle of Wight,

accepting the challenge of the schooner America, proudly flying the New York Yacht Club burgee

I later discovered the schooner was the first American yacht to race in British waters and one of the first to come to Europe, that honour going to Cleopatra's Barge owned by George Crownin-shield, who visited the Mediterranean in 1817.

The New York Yacht Club sesquicentennial in the third week of July, 1994 was a great success. Charlie Leighton and Chip Loomis, Commodore and Vice Commodore of the New York Yacht Club, were keen to join with the Squadron in celebrating the 150th anniversary of the America's Cup. Furthermore, the New York Yacht Club showed the way by putting on a world class event. It soon became clear that if the America's Cup Jubilee was to be a success there was a great deal of planning and action required. Improved facilities would be needed in both Cowes and the Royal Squadron, for the Castle, for all its grand name and old stones, was beginning to feel crowded during Cowes Week, or when other big events were taking place. We also needed to bring aboard the Island - the Isle of Wight. So many events were organised without their participation. The time had come to change all this. The local authority, the Isle of Wight Council, was pleased and joined in the plans with enthusiasm and gave us our first grant. They realised that if the event was going to be the success we all hoped, it would be a great thing for the whole of the Island and not just for the port of Cowes.

Antony Matusch, the Chairman of the Regatta Committee, went backwards and forwards to New York. I particularly remember on one of my visits the enthusiasm that was developing amongst American yachtsmen, the foremost among these was Elizabeth Meyer who headed the J Class with her Endeavour, a past British Challenger for the America's Cup. Elizabeth was one of the first to promise support. With her energies, I knew we were well on the road to success. Bob Tideman of the American 12 Metre Association, who brought together all the old 12's and the America's Cup challengers in that Class, called a meeting at the New York Yacht Club. One member asked, "Do the committee realise that the third week in August will be in the middle of the school holidays?" "The school holidays! This is going to be the greatest event in the world" exclaimed Bob, "bring your children with you, they will remember the experience forevermore." That set the scene. Dr. John Bockstoce, the Arctic archaeologist and the first to sail his yacht from west to east through the Northwest Passage, became Chairman of the American side of the America's Cup Jubilee. Letters and e-mails flashed backwards and forwards. Super Servant III, the submersible floating dock that could carry fragile yachts across oceans, was chartered. Peter Nicholson, who had taken over as Commodore of the Squadron in 1996, made the best of every opportunity and pushed ahead with the plans for a new Pavilion at the Squadron. Antony Matusch visited yachting ports in the Mediterranean, for the plan was for the fleet to move southward and take in two September regattas. Entries flowed in.

The original concept of celebrating the 150th anniversary of August 22nd, 1851 with a race east-about round the Isle of Wight soon became a week of races. Sponsorship was a little slow, perhaps because large, high profile companies needed to be convinced the great event would grow to the size predicted by the America's Cup Jubilee team. However, Bruno Troublé of Louis Vuitton grasped the opportunity and brought Moët & Chandon, Hennessey and Phillips along too. Prada joined in enthusiastically, sponsoring the 12 - Metre World Championship that would be fought out during The Week, bringing 37 of the Class together, itself a world record. Australia II, the yacht that ended 132 years of American domination of the Cup in 1983, was among them. The Lexcen winged keel yacht was taken out of the Australian Maritime Museum, tuned and shipped to England for the event.

Excitement was building in Europe. Agnelli's black wonder Stealth would be coming along with Prada's Luna Rossa, victor of the Louis Vuitton Cup, who fought it out with Team New Zealand, the eventual winner of the America's Cup Series in 2000. Pride of place was awarded to the J's - Endeavour, Shamrock V, Velsheda and the near J, the 23 metre Cambria. They are the swans of the racing fleet, the embodiment of beauty afloat. However, it wasn't only boats that would be there, but world famous designer and helmsman Olin Stephens, Dennis Conner and seven other victorious America's Cup helmsmen promised to be in Cowes. The "Auld Mug", the America's Cup itself, was to be brought ashore with full Maori ceremony at 5.30 a.m. Lord and Lady Dunraven, whose ancestor challenged for the Cup in his Valkyries, promised to come over from Ireland. History was soon to be re-run for all to see. As if to emphasise this, the replica of the schooner America, built by the Shaeffer Brewing Company in the late 1960's, now owned by a Swiss charity, was to be with us, crowning the Jubilee.

In the final event, 184 competitors took part in the celebration, along with a number of large motor yachts, acting as tenders. All of these had to be fitted with great skill into Cowes' small harbour. The large, dark blue Herreshoff schooner, Mariette, the overall winner of the Concours d'Elégance, presented by Yachting World, for example, was tendered or looked after by the superb 1930's motor yacht Atlantide, both owned by Tom Perkins. The 250' Leander was anchored in the Roads, along with the new Jubilee Sailing Trust's square rigged Tenacious. Trinity House's ship Patricia, on which the Patron of the Regatta, Prince Philip, Duke of Edinburgh, stayed for the opening ceremony, lay on her buoy. Prince Philip's interest in Cowes and yacht racing goes back

to 1947. The British Royal Family have a long salt-water history. William IV declared The Royal Yacht Club an "institution of such national unity that it should henceforth be styled the Royal Yacht Squadron". The King graciously added that he would be pleased to consider himself the head of the Club. King Edward VII, when Prince of Wales was Commodore and later Admiral of the Squadron. This post was also held by King George V, Edward VIII, George VI and the Duke of Edinburgh. The crown in the center of the Squadron's burgee, therefore, is truly Royal. The Aga Khan's fast Shergar and the Danish Royal Yacht Dannebrog also decorated Cowes' Roads. They all added to the superb salt-water panorama.

Many members of the New York Yacht Club were aboard their chartered square rigger Sea Cloud II. On the other side of the main shipping channel, Black Watch, the Olsen Line cruise ship of 28,492 tons, acted as an hotel, providing much needed extra accommodation, as hotels and guest houses ashore were full to bursting.

A visitor, gazing down at the assembled 12-metres, preparing to race on a sun soaked morning, could not contain himself and exclaimed, bright eyed. "Look, look, here are all the yachts I have ever read about, famous names I thought I'd never see, all here in Cowes." Turning, his arm swept the horizon, "and more and more out there. It is a dream, just unforgettable".

So it was. Strong winds, wild sea and broken spars marked Sunday. Light breezes from Monday to Saturday and on Tuesday, for the UBS sponsored Race Around the Island, glorious sun, sparkling seas and sails stretching to the horizon. A fleet that will never be surpassed in beauty and reflected gleam, going eastabout, as America and the fleet had done 150 years before.

Sun and moon conspired together to take day into night at Queen Victoria's glorious Osborne, the grounds of which touch the sea. The outside of the House had been newly painted in its original colours and the grounds restored to their former glory, in time for the Jubilee Ball. A fine cabinet of Hennessy cognac, each bottle of the date of an America's Cup Race, 30 in all, was auctioned for $450,000, the proceeds going to the Royal National Lifeboat Institution, which is dedicated to saving life at sea around the British Isles and the Irish Republic. Two thousand two hundred diners, exhilarated then danced away the night.

America's victory in 1851, the America's Cup and Louis Vuitton series were magnificently celebrated. Her triumph not only started the America's Cup series but was the stimulus that began international competitive yacht racing all over the world. There was much for which to be thankful. The smiles paid tribute to this afloat and ashore, where sailors rubbed shoulders with those who perhaps had never felt the heave of the deck on a yacht under sail, but who loved just being there. They could join in the excitement and gaze for themselves at towering masts, taut and singing ropes and straining canvas.

Maldwin Drummond, Chairman
America's Cup Jubilee, Cowes 2001

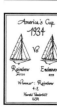

The America's Cup Saga
DEFENDERS & CHALLENGERS
1851-2000

Year	Winning Yacht (Syndicate Head)	Winning Yacht Club (Skipper)	Losing Yacht (Syndicate Head)	Losing Yacht Club (Skipper)
1851	**America** (John Stevens)	New York Yacht Club (C. Brown)	**Fleet of yacht**	Royal Yacht Squadron
1870 1-0	**Magic** (Franklin Osgood)	New York Yacht Club (A. Comstock)	**Cambria** (James Ashbury)	Royal Yacht Squadron (J. Tannock)
1871 4-1	**Columbia*** (Franklin Osgood)	New York Yacht Club (N. Comstock)	**Livonia** (James Ashbury)	Royal Harwich Yacht Club (J.R. Woods)
1876 2-0	**Madeline** (John Dickerson)	New York Yacht Club (J. Williams)	**Countess of Dufferin** (Major Charles Gifford)	Royal Canadian Yacht Club (J. E. Ellsworth)
1881 2-0	**Mischief** (Joseph Busk)	New York Yacht Club (N. Clock)	**Atalanta** (Capt. Alexander Cuthbert)	Bay of Quinte Yacht Club (A. Cuthbert)
1885 2-0	**Puritan** General Charles Paine	New York Yacht Club (A.J. Crocker)	**Genesta** (Sir Richard Sutton)	Royal Yacht Squadron (J. Carter)
1886 2-0	**Mayflower** General Charles Paine	New York Yacht Club (M. Stone)	**Galatea** (Lieut. William Henn)	Royal Northern Yacht Club (D. Bradford)
1887 2-0	**Volunteer** (General Charles Paine)	New York Yacht Club (H.C. Haff)	**Thistle** (James Bell)	Royal Clyde Yacht Club (J. Barr)
1893 3-0	**Vigilant** (Oliver Iselin)	New York Yacht Club (W Hansen)	**Valkyrie II** (Earl of Dunraven)	Royal Yacht Squadron (W. Cranfield)
1895 3-0	**Defender** (Oliver Iselin)	New York Yacht Club (H.C. Haff)	**Valkyrie III** (Earl of Dunraven)	Royal Ulster Yacht Club (W. Cranfield)
1899 3-0	**Columbia** (J Pierpont Morgan)	New York Yacht Club (Charlie Barr)	**Shamrock I** (Sir Thomas Lipton)	Royal Ulster Yacht Club (A. Hogarth)
1901 3-0	**Columbia** (J Pierpont Morgan)	New York Yacht Club (Charlie Barr)	**Shamrock II** (Sir Thomas Lipton)	Royal Ulster Yacht Club (E.A. Sycamore)
1903 3-0	**Reliance** (Oliver Iselin)	New York Yacht Club (Charlie Barr)	**Shamrock III** (Sir Thomas Lipton)	Royal Ulster Yacht Club (R. Wringe)
1920 3-2	**Resolute** (Henry Walters)	New York Yacht Club (Francis Adams)	**Shamrock IV** (Sir Thomas Lipton)	Royal Ulster Yacht Club (W. Burton)
1930 4-0	**Enterprise** (Harold "Mike" Vanderbilt)	New York Yacht Club (Harold "Mike" Vanderbilt)	**Shamrock V** (Sir Thomas Lipton)	Royal Ulster Yacht Club (N. Heard)
1934 4-2	**Rainbow** (Harold "Mike" Vanderbilt)	New York Yacht Club (Harold "Mike" Vanderbilt)	**Endeavour** (Sir T.O.M. Sopwith)	Royal Yacht Squadron (Sir T.O.M. Sopwith)
1937 4-0	**Ranger** (Harold "Mike" Vanderbilt)	New York Yacht Club (Harold "Mike" Vanderbilt)	**Endeavour II** (Sir T.O.M. Sopwith)	Royal Yacht Squadron (Sir T.O.M. Sopwith)
1958 4-0	**Columbia** (Briggs Cunningham)	New York Yacht Club (Briggs Cunningham)	**Sceptre** (Graham Mann)	Royal Yacht Squadron (Graham Mann)
1962 4-1	**Weatherly** (Henry Mercer)	New York Yacht Club (Emil "Bus" Mosbacher)	**Gretel** (Sir Frank Packer)	Royal Sydney Yacht Club (J. Sturrock)
1964 4-0	**Constellation** (Robert Bavier)	New York Yacht Club (R. Bavier/E. Ridder)	**Sovereign** (Tony Boyden)	Royal Thames Yacht Club (P. Scott)
1967 4-0	**Intrepid** (J. Burr Bartram)	New York Yacht Club (Emil "Bus" Mosbacher)	**Dame Pattie** (Emil Christensen)	Royal Sydney Yacht Club (J Sturrock)
1970 4-1	**Intrepid** (William Ficker)	New York Yacht Club (William Ficker)	**Gretel II** (Sir Frank Packer)	Royal Sydney Yacht Club (James Hardy)
1974 4-0	**Courageous** (Ted Hood)	New York Yacht Club (R. Bavier)	**Southern Cross** (Alan Bond)	Royal Perth Yacht Club (J. Cuneo)
1977 4-0	**Courageous** (Ted Turner)	New York Yacht Club (Ted Turner)	**Australia** (Alan Bond)	Sun City Yacht Club (Noel Robins)
1980 4-1	**Freedom** (Dennis Conner)	New York Yacht Club (Dennis Conner)	**Australia** (Alan Bond)	Royal Perth Yacht Club (James Hardy)
1983 4-3	**Australia II** (Alan Bond)	Royal Perth Yacht Club (John Bertrand)	**Liberty** (Dennis Conner)	New York Yacht Club (Dennis Conner)
1987 4-0	**Stars & Stripes** (Dennis Conner)	San Diego Yacht Club (Dennis Conner)	**Kookaburra III** (Kevin Parry)	Royal Perth Yacht Club (Iain Murray)
1988 2-0	**Stars & Stripes** (Dennis Conner)	San Diego Yacht Club (Dennis Conner)	**New Zealand** (Michael Fay)	Mercury Bay Boating Club (David Barnes)
1992 4-1	**America 3** (Bill Koch)	San Diego Yacht Club (Bill Koch)	**IL Moro de Venezia** (Raul Gardini)	Compagnia della Vela (Paul Cayard)
1995 5-0	**Team New Zealand** (Peter Blake)	RNZYS** (Russell Coutts)	**Young America** (Dennis Conner)	San Diego Yacht Club (Dennis Conner)
2000 5-0	**Team New Zealand** (Russell Coutts)	RNZYS** (R. Coutts/D. Barker)	**Prada** (Patrizio Bertelli)	Yacht Club Punta Ala (Francesco de Angelis)

*Sappho (Colonel William Douglas)   **Royal New Zealand Yacht Squadron

Labels courtesy of Hennessy

Back to Cowes
where it all began...

America crossing the finishing line off the Squadron, surrounded by a fleet of spectator craft.

Oil on canvas by Edward Holt. Courtesy of Geoff Banks, Mayor of Cowes.

Oil on canvas by Theodore Walker. Courtesy of Phillips Auctioneers.

*America
in 1851
on the Solent.*

What happened in 1851?

In the mid-19th century - at the peak of British domination of world trade - Queen Victoria's husband, Prince Albert, had the idea for a large exhibition of trade, commerce and inventions in London, and invited all nations to take part. The 'Great Exhibition' was opened by Queen Victoria on 1 May 1851, in what became known as the Crystal Palace. American industry, participating in the Great Exhibition decided to build a seagoing yacht faster than any vessel in America. She was designed by George Steers, at William Brown Shipyard, at a cost of $30,000, and named *America*. With her innovative and unusual design - 180 tons, 112ft LOA - a bluff bow, thin overhanging stern and racked back masts, she was meant to represent America's boat building skills at the Great Exhibition. In those days American ships had to be fast for speed was important for commerce and trade but also because of the slave trade - they had to be able to escape the patrols from the British warships. *America* was called "a rakish, piratical-looking boat", "a sparrow-hawk" - a violation of the old-established ideas of naval architecture with its low freeboard and concave bow sections. She had a small rig and mechanical-woven cotton sails - in contrast to the British sails which were made of flax, hand-woven and semi-porous to the wind. She was so fast that when she arrived at Cowes, from Le Havre, people thought she had a hidden propeller. All this made the old Marquis of Anglesey comment: "If she is right, then all of us are wrong." And she *was* right, and she won against all the British yachts, at a time when the British Navy dominated the seas of the world. On that famous August morning - 22 August 1851 - 15 yachts, 14 of them British, set off to race eastwards around the Isle of Wight for the Royal Yacht Squadron Cup, also called the 100 Guineas Cup. The historic race had arisen from a challenge made by the Royal Yacht Squadron to all nations of the world and *America* from the New York Yacht Club was the only yacht to take up the challenge. She won the race and the Royal Yacht Squadron Cup. The cup - made by

Queen Victoria congratulates John Cox Stevens, Commodore of the New York Yacht Club aboard the yacht America, winner of the 100 Guineas Cup - the event later to be known as the America's Cup

© Louis Vuitton Media Center

Garrards, the Royal jewellers - soon became known as the America's Cup, after the yacht which had won it. Queen Victoria witnessed the race and is reputed to have asked who had won. The yacht *America*, she was told "And who is second?" she asked. "There is no second, ma'am," was the reply and to this day that statement is said to encompass the competitive spirit of the America's Cup, where the winner takes all.

Of kings and grocers

The day after the yacht *America* won that first cup race in 1851, Queen Victoria and Prince Albert visited the winner and asked to go below deck. Captain Dick Brown asked the Prince to wipe his feet, saying: "I know who you are but you have to wipe your feet." It's a tradition that still remains today. For more than 30 years Sir Thomas Lipton - owner of the famous J-Class yacht, *Shamrock* - challenged for the America's Cup, losing every time. King Edward VII was guest on his yacht at Cowes, which made his nephew, Kaiser Wilhelm II of Germany, ask why he went boating with his grocer. When the King proposed Lipton for membership at the Royal Yacht Squadron, the application was turned down - tradesmen were not acceptable. When he did eventually become a member, at the age of 80, although privately pleased, he refused to set foot in the clubhouse.

Anecdotes

Money continues to rule the America's Cup. After the likes of the Vanderbilts, the Rockefellers, Packers from Australia, French Baron Marcel Bich, Americans Bus Mosbacher, Bill Koch and Ted Turner have been among some of the famous participants. Ted Turner is said to have "a temper and a vicious tongue. He tells dirty jokes and loves to speak Latin or Greek, quote Shakespeare and natter about the Civil War". The America's Cup remains a democratic contest in which anyone can challenge, provided they can pay for it... and accept having to wipe their feet! Since the start, the contest has baffled, amused and fascinated tycoons, sportsmen and the public alike.

The 'Auld Mug'
the fascination of the America's Cup

The trophy that celebrates one of the world's truly exhilarating sporting events is neither American nor a cup. It is, in fact, a sterling silver ewer and was made in London in the workshop of Garrard, the Crown Jeweller, in 1848.

After it was won by **America** in that historic Round-the-Island race of 1851, the trophy took the name of the winner and has been known since simply as the America's Cup. It was donated to the New York Yacht Club by the original winner in 1857, and remained for 132 years well protected under its glass case.

For 150 years, since those upstart American ex-colonials of the New York Yacht Club came to Cowes and beat the Royal Yacht Squadron on their home waters - in days when the British Empire was flourishing, Britannia ruled the waves and the Navy dominated the seas of the world - there has been determination to wrest the 'Auld Mug', as the America's Cup has been called, from them. For many years there were expensive challenges from England, sending yachts to America's East Coast aiming to wrest the trophy from its pedestal in the New York Yacht Club, but the expenditure was all to no avail and the trophy remained bolted down in New York, a sort of unobtainable 'Holy Grail' of yachting. In the 1930s the British challenge from T.O.M. Sopwith and the J-Class **Endeavour** came tantalisingly close and was followed excitedly in daily news bulletins in this country. The America's Cup has become the Formula 1 Grand Prix of the yachting world, with syndicates backed by millionaire businessmen spending tens of millions of dollars - and pounds - to come up with the ultimate boat and top-performing crew for the four-yearly challenge.

Photo © MCvA

Asprey & Garrard security guards.

Cup smashing
On 14 March 1996, independent Maori activist Benjamin Peri Nathan walked into the Trophy Room at the Royal New Zealand Yacht Club in Auckland. Before he could be restrained he repeatedly smashed the America's Cup with a sledgehammer, damaging it seriously. It was repaired by Asprey & Garrard, the original craftsmen, and returned to Auckland in even better condition. Since then tight security measures have been taken.

Photo: Asprey & Garrard.

The trophy has attracted the most glamorous personalities, amateurs and ruthless professionals in the sport, involving the biggest budgets of any sailing event, cheating and even legal chicanery. High society, big money, drama, insult, snobbery and controversy have always been part of the game.

In 1983 Alan Bond's **Australia II**, from the Royal Perth Yacht Club and skippered by John Bertrand, became the first non-US yacht to win the America's Cup, from US helmsman Dennis Conner, ending America's 132-year winning streak, and this victory has turned the contest into a hotly contested world-wide challenge.

The America's Cup is currently held by the Royal New Zealand Yacht Squadron and the next challenge for the America's Cup will take place in the waters of Auckland, New Zealand, in 2003. To win the right to challenge the holder, foreign clubs first race for the Louis Vuitton Trophy. The winner of this then challenges the holder of the cup (the defender). The final is a match race between the challenger and the defender, on the defender's home waters. The winner will then host the next America's Cup.

The cup itself is a 24-inch solid silver victorian ewer - wine server - crafted by Royal jeweller Garrards. The America's Cup was originally known as the 100 Guineas Cup. History doesn't tell us the origin of the epithet although one theory is that it was initially valued at 100 guineas, although it cost 100 sovereigns and not guineas. Another is that the winner received a purse of 100 guineas. It was purchased by the 1st Marquis of Anglesey who presented it to the Royal Yacht Squadron as a racing trophy. It has been written that the Americans had considered melting down the cup and having commemorative medals struck, but then decided to keep it.

On the plane from New Zealand to the United Kingdom, Peter Taylor, Commodore of the Royal New Zealand Yacht Squadron and his wife, Rita had to keep it on a seat between them, held in by a special safety belt, for the whole flight. In Cowes, after being exhibited in different places it was guarded overnight at Benzie Jewellers by security guards paid for by Asprey & Garrard.

Absolutely!

The Event of the Year
never seen before and never to be seen again

*The America's Cup Jubilee was born from a desire to celebrate the 150th anniversary
of the first race for the America's Cup,
an event often said to mark the start of international yacht racing.*

Two yacht clubs were involved in 1851 - the Royal Yacht Squadron at Cowes and the New York Yacht Club. Together these prestigious clubs envisaged a gathering of yachts and personalities, past and present, for a week of racing and celebrations at Cowes in August 2001. The Jubilee Regatta was to bring together sailors from those 48 clubs which had challenged for the America's Cup over the past 150 years, with classes for classic, vintage and modern racing yachts. The only stipulation was that the boats should be more than 40ft in length.

To transport some 100 yachts across the Atlantic, the New York Yacht Club had chartered a semi-submersible vessel. On arrival in the Solent, this was deliberately flooded and partially sunk to allow the fully-rigged yachts to sail off to their berths. Another freighter was chartered by the International Committee of the Mediterranean (CIM) to bring 11 classical boats (among them *Nyala*, *Luna Rossa*, *Partridge* and *Tuiga*) with their masts and rigging in place.

More than 30 clubs, from the USA, Britain, France, Italy, Spain, Switzerland, Australia and New Zealand, accepted the challenge with 208 yachts (201 actually participated) from 20 countries - spread over five classes - taking part in the America's Cup Jubilee. Average length of the boats was a staggering 72 feet: an overwhelming collection of majestic J-Class boats rubbed shoulders with beautiful 12-Metre and delightful old vintage boats, as well as state-of-the-art technology monster carbon-fibre yachts. It was a sight unlikely ever to be seen again, with the most spectacular yachts - owned by the richest and the most exciting personalities and captained by the most talented skippers - gathered together in the historic maritime centre of Cowes, the home of world yachting - watched by hundreds of spectator boats and photographers' RIBs. In the words of one of the organisers, Antony Matusch, it was "like having the history of yachting right before your eyes" - a regatta worthy of a Hollywood movie. Much was written about some "happy few" who attended the event and those who witnessed it will remember it for the rest of their lives. There were many moving moments

which made one spectator say: "the breathtaking sights brought gasps of wonder and sent shivers down my spine". Never again will such an unprecedented array of racing yachts be seen together - a fleet full of so much history, prestige and decorum assembled together for spectacular sailing and friendly competition, where Royals mixed with the world's business élite, united in their shared love of sailing.

Two hundred of the world's biggest and most valuable yachts were accommodated in Cowes Harbour for the Jubilee, in addition to the luxury superyachts brought along by rich owners as accommodation for the week and even a cruise ship, the Fred Olsen *Black Watch*, was there as a floating hotel. The New York Yacht Club had hired a tall ship, *Sea Cloud II*, to provide cabins for 150 Club members. As many yachts were too big to go on berths in the Yacht Haven or the river, special moorings had to be set up in the harbour by Harbour Master Capt. Stuart McIntosh and his team, with the help of Trinity House. Big motor yachts were moored in the Solent - Sir Donald Gosling's *Leander*, the Aga Khan's *Shergar*, *Dannebrog*, the Danish Royal yacht, Tom Perkin's *Atlantide* and the eye-catching Irvine Laidlaw's *Lady Christine*.

The J-Class yachts *Velsheda*, *Endeavour* and *Shamrock* and the 23-Metre *Cambria*, provided a great spectacle from the shore, moored off The Green at Cowes alongside beauties such as *Mariette* of 1915, *Mari-Cha* and *Rebecca* and the modern America's Cup Class racers, including the two GBR yachts, the Italian Prada *Luna Rossa*, *Team NZL 32* and *America 3*. The 37 12-Metre yachts were berthed in the Yacht Haven north basin, providing a once-in-a-lifetime spectacle for visitors who could admire the beautiful racing yachts from the pontoons and from the breakwater walkway alongside the yacht basin, where the magnificent three-masted *Adix* was moored.

"A bit like putting together a jigsaw," was how Captain McIntosh described planning where the yachts should be moored for the week. A tricky exercise indeed for the organisers.

*In the background, the cruise liner, **Black Watch***

Photo: Colin Kelly

Photo © Edmiston

Splendour of the Harbour
the most splendid yachts ...

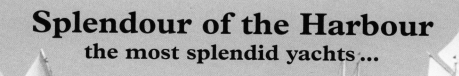

Photo: Colin Kelly

Photo: Colin Kelly

Photo: Colin Kelly

Tenacious

A spectacular ship in the Solent

Special moorings had to be provided

Sea Cloud and Black Night
Photo © Beken of Cowes

Atlantide
Photo © Beken of Cowes

Dannebrog
Photo © Beken of Cowes

Shergar
Photo © Beken of Cowes

Lady Christine
Photo © Kos

Leander
Photo:Colin Kelly

Main photo: Colin Kelly – West Island Group

The America's Cup Arrives in Cowes
accompanied by a 29-strong Maori Ngati Ranana

The America's Cup came back to Cowes - for only the second time in 150 years - at the Jubilee in August 2001 with an escort of Maori warriors. It had been flown from New Zealand - the current holders - with Peter Taylor, Commodore of the Royal New Zealand Yacht Squadron and his wife, Rike, who had to keep it on a seat between them, held in by a special safety belt, for the whole flight. In Cowes it was carried ashore at dawn to The Parade, surrounded by Maori warriors brandishing flares to light the way ashore.

The cup was escorted by Commodore Peter Taylor of the Royal New Zealand Yacht Squadron and senior members of Team New Zealand, led by head of syndicate, Tom Schnackenberg.

The 29-strong Maori Ngati Ranana performed a contemporary Maori challenge, or *Te Wero*, to Royal Yacht Squadron Commodore Peter Nicholson, Commodore Charles Dana of the New York Yacht Club and the flag officers, then carried the cup to the New Zealand Pavilion where it was displayed during the Jubilee.

Every night the cup was taken to the High Street premises of jewellers Benzie, where it was carefully guarded by security guards paid by Asprey & Garrard. The cup was displayed at many occasions in different places and it was, each time, replaced carefully in its wooden box for transportation.

Photo © Isle of Wight County Press

On The Parade
Opening ceremony in the presence of HRH The Duke of Edinburgh

Photo © Isle of Wight County Press

Photo © MCxA

Focal point for the Jubilee shoreside events was the tented village set up on The Parade, alongside the Royal Yacht Squadron, with a 70-metre landing - sponsored by Edmiston - specially constructed to provide a waterfront gateway to the village. The champagne opening and closing ceremonies and daily prizegivings were held in this cosmopolitan tented village HRH the Duke of Edinburgh joined the participants and a "Hall of Fame" line up from the America's Cup for the official opening ceremony, in the presence of HM the King of Spain, Juan Carlos II - who was continuing an old Spanish Royal Family tradition of racing at Cowes - Prince Henrik of Denmark, Consort to the Queen of Denmark, HSH the Aga Khan, Honorary President of the 12-Metre Association, Sir Donald Gosling, and hundreds of personalities, Commodores and members of yacht clubs from all over the world.

The final prizegiving and closing ceremony, another sparkling event glittering with an impressive collection of historic silverware, was carried out by HRH the Princess Royal, Princess Anne. It was an incredible and unique assemblage of Royalty, historic boats, sailors and titans of industry. At the heart of the action in Cowes was the Royal Yacht Squadron, the Club which started it all and originally presented the spectacular trophy. Thus it was only fitting that it should play host to the anniversary celebrations.

A brilliant and prestigious social programme saw Cowes put on its greatest and most glorious show since the 1930s in this "Mecca of World Yachting," with many dinners hosted in private Cowes yacht clubs and the fantastic Jubilee Ball, which was held at Osborne House.

Commodores and Clubs

It was the Royal Yacht Squadron which organised the racing during the Jubilee and this meant a busy time for Commodore Peter Nicholson and Rear Commodore, Dr Jeremy Cuddigan, principal race officer. Together with Commodore Dana of the New York Yacht Club they ensured that everything was shipshape to welcome the visitors.

Commodore Peter Nicholson

The Royal Yacht Squadron

The history of the Royal Yacht Squadron at Cowes - host of the America's Cup Jubilee 2001 and instigator of the first race in 1851 - is almost that of yacht racing itself. On 1 June 1815, a group of gentlemen met at the Thatched House Tavern in St James Street, London. They agreed to form a club, for those interested in salt-water yachting, to meet twice a year at London and Cowes. It was to be called The Yacht Club. This grew into the Royal Yacht Squadron - probably the most famous and exclusive yacht club in the world. During the reign of Queen Victoria the Club was a stronghold of exclusivity, not afraid to blackball Cabinet Ministers and Dukes. But at the same time it was establishing the rules of yacht racing and handicapping. It was the Royal Yacht Squadron which invited foreign yachts in 1851, to come to Cowes to compete for the 100 Guineas Cup and accepted an entry from the yacht *America*. She beat the local yachts and the rest, as they say, is history. The America's Cup was born. At that time there were only 18 yacht clubs in the world, almost all of them British. Britain's Navy dominated the world. The Royal Yacht Squadron, which occupies the old Cowes Castle site on the seafront, has always had a close relationship with the Royal Family and the Royal Navy. Kings and Princes have been an important part of the Squadron and its protocols. Many naval officers, from Commodores to Admirals, are members. Captain Scott flew the Squadron's burgee on his last ill-fated expedition to the South Pole and today the Club has round-the-world sailors, Olympic medallists, powerboat champions and ocean sailing experts as members. At the heart of the Club stands the Castle itself, with its lovely marine paintings and agreeable country house atmosphere.

Photo © New York Yacht Club

The New York Yacht Club

Commodore
Charles Dana III

The New York Yacht Club and its various Commodores were very involved in the organisation of the Jubilee since Maldwin Drummond's first visit in 1994 to the Club.

The story of the New York Yacht Club begins on 30 July 1844, when the New York industrialist John Cox Stevens invited eight friends aboard his yacht, *Gimcrack*. They decided to form a club, with the purpose of racing sailing boats, with Stevens as Commodore. It was the first club of its kind in the States. Several years later Stevens and some other members decided to build the yacht *America* and to transport her to England to take up the Royal Yacht Squadron's challenge to race around the Isle of Wight. *America* won the race and in 1857 Stevens and the *America* syndicate decided to donate the cup - called the America's Cup in honour of the yacht - to the New York Yacht Club. Boats flying the Club's burgee successfully defended the America's Cup for 132 years, until it was taken from them in 1983 by the Perth-based *Australia II*. During that time New York Yacht Club boats won 81 of 93 races. The NYYC also has a long history in offshore racing and has organised many transatlantic races. In 2003 the Club will be represented at the America's Cup as a challenging club by Dennis Conner and his *Stars and Stripes* team.

Charles Dana III

Charles Dana met up with Maldwin Drummond in New York in 1994, at the celebrations to mark his Club's 150th Anniversary. Charlie Leighton was then the Commodore of the New York Yacht Club. The Jubilee was discussed at this time but work really started in 1997. It was vital to convince members of various yacht clubs to make the trip across the Atlantic to Cowes in 2001 and it was the task of the New York Yacht Club to organise the transport of some 100 yachts from New York. "The Jubilee was the best thing ever done in history and was organised fantastically well, from the sailing and the social point of view," said Commodore Dana. "We had the great ball at Osborne House and the parties in the clubs, along with fantastic yachts such as *Leander* and *Atlantide*." During the Jubilee Week, Charles Dana managed to fit in some sailing and stayed aboard *Black Night*, the yacht on which America's Cup helmsman Dennis Conner, who heads the current New York Yacht Club *Stars and Stripes* challenge, also stayed. Commodore Dana lives at Newport, Rhode Island, where he owns what he described as the last shipyard in the city - where boats of up to 500 feet are built. Dana loves sailing and is involved in a lot of charity work. His great aim is to bring the America's Cup back to the USA. He is also looking forward to the next Transatlantic Challenge.

*The next Transatlantic Challenge sponsored by Rolex, is being organised by the New York Yacht Club with the Royal Yacht Squadron. It was going to set off from New York on May 18, 2002 and finish off The Needles, Isle of Wight, around two weeks later. For the occasion the Royal Yacht Squadron had planned to charter **Eleonora**, a replica of the 1909 Nat Herreshoff-designed **Westward**, famous for her tradition of racing against the Royal Yacht **Britannia**. Because of the events of 11th of September it has been postponed till 2005.*

The Challenge was first organised many years ago and a gold cup was offered by the Kaiser of Germany. However, he imposed one condition - the Challenge was never to finish at Cowes. However, some years later it was discovered that the cup was not real gold, so the Kaiser's wishes no longer had to be respected and the Challenge could finish at the Isle of Wight!

*H.M. The Lord Lieutenant
Christopher Bland*

Photo © Michael Dunkason

Maldwin Drummond

Photo ©MCxA

Antony Matusch and Nigel Croney in 1999

Dr. Jeremy Cuddigan

The Organisers

The America's Cup Jubilee celebrations were the culmination of seven years' planning for the core group of hard-working organisers, on both sides of the Atlantic, with co-operation between the Royal Yacht Squadron at Cowes and the New York Yacht Club. They formed Cowes 2001 Ltd., the company responsible for organising the event, chaired by Maldwin Drummond.

Maldwin Drummond

OBE, JP, DL, Hon.DSc.
Chairman of Cowes 2001

Among the many people involved in making the Jubilee happen were Maldwin Drummond, former Commodore and the then Commodore Peter Nicholson of the Royal Yacht Squadron; Charles Dana III, Commodore of the New York Yacht Club; Antony Matusch, Chairman of the America's Cup Jubilee Regatta Committee; Dr Jeremy Cuddigan, Rear Commodore of the Royal Yacht Squadron, and Chairman of the Jubilee Race Committee; Geoff Banks, Mayor of Cowes; Capt Stuart McIntosh, Cowes Harbour Master; Felix Hetherington, Cowes Harbour Commission Chairman; Morris Barton, former leader of the Isle of Wight Council; John Power, Chairman of Cowes Yachting; Paul Bertie, Managing Director of Ocean World, Nigel Croney of Mumm Champagne, and Tim Jones, Chief Executive of the Jubilee.

Maldwin Drummond recalls how veteran Cowes photographer Keith Beken reminded him, in 1993, about the approaching 150th anniversary of the America's Cup. At that time Mr Drummond was Commodore of the Royal Yacht Squadron and his reply was: "We must certainly do something to celebrate that." So when he went to New York in 1994, to celebrate the 150th anniversary of the New York Yacht Club, he suggested that the clubs work together for a joint celebration in 2001. A committee was formed and work started. It was not easy to convince people and get everyone's approval but slowly individuals and associations became involved - the Royal Yachting Association, Cowes Combined Clubs, many volunteers and the Isle of Wight Council, which put in the cash to get things started. It was also necessary to find high-profile sponsors: the LVMH Group (Louis Vuitton Moët Hennessy), Prada and Jour J were very helpful here. "Today, everyone is happy and proud of the event, which was extremely successful and brought great publicity to Cowes and the Isle of Wight. It will be a good example for future events."

Maldwin Drummond lives in Hampshire and has written several books about the sea. His latest, "The Book of the Solent", edited by Maldwin, with respected coastal expert Robin McInnes, was published just before the Jubilee. It contains informed articles on every aspect of land and seascape in the Solent area. This important book costs £26. To order, telephone +44 (0) 1983 854865 (evenings).

Antony Matusch

Chairman of the America's Cup Jubilee Regatta Committee

We first talked to Antony Matusch over a drink with our late friend Ian Cullerne-Bown, in 1999, on the roof deck of Patrick and Lindsay Chisholm's house, high on the hill overlooking the busy harbour. Antony Matusch, who had completed his term as Royal Yacht Squadron Flag Officer, Rear Commodore Yachting, was Chairman of the Organising Committee for the Jubilee Regatta, which celebrated the 150th anniversary of Queen Victoria's Great Exhibition, organised by her consort, Prince Albert, and the 150th anniversary of the first America's Cup race. His task was to oversee arrangements for the sailing and facilities for the visitors to provide faultless and enjoyable racing.

Geoff Banks

Mayor of Cowes
Chairman of the
Shoreside Facilities Committee

Geoff Banks was a member of Cowes 2001 for several years in the run-up to the big event, which he says proved to be such a brilliant week for the nautical town. Beforehand, some people had been a bit apprehensive about the scale of the event and how it would work. But everyone was delighted with the eventual success. His only regret was the poor national press coverage which the Jubilee received in Britain compared with the interest worldwide. Geoff Banks is a building consultant and contractor who specialises in renovating old properties. His dream would be to build a Maritime Heritage Centre in Cowes.

Tim Jones

Geoff Banks

Photo © MCvA

Felix Hetherington

Photo © Claridge & Claridge

Captain Stuart McIntosh

Photo © Claridge & Claridge

Morris Barton

Photo © Isle of Wight Council

Philip Thwaites

Paul Bertie

Photo © MCvA

John Power

Photo © MCvA

The Jubilee Committees

Quite a few other organisations and individuals played key roles in making the Jubilee Regatta such a success. *Felix Hetherington*, Chairman of Cowes Harbour Commission, chaired the General Purposes Committee, which was responsible for on-shore arrangements, including the prestigious opening and closing ceremonies with their Royal connections. *John Power*, Chairman of Cowes Yachting, oversaw the Jubilee's Education Programme*, which saw schoolchildren involved in the event with a chance to learn about the Island's rich yachting tradition. Cowes Harbour Master, *Capt. Stuart McIntosh*, chaired the Harbour Facilities Committee and had the task of overseeing arrangements on the water for the hundreds of valuable visiting yachts, their support boats and the superyachts - including Sir Donald Gosling's 247ft **Leander**, the Aga Khan's **Shergar**, the Danish Royal yacht **Dannebrog** as well as the cruise liner **Black Watch** and New York Yacht Club's imposing charter, **Sea Cloud II** - which provided floating accommodation for the week. *Paul Bertie*, a Cowes Town Councillor and local business-man, was Chairman of the Jubilee Village and former Isle of Wight Council Leader, *Morris Barton*, was also a key figure in the planning. *Nigel Croney* of Champagne Mumm, was in charge of Marketing and Sponsorship. Useful information on the America's Cup Jubilee was provided in the Cowes Port Handbook and the associated Cowes website - www.cowes.co.uk - put together by Cowes Harbour and Marinas Managing Director, *Philip Thwaites*. This gave details of all the local services and facilities, enabling visitors worldwide to plan and make the best of their time in Cowes.

Tim Jones
Chief Executive of
the America's Cup Jubilee

Tim Jones and his very efficient team were busy for months before and after the Jubilee, co-ordinating the great efforts of the different bodies involved, dealing with all sorts of administrative work, such as book-keeping, security measures, sending out information to participants, and putting together programmes, brochures and various maps. They liaised with the 208 yachts taking part, which requested information and accommodation. During the Jubilee they were in charge of all the on-shore facilities and co-ordinated the social events, including the opening and closing ceremonies plus the setting-up of facilities on The Parade. The 'spectator' management also had to be dealt with on a daily basis, liaising with the ferries, highways authority, car parks, heliports and ambulances, among others, along with the Police and the Harbour Master, to make sure that proper security measures were taken. They closed the Cowes office in mid-November but Tim Jones is still following up from his own office at Lymington.

The Cowes Business Association

Although not involved in the organisation of the Jubilee, helped a lot in the final stages with other local organisations which were also not primarily meant to be involved. "It avoided lots of problems which had not been dealt with," said Chairman, Andy Willard.

* The America's Cup Jubilee Education Programme

This was developed for the America's Cup Jubilee under the instigation of local retired businessman John Power as a means of stimulating the imaginations of children and young people throughout the Isle of Wight. A literacy pack entitled 'Blue Days at Sea' written by Lydia Fulleylove contained all aspects of nautical activity ranging from poetry to knot tying instruction. Isle of Wight school children had experience of working with sailmakers and drama workshops obtaining a collection of material to form a maritime archive.

*The Royal Yacht Squadron was anxious to raise the profile of the America's Cup Jubilee throughout the UK with a view to further UK challenge bids in the future. This resulted in twelve young talented sailors aged between 18 and 21 being selected from all over the UK to race on 12- Metre Class yachts participating in the Regatta. In addition, the Jubilee Sailing Trust introduced 32 disabled and able-bodied youngsters to the sea on board the Trust's new sailing ship **Tenacious**. This was supported by the Gosling foundation whose Chairman is Sir Donald Gosling.*

Meet them all over the next pages

Who was there?

During that third week of August 2001 the little maritime town of Cowes welcomed the "crème de la crème" of sailing and the pinnacle of yacht racing. Millionaire yacht owners, Royalty and legendary heroes of sailing history all rubbed shoulders in the narrow streets of the historic sailing town as it once again demonstrated its claim truly to be the home of world yachting. Royal visitors included HRH Prince Philip, the Duke of Edinburgh, and HRH Princess Anne, the Princess Royal, who performed the opening and closing ceremonies of the Jubilee. HM Juan Carlos, the King of Spain, was there sailing on his yacht *Bribon,* HSH Prince Henrik of Denmark stayed aboard the Danish royal motor yacht, *Danneborg* and HSH Karim Aga Khan was on his luxury yacht, *Shergar*. Italian industrialist Gianni Agnelli, boss of Fiat and Ferrari, took part in the Jubilee racing in his distinctive 92ft black-hulled yacht *Stealth* and won the most prestigious race of the week, as first yacht to finish the UBS Round-the-Island Race on the Tuesday. German industrialist Plattner Hass was racing on his yacht *Morning Glory*, another speed machine. The world of high fashion was represented too, with Giorgio Armani, who sailed aboard the beautiful yacht *Shenandoah* with industrialist Francesco Micheli, Prada head Patrizio Bertelli racing his own award-winning 12-Metre yacht *Nyala*. and Allegra Gucci, youngest daughter of Maurizio Gucci, on vintage yacht *Tuiga*. Swiss pharmaceutical millionaire Ernesto Bertarelli, head of the Team Alinghi America's Cup campaign which signed up Russell Coutts and others of the 2000 winning New Zealand Team, raced and won the *12-Metre Prada World Championship* on *South Australia*. This yacht was so far ahead of its competitors in the world championship that

the team was unbeatable even before the last races were sailed - so decided instead to head for a golf tournament in Switzerland on the final day! Veteran America's Cup competitor Alan Bond, whose Australian team was the first to take the cup away from the USA with *Australia II* in 1983, made a rare appearance, sailing on the yacht and taking centre stage at the final prizegiving when *Australia II* was awarded a special prize for the yacht which had added most to the Jubilee. Head of Nautor Swan Yachts, Leonardo Ferragamo, was there, as was Luca Bassani, Chairman of Wally Yachts, Gilles Hennessy and Christophe Navarre, Hennessy Chairman, and Jean-Marie Laborde, Chairman of Moët & Chandon, as well as Yves Carcelle, Chairman and Chief Executive of LVMH. American oil billionaire and fanatical sailor Bill Koch, head of the *America 3* America's Cup challenge, not only had a successful week racing but went into the history books when he paid £310,000, at a charity auction in aid of the Royal National Lifeboat Institution, for 31 Hennessy cognacs, each laid down in the year of an America's Cup final. Peter Harrison, the British sailing millionaire who got the current British America's Cup GBR Challenge going with the backing of his own fortune, was racing on one of the GBR yachts and had the thrill of winning the ACC Class in the UBS Round the Island Race. American TV presenter Gary Jobson, an America's Cup sailor in his own right, had the pleasant task of introducing the celebrity guests at the opening ceremony and these famous names, all in Cowes for the Jubilee, made up a who's who of yachting to rival any. First was Olin Stephens, one half of the Sparkman & Stephens design team responsible for so many elegant but seaworthy racing

*HSH
The Aga Khan*

*HSH Prince Henrik
of Denmark*

Photo © Michael Green, Lausanne

HM King Juan Carlos of Spain

His Majesty, King Juan Carlos of Spain, was in Cowes racing his yacht **Bribon** for the America's Cup Jubilee. As well as mixing freely with the sailors and partygoers, the King was happy to give a press conference at the Royal Yacht Squadron. King Juan Carlos seemed to enjoy being in Cowes and mixed simply with everybody - although his bodyguards were watching closely and tried to keep photographers away from him. The King humbly accepted a third prize at the final prizegiving ceremony, where Princess Anne greeted him personally when she arrived. He also attended the ball. He said he was very happy to be helping the sport of sailing by participating in the event and spoke of his strong emotions, as a competitive sailor, taking part with so many of the best sailors in the world in the Round-the-Island Race which marked the 150th anniversary of the first cup challenge. Both his parents had loved the sea, he said, and ever since his childhood he had sailed, first on **Saltillo** and then on **Giralda**. The King said he believed the Louis Vuitton Cup - awarded to the top challenger in the America's Cup preliminary rounds - had been very positive for Spanish sailing. "I know it is important to participate in the America's Cup and I do hope Spain will be able to participate again in the future," he added. The King, who is known as an excellent skipper, admitted that he sometimes got seasick. He said he loved sailing for its own sake and racing - but there was more of the racer in him, as he preferred competitive sailing. "Sailing teaches you to be prepared to win and lose and that teamwork is extremely important - and this teaches you to work with and to trust one another and to be united towards the same goal. A boat unites a lot," he said.

yachts and an America's Cup winner in 1937, before most of those present at the Jubilee were born. The list of winning skippers there in Cowes was awesome, as Gary Jobson called them up on stage: Americans Briggs Cunningham, with **Columbia** in 1958; Buddy Melges, boat builder, and sailmaker Ted Hood, who skippered **Courageous** in 1974; Bill Koch and Dennis Conner from the 1980s; Australian victor John Bertrand, New Zealanders Russell Coutts and Dean Barker, who at 26 became the youngest person to steer a boat in the America's Cup. Head of Team New Zealand's 2003 defending campaign, Tom Schnackenberger, was there too, and so was Kiwi icon, the late Sir Peter Blake, who headed the 1992 and 1995 challenges, paying the entry fee out of his own pocket when no-one else would. Italian Francesco de Angelis, skipper of **Luna Rossa**, Halsy Herreshoff, grandson of legendary yacht designer Nathaniel Herreshoff, Torben Grael, skipper of **Stealth,** just to mention a few. Round-the-world sailors Grant Dalton, Ellen MacArthur, Dawn Riley and Christine Briand, French Olympic medallist Thierry Peponnet, GB Gold medallists Shirley Robertson and Iain Percy, Olympic rower Greg Searle and Silver medallist sailor Ian Walker, now skipper of the GBR Challenge were either sailing or in the watching crowd. The yacht owners who made the event possible - by paying to bring their boats across the Atlantic, and in some cases half way round the world, to take part in the event. Royal New Zealand Yacht Squadron Commodore Peter Taylor and many other Commodores were also there to enjoy the fun of the Jubilee, including Sir Tom Perkins, owner of the beautiful **Mariette** of 1915 and **Atlantide**, and who is next planning to buy an 87-metre long yacht to race across the Atlantic. You will discover them in the following pages.

BRIBON

Telefónica

Photo © Kos

The Racing

Racing took place over six days.
The highlight was the re-enactment on Tuesday, 21 August, of the
original 100 Guineas Cup Race - eastabouts around the Isle of Wight -
which spawned the America's Cup, the most important race trophy
within the yachting world.

For racing, the yachts were divided into three main groups - the modern America's Cup Class, the 12-Metre and the Classics and Moderns, which included restored originals and modern-built replicas. Each group had its own race course, with the ACCs racing off Bembridge, to the east of the Isle of Wight, and the 12-Metre, north-east of Cowes, off Osborne Bay. The Classic and Modern, including the J-Class, started each morning from the Royal Yacht Squadron line off The Parade, racing down the western Solent and finishing back at Cowes. The J-Class yachts and the modern racers are easily capable of reaching 15 knots and, with strong spring tides all week, the race start zones were patrolled by marshals, Police launches and Royal Navy patrol boats, to ensure the many hundreds of spectator boats kept clear of the courses. The 12-Metre Class assembled for the Jubilee was the biggest ever fleet of these classic international racing yachts ever seen together, with 37 contesting the Prada 12-Metre World Championship held during the week. Joining them on the Solent were the beautiful J-Class yachts, the meticulously-restored **Velsheda**, **Endeavour** and **Shamrock V**, together with the 23-Metre **Cambria**. With their towering masts and acres of canvas, these beauties evoked the 1930s heyday of yachting at Cowes, when King George V raced his **Britannia** in full sail. They are living legends and old monuments, about which many pages of yachting history have been written. In Jubilee Week the Js were racing for the J-Class Hennessy Trophy. At the other end of the spectrum, modern America's Cup Class yachts were competing at the Jubilee for the Louis Vuitton Trophy. They will go on to challenge, during 2002-03 in New Zealand, for the Louis Vuitton Cup and ultimately the America's Cup.

Photo: Colin Kolbe - West Island Group

A bit lumpy!

Photo © Yacht Shots

GBR Crew very busy...

Photo © Kos

The First Day

On the first day of racing, 30 knot winds caused collisions and some yachts were unable to continue racing. Several boats lost their masts - ***Blue Leopard***, ***Tuiga***, ***Havsoernen***, ***Blue Peter***. ***Marilee*** broke her boom and was lucky that Mark Spencer of Spencer Thetis Wharf replaced it so quickly with a temporary one, so that she could continue racing. Roy Hart, skipper of the 12-Metre ***Victory***, was taken to hospital after he lost half his thumb. He refused an operation, saying it would take too long, and he would not miss the Jubilee for anything in the world - even half a thumb...!

But the big yachts revelled in the strong winds: ***Mariette***, ***Thendara***, ***Belle Aventure***, ***Mari Cha III***, ***Shenandoah***, ***Zaca A Te Moana***, ***Ticonderoga***, ***Rugosa***, to name a few. As Royal Yacht Squadron Commodore Nicholson said at the Jubilee Ball: "Lady Luck accompanied the event and the weather was, but for the first day, most beautiful."

Going aground...

Photo © Nash

Help...

Photo © Kos

Main photo: Colin Kelly - West Island Group

The UBS Round-the-Island Race

Photo © Kos

Photo © Kos

Highlight of the America's Cup Jubilee celebrations in Cowes was the UBS Jubilee Round-the-Island Race, a re-enactment of the original race of 1851, when 15 yachts raced clockwise (eastabouts) around the Isle of Wight in the contest that is nowadays looked on as the start of international yacht racing and was certainly the beginning of the America's Cup.

In 1851, 14 of the yachts racing were British, from the Royal Yacht Squadron. The 15th, the modern-designed cutter *America*, won the race and gave her name to the trophy forever after called the America's Cup.

The 55-mile historic race actually took place on 22 August 1851, but Tuesday the 21st was decided on for the 2001 re-enactment because of tides. Very large spring tides during the Jubilee would have meant a difficult foul tide hampering the yachts on the 22nd and, if that summer day had brought light winds, the fleet could have had difficulty in making progress.

Getting it right

For the Jubilee in 2001, the Nab Light vessel, a mark in the original race, was put back in the 1851 position - thanks to Louis Vuitton - for the UBS Round-the-Island Race. Ever since that 1851 race there has been controversy over the exact course around the Nab light ship. *America* went inside the light vessel, but outside the Bembridge Ledge buoy, then tacked in towards Culver Cliff to avoid the foul tide. The British yachts went round the outside of the light ship, leaving it to starboard. From that time on *America* was in the lead for the rest of the race. The controversy over the course was confused by contradictory sailing instructions and the different race cards which had been issued, so no-one was able to establish a clear right or wrong course. In 1887, the

Nab Light Vessel was moved eastwards and the Nab Tower, further south east, was only put in place in 1920. Also fortunate for the *America* was the fact that the 1851 race did not use any handicapping. Under the American handicap rules, *America* measured in at 150 tons but, according to the English system she would have measured 190 tons.

Although 'winner takes all' remains the governing principle, there *was* a second-placed yacht in 1851 - *Aurora*. But it could not be seen, obscured by the other side of the Island. She finished some twenty minutes later. It was the first time a foreign vessel had beaten the cream of the English fleet, defeating the pride of British racing yachts.

Stealth

**Winner of the
UBS Round-the-Island Race**

Alongside the historic J-Class and 12- Metre yachts, and a fleet of modern America's Cup yachts that included seven teams and the top two syndicates in the world, Team New Zealand and Prada, GBR Challenge entered GBR 52 and GBR 41. Despite only three months experience of racing these complicated Formula One machines, both of the British crews had a very successful week, making the sailing world take note that Peter Harrison's team could be a dark horse in the 2002/2003 America's Cup.

The re-enactment of the 1851 race proved to be a thrilling encounter. After starting strongly, GBR 52 led for the whole way around, until gear failure allowed Prada to challenge right at the end of the race. GBR 52, with double Olympic silver medallist Ian Walker at the helm, held a boat length lead at the last mark, but Prada luffed the British team into an illegal zone. Although this allowed the Italians to beat GBR Challenge by 2 seconds - a minute margin given the 5hour 17 minutes finishing time - Prada was subsequently disqualified to give the trophy to Harrison's team.In the week long competition, both of the GBR Challenge crews made it through to the semi-finals of the event, where the match racing format simulated the America's Cup races.

Although GBR 41 won their starts against Prada, the superiority of the Italian 2000 generation 'silver bullet' over the 1995 British yacht, ensured the 2000 America's Cup Challengers a place in the final.

There they met GBR 52, after Ian Walker and Andy Green had managed to defeat current America's Cup holders Team New Zealand.

With the wind failing, the Race Committee elected to have only one race as a final, raising the tension between the two teams that had endured titanic tussles during the week. The watching crowd were not disappointed as the British team won the start against the vastly experienced Italians and led around the course. However, Lady Luck intervened on the final leg, as the British spinnaker ripped shortly after being hoisted. Prada took the lead to win by five seconds. Despite this disappointment, the week was a huge success for the British team, establishing them as a potential force in the America's Cup. Harrison's General Manager, David Barnes, explained how the team are ahead of the goals set. "We're comfortably ahead of where we thought we'd be by this time. The UK sailing programme was always going to be about learning how to sail these boats around the course. Looking at the standard of teamwork on our boats, we've more than achieved that." The fact that we've been able to mix it with the big teams on equal terms and almost took the regatta away - we missed by half a boat length - is a huge achievement for everybody in the team. Although we've still got a lot to learn, I'm very excited with our prospects from here."

The UBS Round-the-Island-Race Trophy

Peter Harrison and GBR 52 won the UBS Round-the-Island Race in the ACC Class.

With his family

Photos © MCxA

The 9th America's Cup Hall of Fame

Commodore and Mrs Nicholson,
Halsey C. Herreshoff, Robert Mosbacher

Crew of **Rugosa**

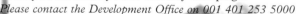

Buddy Melges with his wife
and daughter

The Ninth Annual Induction Ceremony of the America's Cup Hall of Fame, which is normally held at the Herreshoff Museum, Rhode Island, took place during the Jubilee at the Royal Yacht Squadron. The event was sponsored by George Nicholson and his associates at Camper & Nicholson International. The 2001 inductees were firstly the Earl of Wilton, who was Commodore of the Royal Yacht Squadron in 1851. He made yachting history by establishing a race open to yachts of all nations around the Isle of Wight. By extending an invitation to the New York Yacht Club and enabling the yacht **America** to win the cup, Wilton is considered the true founder of the America's Cup competition. The other two were Harry "Buddy" Melges who has an impressive record of sailing championships and Henry Sturgis Morgan who was several times Commodore of the New York Yacht Club and Chairman of its America's Cup Committee. Henry was instrumental in the revival of the Cup campaigns in 12-Metres. The America's Cup Hall of Fame was founded in 1992 by the Trustees of the Herreshoff Marine Museum. It provides a permanent international centre for the exhibition of the history, technology and influence of the America's Cup. Principal emphasis is upon honouring individuals who have had a tangible effect on the record of the Cup. Their achievements are memorialized in the America's Cup Hall of Fame at the Herreshoff Museum. Elizabeth Meyer is the only woman who is a member of the America's Club Hall of Fame Selection Committee. In the next 5 years the museum will undergo many transformations and donations are welcome to the Nathanael Greene Herreshoff Society at the Twenty First Century Campaign.

Please contact the Development Office on 001 401 253 5000

George Nicholson, CNI Chairman,
flanked by Enrico Chieffi and
Leonardo Ferragamo of Nautor Swan

Halsey Herreshoff and John Morgan

Henry Sturgis Morgan

Earl of Wilton

Also see article on the Herreshoff Museum in the America's Cup Saga Section

Photos © Edward Lloyd. Courtesy of the Herreshoff Museum

The Begum, Princess Gabriella zu Leiningen and her Mother

Nicholas Edmiston

Mrs Tim Louis

Mr & Mrs Peter Harrison

HSH The Aga Khan

The Jubilee Ball

Social highlight of the America's Cup Jubilee was the Jubilee Ball, held at Queen Victoria's beloved Island home, Osborne House. The fabulous gala - the most splendid celebrated in more than 100 years - started with a Moët & Chandon Champagne reception, after which the band of Her Majesty's (Queen Elizabeth II, not Victoria!) Royal Marines Beat the Retreat, marching majestically towards Osborne House on a perfect evening.

Mark Lloyd and Bill Koch

Bill Koch at the auction

Invitation to The Ball

David Litchfield wrote in *'All at Sea'* "At the Osborne House Ball, the price for black-market tickets soared to £1000 without anyone knowing why. As a social barometer it was interesting that *Hello* magazine sent a writer and two photographers to the ball but no one to cover the sailing..."

HM King Juan Carlos

Sir Richard Branson

Photo © Kos

Stephen Urquhart

Presiding over the ball were Peter Nicholson, Commodore of the Royal Yacht Squadron, Charles Dana III, Commodore of the New York Yacht Club and Jean-Marie Laborde, Chairman of Moët & Chandon. To the applause of guests on the terrace of Osborne House, overlooking the Solent, Dean Barker, the skipper of Team New Zealand - winner of the last America's Cup - was presented with a magnum of Esprit du Siècle Champagne by M. Laborde. It was an emotional moment for the 2,500 guests who included HM King Juan Carlos of Spain, Prince Henrik of Denmark, HSH Karim Aga Khan, Giovanni Agnelli and Sir Richard Branson, among other guests. After a

good buffet dinner, served in a marquee on the lawns of the great house, Phillips offered the Hennessy cognac in a charity auction (also see other page). After coffee and cognac - not the famous just-auctioned *eaux de vie* - guests danced until - to everyone's regret, the music stopped at 1am. The main charity to benefit from the generosity of visitors to the America's Cup Jubilee -including the £310,000 paid by Bill Koch for the special "Hennessy Cognac Collection" at the Jubilee Ball - was the RNLI, the rescue service which turns out in all weathers to save lives at sea. The RNLI does not receive Government funding, and relies on donations and legacies to buy boats, maintain them and train the brave crews. The RNLI is on call 24 hours a day and, since it was founded in 1824, has saved over 135,000 lives.

HM King Juan Carlos of Spain
at the Louis Vuitton GBR Crew Party

Peter Taylor, Commodore of the Royal New Zealand Yacht Squadron
and his wife Rita with Jean and Dennis Taylor
at the Jubilee Ball. Behind: Princess Eugénie de Serigny.

The Black Watch,
Fred Olsen Cruise Lines

The Senta Crew
at one of the parties

The Jubilee Social Programme

Lavish parties, ceremonies, dinners and prize-givings took place each day.
Throughout Jubilee Week, Cowes became a sort of Monte Carlo in August or St Moritz in February - the jewellery excepted!
Most of them were on an 'invitation only' basis with only a small number of 'Happy Few' invited to all of them.

Jubilee Week started with the arrival at dawn of the America's Cup accompanied by a Maori ceremony described earlier. In the evening of the first day, the opening ceremony took place on The Parade in the presence of HRH The Duke of Edinburgh and the *crème de la crème* of the yachting world. Later on, a private owners' reception, supported by Prada, took place at the Royal Yacht Squadron where Commodores and invited guests from all over the world were present.

The Yacht Clubs had events and dinners reserved for their members and guests and some selected personalities, while the Herreshoff Marine Museum held its ninth America's Cup 'Hall of Fame' induction ceremony at the Royal Yacht Squadron, sponsored by Camper & Nicholson International.

Contrary to usual custom (especially that of the Royal Yacht Squadron), the Clubs allowed the organisation of press conferences in their premises, providing a rare opportunity for journalists to penetrate their inner sanctums. Jubilee and sponsors *oblige* …!

The Jubilee Ball at Osborne House was of course **the** event to be part of. Tickets were even sold on the black market! Hennessy had rented the ground floor of John Terry's Commodore's House to create a Hennessy's Skipper Club where skippers and VIPs were entertained - with cognac and other fine fare - and where they held the Hennessy J-Class dinner. Access was permitted only via a special hand-made metal card.

Very exclusive parties were held on super-yachts **Leander**, **Atlantide**, **Lady Christine** and even on **Dannebrog,** the Danish Royal Yacht . There might also have been some on The Aga Khan's **Shergar**. **Sea Cloud II**, one of the biggest square-rigged sailing ships, now used as a cruise ship, chartered by the New York Yacht Club, also had its own private parties. Entrance to them was carefully controlled from ashore. Commodore Charles Dana used **Black Knight** for interviews and private functions. The 83-foot motor yacht was the starting vessel for many of the America's Cup races in Newport. Louis Vuitton organised a Crew Party at the GBR Challenge base for previous and current America's Cup and Louis Vuitton Cup Syndicate members.

There was also a Jubilee Beach Party at Osborne Bay Beach to which access was not easily obtained and few photographers allowed - no doubt to avoid indiscreet pictures of illustrious personalities enjoying themselves !

Last but not least, on the last day a stunning firework display, sponsored by the New York Yacht Club. was provided by *Pains Fireworks*.

Floating Palaces

*Fred Olsen Cruise Lines provided the cruise liner **Black Watch** for additional accommodation. The luxury ship, which was moored off Cowes during the Jubilee could accommodate 460 passengers and offered a 24-hour tender service for those wanting to go ashore. Meanwhile a series of glamorous parties took place on **Sea Cloud II** which had been reserved by the New York Yacht Club.*

Fred Olsen Cruises:
Tel: 01473 292200
Fax: 01473 292410

Sea Cloud II

The Yachts

The most beautiful yachts in the world gathered for the world's oldest and most famous sporting trophy.

The America's Cup Jubilee Regatta was the largest ever big boat regatta in the UK. The 208-strong fleet, with 110 international entries (43 American and 90 British), included the original yachts or their replicas, elegant J-Class of the pre-war period, 12-Metre Class, Modern America's Cup Class, Vintage, Classic, Spirit of Tradition and Modern IRC and IRM rated 45-ft yachts.

A replica of *America*, the 1851 winner, was there as well as several past winners of the America's Cup: *Ranger* (1937), *Columbia* (1958), *Intrepid* (1970), *Freedom* (1980), *Australia III* (1983), *America 3* (1992), *Black Magic NZL32* (1995). Past challengers were there too: *Shamrock V* (1930), *Endeavour* (1937), *Sceptre* (1958), *Sovereign* (1964), *Kookaburra III* (1987), *Il Moro di Venezia* (1992) and *Luna Rossa* (2000).

Apart from the 23-Metre *Cambria* and J-Class *Shamrock, Velsheda* and *Endeavour*, most of them were 12-Metre. Past winning skippers and owners were present and raced during the Jubilee including Alan Bond, Bill Koch, Dennis Conner, Ted Hood, Russell Coutts, John Bertrand, and the late Sir Peter Blake. Six of the current America's Cup syndicates were represented: GBR Challenge, Team New Zealand, Stars & Stripes, Alinghi Swiss Challenge, Prada Challenge and Le Défi. All these yachts were accompanied by super motor yachts: Sir Donald Gosling's 245ft *Leander*, Irvine Laidlaw's 182ft *Lady Christine*, Tom Perkins 122ft *Atlantide*, HSH The Aga Khan's 153ft *Shergar*, HRH The King of Denmark's 207ft *Dannebrog*, and *Black Night*, the New York Yacht Club race control vessel which was used for the America's Cup in 1983.

America

A replica of the original boat, designed by George Steers, which won the 100 Guineas Cup in 1851, was in Cowes but did not race during the Jubilee. The topsail schooner replica was commissioned by American brewer Rudi Shaeffer from architect Olin Stephens and launched in 1967. She was bought by the US Navy for $1 in very bad shape before Argentinian, Carlos Perdomo gave her a major refit. In 1996, a syndicate headed by Paul Deeth, a member of the crew, had her refitted in Antigua. Recognisable due to her heavily raked masts and a wide ornate transom, she is 31.73 metres long and carries masts of Douglas Pine, which support 500 square metres of canvas. She was featured in the Shaeffer film 'Sail to Glory'.

Photo © Kos

On the right, John David, owner of Cambria

Cambria
K4

Designed by William Fife in 1928 for newspaper owner Sir William Berry (later Lord I. R. Camrose), *Cambria* was built to the 23-Metre International Rule at Fairlie in Scotland. She was to be Lord Camrose's Challenger for the America's Cup but did not have the chance to compete, the New York Yacht Club having introduced the new J-Class. She was the first of many boats to have a Bermudan rig as opposed to a gaff rig.

Cambria was sold to a Belgian who kept her as a cruising yacht in the South of France. She was saved during the war by being kept out of sight. The vessel was seen during the 1987 defence of the America's Cup. Bought by a New Zealand restaurateur, she had been totally neglected and was found lying idle in Townsville, Queensland. She had also been ketch-rigged. Prime Minister Paul Keating found her, and together with a partner, John David bought her. Ian Murray supervised the six-month restoration with dozens of crafts-men working on her. Cambria's Honduras mahogany planks were replaced by teak and blonde mahogany rail cappings and deckhouses. Her hull was strengthened with 6,000 stainless-steel bolts.

The stateroom, four guest cabins and main saloon, panelled through-out in varnished mahogany, were refurbished to the original con-dition. At 135ft long, she has the most graceful lines.

Last June *Cambria's* extended main mast was stepped in Cowes by Spencer Rigging and a longer boom with bronze fittings was made from her mizzen at Spencer Thetis Wharf in just 16 days. She is now a sloop as she was originally, not a ketch. Cambria was ready in time for the Jubilee where she sailed, crewed by young Australians and skippered by Peter Mandin. Adam Gosling was part of the crew and Ian Murray was helmsman for the week. It was her first time back to Cowes after 65 years and she sailed with the J-Class. Unfortunately, on the opening day, she had to retire from the racing in the blustery weather.

Photo © Spencer Thetis Wharf

There was a previous yacht called **Cambria**, *built in 1870. She was the first British challenge for the America's Cup, led by James Ashbury.*

The J-Class

Full of grace and grandiose splendour these magnificent and beautifully lifted 'old ladies' were skippered and sailed by a crew of over 30. The majestic J's and Cambria were undoubtedly the stars of the Jubilee.

Known for their grace, elegance, power and majesty, the J-Class was designed to provide boats for the America's Cup in the 1920's and 30's in the 'Belle Epoque' of yacht racing. Only ten boats were built. Six were modified to fit the rule and four were built as 'trial horses.' Among them Sir Thomas Lipton's **Shamrock V** and Sir T.O.M Sopwith's **Endeavour I** and **II**, all designed by Charles Nicholson and built by Camper & Nicholson in Gosport. They raced during the English summer regattas encouraged by the presence of King Edward's **Britannia** and other men of means who had built similar yachts. **Shamrock V** raced against Vanderbilt's **Enterprise** in 1930. **Endeavour I** and **II** raced against **Rainbow** in 1934 and **Ranger** in 1937, also owned by Vanderbilt and both designed by Starling Burgess and Olin Stephens. The 'J' Boats were stopped when **Britannia**, on 8 July 1936, was scuttled off St. Catherine's Point, according to the wishes of King George V. During the Second World War, most of them were broken up and used for scrap, but three fared better. **Shamrock V** (1930) spent the war years in Italy. **Endeavour** (1937) and **Velsheda** (1933) ended up in mudberths on the Hamble River, and their 90-ton lead keels were used for war efforts. The America's Cup did not take place for 21 years and when it resumed, the J-Class yachts were replaced by the smaller 12-Metre Class. The three remaining J Class yachts have fantastic stories. They have been restored by various owners and have since raced on several occasions in regattas in Antigua, New Zealand and even in Alaska.

Velsheda JK7

128.11ft (39.3m)

*She was built in 1934 by Camper & Nicholson for W. L. Stephenson, the owner of the Woolworth chain, who named her after his three daughters Velma, Sheila and Daphne. With her 128.11ft (39.3m) dimensions, she was the most advanced in design for spars, rigging, sails, deck gear and ropes and the standing rigging was solid rod. Her mast was aluminium and the sails were made from the new Terylene threads. **Velsheda** won many races between 1934 and 1936, but changed hands many times because the new owner could never afford to restore her properly. Banker Royce Poke bought her for £5,000, sold the yacht to Singapore-based Mike Maloney, who sold her to Terry Brabant. There was also a Swiss owner. Finally, in 1997, she was given a proper refit by John Munford. Since then **Velsheda** has been racing all over the world and is now owned by Dutchman Ronald De Waal.*

Endeavour
JK4

129.7ft (39.5m)

Built in 1934 for aviator Sir T.O.M. Sopwith by Camper & Nicholson to sail against **Rainbow** in the America's Cup, **Endeavour** was only 129ft (39.5m) with a mast of 162ft. She was a very fast boat and almost won the Cup (see opposite). Three years later, in 1937, T.O.M. Sopwith tried with **Endeavour II** but lost again. She did, however beat **Ranger** in the New York Yacht Club Cruise. In 1938, **Endeavour** was laid up because of the war and in the next 16 years she passed through many owners, remaining mainly inactive.

In the 1970's she was towed to Cowes but remained moored on the Medina for several years. She was bought in 1977 for £1 by John Amos, who completely rebuilt her hull. He sold her in 1986 to American publisher Elisabeth Meyer, who had her fitted out and rigged in Holland. Harry, Mark and Rafe Spencer organised her launch in the Solent and towed her to Holland. In 1989 she sailed again.

In 2000, new owner Dennis Kozlowski (who is also behind the 'Tyco Team' in the Round The World Volvo Ocean Race) gave her a multi-million dollar refit in the USA, which proved to be very successful. She did very well during the Jubilee, skippered by Mike Beardall with crew including Kevin Shoebridge and Steve Hayles. With her elegant white spinnaker with blue stars she steamed off like a train, leaving the other J's in the wake and won by three minutes over **Shamrock V** in the Round-the-Island Race. New owner Kozlowski says "no one truly owns **Endeavour** she is part of history. I am only her caretaker."

Sir T.O.M. Sopwith had quite a few problems with **Endeavour**. A week before going to America in 1931, the crew went on strike for more pay. They were replaced by an amateur crew, and she crossed the Atlantic under the burgee of the Royal Yacht Squadron, with **Velsheda** as a trial horse. Sopwith followed her on his motor yacht **Aquitania**. In New York, she shared Herreshoff's boatyard with her rival **Rainbow** and Sopwith even went sailing on her with his rival Vanderbilt. During the America's Cup fourth race, **Endeavour** was forced to tack away to avoid collision while she was hoisting her new 'genoa jib'. Sopwith protested but the jury decided that the protest had come too late, which caused indignation and fury. Sopwith decided to withdraw very disillusioned, declaring he would never challenge again (but he did with **Endeavour II** in 1937). The incident made the New York Journal write: **"Britannia rules the waves, but America waives the rules!"**

Shamrock V
JK3

129.7ft (39.5m)

Beautiful bottle-green *Shamrock V* is the only J-Class yacht which has never been out of commission since she was built in 1930 by Camper & Nicholson as fifth Challenger for Sir Thomas Lipton's last attempt to win the America's Cup.

At 119ft (36.5m) long, she was designed by Charles Nicholson and built of wooden planking on composite steel frames. *Shamrock V* challenged *Enterprise* in 1930 and lost. Gallant loser Sir Thomas Lipton died in 1931, aged 80. Sir T.O.M. Sopwith bought *Shamrock V* in 1932 and used her for a benchmark in the design and construction of his challenger *Endeavour*. She was then bought by Sir Richard Fairey. During the war, she was in Italy, where she was renamed *Quadrifoglio* by owner Piero Scanu. She returned to England in 1967 where she was repaired at Camper & Nicholson yard in Gosport (a three-year rebuild) and re-rigged by Spencer Rigging.

The Lipton Tea Company bought her in 1986 and donated her to the Museum of Yachting in Newport, Rhode Island. She was sold in 1998 to Brazilian Marcos de Moraes. In 1999, she beat *Endeavour* and *Velsheda* in the Antigua Classic Regatta.

The J-Class Regatta
The Sir Thomas Lipton Trophy
organised by the
Lymington Town Sailing Club

Mr D.Kozlowski, his wife Karen and Mike Beardall, captain, with the Sir Thomas Lipton Trophy.

During the Jubilee in Cowes, the J-Yachts raced together in the Solent for the first time since 1934. Here they had to compete with high tides, foul weather, 36 knots of breeze and 12 mile beats in open sea. With them was Fife-designed *Cambria* who was competing again for the first time in 65 years! They raced for the "J-Class Hennessy Trophy" which was won by *Endeavour*. Organised by the Lymington Town Sailing Club", a J-Class only regatta took place in Christchurch Bay before the Jubilee, under the auspices of their new J-Class Association formed by the owners of the three remaining J-Class yachts. A good trial test before the Jubilee for these 180-ton monsters. *Endeavour's* £30,000 headsail disintegrated. In spite of that, she was the winner of the "Spencer Rigging Race" and won the "Sir Thomas Lipton Trophy".

J - Yachts
Built in the 1930's

American Yachts
1930 Enterprise *[1]
1930 Weetamoe
1930 Whirlwind
1930 Yankee
1934 Rainbow *[1]
1937 Ranger *[1]

British Yachts
1930 Shamrock V *[2]
1933 Velsheda *[4]
1934 Endeavour *[3]
1937 Endeavour II *[3]

Rebuilt to fit the J-Class rule

American Yachts
Vanity
Resolute

British Yachts
White Heather *[4]
Britannia *[5]
Astra
Candida

Owned by:
*[1] Harold Vanderbilt
*[2] Sir Thomas Lipton
*[3] Sir T.O.M Sopwith
*[4] W. Stephenson
*[5] H.M. King George V

Rosemary Joy, Rear Commodore of the Island Sailing Club in Cowes, has put together fantastic videos on the J-Class Yachts and a very informative commentary on them. "The Rosemary Joy Collection" is a unique treasure trove of old film footage of sailing in the 1920s and 30s, with fascinating glimpses into the world of the J-Class yachts, their construction and life aboard.

Photo © Kos

The Lymington Town Sailing Club

Vintage, Classic & Spirit of Tradition Yachts

During the Jubilee, these classes had a fleet of 76 yachts dating as far back as 1865 all the way up to modern-day replicas of famous boats

The Vintage yachts, built of wood or steel and LOA of 45ft or more were built before 1950, while the Classic Class were built after 1950 and before 1976. The Spirit of Tradition were yachts built or restored since 1970 with new modern materials but preserving the spirit and the appearance of the original design. Some of these yachts were part of the Prada Challenge for Classic Yachts and were racing for various trophies. Some were built in the 19th century: *Valdivia* (1868), *Partridge* (1885), *Thalia* (1889), *Marigold* (1892) and *Nan of Fife* (1896). *The Lady Anne*, built in 1912, was classified in the Spirit of Tradition section and the 1936 *Peter von Seestermuhe*, in the Classic section. Also in the latter section was 1951 *Josephine*, which has an interesting story as well as *Crusade of Dee* which was among the final winners. Beautiful 1983 *Adix* and 1992 *Zaca A Te Moana* were in the Spirit of Tradition. So were newly-built *White Wings* and *Wild Horses*, much to the disappointment of owner Donald Tofias who was hoping to have them classified under a new W-Class which he is trying to develop and promote.

N 1

See various separate articles about some of the above yachts.

Photo © Beken of Cowes

Rugosa

Vintage Yachts
Built before 1950
A Selection seen at the Jubilee

Valdivia, the oldest existing yacht in the world, was built in 1868 and now belongs to Anthony Churchill and Heinrich Kucz.

Partridge, built in 1885, belongs to Alex Laird and James Bishop (See separate page).

Thalia, a 1889 Wanhill-built gaff cutter owned by Ivan and Fe Jeffris, had been refitted and had a new suit of sails for the Jubilee.

Nan of Fife was built in 1896 by W. Fife in Scotland. Her owner Philippe Menhinick, an antique dealer from Saint-Malo, got the original plans from a Scottish museum and spent many years restoring the yacht on which, by great coincidence, his grandfather had sailed!

Shenandoah, built in 1902, has a very interesting story (See separate page).

Véronique, built in 1907, is owned by Dr. Hans Albrecht from Munich, Germany. He also owns *Nordwind*, which used to belong to Admiral Donitz and which is being refitted in Palma de Mallorca. Spencer are designing all masts, rigging and deck work.

Owl, built in 1909, is now owned by Giampiero Grandi (See separate page).

Tuiga, this 15-Metre Class gaff cutter was designed by William Fife and built in 1909 at Fairlie, Scotland for the Duke of Medinacelli, a personal friend of King Alphonso XIII, who also owned the 15-Metre *Hispania**. She was built to compete against the Royal Yacht. In 1995, she was rebuilt by Fairlie Restoration and masted and rigged by Spencer. Since 1997 she has been the flagship of the Yacht Club de Monaco, whose President is H.R.H. Prince Albert. Skippered by Bernard d'Alessandri, Director of the Yacht Club de Monaco.

Marilee was designed by Herreshoff in 1912, but only built in 1926, as a Nat-Herreshoff New York Club 40. There are only three yachts left of the type. One of them is *Rugosa*, which is a ketch, whereas *Marilee* has her original gaff sloop rig. She belongs to four New York Yacht Club members, Larry Snoddon, Mitchel Shivers, Ann Hutchins and Edward Kane. On the first day of the Jubilee her boom broke. Fortunately Mark Spencer, Harry's son, found an old tree in the loft and replaced it in 24 hours. She could then go back to racing with Ted Hood at the helm.

Mariette, built in 1915 belongs to Sir Tom Perkins. (See separate pages).

Rugosa, designed in 1926 by Nathanael Herreshoff, was skippered by his grandson Halsey Herreshoff. (See separate page).

Senta was built in 1928, and belongs to German Holger Schmidt.

Dorade, designed by Olin Stephens and built in 1930 by Nevins of City Island New York, was very narrow (3.12m) and very low, but she won many regattas and became famous - namely for the new ventilation system which was later called the *Dorade Box*. She belongs to Peter Frech.

Blue Peter, built in 1930, belongs to Matthew Barker.

Stormy Weather, designed by Olin Stephens in 1934, was restored recently by her present owner, Italian Giuseppe Gazzoni who had put her up for sale (£750,000) during the Jubilee.

Bloodhound, built in 1936, was skippered by the late Sir Peter Blake during the Jubilee.

Nirvana, which was designed in 1950 by John Alden for the Bermuda Race, was built by Henry Hinckley. Her first owner, Nelson Rockefeller, who sailed her for 23 years, and her current owner, David Warren, for 22 years, have both looked after her well and she has not needed any major restoration.

*Hispania was lifted from the mud where she had been a houseboat for 50 years, and taken to the Hamble by Spencer in 1998 where she is still waiting to be rebuilt. She still belongs to the King of Spain's syndicate.

Marilee

Photo © Yacht Shots

Stormy Weather

Photo © Beken of Cowes

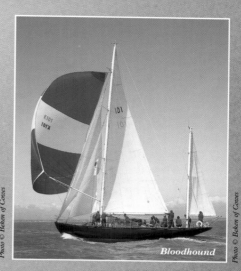

Bloodhound

Photo © Beken of Cowes

Thalia

Photo courtesy of the owner

Valdivia

Photo © Kos

Nan of Fife

Photo © Yacht Shots

Senta

Photo courtesy of the owner

Tuiga

Photo © Yacht Shots

Photo © Kos

Nirvana

Photo © Beken of Cowes

Main photo © MCrA

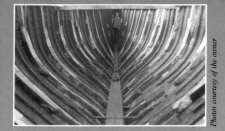

Partridge

Alex Laird, naval architect, who lives in Cowes, and Peter Saxby (Alex's uncle, also originally from the Isle of Wight), spent 18 years restoring **Partridge**, a 50ft, 28 tonne gaff cutter designed by J Beavor-Webb and built at Camper & Nicholson in 1885. They found her lying on the east coast of England. She was about to be burnt by the local council who wanted to make way for a concrete slipway. They paid £200 for the derelict hull. **Partridge** spent the next eight years in Peter's sister's garden and it was here that Alex cast a new ten tonne lead keel and five tonnes of internal ballast for her. He also replaced every oak frame and deck beam with naturally grown timber from Sussex. After much research, **Partridge** turned out to be a historical gem and one of the very few remaining straight-stemmed, lead mine cutters from the late Victorian era. Her designer, J. Beavor-Webb, who was soon to emigrate to the United States, was also designing the two straight-stemmed challengers for the America's Cup: **Genesta** (built in1884, challenged **Puritan** in 1885) and **Galatea** (built in 1885, challenged **Mayflower** in 1886). Since her re-launch in Cowes in 1998, **Partridge** has proved that Mr Beavor-Webb certainly had the ability to design a fast hull. With a beam of a mere 10ft 6ins, **Partridge** slips through the water. Ninety-five percent of her hull planking (pitch pine and teak) is still the original timber and a key factor in her survival was the presence of a completely intact greenheart keelson.

Once restored, **Partridge** raced again with sails by her original sailmakers, Ratsey & Lapthorn. Alex made the mast and spars out of five solid trees from Finland at Harry Spencer's workshop in Cowes, and many craftsmen in the town contributed to the restoration, using skills that are fast disappearing in today's world:

hand-stitched leatherwork, metal-forging, bronze-casting, copper-sheet-work, gold leaf gilding, hand-splicing, pattern-making and wood carving. After one summer in the Solent, **Partridge** was shipped to the Mediterranean in 1999 and won her first regatta at Palma de Mallorca. Since then she has gone on to win many classic yacht races at St Tropez, Cannes, Imperia, Porto Santo Stefano and Antibes, and was awarded the overall *Concours d'Elégance* trophy at Monaco Classic Week in 1999 and in St Tropez in 2001.

Today, **Partridge** represents a yacht from an era that is long gone, but, along with classic survivors such as **Avel** and **Marigold**, the art of sailing these gaff cutters, with no winches, is being maintained. **Avel** and **Partridge** often finish races within seconds of each other (on corrected and elapsed time) and this has helped the two crews of 15 to push for every last fraction of a knot from their respective hulls and rigs.

Partridge, who is currently lying in Antibes, is for sale at $900,000. The full story can be seen on their website.

Joanna and Alex Laird

www.partridge1885.com

Shenandoah

The three-masted gaff schooner, designed by Theodore Ferris in 1902 for New York banker Gibson Fahnestock, has a sailing surface of 700 square metres! Her name comes from a capstan song about an old Indian Chief. The schooner had several owners and several names: *Lasca II*, when she was German, and *Atlantide*, when she had an English owner. In 1952 she was even illegally sequestrated by the French State until bought in 1973 by French Baron Bich, who restored the original name. He was looking for a big boat to follow the regattas of the America's Cup, in which he could launch a challenge with Bruno Troublé at the helm.

Shenandoah was bought cheaply by a young Swiss, Philip Bommer, who was going to re-rig her but eventually sold her to a Japanese for a very large sum. After a period in Phuket, chartering, she was bought by a German owner and taken to New Zealand for not only a refit but a rebuild. Some ten metres of the fore-end, and other very necessary re-planking was also carried out. When cleaned off one could see through both sides. Refit and rebuild was by McMillan & Wing, mast and rig design were done by Spencer as in 1902. Complete masts, spars, blocks and rigging were sent out from England. Raymond Field, Ian McUlly of Spencer Rigging and Rafe Spencer from Thetis stepped and rigged her in New Zealand. After a round the world trip she has been sold again to Serge Guilhauveau. During the Jubilee, Giorgio Armani and Italian industrialist Francesco Micheli were on board.

Thendara

The 40m long gaff-rigged ketch, was designed by Alfred Mylne in 1936 for Sir Arthur Young. She needs a crew of 20 for 900 square metres of sail. Restored in 1994 by Philip Swinstead, she cruised to Cowes from her home port in Antibes for the Jubilee. She is now for sale at Edmiston for almost $7,000,000.

Thendara

Owl
Italy's star of the Jubilee

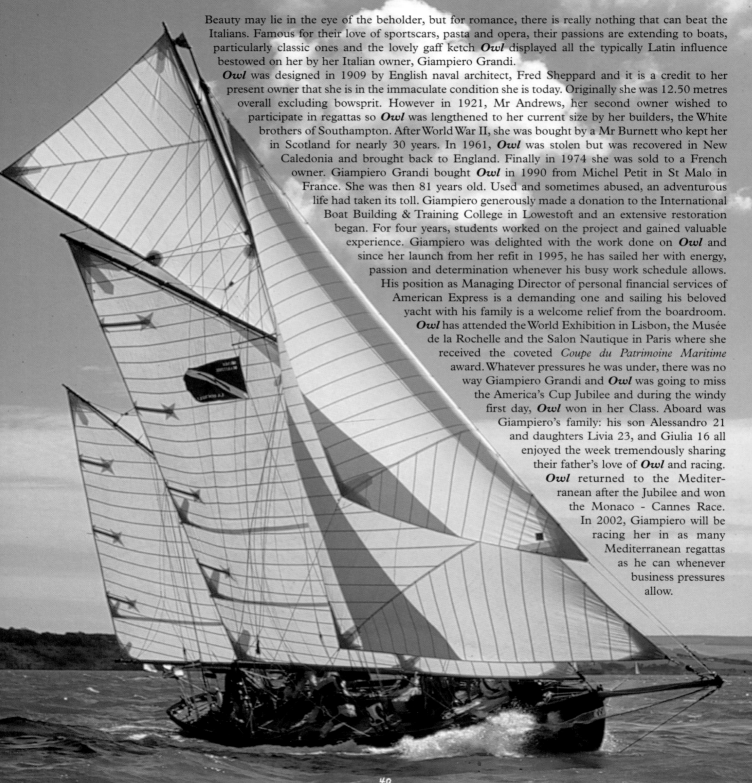

Beauty may lie in the eye of the beholder, but for romance, there is really nothing that can beat the Italians. Famous for their love of sportscars, pasta and opera, their passions are extending to boats, particularly classic ones and the lovely gaff ketch *Owl* displayed all the typically Latin influence bestowed on her by her Italian owner, Giampiero Grandi.

Owl was designed in 1909 by English naval architect, Fred Sheppard and it is a credit to her present owner that she is in the immaculate condition she is today. Originally she was 12.50 metres overall excluding bowsprit. However in 1921, Mr Andrews, her second owner wished to participate in regattas so *Owl* was lengthened to her current size by her builders, the White brothers of Southampton. After World War II, she was bought by a Mr Burnett who kept her in Scotland for nearly 30 years. In 1961, *Owl* was stolen but was recovered in New Caledonia and brought back to England. Finally in 1974 she was sold to a French owner. Giampiero Grandi bought *Owl* in 1990 from Michel Petit in St Malo in France. She was then 81 years old. Used and sometimes abused, an adventurous life had taken its toll. Giampiero generously made a donation to the International Boat Building & Training College in Lowestoft and an extensive restoration began. For four years, students worked on the project and gained valuable experience. Giampiero was delighted with the work done on *Owl* and since her launch from her refit in 1995, he has sailed her with energy, passion and determination whenever his busy work schedule allows. His position as Managing Director of personal financial services of American Express is a demanding one and sailing his beloved yacht with his family is a welcome relief from the boardroom.

Owl has attended the World Exhibition in Lisbon, the Musée de la Rochelle and the Salon Nautique in Paris where she received the coveted *Coupe du Patrimoine Maritime* award. Whatever pressures he was under, there was no way Giampiero Grandi and *Owl* was going to miss the America's Cup Jubilee and during the windy first day, *Owl* won in her Class. Aboard was Giampiero's family: his son Alessandro 21 and daughters Livia 23, and Giulia 16 all enjoyed the week tremendously sharing their father's love of *Owl* and racing.

Owl returned to the Mediterranean after the Jubilee and won the Monaco - Cannes Race. In 2002, Giampiero will be racing her in as many Mediterranean regattas as he can whenever business pressures allow.

Mariette of 1915

This beautiful 1915 Nat Herreshoff designed schooner has been meticulously restored by Sir Thomas Perkins or Tom Perkins as he is generally known.

Sir Thomas Perkins
Ritter OLAF-V*

Sir Thomas Perkins, a graduate of the Massachussetts Institute of Technology and Harvard University's business faculty, is a venture capitalist and Silicon Valley pioneer who looks after many American companies in the computer industry. He was one of the first users of industrial laser technology and synthetic insulin and was the first General Manager of Hewlett Packard's computer divisions, later becoming Director of Corporate Development. He lives in San Francisco but spends most of his time sailing. "I used to work all the time - and more - but now I work just 30% of the time," he says. He also owns the 154-foot Perini ketch *Andromeda*, which he keeps in Florida and is planning to buy an 87-metre long yacht to race across the Atlantic.

Title awarded by the King of Norway.

After her Italian owner Wolf Kitis collided with *Créole* in 1995, Tom Perkins went to see *Mariette* in La Spezia and asked Harry Spencer to rig her. He studied records and drawings at the Hart Museum of the Massachusetts Institute of Technology and had all the equipment restored to the original: even the panelling and a great part of the furniture are original! Sails were provided by Ratsey & Lapthorn. The sail and the deck gear are, of course, modern and with her 24 strong crew, skippered by Chris Gartner, *Mariette* has won many regattas. In 2001, she was overall champion of the classic circuit, winning the Prada season championship, the international Classic Yacht Association championship and the Grimaldi Cup (for the series of "feeder" races). Tom Perkins, who sails her, makes sure that everything is tip top on board. At the Jubilee she was the overall winner of the *Yachting World Concours d'Elégance Vintage Trophy*. Tom Perkins thought the Jubilee was a great event. The only problem for *Mariette* and other deep craft was that the Jubilee coincided with five metre tides. Because of low water she smelt the bottom, losing time, and had to make a two-mile detour on one race, which Tom Perkins thought was "not fair."

MAR

IETTE

Atlantide

Motor yacht **Atlantide,** restored by Camper & Nicholson, is the support boat on which Tom Perkins lives when he sails. She was masted and rigged by Spencer, who also designed all the bronze deck work to match **Mariette**. She has been beautifully restored in her 'Art Deco' original décor. Tom Perkins is very proud of the beautiful panelling, the Lalique appliques, the art pieces and the beautiful reproductions which he has mostly selected himself.

Small wooden boat built by Bugatti for a boat he could never build. They were never used and they are carefully kept on the top deck of Atlantide.

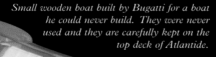

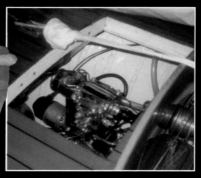

Photos © MCxA

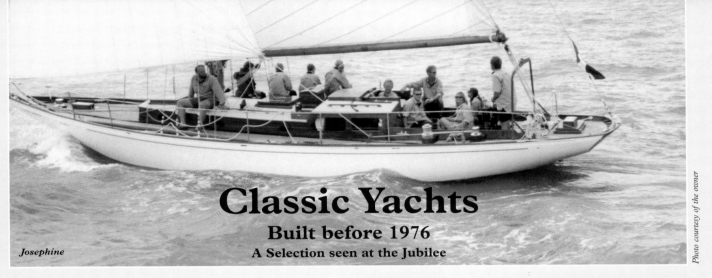

Josephine

Classic Yachts
Built before 1976
A Selection seen at the Jubilee

Josephine
A sad story...

Tim Blackman and his partner, Jo Burr, went to view *Josephine* on Long Island in July 1999. Originally named *Jane Dore IV*, she was a 45ft all wooden classic, built in 1954, but was in a neglected state. Tim's sister Pam and her husband Brian Malcolm, joined as partners in the project and *Josephine* was bought. Their children were now enthralled by the thought of taking part in the America's Cup Jubilee. *Josephine* was taken from Long Island to Marthas Vineyard for a structural refit, beginning at Christmas 1999.

On 2 July 2000, news came that Lucie, the Blackman's eldest child, was missing in Japan. There followed a trail of torture and heartbreak, and a tidal wave of media and intrigue. Surviving on only one or two hours' sleep a day, they dreamed up new initiatives, hassled the Police and the Embassy and kept Lucie's face in the TV news and on the front page of newspapers in Tokyo. By October, *Josephine* was launched from Marthas Vineyard. The twists and turns in Tokyo became more terrible, and it was necessary to ship the yacht home, now requiring a lot of work to reach Regatta standard.

Richard Branson flew Lucie's body home in a Japanese State Ceremonial casket provided by the Japanese Government and, shortly after the funeral, in April, *Josephine* arrived in Southampton Docks. She was motored to the Medina for further work, and thereafter moored in her Jubilee Regatta berth at East Cowes.

During the Jubilee, the family all thought about Lucie, who had loved this stretch of the West Solent so much, and sailed so many times. They carried her memory with them and came second in the race. They were certain Lucie was there with them!

Josephine was designed by Philip Rhodes with the following overall dimensions: LOA 45ft. LWL 32ft. Beam 11ft 9ins. Draft of 5ft and 8ft 3ins. Six of these yachts were built in Germany between 1953 and 1956 at the yards of H. Heidtmann, Hamburg & Abeking and Rasmussen, all for customers in the USA, where their shoal draft was ideal for the waters of the Bahamas and East Coast.

All six are still around, with *Josephine* and her sister, *Undina*, in the UK. *Josephine's* USA owner since 1983 donated her to a maritime sailing trust in New York in 1996 but, due to a lack of sponsorship funds, they were unable to maintain her. When she recently changed hands, her high specification meant that her restoration could be achieved, and next season *Josephine* and *Undina* will be seen 'matching' in the Solent.

Drumbeat, *built by Lallows in 1957 for Sir Max Aitken: owner Alan Dykes*

Crusade of Dee, *built 1969: owners C. O. Liddell and J. A. Boyden*

Zwerver, *built 1956: owner Franz Van Schaik*

The W-Class

The Spirit of the Future - The Soul of the Past

Designed by Joel White, the W-Class, which Donald Tofias is trying to impose as a new class, was classified under the 'Spirit of Tradition' yachts during the Jubilee

That's the W-Class, first seen at Cowes (indeed, it was their first-ever visit to the UK as a whole) for the America's Cup Jubilee in 2001. When **Wild Horses**, the first of the Class, was unveiled to the world as a gracefully sleek descendant of the legendary turn-of-the-century New York 50s, a new era of classic one-design yacht racing was born. The 'W' honours Joel White, the late American naval architect, who designed **Wild Horses**, but sadly died ahead of its launch in 1998. The yacht was built at Brooklyn Boatyard, Maine, USA by Joel's son, Steve, who used the latest construction techniques - cold-moulded, epoxy saturated strips of wood over a form, producing a doubly strong hull lighter than fibreglass.

The Class thus established, **Wild Horses** was quickly followed by a second boat in the series, **White Wings**. The yachts were formally designated as W76 (denoting the length of their hull). By the summer of 2000, the newly-formed W-Class Yacht Company was celebrating the arrival of the smaller W46 design variant. First of these into the water was **Zebra**, followed soon afterwards by **Equus** and, in June 2001, by the third of the series, **Arion**. Since then, the company has developed a full range of hull lengths for the Class, the five variants rising in size from the W46 to the W130. Company President, and the man whose long-time devotion to wooden boats was the original inspiration behind the W-Class, is Donald Tofias. Under his direction, The W-Class Yacht company, based in Boston, Massachusetts, intends to bring back the excitement of big-boat, one design match racing, rekindling the spirit of the early 20th century Corinthians, when gentlemen raced for glory. The idea is to develop strong, fast wooden boats with timeless lines, using the very latest in modern construction techniques. With the emphasis firmly on racing, the deck and cockpit areas of the W-Class yachts are expansive while the accommodation is very much of secondary importance. The company offers a management option, providing experienced captains and reliable crew with racing experience, ensuring that each yacht is delivered, raced and maintained to the highest possible standards. Available for round-the-year charter, the fleet moves effortlessly around the world, sailing from one port to the next, staging match races and working soft breezes season after season.

Wild Horses

The W-Class Yacht Company
Reservoir Place, 1601 Trapelo Road,
Waltham, Massachusetts, USA.
Tel: 001 781 890 5511
Fax: 001 781 890 1512
E-mail: info@w-class.com
Website: www.w-class.com

Adix and *The Lady Ann*,
two beautiful yachts which were skippered by
Paul Goss during the Jubilee,
belong to Spanish bank owner Mr. Botin.

Spirit of Tradition Yachts
Built since 1970
With the appearance of the vintage or Classic designs

Zaca A Te Moana

She was bought in 1997 by Dutchman Baron Steven Bentinck, to navigate the world. He soon discovered that she needed some serious alterations, not only in the interior but also in the engine and other systems. Restoration was started on the East Coast of the USA and after visiting the West Indies, she was sailed to Falmouth in England for further restoration. She was towed by Harry Spencer to Camper & Nicholson for engineering changes and then to Cowes, where Adrian Stone has since been coordinating the interior refit.

In order to raise the sails she was fitted with four stainless steel winches by JMC, along with installing a new anchor windlass and a new hydraulics system to recharge batteries. She was moored for several weeks at Spencer Thetis yard where Harry Spencer and his team were overhauling the rigging and fitting new bronze work and blocks. Harry Spencer is also involved in the design of the new yacht Baron Bentinck is planning to build.

Zaca A Te Moana was to spend the winter in Antigua and to come back to Cowes for Adrian Stone to finalise the restoration work.

Beautiful 140ft Schooner ***Zaca A Te Moana*** *which means 'Spirit of the Sea' was built in 1992 in Holland and is a replica of the Grand Banks Schooners which were used to fish off Newfoundland.*

Mike McMillan was born in England and came to the Isle of Wight when he was aged three. He started professional sailing more than 35 years ago in the Mediterranean and the West Indies and was Captain of the 100ft Camper & Nicholson yacht *Cynara* for five years. He then bought a schooner, which he chartered in the West Indies. Mike returned to England in 1977 with his wife and children and started a hang gliding and corporate sailing business. In 2000 Baron Bentinck asked him to captain and project-manage the refit of *Zaca*. He enjoyed the challenge of the Jubilee and he remembers the day on the way to the Needles when they were sailing against *Shenandoah* in an amazing match. It was a sort of a 'Zaca Haka' (Maori word of war) he says. " We were all very excited, especially Baron Bentinck who was racing for the first time. We crossed the line together, *Zaca* winning by one foot."

Baron Steven Bentinck

Baron Bentinck is half-Dutch with an English mother. His dream is to sail round the world on his yacht with his children being educated on board, discovering unusual places.

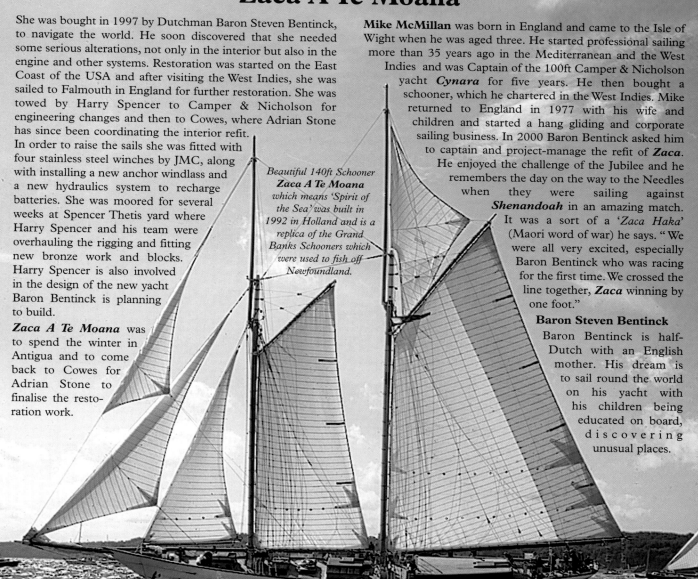

Flica II

Nyala

Photos © Beken of Cowes

South Australia

Photo © Kos

The 12-Metre Class
There were three divisions: Grand Prix, Modern and Classic

The naming of the 12-Metre Class (without an 's' at the end) is a unit of metric rating and not a measurement.
In fact, the yachts have a length of around 20 metres and a sailing surface of 180 square metres.
They are called 'Twelves' because of a formula that was first approved by the International Rating System in 1907.
Since then they have been a trial laboratory for new materials and technologies and the forerunners in
the use of Dacron sails and aluminium masts and hulls.
Here follows a selection seen at the Jubilee.

After the 2nd World War the 12-Metre replaced the J-Class which was considered too expensive. The 'Deed of Gift' had been amended by the New York Supreme Court adopting the 12-Metre Class as more economical to run the Cup. They were started in Europe and became established in America in 1927 when an order from the New York Yacht Club was placed for six boats with the *Abeking & Ramussen* German yard. The 12-Metre raced for the America's cup with smaller crews of 11 to 16 during 29 years until the 1987 series off Freemantle, when they were replaced by the new ACC Boats (America's Cup Class).

During the Jubilee, 37 of them representing four decades of Cup history competed for the Prada 12-Metre World Championship, which is part of a circuit of regattas called The Prada Challenge for Classic Yachts, co-ordinated by the Yacht Club de Monaco, under the aegis of the International Committee for the Mediterranean (CIM). The regattas take place in Porto Cervo, Monaco, Cannes and St. Tropez. They are divided into smaller classes related to Vintage, ranging in age from the 1930s to the 1980s.

Among some of the most famous was of course *Australia II*, the first yacht to win the cup from the USA. Owned by Alan Bond, she was skippered by John Bertrand, who came to

Cowes with almost his entire crew of 1983. She was shipped from the Museum of Western Australia in a container with *Kookaburra*, another America's Cup legend.

Flica II, a 1933 Fife design, owned by German cartography businessman, Alex Falk, was skippered by Olympic Gold medallist and French America's Cup Thierry Peponnet. She is another yacht rigged by Spencer.

Nyala, a 1938 Sparkman & Stephens-designed, pistachio green beauty, owned by *Prada* boss Patrizio Bertelli, was skippered by Brazilian Torben Grael.

Vanity V, designed by William Fife in 1836, and described by Eric Tabarly as the most beautiful 12-Metre he had ever seen, has been completely restored and was skippered by Marc Payot.

Trivia, launched in 1937 by Charles Nicholson, was called *Norsaga* when she belonged to the King of Norway, before being bought by Lord Craigmile. Commodore Peter Hedley, of the Island Sailing Club, remembers racing her with Harry Spencer. Harry was skipper for the Syndicate **Red Duster** for the America's Cup in the early 1960s, but the challenge was never mounted. Restored by Camper & Nicholson, and rigged by Spencer in 1998, she was at the Jubilee with owner/skipper Wilfried Beeck.

Photos courtesy of the owner

Thea

In 1917, the Norwegian shipowner Jakob Stolt Nielsen, grandfather to the present owner with the same name, commissioned a 12-Metre yacht, to be designed by Johan Anker and to be built at Anker's shipyard, Anker & Jensen, in Asger, Norway. The yacht was delivered in May 1918 and Jakob Stolt Nielsen gave her the name *Santa* and kept her until around 1933. The next owner was the legendary Norwegian shipowner Leif Hogh, who kept her until 1969, when the Danish shipowner Ebbe Baron Wedell Wedellsborg bought the yacht and renamed her *Nina*. Baron Wedell owned the yacht for 30 years until he sold her to the Danish shipowner Hans Michael Jebsen, who gave her the name *Thea*.

Thea was designed on the S-Rule, 'S' for Scandinavian and 'S' being the next letter after 'R'. The S-Rule, in 1918, replaced the 1906 R-rule, that in Scandinavian eyes had developed in the wrong direction. In 1919, a year after *Thea* was built, a measurement conference in London embarked on finding a new internationally-accepted rule. Johan Anker and Danish designer Alfred Benzon (one of the fathers of the original 1906 R-Rule) who had been the brains behind the S-Rule, travelled to London and negotiated on the choice between the American Universal Rule and the S-Rule. Thus, in 1919 the new R-Rule was adopted, modifying of the S-Rule. *Thea's* designer Johan Anker has therefore been one of the important influencers of the 1919 R-Rule.

Thea is built in mahogany on oak, and, thanks to the splendid care of her previous owners, 90% of all planking and frames of the hull are still original. *Thea* has a Harry Spencer silver spruce rig, built at Cowes in 2000. She sails under the Danish *Dannebrog* flag and the Royal Danish Yacht Club burgee. *Thea* logs at least 3,000 miles every year, cruising the Scandinavian waters and participating in the increasingly active Scandinavian 12-Metre racing scene.

In Cowes, *Thea* was helmed by Mads Aldertsen. Tacticians were Bjorn Westergaard and skipper, Patrick Howaldt. *Thea* was disqualified in the last two races, which spoiled her chances of reaching ninth place, which would have been a very satisfactory result, taking into account that *Thea* was the second oldest 12-Metre in the fleet.

Ernesto Bertarelli on South Australia

Ernesto Bertarelli

'Alinghi' skipper
Russell Coutts

Michel Bonnefous

South Australia

South Australia *was chartered by Swiss/Italian Ernesto Bertarelli,
whose big money has bought Russell Coutts and some of his men for
the Alinghi Swiss Challenge. They did so well, winning the regatta
with a race to spare, that on the final Saturday they
were playing golf in the Swiss mountains instead of
collecting their trophy at the prize-giving!*

Australia II
Challenger
KA6
63ft (19.2m)

Designed by Australian Ben Lexcen, owned by Alan Bond and skippered by John Bertrand, she was the first boat to take the Cup away from the New York Yacht Club in 1983. Her winged keel and her powerhouse made by New Zealand sailmaker Toni Schnackenberg (now head of Team New Zealand) attracted much attention and controversy.*The NYYC tried everything to eliminate her during the Louis Vuitton Cup but did not succeed. They could feel there was a danger... and there was indeed, because she wrested the 'Holy Grail' of yachting from America for the first time in 132 years! After her victory, Alan Bond sold her to the Australian Government. She was first put on display at the National Maritime Museum in Sydney and is now in Freemantle, where a new Western Australian Maritime Museum is being built for her.

Australia II was on loan from the Museum for the Jubilee in Cowes, where John Bertrand and his entire crew sailed her together for the first time since 1983 with helmsman/skipper Lissi Man, under the supervision of two museum staff who watched her carefully. At the final prizegiving, *Australia II* was awarded the *New York Yacht Club Cup* for the racing yacht that has brought the greatest benefit to the sport.

*Alan Bond revealed the design of the winged keel to the world and many designers copied and adopted it after 1987.

Sceptre

Crusader

Sovereign

Lionheart

Victory

Some 12-Metre Yachts
which participated in the America's Cup

Sceptre (Challenger) 12/K17 65ft 3in (19.81m)
Designed by David Boyd in 1958, she was the first post-war challenge put up by the Royal Yacht Squadron for the America's Cup. After her Cup defeat by *Columbia*, she lay for some years in Lymington. She is owned by the Sceptre Trust and operates in Scottish waters. At the Jubilee, she was skippered by John Roberts.

Columbia (Defender) 12/US16 72ft 6in (22m)
Built of wood in 1958 to a design by Olin Stephens, owned and skippered by millionaire sportsman and racing car driver Briggs Cunningham, *Columbia* inflicted a defeat on Challenger *Sceptre*, steered by Graham Mann. During the Jubilee she was skippered by James Gubilmann.

Sovereign (Challenger) K12 69ft 7in (21.12m)
Also built by David Boyd, she was put up as a challenger by the Royal Thames Yacht Club for the 1961 Cup against *Constellation* but did not win. She now belongs to Frenchman J. Fauroux.

Intrepid (Defender) US22 65ft 1in (19.71m)
Designed by Olin Stephens, she successfully defended the Cup, skippered by Bus Mosbacher in 1967 and Bill Ficker in 1970, defeating Australian *Dame Pattie* and *Gretel II*. When he designed *Intrepid*, Olin made quite a lot of changes. He reduced the wetted surface area, thus increasing the speed. He also separated the rudder from the keel. The other innovation was that four crew operated the grinders simultaneously and only five men could be seen when racing: the helmsman, the tactician, the navigator and two sail trimmers. The sails were made by Ted Hood and set on a titanium mast. She now belongs to John Curtin.

Freedom (Defender) 12/US30 66ft 4in (20.12m)
This beautiful dark blue 12-Metre also designed by Olin Stephens in 1980, was the boat with which Dennis Conner won the Cup. *Freedom* is now owned by Ernest Jacquet who skippered her for the New York Yacht Club at the Jubilee.

Kookaburra III (Challenger) KA11 67ft 4in (20.42m)
Financed by Australian furniture store owner Kevin Parry, built by John Swarbrick and Iain Murray in 1987 and skippered by Peter Gilmour, she defeated *Australia IV* for the right to defend the Cup for the Royal Perth Yacht Club, but was defeated by Dennis Conner's *Stars & Stripes*. During the Jubilee she was skippered by Michael Smith.

Lionheart (Challenger) 14/K18 64ft 4in (19.51m)
After 16 years of British absence, the Lionheart Syndicate challenged in 1980, but without success.

Victory 82 (Challenger) K21 65ft 4in (19.81m)
In 1983, Peter de Savary challenged with the Victory Syndicate but could not win. (See the America's Cup Saga).

Crusader (Challenger) 12 K24 68ft 4in. (19.81m)
This 'old British warhorse', built in 1986 and nicknamed the 'hippo', (because of her radical below the water shape) was designed for the last British Challenge in 1987, where she was skippered by Harold Cudmore. Richard Matthews, Oyster Marine boss, bought her in 1989 in a part-exchange deal for a luxury Oyster cruising yacht. *Crusader* sailed during the Jubilee as a member of the Royal Thames Yacht Club. John Corby, designer of several successful modern racing yachts, had her refitted, partly in the Oyster Yard at Ipswich and partly at the GBR Challenge site in Cowes.

The Modern Yachts
A selection seen at the Jubilee

These boats represented the modern 'end' of yacht racing, from cruise racers such as the perennial Swan line to one-off high-tech offshore and inshore racing yachts (IRC or IMS or the over 45ft LOA). They have been called the "wild young rogue generation."

They had to be owned or chartered at the Jubilee by members of a Club that had competed for the America's Cup or the Louis Vuitton Trophy.

Bribon (2000) owner King Juan Carlos

Morning Glory (2000) owner Hasso Plattner

Leopard (2000) owner Mike Slade.
Spirit of Jethou (1998): owners J. Perry/Peter Ogden

Extra Beat (1998) Alan Bond was on board

Bear of Britain
owners Tim Louis and Kit Hobday

Mari-Cha III

'First among Equals...'

Bear of Britain

Overall winner of the Jubilee

Photo © Yacht Shots

Photo © Yacht Shots

High Voltage US16

High Voltage has had several names: John Caulcutt bought the former *Il Moro 4* from the *Young America* syndicate in New York and renamed her *Right Time*. Together with Oyster Marine Boss Richard Mathews (who had renamed his ACC boat *Tag Hoya About Time*), they were instrumental in encouraging the current British America's Cup Challenge. During the Jubilee, *High Voltage* was sailed by John Caulcutt and a largely amateur but efficient crew, and on one of the days even beat *Team New Zealand NZL32* - something only four other ACC boats have ever achieved.

France 3 FRA37

Le Défi Francais representing "L'Union Nationale pour la Course au Large", a French syndicate with a commercially orientated structure, almost won the Louis Vuitton Cup in 1999. *France 2* (FRA33) and *France 3* (FRA37), built in 1994, were both at the Jubilee with owner/skipper Chris Gordon.

The America's Cup Class
(ACC)

*These yachts have been racing for the America's Cup since 1992 and the Louis Vuitton Trophy. They are about 75 feet long (23m) and weigh more than 20 tonnes. They represent the most advanced performance technology afloat in terms of structure and systems. At the Jubilee, the winner was **Luna Rossa** followed by **GBR52** and **Team New Zealand NZL32**. In the ACC match racing final **Prada Luna Rossa** had only a six-second victory over **GBR52**.*

Luna Rossa ITA45

Built by German Frers and Doug Peterson in 1999 for the 2000 America's Cup, *Luna Rossa* and Francesco de Angelis battled their way through the Louis Vuitton Cup beating *Nippon* and *America One* in the most exciting Louis Vuitton final ever. Unfortunately the best looking boat with its silver painted hull and distinctive red Prada stripe was beaten by *Team New Zealand NZL60* which retained the Cup.

America 3 USA 23

Designed in 1992 by the *America 3* design team, headed by Doug Peterson, technology and big money were the key-words in the design of the new America's Cup Class. The new rule was that there were no restrictions on the number of boats that could be built. In 1992, *America 3*, skippered and owned by Bill Koch, representing the San Diego Yacht Club, beat *Il Moro di Venezia*, owned by Raoul Gardini and skippered by Paul Cayard, representing the Italian Compagnia della Vela. In 1995 Bill Koch passed all his equipment to an almost all-girl team and after they lost, sold most of it to the new Italian Prada Challenge. He bought her back in 2000 from Prada.

Team New Zealand
NZL32

Generally known as *NZL32*, or *Black Magic*, the sleek black-hulled boat, designed by Laurie Davidson and Doug Peterson in 1994, won the Cup in 1995 with skipper Russell Coutts against *Young America*, owned by Dennis Conner. Attention to detail was to the fore in the Kiwi campaign and the boat was far superior and faster than any other in the 1995 series.

Team New Zealand NZL60 won again in 2000, helmed by 26 year-old Dean Barker.

Il Moro di Venezia V ITA 25

Like Bill Koch, Italian millionaire Raoul Gardini spared no expense to have this new America's Cup Class boat built by Argentinian designer German Frers in 1992.

Il Moro di Venezia beat New Zealand in the Louis Vuitton Cup but lost the Cup match against Bill Koch's *America 3*. She now belongs to Bill Koch, who had her returned to original.

GBR Challenge
GBR 41 and GBR 52
(See next page)

Peter Harrison who created **GBR Challenge**, acquired the assets of the Nippon Syndicate including three ACC boats and two of their designers. **Idaten,** one of the Japanese boats, built in 2000, was sailed by the Nippon Challenge to the Louis Vuitton semi-finals. GBR Challenge did very well during the Jubilee considering the team only had three months of training. After the Jubilee GBR 41 and GBR 52 were sent to New Zealand for the team to practice, refining race-winning tactics, during the winter.

GBR Challenge Sponsorship & Partnership Opportunities
- *Make history with the GBR Challenge*
- *Build a global brand awareness campaign around this unique opportunity*
- *Heighten brand awareness in Great Britain and overseas*
- *Become a member of the GBR Challenge Business Club*
- *Purchase exclusive GBR Challenge merchandise via the website or from Musto Stockists*

The GBR Challenge Business Club
During the 2002 London Boat Show, Peter Harrison launched the official GBR Challenge Business Club at the Royal Ocean Racing Club. The Club gives companies who are not in a position to become sponsors an opportunity to support the GBR Challenge. In return for a donation of £25,000, Business Club members will benefit from a range of networking, hospitality and promotional activities for their business and brand.
Tel: 01983 531465
www.GBRchallenge.com
e-mail: info@gbrglobalchallenge.co.uk

The **Bear of Britain** team, Overall Winner with HRH Princess Anne

Photo © Jon Nash

HRH Princess Anne

Photo © Jon Nash

The Prizegiving Ceremony

In the presence of The Princess Royal

Ernest K. Jacquet
(**Freedom**)

Photo © Yacht Shots

Bill Koch
(**America 3**)

Andrew Bray, Editor of Yachting World
with Sir Tom Perkins (**Mariette**)

Photo © Yacht Shots

UBS Managing Director Robert Gillespie
with Peter Harrison (**GBR 52**)

Photo © MCvA

Ken and Keith Beken and Sue Chester

Photo © Yacht Shots

Skip Lissiman (**Australia II**)

Photo © Yacht Shots

Alexander Falk and the **Flica II** crew

Photo © Yacht Shots

Mrs Gilly Drummond and Jim Bishop (**Partridge**)

John Despard

Photo © Yacht Shots

Philippe Menhinick (**Nan of Fife**)

Photo © Yacht Shots

Maldwin Drummond presenting a prize

Photo © Yacht Shots

The Benzie Trophy

Bear of Britain

Australia II

Luna Rossa

Endeavour

South Australia

Societé Nautique de Genève

Stealth

Freedom

Sovereign

Nyala

Rugosa

Crusade of Dee

Trophies & Prizes

The final prizegiving took place the last day in the presence of the Princess Royal, HRH Princess Anne, and many VIPs with a terrific display of fabulous trophies handed out.

Bear of Britain was the big overall winner of the America's Cup Jubilee (and also winner of the Modern IRC Divison 2). Owners Kit Hobday and Tim Louis and the young crew jumped for joy long after the prizegiving. The Louis Vuitton Trophy for current America's Cup Class yachts went to **Luna Rossa** and the Hennessy J-Class Trophy to **Endeavour**. **Australia II** won the 1926 New York Yacht Club Cup and **Stealth** the UBS Round-the-Island Race Benzie Trophy. **Thendara** won the Edmiston Lalique Trophy, **Crusade of Dee** won the Classic Division Overall Prize as well as the ResidenSea Trophy. **Mariette** won the Yachting World Concours d'Elégance Vintage Cup and the Asprey Swan Challenge Trophy was won by **Northern Child of St Peter Port**. The Prada 12-Metre World Grand Prix, Prada Trophy was won by **South Australia**, with **Freedom** taking the 12-Metre Modern Prada Cup and **Sovereign** winning the 12-Metre Classic Traditional Class. The Prada Cup for 12-Metre Classic Vintage went to **Nyala**. The 12-Metre Grand Prix Amateur Helm Trophy, Mrs Hugh Goodson's Whitelegg Cup, was won by the British boat, **Crusader**. Mrs Hugh Goodson's Coronation Cup, for Modern Amateur Helm went to **Intrepid**. **Flica II** won the Classic Amateur Helm Trophy, Captain Michael Boyle's Vanity V Trophy. Among second and third prizes, let us mention **GBR52** which was first in the Round the Island Race in the America's Cup Class and second to Prada in the Cup Match Racing for the America's Cup Class Louis Vuitton Trophy; **Cambria** in the J-Class and 23-Metre; **Mari-Cha III** in IRC Modern was third overall and second in Division 1, with **Chernikeeff 2** third in Division 2. **Aera** was third for the Nautor's Swan trophy, as was **Bribon** in IMS Modern, Division 2. In the Spirit of Tradition, **The Lady Anne** was second (Overall) and first in Division 2, where **Zaca A Te Moana** was second and **Adix** was third. **Wild Horses** was third in Division 1. In the Vintage Class, **Tuiga** came third in Division 2 and **Partridge** was third in Division 4.

Bear of Britain
America's Cup Jubilee Regatta
Overall Winner
"The King's Cup, RYS Regatta
1923 presented by King George V
and won by **Moonbeam**, together
with a presentation collection of
Beken photographs
RYS, Beken and Omnimage

Australia II
The yacht that has brought the
greatest benefit to the sport
through participation in the
America's Cup Jubilee Regatta
1926 New York Yacht Club Cup

Luna Rossa
America's Cup Class★
Louis Vuitton Trophy

Endeavour
J Class and 23 Metre Class
Hennessy J Class Trophy

Stealth
UBS Jubilee
Round The Island Race★
Benzie Trophy with a presentation
of Beken photographs

South Australia
Prada International
Twelve Metre Class World
Championship
Chandler Hovey Memorial Trophy
& the Prada Trophy
International Twelve Metre
Association and Prada

Société Nautique de Genève
The Yacht Club of the
International Twelve Metre
Class World Championship
Azzurra Trophy
Yacht Club Costa Smeralda

Freedom
International Twelve Metre
Class Modern Division
Prada Cup

Sovereign
International Twelve Metre
Class Classic Division
Prada Cup

Nyala
International Twelve Metre
Class Traditional, Vintage
and Antique Divisions
Prada Cups

Rugosa
Overall Winner Vintage
Division
★W. Butler Duncan Constitution
Trophy 1901
The Herreshoff Marine Museum

Rugosa
Vintage Division 1 Large
Bermudian
Queen's Cup, RYS 1839/1838
Sir Geoffrey Shakerley, Bt

Crusade of Dee
Classic Division Large
Bermudian
ResidensSea Trophy

Zwerver
Classic Division Small
Bermudian
Cariad Cup

Thendara
Vintage Division 2 Large Gaff
Edmiston Lalique Trophy

Stormy Weather
Vintage Division 3 Smaller
Bermudian
"Queen Victoria Tureen" 1842
RYS Vice Commodore
Michael Campbell

Marilee
Vintage Division 4 Smaller Gaff
"The Gloriana Trophy" 1891
The Herreshoff Marine Museum

Crusade of Dee
Overall Winner Classic Division
The 1901 Cowes Town Cup
Isle of Wight Partnership, loaned
by the Worshipful Company of
Shipwrights

Diligent
Overall Winner Spirit of
Tradition Division
Phillips Trophy - Rose Bowl 1882

Classic: *Nirvana*
Modern: *America 3*
Overall & Vintage: *Mariette*
Overall and Divisional Winners
Concours d'Elégance
Yachting World
Concours d'Elégance Cups

Gandalf Wight Sorcerer
Overall Winner Modern Class
IMS
RYS Coronation Challenge Cup
1953 and Moët & Chandon
Trophy

Extra Beat
Overall Winner Modern Class
IRC
The Rear Commodore's Cup 1965
RYS

Extra Beat
Modern Class IRC Division 1
United Airlines Trophy

Bear of Britain
Modern Class IRC Division 2
Royal Ocean Racing Club Trophy

Team Tonic
Modern Class IRC Division 3
Blick Rothenberg Trophy

Northern Child of St. Peter Port
The First Swan in the Modern
Class
Asprey Swan Challenge Trophy

★GBR 52 was first in the UBS Round the Island Race
in the America's Cup Class

The Swan Asprey
Challenge Trophy

Zwerver — Thendara

Stormy Weather — Marilee

Diligent — Nirvana

America 3 — Mariette

Gandalf Wight Scorcerer — Extra Beat

Team Tonic — Northern Child of St Peter Port

THE PARTNERS

The gold partners supporting the America's Cup Jubilee were the Isle of Wight Council, Louis Vuitton and Prada.

ISLE *of* WIGHT
COUNCIL

Vic Morey
Chairman
Isle of Wight Council

Photos courtesy Isle of Wight Council

Shirley Smart
Leader of the Council

Louis Vuitton

LOUIS VUITTON CUP

Sir Peter Blake after winning
the America's Cup 1995

Team New Zealand NZL60

© Louis Vuitton Media Centre

The Isle of Wight Council

It was thanks to the foresight and belief of the Isle of Wight Council that plans for the America's Cup Jubilee ever got going. For the Council, ever mindful of the need to use civic money only for the public good, had enough faith in the success of the Jubilee to put in around £200,000 sponsorship to enable planning to get underway at an early stage. The Jubilee brought thousands of people to this lovely little Island, just off the South Coast of mainland Britain - many for the first time. And, charmed by Cowes and the friendly welcome, historic nautical ambience and vivid sailing scene, many vowed to return and explore more of this surprising Island. For the Isle of Wight provides most of what is best about Britain - varied scenery, a rich history stretching back to Roman times and before, a slower pace of life than mainland Britain and an economy still anchored in agriculture, boatbuilding and tourism. Cowes has always been the top attraction for yachtsmen and women, with Skandia Life Cowes Week in August one of the world's most famous regattas. Almost every Olympic or America's Cup champion has raced at Cowes Week at some time. The Isle of Wight Council was one of the first to support the Jubilee, seeing it as an important shop window for key foreign visitors to the Island, be they potential business investors or potential tourists. This support made possible much of the infrastructure improvements around the Cowes waterfront. The Council was keen that the event would be of lasting benefit to the Island and, with this in mind, a wide-ranging education programme for local schools was included. Many children were involved in projects with a maritime theme and all Island schoolchildren aged 10 and 11 were offered the chance to try a day's sailing, with tuition.

Louis Vuitton

To win the America's Cup, first win the Louis Vuitton Cup.
That is the truth facing all challengers for the 'Auld Mug'. The Louis Vuitton Cup is the vital goal which must be secured, the trophy awarded to the top challenger who will then go on to race the current holder of the America's Cup. The first Louis Vuitton Cup was awarded in 1983, an historic year for the America's Cup. It was the year ***Australia II*** having claimed the Louis Vuitton Cup, went on to be the first challenger to take the cup away from the USA, which had held on to the trophy since it was first won in 1851 by the yacht ***America*** in that historic race around the Isle of Wight. ***Stars and Stripes*** was another winner of the Louis Vuitton Cup and, for the second time in a row, the Louis Vuitton Cup winner took the America's Cup away from the defender. For more than a century, Louis Vuitton - the world's best known trunk maker - and the America's Cup have both been synonymous with excellence in technical and avant-garde design along with modern values. Louis Vuitton became responsible for the media operations for the Challenger series and later the America's Cup itself and brought in a lot of technical innovations. Former America's Cup skipper Bruno Troublé has been a major force in building the powerful media relations operation. In 1999 Louis Vuitton introduced a product called Virtual Spectator, allowing Internet users the world over to view all races from the screens of their own computers. For the 2002-03 America's Cup, winning the Louis Vuitton Cup will again be a mandatory passage for any challenger wishing to race for the America's Cup. For the America's Cup Jubilee, Louis Vuitton ran all media operations and hosted many social engagements, among them the Jubilee Ball. The Louis Vuitton exhibition featuring the rich history of the America's Cup, was on show at the Trinity Theatre. The state-of-the-art show was in four parts, with a multi-media presentation which included continuous film footage, still photographs and interpretation. The first part traced the 1851 origins of the Cup while the second section showed the noble age of the J-Class yachts.

Presentation of the bollard

Yves Carcelle, LVMH Chairman

Luna Rossa

Patrizio Bertelli

The Third examined the recent history of the Cup, from 1983, tracing Louis Vuitton's sponsorship and the contests in Newport USA, Perth, San Diego and Auckland. The final part of the exhibition offered a fascinating insight into the tycoons and personalities associated with the Cup, from Lipton and Sopwith to Alan Bond and Peter Harrison. Created to celebrate the 20th anniversary, in 2003, of Louis Vuitton's involvement in the Cup, the travelling presentation went on show in Paris, Venice and New York before it arrives in New Zealand - at the National Maritime Museum in Auckland - in time for the Louis Vuitton Cup and America's Cup.

A commemorative mooring bollard was presented by Louis Vuitton to celebrate the 150th anniversary of the first race around the Isle of Wight in 1851. It was unveiled at a special ceremony below the Royal Yacht Squadron battlements by Yves Carcelle, Chairman and Chief Executive of the company and the LVMH Group, with Commodore Charles Dana III of the New York Yacht Club and Commodore Peter Nicholson of the Royal Yacht Squadron. Created by Paris artist Gregory Ryan, the tall, slim contemporary artwork has been planted into the pavement of the gun emplacements fronting the Squadron.

LVMH

LVMH is the world's leading luxury products group, represented in wines and spirits by brands which include Moet & Chandon, Dom Perignon, Veuve Clicquot Ponsardin, Krug, Pommery, Château d'Yquem, Hennessy and Hine. The fashion and leather goods division includes Louis Vuitton, Celine, Loewe, Kenzo, Givenchy, Christian Lacroix, Thomas Pink, Fendi and Pucci. In addition, LVMH recently finalized the acquisition of Donna Karan. LVMH is also represented in the fragrance and cosmetics sector with Parfums Christian Dior, Guerlain, Givenchy and Kenzo, and has recently acquired five promising cosmetics companies Bliss, Hard Candy, BeneFit Cosmetics, Urban Decay Make-up for Ever and Fresh. LVMH is also active in retailing through DFS, Miami Cruiseline, Sephora, Le Bon Marché and La Samaritaine. The Group has established a watches and jewellery division comprising TAG Heuer, Ebel, Chaumet, Zenith and Fred, as well as Omas, the prestigious Italian writing instruments company. Phillips, one of the world's largest auction houses, which has teamed up with Etude Tajan and Geneva art dealer de Pury & Luxembourg Art was recently renamed Bonhams after merging with Bonhams & Brooks auctioneers. Connaissance des Arts and Art Auction Magazine, two specialized publications, also joined the Group. LVMH has recently launched eLUXURY, the authoritative online source for luxury goods and services on the Internet. LVMH shares (LVMH.PA) are listed on the Paris stock exchange and the NASDAQ in New York. For more information www.lvmh.com.

Prada

The other main gold partner in the America's Cup was fashion icon Prada, which is strongly associated with the vintage and classic boat series organised in the Mediterranean, by the CIM. *Luna Rossa*, the Louis Vuitton Cup winner and challenger for the America's Cup in 2000, was in Cowes for the Jubilee. Patrizio Bertelli owner of Prada, is known for his intense love of sailing and is backing the next Italian America's Cup Challenge for 2003 through his company for around $50 million. Bertelli is also the proud owner of one of the most beautiful of the 12-Metre yachts, **Nyala**, built in 1938, which was also racing at Cowes. Prada was the sponsor of the prestigious Prada International 12-Metre Class World Championship, held during Jubilee week. The event attracted the largest fleet of 12-Metre ever to race together, with 37 gathered together at Cowes. They were divided into five categories: *Grand Prix*, built since 1983; *Modern*, built between 1968 and 1983; *Traditional*, built before 1967; *Vintage*, built before 1950 and *Antique*, with gaff rigging. Bertelli had also provided Prada's sponsorship for the Prada Challenge for Classic Yachts, a series of classic races held in the Mediterranean and co-ordinated by the Yacht Club de Monaco and other local clubs. For the Jubilee, the Royal Yacht Squadron and the New York Yacht Club were also involved. The classic yacht scene encompasses a wide variety of vintage craft, with hundreds restored and now sailing and racing around the world. Some of them, such as **Partridge** and **Avel**, are more than 100-years-old. The yachts, between six and 60 metres long, are divided into *Vintage*, *Classic* and *Spirit of Tradition* - those built along classic lines with modern techniques and materials. The classic circuit is overseen by the *Comité International de la Méditerranée* (CIM) and sponsored by Prada, with four or five events a year. In 2001, many of the Mediterranean fleet made their way to Cowes for the Jubilee, where they met up with classic yachts from Northern Europe and the East coast of the US. After the Jubilee, many went back to the Mediterranean, some on a submersible ship, for the Prada Veteran Boat Rally, held at Porto Cervo in September and organised by the Costa Smeralda Yacht Club. From there the yachts sailed to Monaco for the Monaco Classic Week. The Monaco-Cannes stretch represented the second leg of the 2001 Trophée Grimaldi-Coupe Prada, with participants at Cannes for the Regates Royales-Trophée Prada. The final and prizegiving was held at Les Voiles de St. Tropez in October, for the final Coupe Prada prizegiving.

Gilles Hennessy, Bruno Troublé and Dennis Conner

Bill Koch who bought the Hennessy Collection at the auction

Gilles Hennessy

America's Cup Jubilee Collection

150TH ANNIVERSARY OF THE AMERICA'S CUP

AUCTION OF THE UNIQUE HENNESSY EAUX-DE-VIE COLLECTION 22 AUGUST 2001

Cover of the auction catalogue

HENNESSY SKIPPERS' CLUB AMERICA'S CUP JUBILEE 1851 - 2001 MEMBER

PRIVATE ACCESS 11 AM - 7 PM   COMMODORE'S HOUSE COWES

Silver Partner

Hennessy Cognac

"We have to leave to time what the present cannot accomplish"
Richard Hennessy.

Hennessy Cognac has been associated with the sea from its origins. Since Richard Hennessy established the company in 1765, the house of Hennessy has collected more than 200 years of *eaux de vie*, the physical ingredient of cognac, assembling the best cognacs over that time. At the America's Cup Jubilee Regatta, Hennessy supported the legendary J-Class fleet. It was the first time these historic yachts had raced together in the Solent since 1934. The J-Class Hennessy Trophy, a special bottle of Richard Hennessy cognac in an Italian silver box, was presented to ***Endeavour***, the yacht with the best score. For the Jubilee, Hennessy had created the America's Cup Jubilee Collection, a set of 31 bottles of its rarest *eaux de vie* - one for each America's Cup raced - presented in a specially-commissioned oak and teak cabinet, with chrome hardware and stainless steel cables. It was created by Thierry Drevelle. Auctioned by Phillips at the Jubilee Ball, in aid of the Royal National Lifeboat Institution (RNLI), the America's Cup Jubilee Collection was bought by American oil billionaire and cup sailor Bill Koch for a staggering £310,000! The price expected had been £20,000. Each bottle - distilled in the year of an America's Cup match, starting with 1851 - had a special label with drawings of the challenger and the defender and the winning skippers' names - including Bill Koch, on the 1992 bottle.

Before the sale he had said: "I'm debating on whether I will bid or not. Because, you know, I collect fabulous wines. I love it." He added: "This is an absolutely magnificent event. Even though the sailing is tough, difficult and challenging, and the Brits are superb sailors and tough competitors, the hospitality here, the warmth and the magic of it... it's like falling in love for the first time!" At the ball, however, Koch made it clear that he wanted the collection and stood before the podium, programme in the air, vigorously responding to each counter bid by Mark Lloyd who was probably bidding for one of his wealthy clients or friends. Bill Koch said: "The RNLI has rescued thousands of sailors over the years, for which I am extremely grateful. After spending £68million on the America's Cup, this was rather cheap!" The idea for the collection and its auction was the brainchild of Bruno Troublé and Marcus Hutchinson of *Jour J*, the Paris-based agency which worked extensively with the Jubilee organisers. A hand-made exclusive card gave access to the Hennessy Skippers' Club located at the Commodore's House in Cowes, belonging to John Terry , where pirate parties also took place.

Richard Hennessy

Richard Hennessy was the son of the Lord of Ballymacmoy and had left County Cork to serve Louis XV in the Irish Brigade of the Clare Regiment. The Count de Thomond in 1757 described Richard Hennessy, recently promoted to the rank of Captain, as a "brave and gallant man." But after a distinguished army career he decided to abandon his uniform for the eaux de vie trade, moving to Tonnay-Charente in 1765. So the Hennessy dynasty was born...A dynasty which perpetuated the spirit of its founder. Being Irish did help to make England Hennessy's largest export market.

Team New Zealand with Dean Barker holding the bottle of Esprit du Siècle

Phillips Prizegiving

Christopher Thomson, Chief Executive of Phillips and Ellen MacArthur

Christophe Navarre, Chairman of Moët Hennessy and Jean-Marie Laborde Chairman of Moët & Chandon

Jean-Marie Laborde, Tony Thomas and Tom Schmackenberg of Team New Zealand

Jean Berchon Moët & Chandon

Tom Perkins and his crew

The Bear of Britain Team

Silver Partner

Moët & Chandon

Moët & Chandon, the official Champagne for the America's Cup, organised the social highlight of the week - the America's Cup Jubilee Ball. Having been present at all of the crowning moments in recent America's Cup history, it was only natural that the prestigious Champagne brand would want to celebrate the 150th anniversary of the world's oldest sporting trophy, the America's Cup. At the ball, Moët & Chandon honoured the youngest and current winners, Team New Zealand, with a magnum of their *Esprit du Siècle Champagne*.

Esprit du Siècle is a blend of eleven of the most extraordinary vintages from the 20th century - 1900, 1914, 1921, 1934, 1943, 1952, 1962, 1976, 1983, 1985 and 1995. The blend, once assembled, underwent a new in-bottle third fermentation. Only 323 magnums were produced, undergoing a further three years maturation in magnums specially created for the occasion. To create these bottles, Moët & Chandon called on contemporary talents. The glass presentation case is both a coffret and a showcase. Through it, the *Esprit du Siècle* magnum is visible - blown glass, engraved tin cap and cork secured with metal clip rather than wire.

Phillips Auctioneers

Phillips Auctioneers (now Bonhams), founded in 1976, holds more than 600 sales a year, including specialist marine auctions during the London Boat Show and in June, during the Henley Royal Regatta. Phillips sponsored the first day of sailing on Sunday, 19 August, known as Phillips Day. The day - a breezy start to the week which saw some damage, with several boats dismasted - culminated in a prizegiving performed by round-the-world solo sailor Ellen MacArthur MBE. The 'Spirit of Tradition Class' comprised 11 yachts built since 1970 but with the traditional spirit in mind. The winner received the Phillips Spirit of Tradition antique silver trophy. Phillips also auctioned the unique collection of Hennessy cognacs at the Jubilee Ball and had waived all auction fees.

To mark the Jubilee, Phillips also produced a unique collector's item - a map depicting the Isle of Wight in 1851 and charting the route of the original race in that year. It incorporated drawings and profiles of each of the 31 America's Cup winners since. Limited edition prints were signed by legendary winning skippers and presented by Phillips to the Royal Yacht Squadron and the New York Yacht Club.

Nicholas Edmiston
and his two sons,
Woody and Jamie

Photo © Edmiston

Jamie Edmiston and his team at the Jubilee

Photos © MCvA

The late Sir Peter Blake

Silver Partner

Edmiston

Edmiston & Company is a name synonymous with some of the largest and finest yachts in the world, whether sail or power, buying or chartering. The company handles brokerage, new construction and charter, with headquarters in Monte Carlo. Its new offices in the heart of London, designed by Jon Bannenberg, feature furniture from the David Linley Marine Collection. During the Jubilee the name of Edmiston - previously unknown to many at Cowes - was highly visible. As silver sponsors, Edmiston sponsored the landing stage at the front of the tented village on The Parade. The Edmiston pavilion nearby was furnished by Summit, David Linley and Linn and Thomas Goode. It was the meeting point for crew members, owners and VIPs. They also manned the helicopter facilities and provided vehicles (Range Rover and Smart cars) to transport guests. All competitors, participants and passengers on the *Sea Cloud II* wore an Edmiston VIP card. Copies of the *Financial Times* were offered every day, compliments of Edmiston. They also gave the *Lalique Trophy*, a beautiful crystal sculpture worth £20,000 to *Thendara*, winner of Vintage Division Large Gaff at the final prizegiving. After one year, the trophy will be handed back to be given to the winner of a race still to be decided by the *Lalique* Committee. Edmiston also entertained on picnic boat *Hinkley* (of which they are the European agents) which they brought from the States. The Aga Khan, Commodore Charles Dana, Mark Lloyd and others were its VIP guests. Edmiston is a world leader in the sale and charter of large yachts and in just five years has evolved from a bright, enthusiastic new company into one of the pre-eminent names in yachting. The company sells some of the largest yachts in the world, has a charter division and is involved with spectacular new construction projects, becoming a major force in the industry with speed of thought and action. The company has sold some of the most high profile yachts in the world, such as the *Lady Christine*, which attracted much admiration during the Jubilee at Cowes. Edmiston also has a remarkably broad spectrum of experience in new construction. For such work, or the refitting of an existing yacht, Edmiston uses the best designers, engineers and shipyards, working as a team. When it comes to chartering a yacht, the company has an impressive list, from fast day boats to magnificent motor yachts, from intrepid discovery yachts to classic sailing yachts - and they can also research locations and itineraries. Edmiston says large yachts should be professionally managed, since this involves safety and security issues as well as legal and logistical matters. Its package includes reliable and experienced captains, with full support, technical back-up, maintenance schedules, shipyard planning and supervision; full accounting programmes; recruitment of crew and other detailed issues - to say nothing of chefs to provide the finest cuisine! Edmiston will also co-ordinate the production of yacht brochures and feature these yachts in its charter annual, newsletters and advertising. The Chairman and founder is Nicholas Edmiston, whose son, Jamie, is in charge of marketing. Jamie was delighted with the success of the Jubilee sponsorship and said he wants to see Edmiston become to yachting what Ferrari is in the car business! Edmiston aspires to the perfect balance: young enough to be dynamic, enthusiastic, entrepreneurial and experienced enough to have the contacts, confidence and reliability of an established name.

Website: www.edmistoncompany.com

Edmiston provided Rovers, Smart cars and helicopters for the transport of Vips

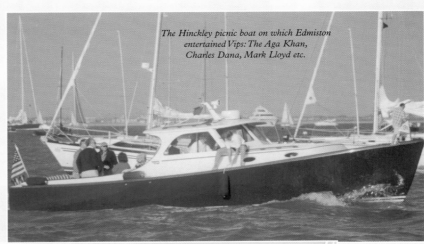

The Hinckley picnic boat on which Edmiston entertained Vips: The Aga Khan, Charles Dana, Mark Lloyd etc.

Photo © Omega

Dean Barker and Nicholas Hayek, Chairman of Omega

Photo © MCvA

*Stephen Urquhart
President of Omega*

Silver Partner

Omega

Another silver sponsor was Omega, the official timekeeper of the most recent America's Cup - and official watch of the victorious Team New Zealand for the past two events, in 1995 and 2000. It is also linked to *Cowes Week* and *Les Voiles de St Tropez*. The America's Cup dates back to 1851 but the Omega brand was born three years earlier. Born in 1848 in Louis Brandt's modest assembly workshop in La Chaux-de-Fonds, the heart of Switzerland's watchmaking country, Omega can also look back on an eventful century-and-a-half of history, during which it has, like the America's Cup, assumed a pioneering role in its field. Among its numerous firsts are - the first watch to be qualified for use in outer space; the first watch with a Central Tourbillon movement; and the world's first series-produced watch with a Co-Axial Escapement, launched in 2001. Omega watches even have some materials in common with the latest racing yachts, such as resilient Kevlar and carbon fibre. Omega's long association with the ocean has led to numerous pioneering developments for divers' watches, such as the helium escape valve and the world's first chronograph with push-buttons, which function at depths up to 300 metres - attributes of the Omega Seamaster. During the Jubilee, Omega announced that it will once again be official timekeeper for the America's Cup in 2003, continuing the brand's close relationship with this prestigious event. Whilst the America's Cup remains a challenge of design, boat-building and technology, it certainly places considerable demands on the yachtsmen's knowledge of tactics, strategy and seamanship, as well as timing. The ability to hit the starting line at the gun and the capacity to time manoeuvres on the course often decides the race. Omega has a history of timekeeping for some of the world's leading sailors, such as Team New Zealand and the late Sir Peter Blake, with the Omega Seamaster. The Seamaster diver has served some of the greatest athletes on the sea since its beginnings in 1948. The renewed partnership was introduced during the Jubilee by Omega President, Stephen Urquhart, at a press conference with Team New Zealand defenders Ross Blackman, Dean

Barker and Tom Schnackenberg, at the Royal Yacht Squadron. A great part of Team New Zealand was in Cowes, where they sailed their 1995 cup winning yacht NZL-32. For the Jubilee Regatta at Cowes, a new timing system was brought to the Island by Omega which enabled all clocks to synchronise to exactly the same time across the Island. The Powertime hand printer was used to synchronise all boats at the beginning of each race. Powertime also allowed the operator to enter sail numbers of each boat into the timer as they crossed the finish line, to record the time and position of each competitor on the day.

The Omega Seamaster

To celebrate its role as official timekeeper of the America's Cup 2000, a limited edition timepiece was created, enhancing the standard stainless steel Seamaster Professional 300m chronometer, with a white gold bezel and embossed markers. A special limited edition of 10,000 pieces was produced, 5,000 with a steel bracelet and 5,000 with a sporty rubber strap - all with the America's Cup logo. They quickly sold out and Omega decided to incorporate this refined Seamaster in its standard collection, with the same exacting specifications as its predecessor: self-winding certified chronometer movements with 44-hour power reserve, helium escape valve, high-legibility hands and hour markers with Super Luminova coating, anti-reflective, scratch-resistant sapphire crystal and water resistance guaranteed to a depth of 300 metres. For the America's Cup 2003, a new model has been developed in conjunction with Team New Zealand, which assisted with the specifications. The result is a highly robust watch with a regatta countdown timer, for the period when the skipper aims to position his yacht so that he crosses the start line as near to the gun as possible. A sturdy case with a large 43mm diameter allows clear legibility to read off remaining time in an instant. This exclusive watch will come with the familiar features of the Seamaster range. The new Seamaster will surely become a genuine master of the sea.

Seamaster

Photo © Omega

Omega and Blakexpeditions

*Following his victory with Team New Zealand in the 1995 America's Cup, Sir Peter Blake retired from competitive sailing to concentrate on the wellbeing of the waters of the world, with Blake Expeditions. Omega was his official partner in the venture, until Sir Peter Blake sadly died recently. During the Jubilee regatta, at a press conference held at the Royal Corinthian Yacht Club, Sir Peter Blake had revealed his findings from the first part of his expeditions. The first voyage, to the Antarctic Peninsula, was completed in March 2001. The crew of the vessel **Seamaster** were surprised to be able to navigate so far south, due to the lack of ice, and this was viewed with some concern by ministers at the United Nations Environmental Programme (UNEP).*

To find out what will happen to the Blakexpeditions www.omegawatches.com or www.blakexpeditions.com

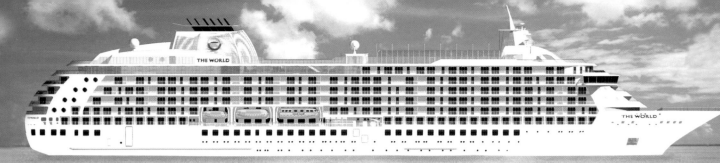

The World of ResidenSea was pronounced the winner of the "Ship of the Year 2001" award, by the Norwegian Minister of Trade and Industry, in the presence of HM King Harald of Norway.

Fredy M. Dellis
President & CEO

Knut Kloster
Founder

Henning Oglænd
Chairman

Anna Synnove-Bye
Owner Fosen Mek.
Verksteder AS

The first cruise from Lisbon to Rio de Janeiro which was supposed to take place in January 2002 was postponed.

THE WORLD
of ResidenSea

Imagine being able to travel the world without leaving home, to attend the greatest international events and see the wonders of the world on your doorstep, following the sun to climates perfect for exploration or relaxation. It may sound like a dream but it is now possible with *The World of ResidenSea*. The first ocean-going luxury resort, *The World of ResidenSea,* has 110 spacious, fully furnished and equipped residential apartments and 88 guest suites available for vacation excursions. The ship combines the comforts of a private home with the best features of ocean travel and the environment of an exclusive resort. It will continuously navigate the globe, including in its itineraries major world events, such as the Carnival in Rio de Janeiro, the Cannes Film Festival, the Grand Prix of Monaco, the British Open in Scotland, etc. With extended stays of two to five days, residents will experience all the sights, sounds and flavours of the world's most exciting port cities. *The World of ResidenSea* can take 285 residents and guests, of which 40 per cent are expected to come from the United States and 60 per cent from Europe and the rest of the world. Her innovative design has been developed by renowned naval architects and ship designers Yran & Storbraaten and she will have a full-time crew of 252 seafarers and hospitality staff to run the ship and serve the residents. It was conceived and developed by Norwegian Knut U. Kloster Jr, former chairman of Royal Viking Line and Norwegian Cruise Lines, who, together with other investors, has funded the company ResidenSea Ltd which is based in Freeport, Bahamas. Fosen Mek. Verksteder AS in Norway is the ship's builder and they also have the contract to build *The World of ResidenSea's* sister ship. The NOK 2.5 billion contract is foreseen for delivery in 2003.

The World of ResidenSea offers an exclusive lifestyle, together with the comforts, facilities and activities of the world's best resorts. Members enjoy the privacy and camaraderie of the most discriminating private clubs and the opportunity to come together in public areas. Unique onboard facilities include a full shot driving range, golf simulators, real grass putting greens and a full-time pro. A 5,000 square foot spa, health and fitness centre and beauty salon is operated by renowned Swiss specialist *Clinique La Prairie*. There is an unparalleled programme of cultural activities, including lectures and seminars, recitals and concerts, and a wide variety of classes ranging from dance to computers and from photography to navigation, together with theatre, live concerts and films. A nightclub and a luxury casino operated by Century Casinos are available. Apartments range in size from 1,106 to 3,242 square feet and unit prices range from approximately US$2,000,000 to US$6,840,000. Five standard floor plans and several interior design concepts were developed exclusively by four internationally renowned designers - Nina Campbell, J. P. Molyneux, Luciano Di Pilla and Yran & Storbraaten. The 110 private apartments have spacious living and dining areas; two or three bedrooms, each with en-suite bathroom; a terrace with an optional jet pool and advanced audio/visual equipment. Round-the-clock restaurant delivery and private chef services are available. Eighty-eight spacious guest suites are available for rental by residents' friends and families, business associates and other travellers. The luxury and comfort of these suites has been designed by Hirsch Bedner Associates and they are marketed and managed by Silversea Cruises.

The ship's concierge can assist residents in arranging every aspect of their stay. All services and facilities to maintain a home are provided: the village market, daily housekeeping service, travel agency, hair and beauty salon, laundry/dry cleaning service and gift boutiques - including the prestigious *House of Graff* Jewellers. Residents can do business as though they were in their offices ashore, and the ship has its own business and conference centre.

Further Information: www.residensea.com.

Photo © Jon Nash

*Marcus Hutchinson and
Bruno Troublé of Jour J*

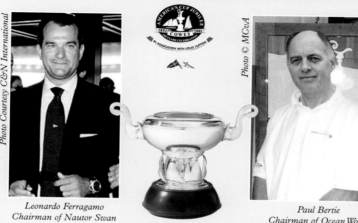

Photo Courtesy C&N International

*Leonardo Ferragamo
Chairman of Nautor Swan*

*The Asprey Swan
Challenge Trophy*

Photo © MCvA

*Paul Bertie
Chairman of Ocean World*

Franco Costa paintings

Bronze Partners

BT Openworld was one of the Bronze sponsors for the Jubilee. BT's new mass-market Internet business was the official communications sponsor and, in association with Louis Vuitton, equipped a state-of-the-art media centre for the international media.

Lewmar has, since 1980, developed radical technologies for five of the seven winning America's Cup yachts. For the Jubilee, Lewmar sponsored the launch service and presented trophies for the UBS Round-the-Island day. The company also ran a winch-grinding competition at the tented village on The Parade.

Nautor Swan, builder of the unique and lovely Swan yachts, presented the Asprey Swan Challenge Trophy to the owner of the winning Swan, **Northern Child of St Peter Port**, at the final prizegiving.

ResidenSea, the first luxury residential community at sea, also presented an award. This unique ship, which combines the comforts of a private home with the magic of travelling the globe, and the environment of an exclusive resort, was due to be delivered in early 2002 and will sail around the globe in pursuit of fair weather and world attractions.

United Airlines was another bronze sponsor of the Jubilee. The company is a long-time supporter of sailing in the UK, including the United Airlines RYA Match Racing Open at Weymouth last September, where six of the America's Cup syndicates had teams sailing.

Wightlink, last but not least, a main operator of ferries to the Isle of Wight, with more routes, more ships, more sailing times and the fastest catamaran and ferry services, was also involved as a Jubilee sponsor.

Other bronze partners included: **Asprey & Garrard** (sponsored the security for the America's Cup), **Blick Rothenburg** and **Ernst & Young** (for the accounting) and **Bouchard Wines** (gave special conditions for the Ball), **Jour J**, the Parisian agency headed by Bruno Troublé and Marcus Hutchinson, was in charge of the Louis Vuitton Media Centre. In addition they brought in the LVMH sponsorship and organised the Jubilee Ball. **Henri Lloyd** supplied clothes for the racing officers, **Camper & Nicholson International** sponsored the Herreshoff 'Hall of Fame' Ceremony, **Cowes**

Trading managed The Parade, **Red Funnel** organised the ferries and offered a free ferry to carry guests to the Ball. *Abordage Models, Benzie of Cowes* (jewels), *Chatham Marine, Five Star Catering,* painter *Franco Costa, Henri Lloyd, Ocean World, T & G Clothing Ltd, Washington Promotions International* and *World Leisurewear Ltd.* all bought licences to produce articles with the America's Cup logo.

Franco Costa

The original painting by Franco Costa, on which the Jubilee logo was based, was displayed during the week at his marquee in the Jubilee Village, with a set of 150 limited edition numbered graphics available. Franco has been involved with the America's Cup for nearly 15 years. He was also official artist to the Volvo Ocean Race, for which he created five paintings. Prints and limited editions were on sale during the Volvo Race assembly week in Southampton and will be on sale at every stopover port until the race finishes in Kiel, Germany, in June 2002.

Ocean World

The official logo for the America's Cup Jubilee was designed by Paul Bertie, proprietor of Ocean World, based on a design by painter Franco Costa. Paul had been involved in planning the event from the beginning, when he was Chairman of *Cowes Business Association.* He was in charge of the Jubilee Village, the official licensees and suppliers. Ocean World in Cowes High Street offered a very popular range of merchandise for the Jubilee, bearing the official America's Cup Jubilee logo - everything from a key fob to crew shirts, sailing jackets and bags. Also on display at Ocean World during the Jubilee was a half-sized replica of the America's Cup, produced by Royal jeweller Asprey & Garrard, who made the original trophy in 1848. The replica, hand-made from silver, was on loan from Bill Koch. Replicas are made to measure only at the request of people who have sailed or won the America's Cup. Ocean World also displayed models of the America's Cup yachts, with prices starting at £1,000. It was the official clothing supplier to **White Crusader** in 1987 and to the **Blue Arrow** challenge - two British contenders for the America's Cup.

Kenny Jones, Lorraine Chase & Kos

Sue Saville ITV news reader

Elisabeth Meyer

Irvine Laidlaw & Don Wood

Graham Walker

Ellen MacArthur & Kos

Mr & Mrs Alan Bond

Harold Cudmore & Kos

Mr & Mrs Reynolds

Peter Harrison

All photos Courtesy Kos & C. Borlenghi

LADY CHRISTINE

Coming on board

Kenny Jones & Philip Amadeus

Irvine Laidlaw & Elizabeth Meyer

Mr & Mrs Leask & Rod Carr

Roger Maingoe & Chris Savage

Steve Mead & Kos

20" x 20" by Kos
Book Launch
on
Super Yacht Lady Christine

Alan Bond & Bill Koch

This large carbon fibre book, which celebrates 20 years of Kos's marine photography, must be one of the most extraordinary books ever published, both in content and sheer enormity (520mm x 630mm). It weighs nearly 10 kilos and costs £750. Many of the 200 beautiful images have been taken from the top of a 180ft mast - one of Kos's favourite vantage points. It was printed as a limited edition of only 1,000 copies with a foreword by HSH The Aga Khan.

Absolutely!

Maldwin Drummond, Paul Mason, Anne Tyrrell and Mr & Mrs Augustin Edwards

Kit Hobday, Anne Louis, Hugh Hamilton (the Piper), Susie Hobday & Tim Louis

Mrs Peter Cove

Diana Bond

Alan Bond

Geoff and Geraldine Dawson

Deida Acero, The Rt Hon Paul East QC and Nancy Jong Miller

Photos @ Michael Dunkason (Ryde. Tel: 01983 612129). Courtesy of the Paul Mason Gallery

Mavis Patterson

Elizabeth Meyer

Sue Chester & Nick Bonham

Larry Friedman, Paul Mason's Partner

Johan Sylvan of the Royal Gothenburg Yacht Club

Shane Michael Couch, the artist.

The First Defence 1870

Windward of America are Silvie and Magic, astern come Dauntless, Idler & Cambria

Thistle and Volunteer off New York 1887

Paul Mason Gallery

During the America's Cup Jubilee, Paul Mason Gallery had an exhibition of Maritime Art at the Marine Gallery in Cowes. The exhibition featured oil paintings by Shane Michael Couch depicting scenes inspired by historical contests for the America's Cup, a collection of over 100 books on the subject and antique Marine Paintings as well as furniture, jewellery and artefacts. Maldwin Drummond, Chairman of the America's Cup Jubilee, opened the exhibition and the inaugural reception which was attended by a 'who's who' in Cowes and the world of yachting. Paul Mason Gallery, established over 38 years, specializes in 18th to 20th Century marine paintings.

149 Sloane Street, London SW1X 9BZ
Tel: 0207 7303683 Fax: 0207 7307359 E-mail: paulmasonart@aol.com

The First Challenge
for the
America's Cup 1870.

*Painting by
Rodney J.K. Charman
www.maritimeartist.co.uk*

The America's Cup Saga
& The British Challenges
1851 - 2003

Britain has a special place in the history and heritage of the America's Cup, since it was around the Isle of Wight that the first race was held in 1851 when (as recounted elsewhere) the yacht **America** won, a humiliating defeat for the British racing fleet. Over the next 132 years, Britain regularly challenged the New York Yacht Club, holder of the 'Auld Mug', but without success. Britain challenged no fewer than 14 times up until the Second World War, almost winning the Cup on two occasions. The first to challenge was James Ashbury with **Cambria** in 1870 and **Livonia** in 1871. In 1885, Sir Richard Sutton challenged with **Genesta** and in 1887, James Bell with **Thistle** under the burgee of the Royal Yacht Squadron. In 1886 there had been another challenge with **Galatea**, under the burgee of the Royal Northern Yacht Club. Lord Dunraven challenged in 1893 and 1895 with **Valkyrie**, creating an enormous international scandal from a "simple misunderstanding." Tea magnate Sir Thomas Lipton challenged five times between 1899 and 1930 with five boats called **Shamrock**, earning the sporting respect of the whole of the United States as a trier but, unfortunately, a loser. The aviation pioneer and manufacturer T.O.M. Sopwith challenged twice in the 1930's with **Endeavour**, coming as close as anybody

ever had to beating the Americans on the water without actually doing it. Most of them sailed under the burgee of the Royal Yacht Squadron, except James Ashbury who in 1871 chose the Royal Harwich Yacht Club. In 1895, the Earl of Dunraven, and later, Sir Thomas Lipton chose the Irish Royal Ulster Yacht Club. After the Second World War, Graham Mann challenged with **Sceptre** in 1958 and Tony Boyden with **Sovereign** in 1964, **Sceptre** representing the Royal Yacht Squadron and **Sovereign**, the Royal Thames Yacht Club. It took Britain 16 years before becoming a challenger again in 1980 with the **Lionheart** Syndicate and in 1983 with Peter de Savary and the **Victory** Syndicate. Neither of them made it to the final America's Cup race. There was a last and unsuccessful British challenge by Graham Walker's **White Crusader** Syndicate with skipper Harold Cudmore in 1987.

After an absence of more than 15 years, yachtsman and successful businessman Peter Harrison is bringing Britain back to the America's Cup. In 2000, he created GBR Challenge and selected Cowes as its UK base and the burgee of the Royal Ocean Racing Club. Peter Harrison has re-united the best of British sailors, who will first have to beat nine other challengers in the Louis Vuitton Cup in order to become the challenger for the 31st America's Cup.

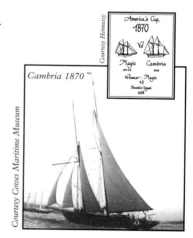

Courtesy Cowes Maritime Museum

Cambria 1870

Courtesy Paul Mason Gallery

Livonia 1871

Thistle

Galatea

When the winners of the 100 Guineas Cup returned to America in 1851, the syndicate donated the Cup to the New York Yacht Club (NYYC) with a Deed of Gift stating that the trophy was to become "a perpetual challenge cup for friendly competition between foreign countries." After the defeat, the British yachts were remodelled and built to look like *America*.

Because of the American Civil War, the first challenge did not come until 1870 with Englishman James Ashbury of the Royal Yacht Squadron (RYS) and his 108ft (37.2m) Cowes-built schooner *Cambria*. He was defeated by Franklin Osgood of the NYYC on *Magic*. Ashbury returned in 1871 under the burgee of the Royal Harwich Yacht Club with *Livonia*, but was beaten again by the same owner, this time on *Columbia*. Ashbury placed several protests during the races and, when he lost, issued a pamphlet describing what he called the abuses he had suffered. The next two challenges came from Canadian clubs in 1876 and 1881.

It was only in 1885 that Sir Richard Sutton of the RYS challenged with *Genesta* and lost against *Puritan*, built by E. Burgess, (who had actually been seen on the Isle of Wight studying the latest British yachts...). In 1887, Scotsman James Bell challenged through the Royal Clyde Yacht Club with *Thistle*. It was written that *Thistle* had been built by G. L. Watson "in great secrecy" and that a false set of plans had even been sent to America! However American *Volunteer*, built by E. Burgess for General Paine, won the race.

Genesta

Valkyrie III 1895

Valkyrie II 1893

The Dunraven Affair

In 1893 and 1895 the Earl of Dunraven, once under the burgee of the RYS and then the Royal Ulster Yacht Club, challenged with *Valkyrie II* and *III*, designed by Watson. In 1893 he was beaten by *Vigilant* and in 1895, by *Defender*, owned by New York banker, Oliver Iselin, of the New York Yacht Club, and designed by Herreshoff.

In 1893, Dunraven had been unhappy with the spectator fleet, which he said crowded the racers too much. In 1895, in the second race, *Valkyrie III* swept the deck of *Defender* and tore out her starboard topmast shroud. She won the race but the win was overturned on protest. Dunraven started the third race but quickly lowered the sails and retired from the race, showing his own protest over the decision. He was blamed and later, after various exchanges of letters with the New York Yacht Club, he was expelled and asked to give back his honorary membership card to the Club. In 1895 the unfortunate 'Dunraven Affair' led to his expulsion from the NYYC. Windham Thomas Wyndham-Quinn, 7th Earl of Dunraven and 2nd Baron Kenry, was accused of "distrust, suspicion, unfounded reputations of fraud and refusal of reparation." He had, among other things, accused *Defender* of carrying illegal ballast. This was one of the many 'highs and lows', deep intrigue and drama which have embittered the history of the America's Cup over the years

Valkyrie III

In 1901 the era of Scottish tea baron Sir Thomas Lipton began when he entered a challenge with **Shamrock II** under the flag of the Royal Ulster Yacht Club. Lipton challenged five times with five successive **Shamrocks**. He lost each time but the American people loved the "gallant loser" as he was called, and his tea business thrived.

Lipton lost against the following boats, which were all under the burgee of the NYYC: in 1901, against **Columbia**, owned by J. Pierpont Morgan; in 1903, against **Reliance** owned by Oliver Iselin; in 1920, against **Resolute**, owned by Henry Walters, and in 1930, against **Enterprise**, owned by Harold 'Mike' Vanderbilt. **Columbia** and **Reliance** were skippered by Charlie Barr.

The Edwin Levick Collection, Mariners' Museum

Sir Thomas Lipton
The 'boating grocer'

Sir Thomas Lipton, who had started out earning a shilling or two a week, became a millionaire by the age of 30. He was described as a "romantic, attractive man with great personal charm." A real one-man show, he never married, probably too busy and "too wrapped up in himself to share his life." He was very elegant, wearing spotless stiff white shirts, and entertained lavishly - offering "gorgeously ornate boxes of chocolates".

Aboard his various yachts, he entertained Royalty - Edward VII, who was his friend, the King of Spain, millionaires and political figures such as Winston Churchill. Anthony Heckstall-Smith, in his book 'Sacred Cowes' wrote: "He collected celebrities as others collect stamps ... A non-smoker, non-gambler and a teetotaller, he was surrounded by a glittering crowd who lived largely to smoke, drink and played cards for high stakes." Everyone liked him - he was a "refreshing change from their toadying courtiers" and he was a good raconteur, telling stories about his humble background and many anecdotes about himself. He always joked about the way he had got his title for nothing and had it paid for by someone who wanted to become a peer! After all he was "no Scotsman for nothin'."

Shamrock II 1901

Photos © Beken of Cowes

Shamrock III 1903

Shamrock IV 1920

The story about his being blackballed from the RYS is not quite accurate. In fact Edward VII did not propose him and withdrew his name, knowing he would probably be blackballed. However, when he was close to 80 (almost 50 years later) Tommy was elected unanimously in 1931, "in recognition of his great services to yacht racing" but he never set foot in the Club. He was not really a great sportsman and he went yachting because it was part of his great advertising campaign to sell Lipton Tea. In fact, he used the America's Cup and challenged five times on his **Shamrocks**, spending his own fortune against syndicates of American millionaires (Morgan and Vanderbilt did not spend their own money but had the syndicate pay for the defending yachts). Win or lose the name of Lipton was on all the front pages. Nobody could have afforded such expensive advertising space! He became such a legend in America when he was presented with a golden cup as the 'World's Best Loser', that it was better to lose than to win! He claimed he was the only foreigner without a voice for whom an audience at the Metropolitan Opera in New York would ever rise to cheer while he was brought down Broadway with screaming escorts of motorcycle police. He enjoyed the cheering crowds welcoming him everywhere. It was all part of his publicity and he loved it. He seldom went racing himself and would watch aboard his steam yacht **Erin**. He always lived in great luxury but his palatial steam yachts, racing cutters and huge motor cars were just part of his business and helped to increase the sales of his goods.

Lipton is recorded as saying: "*It is like this: when a chicken lays an egg, she cockles an' tells the whole farmyard. But when a duck lays an egg, she makes no' a sound. An' how many people eat ducks' eggs? Did ye never ask yourself yon question?*" That was his theory of self-promotion and the America's Cup did make the name Lipton very well-known!

Charlie Barr

Born in Scotland, Charlie Barr became an American citizen in order to be able to defend the Cup. A master of tactics and technology, he won the Cup three times in 1899, 1901 and 1903 with nine straight victories. Being British, he was not very popular in America.

During the 1899 Cup William Marconi developed his new wireless telegraph by sending match reports to shore from the race course.

© The Edwin Levick Collection, Mariners' Museum

Photos © Beken of Cowes

Shamrock V 1930

Nat Herreshoff

The Herreshoff Museum

Charles Nicholson

Olin Stephens

The America's Cup Yacht Designers

The Herreshoff Marine Museum America's Cup Hall of Fame

From 1863 to 1945, the Herreshoff Manufacturing Company, on the site of the present-day Museum in Bristol, USA, produced the world's finest yachts at the cutting edge of design and engineering. The genius of naval architect Captain Nathanael Greene Herreshoff along with the business acumen of his blind older brother, John Brown Herreshoff, truly built the "better mousetrap," as well as the first United States Navy torpedo boats, the finest light-weight steam machinery, pioneering fin-keel spade-rudder boats in the 1890s, mammoth schooners and the principal one-design racers of the New York Yacht Club. Their most significant record was the construction of eight consecutive successful defenders of the America's Cup from 1893 to 1934. The Herreshoff Marine Museum/America's Cup Hall of Fame, which is open from May until the end of October, celebrates the unique accomplishments of the Herreshoff family and the related drama of the America's Cup races. Contact details are as follows:

*PO Box 450,
Bristol, RI 02809-0450 USA
Tel: 001 401-253-5000
Fax: 401-253-6222
Website: www.herreshoff.org*

American Designers

The Herreshoff Brothers

Reliance was the biggest yacht ever built for the Cup. The longest racing sloop ever built at 144 feet (44 metres), she stretched 200ft (61m) from the top of her bowsprit to the end of her boom. The yacht had more than 1,500 square metres of sail area and a fantastic 88ft spinnaker pole. **Reliance** had 64 crew on board. She was designed and built by the Herreshoff brothers, Nathaniel (Nat) and his blind brother John Brown. They designed and built six yachts for the America's Cup between 1893 and 1920.

In the 1890's George Watson in Britain and Nathaniel Herreshoff in the USA developed the new, powerful Big Class yachts which were sometimes over 120 feet long, with a towering gaff rig.

Olin Stephens

Olin became known when he designed **Ranger**, the last of the J-Class to contest the Cup in 1937. H.M. Vanderbilt won it against Sopwith's **Endeavour**. He also designed **Columbia** in 1958, **Intrepid**, a 12-Metre, which won the Cup in 1970, and **Courageous** in 1977. He designed all but one of the successful NYYC defenders - **Liberty**, which lost the Cup was not designed by him. He also designed many offshore and cruising boats until 1987, when, after 50 years, he decided to retire.

British Designers

Charles Nicholson

Naval architect Charles Nicholson was born at Gosport, Hampshire in 1868 and designed his first yacht, the ten-tonner **Lucifer**, before he was 20. Until 1938 he designed 235 yachts, some very famous such as **Istria**, the 15-Metre racing cutter owned by Sir Charles Allom, the first yacht to carry a *Marconi* rig* in 1912. He also designed Cup challengers **Shamrocks IV** and **V** for Thomas Lipton and two **Endeavours** for Sopwith. **Flica**, a 12-Metre, was made for Dick Fairey. Nicholson was quoted as saying: "Building yachts always has an element of fascinating uncertainty in it. It is one of the few crafts left in the modern world where arts, sport and work are all combined. Yacht designing is still more of an art than a science. The speed of our yachts depends upon the harmony of line, upon sail area, efficiency, and wind, and upon not least seamanship."

William Fife

Fife built many famous yachts, amongst them **Cambria** in 1928, for Lord Camrose (Sir William Berry). It was said of the yacht that "she was perfectly constructed and that no door in her ever jammed and no drawer ever stuck. She was a specimen of British shipbuilding and craftsmanship, but she was too well built to be a racer." Another of Fife's masterpieces was **Moonbeam**. He also re-rigged **Britannia** in 1927 among other yachts.

*A single-pole mast, resembling a Marconi transmission mast, instead of a lower mast, topmast and top-sail yard. Around 1928 this led to the 'Bermudian' rig which eliminated the gaff and topsail altogether.

Endeavour's amateur crew for the 1934 Challenge

Sir T.O.M. Sopwith at the helm of his J-Class Endeavour in 1934

In the 1930's the Big Class yachts were replaced by the J-Class. With **Enterprise** (1930), **Rainbow** (1931) and **Ranger** (1937), Harold 'Mike' Vanderbilt of the New York Yacht Club, who skippered his boats, won the Cup three times, once against Sir Thomas Lipton and twice against **Endeavour**, owned and skippered by Sir T.O.M. Sopwith. Sopwith sailed under the burgee of the Royal Yacht Squadron.

In 1934, **Endeavour**, designed by Charles Nicholson, almost beat **Rainbow**, but lost mostly because of her hastily-assembled amateur crew, after a strike of professional sailors. There was also an incident during the third race when the sailing committee decided that **Endeavour** had not hoisted her protest flag early enough and that her protest was disallowed. He, however, went back in 1937, but **Endeavour II** was beaten by **Ranger**.

The 12-Metre Class

*With the defeat of **Endeavour**, the J-Class came to an end. After the war, they were replaced by the 12-Metre, which had already become well established, first in Europe and later in America, when in 1927, the NYYC had placed an order for six boats with the German Yard of Abeking & Rasmussen. No longer wood but aluminium (and later glass fibre) masts, synthetic and no longer cotton sails, composite construction boats and sophisticated instrumentation were some of the characteristics of the new 12-Metre.*

During the same period, Dick Fairey had tried to issue a new 'K' or 'L' Class yacht with a smaller vessel. He considered the 'J' unseaworthy and too expensive to build and maintain, but the NYYC declined his challenge with a new Class.

Mr & Mrs Harold Vanderbilt

Endeavour I and II (1937)

Sovereign

Lionheart

Crusader

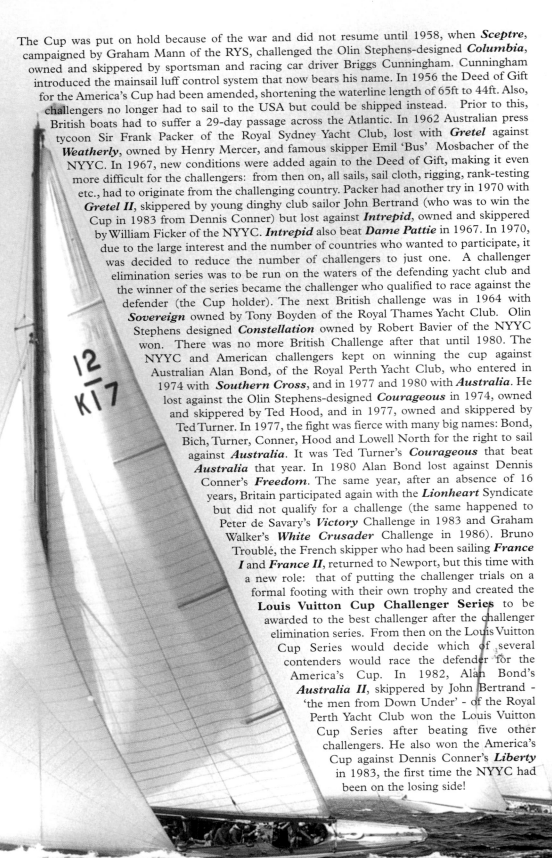

The Cup was put on hold because of the war and did not resume until 1958, when *Sceptre*, campaigned by Graham Mann of the RYS, challenged the Olin Stephens-designed *Columbia*, owned and skippered by sportsman and racing car driver Briggs Cunningham. Cunningham introduced the mainsail luff control system that now bears his name. In 1956 the Deed of Gift for the America's Cup had been amended, shortening the waterline length of 65ft to 44ft. Also, challengers no longer had to sail to the USA but could be shipped instead. Prior to this, British boats had to suffer a 29-day passage across the Atlantic. In 1962 Australian press tycoon Sir Frank Packer of the Royal Sydney Yacht Club, lost with *Gretel* against *Weatherly*, owned by Henry Mercer, and famous skipper Emil 'Bus' Mosbacher of the NYYC. In 1967, new conditions were added again to the Deed of Gift, making it even more difficult for the challengers: from then on, all sails, sail cloth, rigging, rank-testing etc., had to originate from the challenging country. Packer had another try in 1970 with *Gretel II*, skippered by young dinghy club sailor John Bertrand (who was to win the Cup in 1983 from Dennis Conner) but lost against *Intrepid*, owned and skippered by William Ficker of the NYYC. *Intrepid* also beat *Dame Pattie* in 1967. In 1970, due to the large interest and the number of countries who wanted to participate, it was decided to reduce the number of challengers to just one. A challenger elimination series was to be run on the waters of the defending yacht club and the winner of the series became the challenger who qualified to race against the defender (the Cup holder). The next British challenge was in 1964 with *Sovereign* owned by Tony Boyden of the Royal Thames Yacht Club. Olin Stephens designed *Constellation* owned by Robert Bavier of the NYYC won. There was no more British Challenge after that until 1980. The NYYC and American challengers kept on winning the cup against Australian Alan Bond, of the Royal Perth Yacht Club, who entered in 1974 with *Southern Cross*, and in 1977 and 1980 with *Australia*. He lost against the Olin Stephens-designed *Courageous* in 1974, owned and skippered by Ted Hood, and in 1977, owned and skippered by Ted Turner. In 1977, the fight was fierce with many big names: Bond, Bich, Turner, Conner, Hood and Lowell North for the right to sail against *Australia*. It was Ted Turner's *Courageous* that beat *Australia* that year. In 1980 Alan Bond lost against Dennis Conner's *Freedom*. The same year, after an absence of 16 years, Britain participated again with the *Lionheart* Syndicate but did not qualify for a challenge (the same happened to Peter de Savary's *Victory* Challenge in 1983 and Graham Walker's *White Crusader* Challenge in 1986). Bruno Troublé, the French skipper who had been sailing *France I* and *France II*, returned to Newport, but this time with a new role: that of putting the challenger trials on a formal footing with their own trophy and created the **Louis Vuitton Cup Challenger Series** to be awarded to the best challenger after the challenger elimination series. From then on the Louis Vuitton Cup Series would decide which of several contenders would race the defender for the America's Cup. In 1982, Alan Bond's *Australia II*, skippered by John Bertrand - 'the men from Down Under' - of the Royal Perth Yacht Club won the Louis Vuitton Cup Series after beating five other challengers. He also won the America's Cup against Dennis Conner's *Liberty* in 1983, the first time the NYYC had been on the losing side!

Photo © Beken of Cowes

Sceptre

Peter de Savary
The Victory Challenge

The British Challenge in 1980 was led by Tony Boyden with the 12 metre yacht 'Lionheart'. Peter de Savary participated in this challenge and was determined thereafter to lead a challenge himself for the 1983 America's Cup. As part of this programme he commissioned Ed Dubois to design a yacht for the 1981 Admiral's Cup. The production of this yacht and the experience of an Admiral's Cup Campaign was felt to be a good precursor to the America's Cup. The 1981 Admiral's Cup was won by the British team with the de Savary yacht 'Victory' being the top boat of the overall series.

For the 1983 America's Cup, de Savary commissioned both Ed Dubois and Ian Howlett to each design a 12 metre yacht (both called Victory). Both yachts were produced and sailed vigorously against both 'Lionheart' and 'Australia' both of which had been purchased as training horses.

The 'Victory' Challenge for the America's Cup was the best funded British effort since the days of Sir Tommy Sopwith. The sailing crew and shore crew were drawn from the best of British sailors, young boys and girls from the Duke of Edinburgh award scheme, the British Armed Forces, the unemployed of Great Britain and technical and back-up personnel drawn from all walks of life and diversified employments. It was a great British Team representing people from all over the country with a

determination to win the cup and at the very least put on a good show. Included in the sailing team were Rodney Patterson (triple Olympic gold medallist), Laurie Smith, Phil Crebbin, Harold Cudmore and numerous others representing the best of British talent. The best of British technology was utilised in the design and construction of 'Victory' and in the opinion of most people, there was every likelihood that 'Victory' could have beaten the American defender due to both yachts being of comparable performance and the crews being of equal ability. Britain could and should have won the America's Cup had it not have been for the Australian Alan Bond, and his radical winged keel; this keel of dubious legality under the America's Cup rules, enhanced the performance of a 12 metre yacht so considerably that together with excellent sailing the Australians won the America's Cup.

The 'Victory' challenge had spent the summer of 1982 training in Newport and the winter in the Bahamas. During the 1983 campaign in Newport, Rhode Island the British Team, losing only to the ultimate victor, provided the British public with all the excitement of a vigorous sailing campaign and are certainly remembered in Newport for hosting a social programme of style and excellence culminating in the 'Victory Ball' which was attended by His Royal Highness, Prince Andrew.

Peter de Savary aided by his Deputy Kit Hobday devoted 2 years in an attempt to bring the America's Cup back to Britain for the first time. 1983 was probably the last America's Cup where enthusiastic amateurs joined together in a great sailing regatta; thereafter professionalism and major corporate sponsorship has taken over the event. Without regrets, de Savary returned quietly home to enjoy sailing for pleasure only.

Ted Turner
*also made himself
known by
winning the
Sydney to Hobart
race with*
**American
Eagle** *and in
winning the
Fastnet race with*
Tenacious.

Graham Walker

Alan Bond

Ted Hood
*boat designer,
boatbuilder and
sailmaker has built
one of the most
diverse marine
businesses in
America.*

Bruno Troublé

*Buddy Melges, Bill Koch, Sir James Hardy, Sir Peter Blake, Bill Ficker, Dean Baker, Olin Stephens, Russell Coutts,
Dennis Conner, John Bertrand, David Barnes, Francesco de Angelis
Right: Patrizio Bertelli, Prada Challenge and Peter Harrison, GBR Challenge*

Finally, after 132 years,
the sport's longest winning streak had been broken and
the Americans had lost the Cup!

The ACC Boats

By 1992 a new Class had been developed: "The International America's Cup Class" (ACC Boats) putting an end to the 12-Metre era. The new boats involved new technology and materials such as carbon fibre and Kevlar with epoxy resins, new sails made with a product called 3DL. Even the rigs had changed and the "Millennium Rig" featured a relatively long chord length but at the same time only three levels of spreaders. From the earliest days, boat design and sailing techniques have been crucial to success. Even in the 1930's British wartime aircraft manufacturer T.O.M. Sopwith had developed a design office to develop specific equipments for his boats Endeavour. More than ever before the America's Cup represented the fruit of the most advanced studies, techniques and technologies available. Today as before, major high tech engineering and science agencies as well as big industries invest millions into developing, testing and building sailing boats. Huge fortunes continue to be spent to defend it and trying to win the America's Cup has been a saga of technology but also of controversy and personalities. Reputations were built but also destroyed for the people involved. The yachting's greatest trophy has been an obsession for many but such a reward to the few who have managed to win it.

The next event was to be hosted in Australia by the Royal Perth Yacht Club (RPYC). In 1986, 13 syndicates raced for the second Louis Vuitton Cup in Perth against Graham Walker's **White Crusader** syndicate. It was won by Dennis Conner, sailing **Stars & Stripes** and since then it is said *"to win the America's Cup, first win the Louis Vuitton Cup."* In 1987, **Stars & Stripes** and Dennis Conner won against Kevin Parry's **Kookaburra III**. The America's Cup was back in America! But this time under the burgee of the San Diego Yacht Club. Dennis Conner won again in 1988 with **Stars & Stripes** against Michael Fay's **New Zealand** skippered by David Barnes of the Mercury Bay Boating Club. There was an interesting court case around the 1988 Cup, too long to explain here. In 1992 the loser was **Il Moro di Venezia** owned by Raoul Gardini and skippered by Paul Cayard. The three-second winning margin was the closest ever in an America's Cup, but Bill Koch had won on **America 3**. He later sold his boats to the Prada Challenge in 1995. Again in 1995 the Americans were defeated. Peter Blake's **Team New Zealand NZL 32 (Black Magic)** skippered by Russell Coutts, after winning the Louis Vuitton Cup won over Dennis Conner and helmsman Paul Cayard's **Young America**, taking the Cup to Auckland, the City of Sails. Sir Peter Blake who was asked by Sir Michael Fay to help run the 1992 Challenge, had to pay the entry fee for 1995 from his own pocket and look for sponsors when Fay decided to pull out. Blake ran the team, got the sponsors and even sailed on the

boat as a grinder, winding a winch during the Cup. It took five years before the New Zealanders were ready to defend. They wanted to have the right facilities and developed a spectacular Cup basin in the old fishing boat harbour at Auckland, where a complete America's Cup Village was built, ready to receive 10 Syndicates for the Louis Vuitton Cup in 1999. In 2000, **Team New Zealand** with **NZL 60**, owned this time by Russell Coutts, who skippered with Dean Barker, won the Cup again! This in spite of the fact that the **loser**, the Italian Prada Challenger **Luna Rossa**, owned by Patrizio Bertelli and steered by Francesco de Angelis, representing Yacht Club Punta Ala, had won the Louis Vuitton Cup! This was the first time ever that the Cup match was held without an American boat present! They had been ousted by the French Team Le Défi!

What will happen in 2003?

*Which of the ten challengers from seven countries will win the Louis Vuitton Cup which will take place in Auckland from mid-October 2002? Will the winner of the Louis Vuitton Cup in February win the America's Cup in 2003? Will **GBR Challenge**, the first British Challenge for 15 years, bring the America's Cup back to Great Britain? Only time will tell.*
No other trophy has ever cost British sportsmen so much money, but British challenges have always failed. Why? Lack of thoroughness, lack of a good designer, lack of a good helmsman or naval architect? Or could no-one master the local conditions?

THE 31st AMERICA'S CUP

GBR Challenge did very well during the Jubilee considering the team only had three months of training. After the Jubilee, GBR 41 and GBR 52 were sent to New Zealand for the team to practice, refining race-winning tactics, during the winter.

www.gbrchallenge.com

After an absence of almost fifteen years, yachtsman and businessman Peter Harrison is bringing Britain back to the America's Cup. In 2000, he created *GBR Challenge*, selecting Cowes as its UK base and the burgee of the *Royal Ocean Racing Club*. He acquired the assets of the Nippon Syndicate including three ACC boats and two of their designers. He also bought the former FBM yard in Cowes where the Syndicate has been training and where the new boat *ACC* is being built, with cutting-edge materials, by Cowes-based designer Jo Richards and two Japanese designers. After a series of tests on quarter size models in the tank testing unit at Gosport, work on the new yacht started in 2001. Once built, the boat will be tested in the Solent by the team, who will come back from Auckland. It will then be shipped to New Zealand again for the Louis Vuitton Cup.

Photo © Jon Nash

THE 31st AMERICA'S CUP

October 2002 - March 2003

The America's Cup is one of the biggest sporting events and certainly the biggest for yachting, in the world with the oldest trophy to be won. The race takes place every three to five years.
The challengers must first enter the Louis Vuitton Cup. The winner will then face the defender for the next America's Cup. The winning country then wins the right to stage the next America's Cup. Ten syndicates from seven countries have challenged the Royal New Zealand Yacht Squadron, current holders of the America's Cup, for the next America's Cup. The ten challengers have to compete in the challenger elimination series for the Louis Vuitton Cup, which will start in October 2002. The winner will then race against the defender in the 31st America's Cup Match in March 2003.
Seven of the ten challengers come from Europe, the strongest-ever representation from the 'Old Continent'.

The Defender

The Royal New Zealand Yacht Squadron and Team New Zealand

The current holders of the Cup lost a great part of their syndicate after winning it. Russell Coutts and his core crew left Team New Zealand to join the Swiss Challenge Alinghi. They chose to trade their national hero status for a multi-million dollar offer. Among those who remained, Dean Barker skippered *NZL-60* in the last race of the 2000 Cup match against *Luna Rossa* when Russell Coutts handed the helm to him making the 26-year-old Kiwi, the youngest person to win the Cup. He will be helmsman for the 2003 Cup defence and is now managing and running the sailing team in liaison with the design and management teams. Syndicate head and design co-ordinator Tom Schnackenberg and Dean Barker have built a new team. Ross James Blackman, Chief Executive, is in charge of the overall management of the syndicate and defence campaign. Anthony Thomas, Executive Director, is responsible for fund-raising, sponsorships, the brand and general management.
www.teamnz.org

The Challengers

Many of the challengers are financed by multi-millionaires and billionaires who are investing money in what seems to be for some, a personal challenge: Swiss Ernesto Bertarelli, Italian Patrizio Bertelli, Americans Larry Ellison and Craig McCaw, Briton Peter Harrison, German Michael Illbruck and Swede Jan Stenbeck.

● **Yacht Club Punta Ala** and the **Prada Challenge** supported by Patrizio Bertelli, owner of *Prada*, won the last Louis Vuitton Cup but lost the America's Cup on *Luna Rossa*. The Syndicate, with Francesco de Angelis as skipper and Doug Peterson leading the design team, have not stopped training and bought the *Young America* assets, including two Bruce Farr designed yachts. www.prada-americascup.com

● There is another Italian challenge, the **Onorato Challenge** of the **Reale Yacht Club Canottieri Savoia**, supported by Vincenzo Onorato. They are using the Spanish boat from the 1999-2000 Cup to train. www.onoratochallenge.com

● **Team Dennis Conner** and his **Stars & Stripes** Syndicate represent the **New York Yacht Club** (the first time since he lost the Cup with *Liberty* in 1983). Involved in the Cup since 1974, Dennis has delegated the management to Bill Trenkle, the sailing to his skipper Ken Read and the design to John Reichel. www.stars-stripes.com

● **Team One World** of the **Seattle Yacht Club** is supported by telecommunications tycoon Craig McCaw, who recruited a group of talented sailors from other syndicates, among them Laurie Davidson, to lead the design office. Peter Gilmour is the skipper. He bought *America 3* and *Stars & Stripes*, semi-finalists in the 2000 Louis Vuitton Cup (renamed *USA-51* and *USA-55*) to train the team.
www.seattleyachtclub.org/sycmcup.htm

● **GBR Challenge** (*See previous page*)

● **Team Oracle Racing** of the **Golden Gate Yacht Club** financed by software guru Larry Ellison, also owner of Maxi yacht *Sayonara*. Oracle Racing has bought the boats and assets of *America One*. The design team is led by well-known Bruce Farr and the sailing team, by Chris Dickson with Cup veteran Paul Cayard. www.oracleracing.com

● **Le Défi Francais** representing **L'Union Nationale pour la Course au Large**, a French Syndicate which has a commercially orientated structure. They almost won the Louis Vuitton Cup in 1999. Past skipper, Bertrand Pace, has joined Team New Zealand. www.ledefi.com

● **Victory Challenge** of the Swedish **Gamla Stans Yacht Sällskap** is financed by Jan Stenbeck, who bought *NZL-38* to train his international team. The design team is led by German Frers. Among the new and possible skippers are Magnus Holmberg, Jesper Bank and Mats Johansson. It is the first time that Sweden has taking part since 1992. www.victorychallenge.com

● **Illbruck German Challenge** of the **Dusseldorfer Yacht Club** is financed by Michael Illbruck bringing Germany to the Cup for the first time ever. The team led by Cup veteran John Kostecki and managed by Glenn Bourke will have just a few months to recover from the Volvo Ocean Race, which Illbruck is also financing. The design team is led by Michael Richelsen. www.illbruck-pinta.com

● **Alinghi Swiss Challenge** (*See next page*)

During the America's Cup Jubilee in Cowes, Team Alinghi sailed *South Australia* which was skippered by Russell Coutts and won the "Prada 12-Metre Championship".

Alinghi Swiss Challenge representing the *"Société Nautique de Genève"* in landlocked Switzerland, is financed by tycoon Ernesto Bertarelli who hired Russell Coutts and seven elements of Team New Zealand after they won the Cup in 2000. The crew includes sailors from other countries: Switzerland (3) including Ernesto Bertarelli himself, France (3), Holland (3), the USA (2), Canada (2), Australia (2), Denmark (1), Italy (1) and Germany (1). This makes the Swiss Challenge a strong contender for the "Louis Vuitton Cup" and the America's Cup itself. *SUI 59,* the Swiss boat used in the last America's Cup is being used for training. The Swiss Challenger has two state-of-the-art ACC boats under construction at the 'Decision' boatyard in Cordier-sur-Fenil (Vevey). Team Alinghi is sponsored by UBS Financial Services Group, Infonet, Audemars Piguet Watches and zip manufacturers Riri. www.alinghi.com

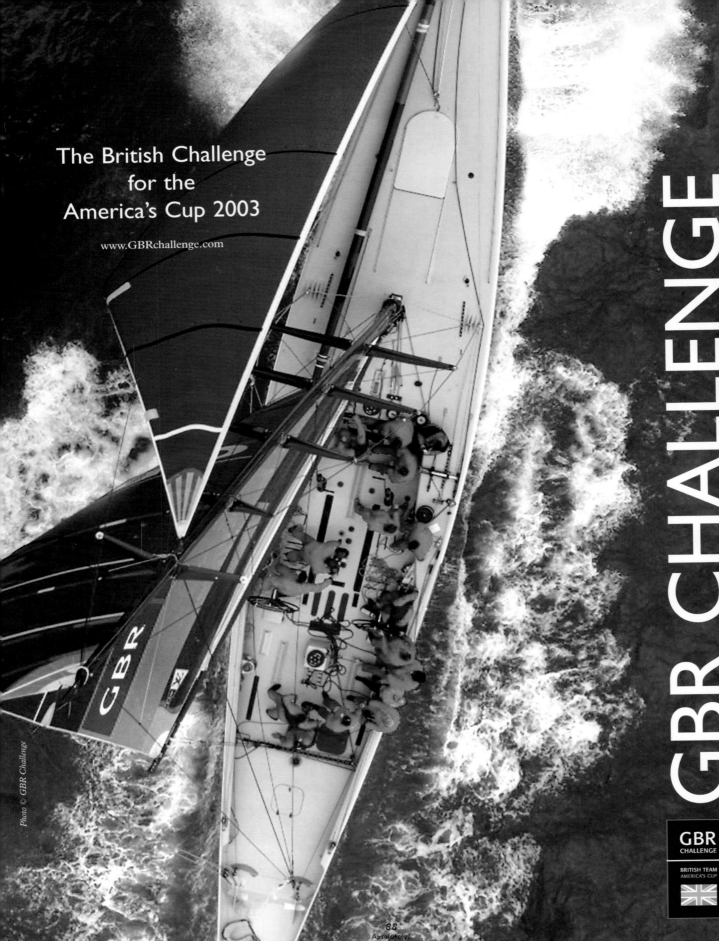

The British Challenge
for the
America's Cup 2003

www.GBRchallenge.com

GBR CHALLENGE

GBR
CHALLENGE

BRITISH TEAM
AMERICA'S CUP